The
Buddha
from
Brooklyn

Martha Sherrill

The
Buddha
from
Brooklyn

RANDOM HOUSE

NEW YORK

Grateful acknowledgment is made to the following for
permission to reprint previously published material:

Louisiana State University Press: "Sometimes, When the
Light" by Lisel Mueller from *Alive Together: New and Selected
Poems* by Lisel Mueller, copyright © 1996 by Lisel Mueller.
Originally published in *The Need to Hold Still.* Copyright ©
1980 by Lisel Mueller. Reprinted by permission of Louisiana
State University.

Universal-PolyGram International Publishing, Inc.: Excerpt from
"Who Am I" (from the musical *Peter Pan*), words and music
by Leonard Bernstein. Copyright © 1950 by Universal-
PolyGram International Publishing, Inc., a division of
Universal Studios, Inc. (ASCAP). Copyright renewed.
International copyright secured. All rights reserved.
Reprinted by permission.

Library of Congress Cataloging-in-Publication Data
Sherrill, Martha.
The Buddha from Brooklyn / Martha Sherrill.
p. cm.
ISBN 0-679-45275-3 (hc.)
1. Ahkön Norbu Lhamo, Jetsunma.   2. Buddhist women—
United States.
3. Buddhism—Social aspects—United States.   I. Title.
BQ734. S44 2000
294.3'923'0973—dc21
99-045346

Random House website address: www.atrandom.com
Printed in the United States of America on acid-free paper
24689753
First Edition

Book design by Barbara M. Bachman
Map design by Jackie Aher

To my mother, Peggy Bonini Sherrill,

and in memory of my friend Nina Hyde

Sometimes, when the light strikes at odd angles
and pulls you back into childhood

and you are passing a crumbling mansion
completely hidden behind old willows

or an empty convent guarded by hemlocks
and giant firs standing hip to hip,

you know again that behind that wall,
under the uncut hair of the willows

something secret is going on,
so marvelous and dangerous

that if you crawled through and saw,
you would die, or be happy forever.

—Lisel Mueller

Contents

Part Four: The Nun

Prologue

A stupa is a holy thing, a monument to peace and harmony. It is a place where the Buddha's mind is alive on earth. That's what I was told, anyway, when I first came to Poolesville, Maryland, and what I still believe—in spite of everything else I know.

The moon was rising in the dark blue sky. It was a harvest moon, a warm moon, full and golden. It was the fall of 1996. The next morning a retreat would begin, a *bodhicitta* or compassion re treat. I arrived on the temple grounds very late, parked my car, and walked past the main building of the temple, a large white plantation-style mansion. The temple looked quiet behind its spread of green grass. Only a few dim lights were still on. Through a window I saw a flash of a burgundy robe inside the Dharma room—a monk or nun was cleaning the altar bowls. Instead of going inside, I walked down the long driveway in the direction of the dark woods. I went to the Migyur Dorje stupa when I was confused, when my mind needed clearing, simplicity, a broad brushstroke, a big picture. When I needed to relax.

I'd been told that if you walk around a stupa, clockwise, you will receive blessings. I still believe that, too. There are all kinds of explanations of what a stupa is, of course, and how one works. There are academic tracts with detailed diagrams, discussions of the various types of stupas, and essays about the metaphysical properties of these compelling shrines. You can be as highbrow as you want about stupas—just as Buddhism itself can be terribly highbrow—or you can try to comprehend a stupa simply and forget the details. You can walk around one, clockwise, as the Tibetans do, and just soak up the blessings. I had purchased miniature stupas from the temple gift shop in Poolesville. I collected photographs of stupas and books about them. I became fascinated with the inner chambers of the stupas, and the secret contents. Sometimes my passion was a little hard to explain to my journalist friends. To the unromantic eye, I suppose, a stupa doesn't look like much. The Buddha's mind is just a monolith, really—an obelisk with a pagoda roof and a spire. At the highest point, there is a crystal ball pointing to the sky.

I took the shortcut in the woods and found the narrow dirt road that led to the great stupa. When I had started coming to Poolesville regularly, just a year before, there had been plans to pave the road—but it was still potholed and loaded with hazardous puddles and large rocks. Vines were curling out of the forest, too, dangling down from trees and growing back into the path.

A stupa is a magical thing, seductive and mysterious, but also very simple. Maybe that's what I like about them. There was no debate raging about stupas—no controversies swirling within the rarefied world of Tibetan Buddhism about what a stupa really is. A stupa is perfection. A stupa is emptiness, and a stupa can't break your heart.

A *tulku* is a little harder to comprehend. Like a stupa, a tulku is also a living Buddha and supposed to be perfect. That's what I was told, at any rate, when I first arrived in Poolesville. But a tulku is a human being—a person with a childhood, with parents, with loves and losses, with regrets, with needs and dreams. Which brings me to Jetsunma. She is a tulku. And she is the one who lured me to Poolesville and to this place called Kunzang Odsal Palyul Changchub Choling, or Fully Awakened Dharma Continent of Absolute Clear Light. For a year I had been coming to Poolesville as a journalist, and this mysterious woman called Jetsunma—an American woman and a Tibetan Buddhist lama—was my subject.

I had met Jetsunma in 1993, when I came to interview her for a profile in a magazine. She was in her midforties at the time and wore her dark hair long and curly. I couldn't help but notice her eye makeup, and the red polish on her nails. She was earthy, worldly, a shade tacky. She cracked jokes and seemed to tell the truth, even if it was unflattering—confessing to me at one point that she'd bought her long, flowery-print skirt on sale at The Limited. I was charmed by her good humor and wisdom. She seemed without pretensions or pious sanctimony. To me, there was something very special about her. And, clearly, I wasn't the only one. Within the hierarchy of Tibetan Buddhism, she held a revered position, particularly for a Western woman. She was thought to be a reincarnated saint, an enlightened lama. Her long Tibetan name, Jetsunma Ahkön Norbu Lhamo, carries the honorific Jetsunma—one of the religion's most regal titles. And the Tibetan Buddhist center she had founded in 1986 had quickly become one of the most prominent in the United States. It was crowded with families and lay practitioners—nearly all Westerners—who had come to study Tibetan Buddhism with Jetsunma. She was also running the largest monastery of Tibetan Buddhist monks and nuns in America.

I knew next to nothing about Tibetan Buddhism when I first ventured to Poolesville, apart from what I'd picked up in mainstream media and what I'd witnessed during a childhood spent in California, where the practice of various kinds of Buddhism seems more prevalent. I was naïve, I suppose, and pulled toward Jetsunma by something in me not entirely rational. She seemed to have created an enchanted world and a radical place beyond the laws of physics and government. And at the same time it seemed happy in a way that the newsroom world—where I had spent the last ten years—did not. Bitterness is rampant in journalism, as is a vague malaise: My desk at the newspaper was surrounded on all sides by the desks of people taking antidepressants. Was there something special about Tibetan Buddhism that made people content, or was it simply the lush temple grounds? At KPC—as it is called by the students—there were seventy-two acres of woods and gardens to walk in, hidden shrines to peek at, prayer wheels to spin, and benches to rest your legs. Everywhere, it seemed, pale-colored prayer flags were blowing softly in the breeze. Outside the main building there were shoes scattered about. Inside there was a funky gift shop selling Buddhist books, crystals, and postcards of His Holiness, the Fourteenth Dalai Lama of Tibet (does he ever not smile?). There was a buzz in the air, a freshness and vitality. The nuns and monks, dressed in long burgundy and saffron robes, were for the most part Americans, and they went about their duties with a playfulness and wit that surprised me. The rooms were crowded with colorful Buddhist icons and artifacts and ritual instruments, but at the same time they had a feeling of warmth and familiarity, a feeling of home.

And there were a number of exquisite spire-topped stupas to circumambulate in Poolesville, too—all conceived by Jetsunma and executed by her students—but nothing compared in beauty and magnitude with the great Migyur Dorje stupa. Early in the summer of 1995, His Holiness Penor Rinpoche had visited Poolesville from India and had given Jetsunma a rare collection of ancient relics, perhaps the rarest and most potent combination of Tibetan Buddhist relics in the West. And Jetsunma had set out to build a stupa worthy of them.

When I arrived in the clearing in the woods where the stupa stood, the moonlight was streaming down on the magnificent monument like liquid from the sky. I could see the roughness of the concrete—it still hadn't been sanded or painted. And the impressive landscaping plans, for an amphitheater and waterfall, for shrubs and well-placed spotlights, were still on hold. The money had run out—or had been spent on other things.

But even so, in the darkness and surrounded by the woods, the stupa had an unworldly loveliness. Neglect didn't mask its power but almost emphasized it, as though it were as natural and alive as the forest. I liked the way the concrete was stained and imperfect. And in the bright moonlight I could see the crystal ball glowing quietly at the top. Standing on the ground and looking up, I was moved—the stupa moved me like no historical monument in Washington ever had.

I had seen this stupa come from nothing. I'd seen the place in the woods before the trees were cleared. I'd seen a deep hole dug in the summer heat. I'd seen an eclectic young crew of six Americans work tirelessly, selflessly—with the sort of energy and devotion and faith that gave me a kind of hope myself. There had been aching elbows and knees and shoulders. There had been accidents and sleepless nights. They had poured buckets and buckets of concrete. They had bent rebar and made molds. And as the stupa had come to life, inch by inch, and grown taller and taller, I had seen bags and bags of rice and beans passed person by person and then lowered into its belly. I had seen a long cedar tree lying on its side in the prayer room—its branches shorn, its body smooth—and seen it painted red with gold Tibetan lettering. The relics were placed in little clear plastic boxes and carefully tied to the painted tree with silk string. One box contained an ancient fingerbone of Migyur Dorje; another housed the "brain pill" of another great wisdom being. And one small clear box was said to hold the crystallized breath of the Buddha himself.

In the darkness and moonlight, as I began to walk around the stupa, clockwise, a thought came into my mind. It was as though the stupa itself had whispered it to me. *There are sacred things. There are sacred towers and sacred texts and sacred teachings and sacred traditions. And the truth is, absolutely everything sacred has some people behind it.

Cast of Characters

THE LAMA AND HER CHILDREN

Jetsunma Ahkön Lhamo—
Alyce Zeoli/Alyce Cassara/Catharine Burroughs
Atira Zeoli
Ben Zeoli
Christopher (Rigdzin) Zeoli

THE LAMA'S HUSBANDS

Michael Burroughs
Karl Jones
Pat Mulloy
Jim Perry

THE LAMA'S ATTENDANTS

Alana—Elizabeth Elgin/Betsy Elgin
Ariana—Judith Kreitemeyer
Atara—Holly Heiss

THE NUNS OF KPC

Aileen—Karen Williams—Ani NBC
Alexandra—Diane Johnson
Arene—Maria Windolph
Catharine Anastasia—Jalee
Dara—Karen Tokarz
Dawa—Sophie Dellamula
Dechen—Michelle Grissom
Ella—Vicky Windolph
Palchen—Jan Hoge

Rene—Deborah Larrabee
Rinchen—Janice Newmark
Samla—Catherine Windolph
Samten—Shannon Swift
Sherab Khandro—Teri Milwee
Sophia—Angela Windolph

THE MONKS OF KPC

Jampal Rowe
Kamil—Roger Hill
Konchog Norbu—Tom Fry
Richard Dykeman
Sangye Dorje—Jay Allen
Tashi—Tom Barry
Yeshe Nyonpa—Jon Randolph

THE LAY PRACTITIONERS OF KPC

Bob and Linda Colacurcio
Chris Finney—Chris Cervenka
Eleanore Finney
Rick Finney
Ted and Linda Kurkowski
Ayla Meurer
Wib Middleton
Jane Perini
Eleanor Rowe
Doug Sims
Shelly Sims—Shelly Nemerovsky
David Somerville
Sylvia Somerville—Sylvia Rivchun

THE VISITING TIBETANS

Gyaltrul Rinpoche
Khenpo Tsewang Gyatso
Kunzang Lama

Kusum Lingpa

His Holiness Penor Rinpoche—
Drubwang Pema Norbu Rinpoche

Tulku Rigdzin Pema—the Stupa Man

Yantang Tulku

Plans for the Migyur Dorje Stupa with all the phases complete

KEY TO RENDERING

A. Waterfall to the stream below

B. Two-foot curved wall, defining the
   interior garden

C. Open, natural, amphitheater seating

D. Partially protected shelter

E. Wheelchair access ramp and walkway

F. Circular stone pathway (korwa path)
   around the stupa

Part One

The
Lama

1.

The Lady Lama Appears

I HAVE NEVER MET SUCH WEIRD
YET SERIOUS AND EARNEST PEOPLE.

—JACK KEROUAC, *The Dharma Bums*

The drive to Poolesville takes forty-five minutes from downtown Washington, D.C., mostly on a winding two-lane road that runs from the northern heart of the district to the farthest reaches of Montgomery County. The road takes you quickly out of the district, away from taxicabs and pedestrian traffic, and into suburbs of Maryland, where the view out the windshield becomes a blur of fulgent green grass and white fences. Country clubs and private schools, churches and synagogues. Everybody seems to have white fences at the roadside, and as you drive on, the fences only get newer and longer and fancier. There are large horse farms in Potomac, whose owners favor split-rail fences and showy stone gates. And where farmland has been sold off, mansions have gone up cheek by jowl, each as grotesque as the next. It puzzled me, as I made the drive to Poolesville to hear Jetsunma teach, that anyone with enough money to buy a house that large wouldn't want some grounds around it, or even the shade of a few big trees, but the orange earth was upturned on either side of River Road—to accommodate mansions crowded together and very close to the curb, and to accommodate all the people getting rich by doctoring and lobbying and lawyering and investing in the stock market. These people were retreating, searching for a better and calmer life, away from the District of Columbia and its seemingly insoluble problems. People were looking for a place that felt safer, and more like home.

Samsara. That's what I started to think, after the drive had become a commute for me. Samsara is what Tibetan Buddhists call this world we live in, the accumulating and spending, the jobs and cars and houses, the white fences and green grass. It is the world around us, always dying, always being reborn, and the reality that scientists are so busy studying and tracking and testing and proving. Samsara is suffering, sickness, and old age. And on my drive samsara was the labor and delivery ward at Sibley Hospital, the National Cancer Institute in Bethesda, the quaintly appointed mortuary on the side of the road in Potomac Village. And from what I could tell from my limited exposure to Tibetan Buddhism at that point, samsara was all the things I cared about—my family, my cats, the plants growing in my garden, my job at the newspaper, my rented house in Georgetown. Only the Tibetan Buddhists don't think of *it* as real. Samsara has only the illusion of reality. It is a hallucination fed by desire. "We are living in a realm of desire," Lama Yeshe says at the beginning of *Introduction to Tantra: A Vision of Totality,* "from the moment we wake up until the moment we fall asleep at night, and even throughout our dreams, we are driven by desire . . . and behind all our desires is the wish to be happy."

Beyond the village of Potomac, the road becomes rural again. As I reached the edge of Poolesville, there were woods and pastures, and I passed vegetable stands and rusted cars, and heard crickets in the dark parts of the forest.

The sign outside the center was faded and rusting. KUNZANG ODSAL PALYUL CHANGCHUB CHOLING, it said rather exotically, with no further explanation. VISITORS WELCOME SUNDAY SERVICE. A long line of cars and four-wheel-drive trucks had parked on either side of River Road. Many of the cars advertised a Buddhist bent, with bumper stickers that read FREE TIBET or PRACTICE RANDOM KINDNESS AND SENSELESS ACTS OF BEAUTY. There were more cars than I'd seen in Poolesville on any other visit to KPC. Since 1993, when my friend

Martin Wassell first told me about the center and suggested that Jetsunma might make a good story, I'd sort of circled the place with fascination. Eventually, I did interview Jetsunma for *Elle,* and I'd written about Penor Rinpoche—Jetsunma's mentor and Tibetan teacher—for *The Washington Post.* I'd also spent some time with one of the nuns in Poolesville, a woman named Rinchen, for an essay about happiness.

Jetsunma had decided to begin teaching again in September 1995, every other Sunday. Over the summer a television set had been wheeled into the large Dharma room and videotapes of her old teachings played; then only the diehards and the ordained tended to show up. But Jetsunma live and in person had a wholly different appeal.

The temple itself was set back from the road, at the end of a cracked asphalt driveway and a stretch of grass. Not that long ago, in the 1970s, it had been a new colonial mansion, too, belonging to a rich gay couple who had had a twelve-seater hot tub in what was now a large prayer room. The facade was a modern cliché of a southern plantation—white columns and brick—but there were signs that something else was going on. Atop the roof was a sculpture of deer sitting on either side of what looked like a golden wagon wheel—a traditional Tibetan Buddhist symbol for the wheel of Dharma, the wheel of teachings and transformation. Tibetan prayer flags were up, too, blowing about poetically. The idea is that the wind will loosen the prayers from the cloth and carry them across the world.

Rinchen was standing at the front door and greeted me with her luminous, childlike smile. Her burgundy robes almost overwhelmed her small body. Her hair was glossy black, shorn to an inch, and flecked with white. During our previous talks she had described her life to me—all the years she dreamed of being an artist. All the years she was miserable. Since becoming a nun or *ani,* seven years before, she had given up wearing jewelry or fragrance or makeup. She had given up having hair even long enough to curl and look soft around her head. She had forgone a sex life and vowed not to drink alcohol or take drugs, or listen to music or dance for pleasure. She had given up dreaming of being an artist, too. In Poolesville she was paid a small salary to answer the phones and to keep the temple clean. All this, and the practice of Buddhism, had brought her deep contentment.

"Did you come for the carnival, or did you just find your way out here today?" Rinchen asked. When I said I didn't know anything about a carnival, she explained that it was being run by the children of the temple to raise money for the stupa. A small auction was also being held. On the table to Rinchen's left there were necklaces, crystals, polished stones, rings, a Timex watch—the kinds of offerings I had seen on the altars inside, next to bowls of water and bowls of rice, or outside on the steps of the stupas, next to burning incense and flickering candles. Indeed, these had been offerings, left by members and visitors, and now, after having been blessed, they were being sold.

Inside, people crowded into the small foyer. The early morning prayers and meditation class had ended, and there must have been eighty or a hundred people waiting to find their seats for Jetsunma's teaching. Polished-looking professionals, men with expensive haircuts and women in long gabardine dresses, stood near each other and talked. There were teenage girls in Indian print skirts and black nail polish, and their boyfriends in baggy jeans. The ordained, wearing long maroon and saffron robes, made their way through the press of flesh, attending to various duties they had been assigned on Sundays.

Buddhists don't worship on Sundays traditionally, but in America the Sunday "church thing" works, as Wib Middleton liked to say. Wib was the spokesman for the temple, the public relations guy. And ever since I'd first stumbled out there, he'd been my tour guide, generously helping me navigate the foreign waters of Tibetan Buddhism. He had set up my first interview with Jetsunma two years before. He had helped me find Rinchen, too, when I was looking for "happy people." He was affable and easygoing, tall and tan, and wore his thick head of prematurely gray hair like a fashion accessory. On most days Wib also wore a starched striped button-down shirt and jeans, and looked as WASPy and trust-fundy as his nickname, short for Edward Willoughby Middleton III.

I caught sight of Wib across the foyer, standing with his pretty wife, Jane, and their two daughters. I waved, but the crowd was so thick it seemed pointless to try moving closer. There were many faces I hadn't seen before, visitors who, I imagined, were coming to the temple for the first time to check things out. "Tire kickers" was Wib's expression for them. People who showed up, sniffed around, looking for a new spiritual practice, and after a certain number of weeks they moved on, presumably to try something else. But the *sangha*—the community of students at the center, both lay practitioners and the ordained—had remained fairly constant over the years, hovering around 100 or 120. I noticed Eleanor Rowe in the foyer, too; she was an elegant older woman, a former Russian literature professor at George Washington University, who had helped found KPC with the Middletons. And next to Eleanor there was a tired-looking blond woman with three little girls jumping around her—Sylvia Somerville, the wife of David Somerville, chief of the stupa construction.

News of the stupa was everywhere, and the excitement about the project was palpable. There was a stack of palm-sized maps printed on blue paper so visitors could make the ten-minute walk to the woods and find the stupa site. There was a poster push-pinned to a bulletin board with a sketch of the stupa as it would look finished—with a spire and a faceplate with the image of a man I assumed was one of the incarnations of the Buddha. On the sketch was also a rendering of impressive landscaping planned for the stupa area, shrubs and pathways, an amphitheater, and elegant benches. MIGYUR DORJE STUPA, the poster announced. PROJECT COST: $250,000.

The walls were dotted with photos of Jetsunma. In one she was seated on a throne and a crown was being lowered onto her head. In others she was standing next to various golden-skinned Tibetan men in robes, one of whom, a stocky man in heavy eyeglass frames like Cary Grant used to wear, I recognized as His Holiness Penor Rinpoche. It hadn't taken me many phone calls to Tibetan scholars and practitioners at other centers to learn he was a rather unassailable figure in Tibetan Buddhism, a lama so revered in India that people saved the clods of earth he walked on. Here, standing with his great American discovery—it was Penor Rinpoche who had met Jetsunma on his first trip to the United States, declared her a tulku, and later enthroned her and consecrated the temple—he looked sort of pleased, almost beaming. Jet-sunma had a pudgy, beautiful face and warm almond-shaped brown eyes. Her hair was long and wet-curled. In the photograph with Penor Rinpoche, she was smiling hugely, exuding a blossoming unrestrained joy, as though two seconds before she'd heard the silliest joke. I detected a hint of awkwardness, too. She was a robust American woman, part Jewish, part Italian, with big hair and a big face, and as happy as she seemed to be with Penor Rinpoche, somehow she didn't belong. Or maybe that was me, too stuck on appearances. Maybe I saw only the surface and wasn't seeing something else, way below, some sign that she was Ahkön Lhamo, a reincarnation, a realized saint, and that she was ultimately not Jewish or Italian or American—deep inside, she was a tulku, or her essence was, her energy and her spirit, and she had been born in New York City to bring the teachings of the Buddha to the United States. This seemed to be what Penor Rinpoche believed.

Most of the seats were taken by the time I wandered down the aisle and found mine. Gray metal folding chairs were set up in rows, in three sections that had, I was told, no significance. Anybody could sit anywhere. The monks and nuns were all sitting on the floor near the far wall and looked like an explosion of maroon and saffron fabric. And in the middle of this, one stout nun remained on her feet—they called her Ani NBC because she worked as a sound technician at the NBC news bureau in Washington—standing behind a video camera on a tripod.

In those first few visits the Dharma room was confusing to me. In a church or synagogue you are directed, usually by architectural design, to a central point of focus, like a pulpit or altar. But once inside the Dharma room, from any of the three sections of metal chairs, I had no idea where I was supposed to be looking. Everywhere my eyes fell there was an array of circus-colored stuff, golden Buddhas, wall hangings, and tubular kites, which dropped from the ceiling. There were two empty thrones—painted wild colors. One was very large and had a picture of Penor Rinpoche on its seat. The other, smaller throne had a glass of ice water nearby. Along a different wall there was a large altar with a statue of the Buddha where candles had been placed, bowls of water and rice, and assorted offerings, including a box of Cap'n Crunch cereal. And sprinkled about the room enormous crystals were spotlighted with tiny halogen lights so they glowed, almost throbbed, as if from some kind of natural power.

Tibetan Buddhism is sometimes called the Short Path, as Wib Middleton had explained to me. None of the other forms of Buddhism advertises so swift a route to enlightenment. You can expect to "incarnate" countless times, as bugs and animals, even descend into the ghost realms and hell realms, before you achieve liberation from the endless hamster wheel of death and rebirth. But in Vajrayana Buddhism, the more formal name for the school of Buddhism practiced in Tibet, the student progresses toward enlightenment by practicing intense introspection and retraining the mind, learning to see the world differently. The student is taught, sometimes rather painfully, to abandon the notion of self (it is a delusion anyway) and to go in search of his or her own Buddha nature. If the other forms of Buddhism are like climbing a mountain by going around it many times, gaining altitude in gradual steps, Tibetan Buddhism is like going straight up one side of Mount Everest without stopping. It is a sure path to wisdom, the lamas say—and the most treacherous. But for impatient Americans, what could be better than the fastest route?

A gong sounded, loudly and suddenly—and we all rose to our feet in a jolt. There were seventy or eighty lay practitioners and visitors, including a group of eight children who were sitting on the floor, plus thirty-three ordained—about twenty-five nuns and eight monks. All at once they turned to face the back door, the way people turn at a wedding when the bride is about to appear. They put their hands together in a prayer pose, their fingers not folding over together, clasped, but pointing to the sky like church steeples. They bowed their heads a bit.

Through the windows I caught sight of Jetsunma, walking on the front porch. She was wearing a red dress and looked considerably thinner than in the pictures on the wall. Her hair looked straighter too, less full. A young man was beside her, a broad-shouldered fellow with straight red hair and a handsome face. He was easily fifteen years her junior. It was Karl Jones—her husband, or sometimes her husband. Their marriage seemed in a state of flux. One minute I was told they had separated, and the next I heard they were working things out.

"Hi," Jetsunma said to the room as she entered.

"Hello!" the audience said back.

She walked quickly down the aisle. I could see she was also wearing stockings and pumps, for upon arriving at the center of the room, just in front of the children and the ordained, Jetsunma got down on her hands and knees and put her head to the floor. Then she rose again. She prostrated herself three times this way, in the direction of either Penor Rinpoche's throne or an altar—I couldn't tell which. Then she took her place at the smaller throne, where the glass of water had been set. I felt a sigh of relief. Finally, I knew where to be looking.

But the relief didn't last long. The people around me began kneeling—in the aisles, in the center of the room, and along the walls—prostrating to Jetsunma. Once, twice, three times. They moved in shifts, took turns in the aisles. The ordained on the floor seemed to do it with a particular focus and intensity. As they rose from the ground, their hands formed the steeples, and they bumped themselves on the crown of the head, then the throat, then the heart. And then they dropped to the ground again, touched their foreheads to the floor, and started over. Jetsunma didn't seem to be watching. She took a fingernail and moved her bangs out of her eyes. She picked up the glass of water and took a sip. Then she adjusted the flowers in a vase at her side.

The stupa was the subject of all temple announcements, which were made after prayers and before the teaching. Shelly Sims, who was married to the stupa crew member Doug Sims, delivered a fund-raising pitch as part of her role as public relations woman of the temple. Shelly had styled blond hair, and in her pale blue suit she reminded me a little of Hillary Clinton.

"The relics we've been given are very, very potent," Shelly said, then flashed an excited smile. "That's the buzz, anyway—what we've heard from the people around His Holiness Penor Rinpoche. The relics bring great results. They are very powerful, and people who have circumambulated stupas and left offerings at stupas with relics this powerful say they have found better lives, and sometimes experienced miraculous healings . . ."

Jetsunma broke in. "When I heard about the existence of these relics, I begged His Holiness for them," she said. "And I promised that we would revere them, respect them, and treat them very, very well. His Holiness was afraid, he said, that Americans wouldn't understand their importance. I told him, I can't speak for everybody, but I can speak for myself. *I will.*"

"We've raised fifty thousand dollars already," Shelly said, "but we need two hundred thousand more. And very soon. There are materials and supplies to buy before it can be finished."

It might be easy to be unimpressed with Jetsunma Ahkön Lhamo if you'd never heard her speak or teach in person, if you'd simply bumped into her at White Flint Mall, where she liked to shop, or you saw her in Gaithersburg at the manicurist, where she had her nails done every week. It was easy to see her as she seemed, like a forty-five-year-old woman with a pretty face who was a little doughy around the edges and trying to keep her weight down, a woman who liked experimenting with eye shadow, who probably kept a stack of mail-order catalogs by her bed and watched TV after dinner with her three kids. And you wouldn't be wrong there either. But if she seemed ordinary, it was a magnificent ordinariness, both defensive and sweet, contrived and genuine.

"I want to talk about conventional wisdom," she said, "and the difference between conventional wisdom and something meatier, a little bit deeper." Her face grew serious, like a mother's face while she's reviewing with her young children, once again, the procedure for crossing the street. "How do we come to assume certain things about life?" Conventional wisdom is based on history, she said. It is based on the accounts of many, many lives.

"But what if all the things we knew—about history, about the lives of all these people—were only snapshots, and not the whole picture? What if the histories we read, and the biographies we read, didn't offer complete explanations? Because they don't, you know. They are snapshots, pieces. . . . It's like watching one scene of a movie and trying to guess the entire plot. This is the little amount of information that we use to base our understanding of life."

She flexed her hands; her nails were long and painted red. The audience barely moved or fidgeted. Jetsunma fixed her eyes on the nun named Sherab for a couple of beats, and Sherab responded with a smile.

"And what does conventional wisdom tell us? We live in a strongly communicative society—we have radio, we have TV, we have the Internet, you know—we have lots of ways in which conventional wisdom is communicated to us. We aren't living out on some prairie. In fact, we know exactly what our society expects from us. And what are the messages? For one thing, in America, they are absolute. This is the way the world is. Period. . . . You might travel to another country, like India or Africa, and realize that people in those places believe a completely different set of rules—the things we value are suddenly not valued there. Many of us have had that experience, I'm sure. But even though we experience this for a brief time, while we are traveling, it is deeply ingrained in us that our way is *the way*. We are totally sold on our own conventional wisdom. We've been programmed, really. By the things our parents told us. The things society tells us. And conventional wisdom is really just our inner programming. . . .

"And what are we told? For the most part, the world we are told about is materialistic. And we are told the path to happiness is materialistic. You need a nice house. You need a nice car. If you are a woman, you need a rich man. If you are a rich man, you need a gorgeous woman. *We all know how it is.* We are told you will be happy if you are a success, and we are told that, to be a success, you have to have more than others. You have to be bigger than everybody else, stronger, more powerful. And we are taught that we have to fortify ourselves. You can't be too rich. That's basically it—you can't be too rich or too thin. . . . And we spend the better part of our lives accumulating, or planning to accumulate—and worrying about our weight."

The audience laughed.

"And then, suddenly, you meet up with the BuddhaDharma. And the BuddhaDharma tells us very different things. We are told, in fact, that accumulation is actually not the cause of happiness. It's a little scary because, up until this time, accumulation might be all we've known. So we are frightened of that information. That information is not welcome. And also, that information puts us back in the beginning of the class—maybe we don't know so much after all—and the beginning of the class is where no adult in America ever likes to be. The beginning is not a comfortable place. We spend so much of our time preparing and growing, and accumulating—we're so proud of every stage of our growth—that it's very hard to think: Oh, I have to relearn everything? It's very, very hard. . . ."

Jetsunma took a sip of water, set down the glass, then wiped the moisture from her fingers on her palm.

"And that's where the conflict comes in. . . . One of the things that Buddhism does is create a kind of programming—or habitual tendency, as we call it—that produces happiness, as opposed to the kind of programming or habitual tendency that we see demonstrated in our lives ad nauseam every day, and that makes us unhappy. And a bit confused. We are periodically happy and periodically miserable—life in samsara just seems to go around in cycles like that. And we can become used to it. . . . We think we know the causes of our suffering. We think we need a better car or a different wife. We think we are suffering because of bad luck or bad timing. And some of that might be true. But we've become so arrogant! We really think we know everything—or everything we know is all that's worth knowing!

"For instance, the BuddhaDharma tells us that in order to attain happiness, we should be generous. Now, see, that is completely contradictory to what we were told as materialists. The mantra for materialists is *Gimme gimme gimme. Gimme, gimme, gimme, gimme. Mine mine mine mine mine. I want I want I want.* That's the mantra. And now, when we begin to practice Buddhism, we're told to let go of that. We should let go, relax, loosen. Have you noticed how tight you feel when you are overwhelmed by self-concern? When we begin to practice Buddhism, we begin working in a broader way, begin to work for the benefit of others, begin to see the equality of all that lives, and begin to act accordingly. We begin to practice generosity, to practice mindfulness, to think of our lives as being potent only if we can work toward the liberation and salvation of other sentient beings, rather than: How many chickens can I get in my Crock-Pot at once?"

The room broke into laughter. And Jetsunma laughed too. A hearty, New York City kind of laugh.

"You see? It's a whole different ball game. And we fight with ourselves. We have difficulty. This is just scratching the surface of Buddhism, really, but already it conflicts with the conventional wisdom—with the programming we've gotten so far. . . . And as we go deeper, this conflict continues. As we go deeper, it can get scarier. When people really begin moving into Dharma, they start having reactions, saying, 'This is good, I like this. Oh, I don't like that. That's too difficult!' We really want a religion that's easy, no trouble, no heavy commitments, just smoothness. Make it nice. I want it nice-nice!"

This time the ordained were chuckling; thirty-three sets of shoulders were jiggling up and down. Jetsunma squeezed her eyes closed with pleasure. "Hopefully, though, you want to go deeper. You want to move into a deeply spiritual life. And when that happens, people often look around at their lives and want to change things. . . . Some things have to go. Some things don't work anymore. You might want to change your job. That might be one thing. Not everybody, but some people. You might want to leave your marriage. And I've seen that happen a number of times on the path. Two people will come and one of them really deepens into Dharma—it becomes the most important element in their lives—but their partners are like, *Not really.* And then eventually, *Not interested.* And they don't stay together. It's no longer workable. I've seen that happen.

"I've also seen lifestyles change, appearances change, attitudes change. There are so many things that change when one really moves into practice. It makes me think of how I feel now, having reached forty-five. The things that were important to me before, the things I pursued . . . I look in the mirror now and go, 'What were you thinking? What?' " She knocked a fist on the wood in front of her. " '*Hell-ooo.*' "

The room exploded in laughter. "Kind of like that. Those of you who have reached forty-five—and you don't have to nod your heads, I know who you are—may be feeling the same thing. You may sort of wake up one day and feel like you're looking at a stranger in the mirror. You just feel like you've completely changed your values—what you want in relationships, what you want in every accord. And that happens in our relationship with the Dharma, too. There is a maturing very much like you see in midlife, when we have gathered more material about life, seen a bit more cause-and-result, when we just have more information in the hopper. And you feel a bit more spacious and relaxed, too. You've either succeeded in some degree, accomplished things—or failed—but you have perspective. You know you will survive after all. And it's the same thing with practice. In the beginning it's all new and scary, and you feel really kind of excited and thrilled and in love with practice. There's a big romance going on. It's just so cool to go to a temple that looks as weird as this place looks! And it's just so cool to go to a place that doesn't look like America at all! So you fall in love with all that and think, Cool, I am here. Cool! And you start acting spiritual and talking differently. Not like suddenly you have a British accent or something, but you do talk differently. And you're playacting being a spiritual person, like dressing up in your parents' clothes. You keep thinking your eyes need to be rolled skyward or something, out of devotion—which doesn't really work in Buddhism at all. There's nobody up there.

"But you move further along in Dharma practice, hopefully, and some of that starts to be shed. We're not playacting anymore, and we're really starting to deal with the meat and potatoes of our lives. We're really starting to use Dharma as a tool. And we begin to see some cause-and-effect relationships. The first big aha comes. You realize that your whole life, all you've been really thinking about is this one thing. What can I do that's really fun that's going to make me happy? What can I do that's really fun that's going to make me happy? Or that other mantra: *What can I do that's really fun that's going to make me happy?*

"And that's about the time your teacher gives you something to take the place of the what-can-make-me-happy mantra. It's a course of study, or a practice. And at first, you think, Oh cool, my teacher gave me something to do! So you do it. And you practice and practice, study and study. But your habit for years has been trying to look for excitement and fun, so practicing and studying is like, *Naaaaaah.* Boring! But you hang in there, you deepen, and deepen some more, and the next big aha comes when you realize you are actually happier when you're doing this practice and this study, this contemplation, this meditation, than when you were out there spastically—and I do mean spastically—looking for a good time."

She paused and looked around the room, at the hundred or more faces looking back at her—looking cheerful, almost giddily so. I looked down at my lap and realized that I had stopped taking notes. Somehow, I had been imagining myself on "the path" as she described it, as though it were a real place, a specific place, and I imagined myself beginning to practice, then deepening in that practice—and I even imagined I knew what "deepening" meant. She was a Buddha, I'd been told several times by her students. She was a living Buddha, they said, an enlightened being.

"Seed always produces fruit," she said. "What goes up, must come down. What goes around, comes around. This is a part of conventional wisdom, too. But not to the same degree. The Buddha-Dharma says that a seed produces an *exact* fruit. Every thought, every action, every word is a seed that will produce an exact fruit. What causes loneliness? What causes unhappiness and poverty and illness?"

Buddhas don't just see snapshots of life, I had been told. They see the whole movie. They can see the past and the present and the future all at once. They see the chain of all events in history, all the causes, all the effects . . .

"And we keep getting chances to repair this. We are offered a chance to change our habits, our tendencies—the patterns of our lives that cause unhappiness and loneliness and even poverty. . . . Keep being unkind, and the outcome is you will be lonely. It doesn't take a great genius to notice this." The audience laughed again. "Even in one lifetime, you'll notice that mean people and selfish people are alone, and lonely."

Money seems complicated, she said, but it isn't. Money is simple. It is just like energy, and breath. You give away things, help people, be generous, and it's like exhaling energy. "We all know what it feels like to take a deep breath, to fill up our lungs, and then not be able to take any more air in. You can't take any more in because you need to exhale, to make room for more." Money is like that, too.

Afterward I waited on the driveway for Wib, who had remained my main contact at the temple. He was giving a tour of the stupa site to newcomers and visitors—to the tire kickers, in other words—and I thought I'd catch him beforehand and say hello. As I waited, a group of about twenty people slowly gathered near me, several older women, a doctor visiting from India, a Taiwanese couple, an Associated Press photographer, and a young man, barely out of his teens, wearing jeans and a T-shirt and very small sunglasses. He introduced himself to me as Roman.

"How long have you been coming here?" I asked Roman.

"Eight weeks. Such a cool place."

I nodded. "Have you been out to see the stupa yet?"

"I'm on the stupa diet!"

Wib appeared, and as he came closer I could see how tired he was. There were baggy circles under his eyes and fine beads of sweat on his face. Along with his other temple obligations, he'd been raising thousands of dollars for the stupa project. "It's been pretty intense around here," he said to me, as we stood out of hearing range of the tour group. "We've been doing practice non-stop. Jane and I were here every night last week."

A few more newcomers arrived, and Wib introduced himself to them. He'd be taking them to the stupa in a few minutes, he said. Then he turned to me again. He asked how my work was going—specifically, how my proposal to write a book about Jetsunma was being received. There were a few editors interested, I told him, at three publishing houses.

"Have you thought about getting Jetsunma's help?" Wib asked.

"What kind of help?"

"We can give her the list of names," he said. "The names of the editors, and the names of the publishing houses."

"And then what?"

"She can see a name, written on a piece of paper," he said, "and have a reaction to it. Sometimes she can see a certain result—or obstacles—or just tell you the name is okay."

This was a generous offer, by Poolesville standards, and I remember feeling flattered. Also, I didn't want to appear rude. Jetsunma received many letters a month from students asking for her guidance. Jobs, houses, boyfriends—even asking which car to buy. What would I do with Jetsunma's advice? What if she were opposed to the very editor I liked the most?

Wib must have sensed that I was equivocating, because, before I could answer, he looked over to the tour group, motioned that it was time to start.

I stayed with the group as far as River Road, where my car was parked. Along the way Wib answered questions the group had—explaining what a stupa is and how the relics had been brought from India. They would be inserted in the stupa during a special ceremony the following week, weather permitting, then sealed away forever.

"What color will the stupa be," one of the older women asked, "when it's finished?"

"Gold," Wib said. "We're looking into gold-leafing it. Jetsunma has gotten the idea into her head to do that—so there's probably no turning back."

As we reached River Road, and I was pulling out my car keys, Wib stopped his tour for a moment to say good-bye.

"Gold? I didn't know a stupa could be gold," I said. The other stupas in Poolesville were all white.

"Neither did we," Wib said. "The Tibetans never offer much information, you know. It's a little like having a conversation with somebody from Maine. Yep. Nope. Not a lot of volunteering. We thought stupas had to be white, too . . . until we asked."

2.

The Stupa Builds Itself

In India they are made of mudbrick. In France the builders tend toward stone and mortar. In America stupas are concrete—like American sidewalks and American condos, American baseball stadiums and American swimming pools. And when the Migyur Dorje stupa was done, the students in Poolesville expected it would be the best, the largest, most perfect stupa, nearly forty feet high with a spire made of concrete—if you can imagine that— and a full moon of a crystal ball on top. Now, in October, they were halfway finished, but the stupa felt like a holy thing already. Once the cedar tree was placed inside it, with all the relics hanging from it like Christmas ornaments, it would heal people, be an avenue for the miraculous, a seat of primordial wisdom. The Buddha's mind would come alive in the woods of Poolesville, Maryland. It would be a twenty-four-hour prayer vigil all in itself. Ceaseless endless effortless goodness. There'd be a paved road in the woods by next year, too, and shuttle buses would come back and forth, bringing the sick, the sad, the suffering—maybe from the National Institutes of Health.

There were seven other stupas in Poolesville, all much smaller and less perfect. They'd built their first one in 1988, the summer Jetsunma was enthroned, but they'd made lots of mistakes—the relics had been accidentally run over by a bulldozer, for one thing. Now, seven years later, they were beginning to get the hang of stupa building. And they were beginning to figure out concrete.

Anybody who knows concrete will tell you this: weird stuff, impossible stuff. It's a little like karma—exacting, unforgiving. Concrete seems mutable while you are pouring, then, suddenly, it's set into place. But not just set: fixed forever, hardened into stone and impossibly heavy. Each cubic foot of concrete weighs one hundred pounds. In the next section of the stupa, the heart-shaped *bum-pa*, there'd be something like twenty-five thousand pounds of concrete in the lower part alone.

The middle chamber of the stupa was now done, stuffed and sealed. Over the weekend it had taken six hours to stuff the cavernous chambers. There had been a great chain of people—like a line of ants—passing the offerings hand to hand. There were nearly three hundred buckets of white rice and dried beans. There were thousands of mantras printed on thin paper that had been sprayed with saffron and rolled and then shrink-wrapped and covered in five-colored cloth and tied with five-colored ribbon. There were wealth bowls filled with gold and silver and jewelry. There were ceramic vases holding a specific blend of flowers and herbs and spices. People unloaded the offerings off the trucks, then handed them to the next person, and the next, down a line that continued twenty or thirty yards to the bottom of the ladder. The offerings were passed up the ladder to the scaffolding and then down again, to the hollow interior of the stupa, where Doug Sims, a forty-eight-year-old lay practitioner and accountant with strawberry blond hair and freckles, was arranging them in some semblance of order. It was a little like an Egyptian tomb. Once all the offerings were unloaded and arranged, the top of the chamber was packed with bales of cedar chips and covered with loose cedar and a final sheet of clear plastic—so when the chamber was sealed over with concrete, everything would be protected.

Sangye, a young monk who had been a student of Jetsunma since he was a teenager, had sealed the throne and middle chambers himself. He was an American, thirty-one years old, and a fresh-faced guy with light hair and slightly sad blue eyes. He made sure that the plastic was carefully placed, mixed a thick batch of concrete, carried the white buckets of wet mortar up the ladder, and bent over the plastic, spreading the concrete, smoothing it out, and then sealing it. Sealing it for eternity.

Sangye Dorje was his Tibetan Buddhist name—Jetsunma had given it to him before he became a monk, during the brief time that he was her consort. *Sangye* means "buddha" in Tibetan. *Dorje* means "thunderbolt" and "indestructible," but there were a few jokes at the temple about the fact it is also Tibetan slang for "penis." His birth name was pretty simple: Jay Allen. Maybe too simple. He'd grown up in California and Maryland, in a broken home and in front of the tube, like everybody else his age, but he had the presence and the voice of an uncomplicated farmboy. In Poolesville people were always talking about him, always saying his name, *Song*-gay this, *Song*-gay that. What Sangye said carried weight, and his observations about Buddhist life were often repeated.

It was late in the month—Halloween Day, to be exact—when Sangye was climbing the ladder and felt a slight wobble in it. He'd just finished sealing the middle chamber and was beginning to worry about how to make the bum-pa. Unlike the bottom chambers of the stupa, which were masculine, straight lines and right angles and relatively easy to pour—as easy as concrete ever is— the bum-pa would be curvy, heart-shaped, voluptuous.

Bum-pa means "vase" or "container of precious energy" in Tibetan. As soon as he was down the ladder, Sangye thought, he was going to start working on it.

The ladder was wobbling a bit under his weight on the way down. Sangye was broad-chested, broad-shouldered. Before he became a fully ordained monk there were always women around, just sort of staring at him hopefully. And he was always looking back, reasonably interested—as any guy would be. But frankly, he said, when people asked, it wasn't women that he missed most about being a regular person. He had taken a vow of celibacy— that was true—but sometimes he thought the other vows were more difficult to keep. He couldn't sing anymore, or dance, or listen to music for pleasure. He couldn't drink alcohol. And the hardest part about being a monk, it sometimes seemed to Sangye, was not being able to sit in a dark bar and drink a beer sometimes and listen to a band play the blues.

Two other monks in the stupa crew, Tashi and Kamil, were on the ground when Sangye fell. Tashi was a pale teddy bear of a guy. He had sold weapons parts to third world countries before becoming a monk. Kamil was the only black monk at KPC, a former schoolteacher from the Virgin Islands, and he was bending down when he heard the ladder banging against the concrete. The ladder was bouncing, and Sangye's legs had lost contact with it. Kamil saw Sangye's golden T-shirt flying in the air, saw Sangye's arms stretched out like the wings of a bird.

It was a clean hit. Sangye landed flat on his back, all parts of him hitting in one solid dull thud. And then he just lay there, perfectly still. Kamil ran into the construction trailer and called 911. Then Kamil made another call—to Jetsunma's private line. She was the lama. The giant stupa had been her idea. And Sangye was her special monk.

Jetsunma herself had picked the stupa site and approved the stupa crew. Her clairvoyance was well known among her students and her Tibetan teachers alike. A couple of people were turned away, gently denied the opportunity to work on the stupa—told they weren't strong enough, or reliable enough. Their karma wasn't right for it in this lifetime. Stupa work is considered auspicious. In India Buddhists might wait in line for hours, or days, just to have a chance to work on an important stupa. They might sleep next to a site, hoping to help with its construction for just a few minutes. There was even an old story about a pig who attained enlightenment: He had mud on his tail and happened to back into an old stupa, thereby mending a hole that ultimately would have caused the shrine to deteriorate. For this the pig was reborn in the next lifetime not just as a human being but as a human being who found the Dharma and became realized.

The word is *meritorious*. That's how you say it—the way you describe the benefits bestowed by stupa work. It's an awkward word, but if you are an English-speaking Tibetan Buddhist, it gets easier to say after a while. And it is always meritorious and nothing but meritorious. You never say "virtuous" or "righteous" or "honorable" or "commendable." Although sometimes you might include the word *activity*, as in stupa work being a *meritorious activity*. This isn't the only Eastern concept that is too subtle to be elegantly translated. You say *auspicious* instead of "lucky," and you don't talk about doing good, or volunteering, or finding a good cause. You talk about *being of benefit*. And generally when you talk about *being of benefit* it is really a shorthand way to talk about respecting life and making the world a better place. The longer and more traditional way of expressing this is *being of benefit to all sentient beings*. Everything in Tibetan Buddhism is about sentient beings—and ending the suffering of sentient beings. You say *sentient beings* instead of "human beings" because you don't want to exclude anybody, and *sentient* is a way of describing all life-forms that are conscious, sensate—all people, all animals, all bugs and fish, including the invisible realms, the ghost realms and the hell realms. There are eighteen different hells in Tibetan Buddhism, and there are countless beings there, too, all hoping to be released.

The Tibetan Buddhist world is largely unseen, the way thoughts are unseen, and ideas. The way love is unseen, and energy.

When Jetsunma chose the site of the stupa, she was shown a topographical map of the property across the road from the temple, but she wasn't too great at reading maps, so she decided to walk around the woods herself. She dressed in jeans and a pair of Doc Martens and left her house on the temple grounds, where she lived with her three kids and her husband, and was guided to two possible locations by members of the stupa crew.

The first site was nice but too large, Jetsunma said. Perhaps, later on, they could use it for something else, like a new temple. The second site was perfect. It was in the deep woods. There were hundreds of trees, vines, rosebushes. There were two streams that converged. It was on a rise of land, which was good for drainage—concrete tends to crack and leak—and the energy there, Jetsunma said, was "very clear."

So electrical lines were laid, a crude road was created, and hundreds of trees were cut down with two chain saws. The stupa crew was joined by thirty or so volunteers, mostly members of the sangha—the group of ordained and lay practitioners at the center. When a bug got killed, they said prayers over the dead bug's body. When squirrels and birds were found dead, there were more *Om Mani Padme Hums*. They prayed for the animals that were relocated, for the birds' nests that were smashed, for the worms chopped in half, for the ants underfoot, for the microbes being shifted, for the invisible beings in the invisible realms. They prayed their work would benefit the world and bring an eventual end to suffering. And then they prayed that the merit they accumulated by doing this work, and even by saying these prayers, would be offered up to bring an eventual end of suffering, too. A sign was stuck by the steering wheel in somebody's Ford Explorer: REMEMBER TO DEDICATE YOUR MERIT.

It was in the dead middle of summer, the end of July, that Jetsunma returned to the woods with a group of crew members to see the cleared land and choose the actual site of the stupa itself. Doug Sims came along, carrying a hammer and a stake, prepared to mark the spot.

As Jetsunma walked around in the clearing, everybody remained quiet. They all watched her look up to the treetops. They watched her listen for the sound of the creeks. Then she pointed, with a long red fingernail, to Doug's shoes. And everybody's head swiveled to look at Doug's shoes, too.

"Right where your foot is," she said to Doug.

So he bent over in the sunlight and pounded the stake. He looked up again, looked at everybody looking back at him, and felt something on his legs and arms: goose bumps.

And so it was on August 1, 1995, that the stupa crew began its work. There were auspicious reasons for choosing that date, although nobody can really remember now what these were, besides that the moon was in a growing phase. You plant seeds and begin new endeavors you hope will bear fruit when the moon is waxing. There are many days in the Buddhist calendar that are considered auspicious, like the Ten Thousand Days. Whatever activity occurs on these days, the good as well as the bad, is magnified ten thousand times.

Each morning the crew would meet at the temple at 7:00, do Buddhist "practice"—sets of prayers and visualizations and prostrations—together, and afterward eat a huge breakfast prepared for them by a rotating team of nuns. A special diet goes along with stupa work, too—a universally acknowledged "stupa diet" followed by Tibetan Buddhists everywhere, who need to be particularly pure while toiling in sacred construction—for the ordained as well as the lay practitioners. No meat, no alcohol, no onions, no garlic, no sex for twenty-four hours before work, and no menstruating women allowed. There could be a serious problem, it is believed, if a person's blood spilled inside the stupa's chambers.

All the nuns who volunteered to do stupa-related jobs had to adhere to the diet and restrictions. Normally, they ate meat—unlike the Zen Buddhists—and Tibetans themselves are famous steak lovers. But if you offered to sew the cloth cases for the rolled mantras, you had to be on the stupa diet and not menstruating. If you were pouring the grain into the five-gallon buckets, you had to be on the stupa diet and not menstruating. If you were helping to sand the cedar tree, you followed these rules, and if you were painting the relief on the faceplate, you did also. Only the volunteers who were one step removed from the process were exempt. The nuns cooking for the stupa crew, for instance, were free to eat garlic.

It didn't take long for Jetsunma's stupa crew to become a cohesive and efficient team. From the start they were working twelve-hour days—and all being paid nine hundred dollars a month. David Somerville, a thirty-seven-year-old professional contractor with dark hair and striking blue eyes, was designated as the brains in charge, although he was not necessarily working on site every day, since he had a wife and three kids at home and other construction jobs to look after. Sangye was number two, since he had the most experience with stupas and concrete. There was Doug, the accountant from Texas. He was a relatively new student but had previous stupa-building experience and would be working on preparing the cedar tree. Kamil Hill would be cutting most of the rebar—he was hardworking and endlessly easy to be around. Karl Jones was chosen, too. He didn't always get along with Sangye, but he was young and strong and married to Jetsunma. And there was Sherab Khandro, a nun and the only woman working on the stupa.

Sherab was loud sometimes—also six feet tall and strong. Before taking robes she had been a personal trainer at Bally Total Fitness. Before that there were stories about drugs and jumping over Cyclone fences in the night, living near the beach in San Diego and falling in love with somebody new every four seconds. Her brown hair was shaved down now and her love life was over and she had finally gotten rid of the silver Ford Probe with the license plates 4EVRFIT, but all other attempts to subdue expressions of Sherab's spirit were pretty much useless. Working on the stupa, she arrived every morning wearing work pants and tool belt, sunglasses and a straw hat, a wet T-shirt wrapped around her neck and a Walkman plugged into her ears. For Sunday services she turned up at the temple with size eleven steel-toed construction boots under her robes.

The work was miserable, hideous, back killing—beginning with the digging of a fifteen-by-fifteen-foot hole in the clay and shale during the peak of the hottest and muggiest summer in memory. The stupa crew had shovels and, for some of it, a backhoe. They tried not to lose their tempers or complain too much—generating negativity could create serious obstacles—but everybody was experiencing sleepless nights and pain. Sherab, who had suffered from back problems in the past, visited her chiropractor before she started on the stupa and was taught how to dig a ditch while squatting so she wouldn't injure herself again. "I know I look like an idiot," she'd yell out while she squatted, "but at least I'm still here."

At midday the crew drove back to the temple, took off their boots, ate lunch in the community room. Afterward Sangye would lie down in front of the big AC unit and close his eyes. Sherab would put her Walkman earphones on and listen to a tape of *The Mists of Avalon,* a book Jetsunma had recommended years before. "I wanted to stay away from the guys during the breaks," Sherab said later. "All that guy stuff, the testosterone flying around, I didn't want to hang out too much with them, or else I might start thinking I was one of them—and do something really stupid and hurt myself."

At night Doug collapsed at home, in agony from swollen hands and fingers and inflamed hip sockets. He tried aspirin and ibuprofen, hot packs and cold packs—but he still woke up at 3:00 A.M. needing a third dose of Advil.

The heat was beyond anything. It was suffocating and unrelenting, an oven in the woods for hour upon hour, and there was no escaping it, nowhere to go but up, farther up the ladder, to pour more concrete.

Underground, in the lower chamber of the stupa, Sangye buried some guns and knives, some photographs of suffering people, wounded animals, cancer cells, and electron microscope images of the Ebola and AIDS viruses. The lower chamber contains all the things the stupa will be suppressing.

By the first of October, when the crew had begun pouring the throne chamber, the Stupa Man had arrived in Poolesville. He was a Tibetan, a tulku who traveled the world as a master stupa builder. He came on special orders, after having been telephoned in the middle of the night and implored by His Holiness Penor Rinpoche, the supreme head of the Nyingma lineage of Tibetan Buddhism. It takes a while to figure the Tibetan power structure out, and the only useful analogy is unfortunately military. If there were a Navy captain of the good ship KPC, it was Jetsunma. If there were a chief of naval operations, it was Penor Rinpoche. Directly over him would be the Dalai Lama, sort of a chairman of the Joint Chiefs of Staff of all lineages of Tibetan Buddhism, of which there are four—like the Army, the Navy, the Air Force, and Marines. The Stupa Man was a Nyingma lama in the same lineage as Penor Rinpoche and well known for making the best stupas, and the most correct stupas, and, although he was a busy man, he'd offered to squeeze in the Poolesville stupa between stupas in Taiwan and France. Tulku Rigdzin Pema was his official name, but early on Jetsunma had started referring to him as the Stupa

Man, and it stuck, although nobody was calling him that to his face exactly. To his face they called him Rinpoche.

Rinpoche is a term of respect, and, in the case of the Stupa Man, it was a bit of a title enhancement. There are rinpoches, jetsuns, *drubwangs*, but they are all tulkus, or reincarnated saints. Tulku Rigdzin Pema had been raised in a monastery and was, according to His Holiness, "a very pure monk." In order to become an expert in stupas, he had performed the Noble Light Rays practice, not just thousands of times but many hundreds of thousands of times. He wasn't a macho sort of lama—out in the woods every day, wielding a hammer and pouring concrete—as the stupa crew had imagined. Instead, the Stupa Man was very quiet, thin as a stick, and, upon arriving in Poolesville, he had gone immediately into his bedroom, where he remained most days, engaged in prayer.

It was his presence, though, that reminded the stupa crew all over again of the importance of their work. And the importance of the stupa. They'd take a spontaneous break from their labor and listen to the creeks, and the rustling of wind in the circle of trees at the edge of the clearing. They felt a fullness in their chests, a sense of completeness, and an exhilaration that made them light-headed.

"There's nothin' in this world I'd rather be doin'," Doug would say in his Texas drawl.

"Nope," Sangye would answer. "Nothin'."

And every so often a sangha member would wander out and watch the crew sweating away and tell them how beautiful the stupa was looking—just a bunker of concrete at this point—and go on and on about the benefit to sentient beings, *the meritorious nature of it all.* The stupa was a holy thing all right, but as the crew struggled and sweated and grunted around it, hauling and digging and pouring the stupa into being, it also seemed as though they had nothing, really, to do with it. The stupa seemed to be getting taller on its own, growing out of the orange earth rather quietly and sweetly. Like a plant.

"It's like we're just showing up," Doug said to David, "and the stupa is building itself."

"Yeah," David said. "I know exactly what you mean."

•

The stupa crew was focused mostly on the exterior, pouring the concrete, getting the spire done right. They were surprised to discover that the Stupa Man hardly seemed to care how the stupa looked. He was mostly intense about the tree—the hidden spine of the stupa, where all the relics would be placed. Doug Sims cut down a tall cedar tree in the woods, and, after the Stupa Man approved it, Doug began shaving the sides of the twenty-foot trunk—making it perfectly round, giving the bottom four flat sides—then belt-sanding, hand-sanding, and filling in the small holes and pocks with wood putty. After the putty dried Doug sanded the tree again, until the surface of the wood was smooth and flawless. Afterward he coated the tree with a red interior-exterior marine enamel paint that was so glossy and so thick—so gleaming and fresh and shiny—that the finish of the tree, when it was delivered to the Stupa Man in the prayer room on October 19, looked like an advertisement for nail polish.

The Stupa Man, who had no English to express his reaction in words, simply smiled broadly and gave the thumbs-up sign. For five or six days afterward, he prayed over the tree—as it lay lengthwise across the floor of the prayer room. After that he began pulling out relics.

One by one he attached them to the tree. They were tiny things, fragments of fragments of relics. He put them in small, clear plastic boxes with magnified tops—the kind of box a child uses to study dead bugs—and tied them securely to the trunk with strands of colored silk. The Stupa Man explained that the tree was like a human body. It had *chakras*, or energy points. In particular parts of the tree, he'd placed certain relics—at other points he'd placed small glass vases filled with beads and semiprecious stones.

The first box of relics contained Kasyapa, or the crystalline ashes of the Third Buddha. The second clear box contained the "brain pill"—no bigger than a lentil—of a Tibetan Buddhist scholar. Toward the bottom of the tree, the Stupa Man attached the three-hundred-and-fifty-year-old skull bone of Kunzang Sherab, the first throne holder of the Nyingma lineage. And last came the most important relic of all: the finger bone of Migyur

Dorje, a *terton* or "treasure revealer" who lived in the seventeenth century. The finger bone was gray, the size and color of a pebble, and sat loose in a box with saffron and diamond chips. The words *Nam Cho Migy* were written in gold paint beside it. *Nam Cho* is Tibetan for "sky treasure" or "sky Dharma," and *Migy* is a Tibetan abbreviation of Migyur Dorje's name. Together these words referred to a series of profound teachings the young terton was said to have pulled from the sky.

The Tibetans believe that Padmasambhava—who brought Buddhism to Tibet in the eighth century—hid many of his teachings and spiritual discoveries inside rocks and caves, and the minds of individuals yet to be born. One of these special Tibetans was Migyur Dorje, who entered his mother's womb, the legend goes, as she dreamt of a golden tortoise radiating light rays in the depth of a vast ocean.*

And as Sakyamuni Buddha had been born without harming his mother or causing her even the slightest pain, so was Migyur Dorje—who also had auspicious markings on his body, in particular, a blue mole on his right hand. Even as a young boy he performed secret yogic exercises, had visions, made proclamations, and by the time he was nine his teachings were so potent he was being followed around by Karma Chagmed, "the minister of treasures," who wrote down all the boy's revelations—many of which would become fundamental to the Nyingma teachings of Tibetan Buddhism.

When Migyur Dorje died at twenty-three, his body was cremated, and afterward astonishing rainbows began appearing in the cloudless sky overhead. His heart and tongue remained intact in the fire—and his bone relics bore the marks of the vowels and consonants of the Tibetan language. These relics were placed inside a number of golden stupas in Tibet, offered by lamas of all the lineages and traditions. And for two centuries they were known as very powerful places—places of refuge and circumambulating, until the Chinese invasion of Tibet.

---

* Tsering Lama Jampal Zangpo, *A Garland of Immortal Wish-Fulfilling Trees: The Palyul Tradition of Nyingmapa* (Ithaca, N.Y.: Snow Lion, 1988).

Penor Rinpoche was an important tulku and just twenty-seven years old when he fled Tibet in 1950, leading two thousand monks along with him. They fought their way out with guns and hand grenades—and the great majority of the monks died. But when he arrived in India, he was still carrying the Migyur Dorje hand relic around his neck in a *gau,* or little box. Thirty-six years later he'd given a finger bone of it to Jetsunma.

A day or so before Halloween, the Stupa Man began spending more time in the prayer room, barely taking a break for meals. Outside the temple, where a circle of stones was arranged, he performed a purification ritual called a fire *puja.* He announced—through a translator—that he was seeing things in his meditations. Powerful obstacles were hurtling through time and space, coming directly at the stupa and KPC.

Usually, people liked to focus on the upside of stupa work. They slaved away and felt good about their meritorious activity, and the benefit to sentient beings. Merit—at least the way Jetsunma had always explained it to them—is a little like airline frequent flier miles. Certain activities award you more points than others. And there are even certain bonus times, like Ten Million Days, when your merit multiplies exponentially.

Stupa work has limitless potential for merit acquisition. From the Buddhist point of view, building one stupa is much more beneficial than, say, building a thousand houses for the homeless. When you build a house for the homeless, you are simply giving a person shelter. When you build a stupa, you don't simply create a mechanism that heals physical problems, cures cancer and AIDS—although the stupa can do that—you create a mechanism that changes a person's karma and, ultimately, can change the root cause of all suffering. Jetsunma liked to call stupas merit machines. Every time somebody walks around the stupa that you built, you earn a little merit, too, kind of like a royalty. And every time somebody does a Buddhist practice while walking around a stupa that you built—even if she is saying only the simplest Tibetan Buddhist prayer, *Om Mani Padme Hum*—you get some more merit. It's like one of those interest-earning bank accounts that's constantly accumulating. "Nearly limitless potential," David Somerville liked to say.

Nobody liked to talk too much about the downsides of stupa work: the problems of impure intention, merit depletion, and the quick ripening of karma. Just to have the chance of working on a stupa, a person has to spend merit—which can cause temporary merit depletion. You spend merit in order to generate more. And when your merit is depleted, you are vulnerable to bad things, to *obstacles.* There is also the sticky problem of motivation or intention. There might be times when you are doing a meritorious activity for the wrong reasons, or even for the tiniest hint of the wrong reason. Like maybe you are building a stupa because you want people to see how good you are. Maybe you want people to admire you. Or you are building a stupa to get your lama's approval. Or to make up for some crummy thing you did last year. In any case, the offering of your labor isn't pure. It is tinged with self-interest. And that can cause some negative things to ripen, too.

The hardest thing of all for the Poolesville stupa crew to face was that by doing such meritorious work—even as purely as possible—you make your karma ripen more quickly. It was said that simply being around a stupa as potent as the Migyur Dorje stupa could ripen your karma very quickly, the way being around Jetsunma for any duration tended to ripen a student's karma. Imagine your karma as seeds inside of you that become fruit on a vine. Imagine grapes coming out all at once, and *ripening.* The problem is, not all the grapes are delicious. Some of them are poison.

"I think of karma coming in chunks," Sherab said. "A chunk of it ripens and can actually cause bad things to happen."

The Stupa Man was interrupted in the prayer room. He was in the middle of prayers when Shelly Sims found him. A monk had fallen from the stupa, he was told. A helicopter was waiting on the front lawn of the temple, to medevac the monk. They feared Sangye had broken his back, or possibly his neck. He was being carried through the woods on a canvas stretcher. The Tibetan closed his eyes, and he remained very quiet, as though he was visiting the place in his mind. He was a tulku, after all—a reincarnated saint. They could often see the outcomes of things, see pieces of the future.

The Stupa Man opened his eyes again and spoke softly to his translator. "He'll be okay," the Stupa Man said. "He'll be okay."

Jetsunma stood next to the helicopter, saying prayers. She grabbed her monk's hand. There was an oxygen mask on Sangye's face and a huge brace on his neck. And then he rode in the sky, all the way to Suburban Hospital.

The impact of Sangye's fall had spread all over his body, which was a good thing. He had two compression fractures in the middle of his back, two sprained ankles, and a fracture of his left scapula. He was in the hospital for five days. Pretty much everybody in the sangha came to see him—Jetsunma came twice. When David visited he had some specific questions for Sangye, because the brunt of the stupa work would now be his. But the monk was too doped up on painkillers to answer them. "Sangye, how were you planning to build the bum-pa?" David wanted to know. And, "Sangye, *why did you have to fall?*"

Everyone needed to remember a few things, Jetsunma announced. Building a stupa was like giving birth to the Buddha. It was time to pay attention, be on guard, and it was a crisis.

The Stupa Man never left the prayer room anymore—and Jetsunma said it was time for the entire sangha to join him there, to start doing the Noble Light Rays practice around the clock. It wasn't a practice well known in the West, so it had to be translated into English by a monk and nun in Poolesville who read Tibetan—and it had to be explained in detail to the entire sangha so they'd do it correctly. Jetsunma wanted four members of the sangha to be doing Noble Light Rays in the prayer room at all times. It was up to them whether the stupa could be built or not. It was up to them . . . all the healing that would come from it, all the good, all the benefit. This was the time to show their compassion. And so they came. The Somervilles, the Simses, the Middletons, the Finneys, the Colacurcios, the Rowes. Sherab and the nuns of Ani Farms. Aileen and the nuns of Ani Estates. All the ordained, and most of the lay practitioners. There were teenagers coming after school, mothers and fathers coming after work. People were sleeping on the floor of the solarium. People were arriving at the temple in the middle of the night. Everybody was tired and run down, grabbing dinner, heading back to the temple, and settling into the cushions on the floor of the prayer room again.

Jetsunma stood before a Wednesday night crowd, the private weekly meeting of her students. "The negative forces," she said, "have arrived."

3.

Repeat After Me

SAFETY I HATED—AND ANY COURSE WITHOUT
DANGER. FOR WITHIN ME WAS A FAMINE.

—St. Augustine, *Confessions*

It wasn't exactly easy getting an appointment to speak with Jetsunma privately. While her presence at the Buddhist center seemed pervasive and insistent—perhaps the very thing, like oxygen in the air, that kept the place alive—she was actually never around. Her days were spent mostly with her family, inside her house on temple grounds. There was an old dog, a brown Lab named Charlie, who also lived with them. There was a swimming pool, recently built. She had a Health Rider exerciser—one of those stationary bikes with handles that pump up and down—which she enjoyed riding. But what she did, aside from praying and eating meals and working out on her Health Rider, intrigued me, and haunted me. How does a living Buddha pass the time? I had been told she liked watching *Absolutely Fabulous* and *Star Trek: The Next Generation* on television. She liked listening to Motown oldies. I had heard she often shopped for clothes by mail order. She had two attendants and a private secretary, Alana and Atara and Ariana, all ordained nuns, who kept her life organized. They opened and answered Jetsunma's mail, made sure her house was clean, helped take care of her eight-year-old daughter, Atira, grocery-shopped, and looked after the cooking of the family's dinners.

Presumably it was through these attendants that word of Jetsunma's daily life would occasionally leak out. I'd hear, secondhand or thirdhand, that Jetsunma had enjoyed a certain movie she'd rented (usually sci-fi or adventure tales) or was interested in a certain book (a self-help classic, *Radical Honesty*, was a favorite for a while, and Gail Sheehy's book on menopause). Sometimes I'd hear she was excited by the appearance of a particular new student, or by someone asking to become ordained. Sometimes she'd be craving a certain kind of food, or go on a special diet. Her students would get wind of her new passions—and suddenly there would be a slew of them trying out her diet or buying Health Riders. KPC was its own enchanted world, with its own news bulletins and trends, its own royalty. It was as if a long invisible wall traced the boundaries of the Tibetan Buddhist center, keeping its spell intact, and within that wall was another wall protecting Jetsunma herself. She seemed to live not simply yards away from the front door to her temple but worlds beyond.

When I'd first met Jetsunma a couple years before, she hadn't seemed so remote or exalted. Our interview felt relaxed—and was in an informal temple sitting room upstairs. She was jolly, easygoing, and I liked her immediately. I felt completely comfortable around her. The only thing that puzzled me was how Wib seemed to throw himself on the floor when he entered the sitting room where Jetsunma was waiting for us, and how he prostrated three times.

She had little in common with me in terms of lifestyle or background—except that we were both half Italian—but there was, nonetheless, the feeling of a bond or connection between us, a kind of mutual understanding. After my article was published I remained fascinated with Poolesville—and with Jetsunma. I had the nagging sense that there was more to know, and more to write. She came into my mind at the oddest moments—on bumpy airplane flights and when I was writing on deadline. She had even appeared in my dreams. I had learned that my father was dying, and part of me felt vaguely comforted by the idea of her, of a woman familiar with magic and miracles, and one who seemed to know the human heart. It was as though I carried around a piece of her—the sound of her voice, a sense of her, a spirit or presence—that I couldn't shake.

In Poolesville, Wib was my go-between, my conduit to her in those days. Jetsunma's telephone number was unlisted and kept private, even from most of her students. "Otherwise, I'd get calls all day," she explained later, "people asking me which cereal to buy." If I had a question, or hoped to set up a meeting with the lama, I had to call Wib at home—sometimes getting Jane or one of their young daughters on the line first. Wib was always kind and welcoming, always sounded happy to hear from me, but as time passed and my suggestions for meetings were sometimes left hanging for days, weeks, it became obvious to me that "getting to know" a Buddhist lama was a curious and perhaps absurd ambition. Even the experience of covering Hillary Clinton during her reclusive first year in the White House hadn't prepared me for the perplexing process of writing about Jetsunma Ahkön Lhamo. And just as I began to fantasize about giving up, I'd get a call from Wib out of the blue. "Jetsunma thinks the name Random House sounds very good," he'd say, after I'd told him the publisher of my book about KPC. Or "Jetsunma feels very good about this project and seems very excited." One time, in passing, he asked for my new boyfriend's full name—something Jetsunma had inquired about.

As I waited to see her in October and grew increasingly anxious, I checked on the progress of the stupa, interviewed the visiting Stupa Man, and studied the relics in the prayer room. I sat with David Somerville in his construction trailer on the stupa site. I went to see Doug Sims at his home (his Health Rider was prominently placed in the living room). I tried to get in touch with Sangye and learned that he was recuperating in a cottage on the temple grounds, being nursed by a team of nuns. I began my inquiries into Jetsunma's life story and spoke with Shelly Sims and Jon Randolph and Eleanor Rowe, three of her oldest students. And as the weeks passed and my frustration grew, I learned a valuable Buddhist lesson: If I wanted to remain calm and sane, I shouldn't count on seeing the lama at all.

Each visit to Poolesville provided new tidbits of information, though, adding to what I already knew about the temple and its beginnings. Jetsunma's story grew like a vine, too, and the longer it became—the more it twisted and curled in on itself—the more it drew me. Quintessentially American stories are usually material success stories—a class nerd becomes a billionaire, an awkward girl becomes a movie star. Or they are stories of a political rise: a poor man becomes a senator or congressman or the president of the United States. The landscape is crowded with such legends. But each time I learned new things about Jetsunma's story, the more magnificent it seemed. It had a stunning arc, such a *Star Is Born* quality that it was strange it wasn't Hollywood that had found her, created her, lifted her out of obscurity and squalor, but a holy man from Tibet who walked with a limp, couldn't speak English, and knew very little about the West.

She was born Alyce Louise Zeoli, on October 12, 1949, a calm, bright, and imaginative girl—a quarter Dutch, a quarter Jewish, and half Italian—who seemed to thrive and do well in school despite the atmosphere at home. Her mother, Geraldine, was a tall woman, dark haired, with large blue eyes and a prominent nose, something of a beauty in her youth. But she was a single mother who struggled to make money, working in factories and as a grocery store cashier. As a young girl Alyce was often left with her mother's mother, Alyce Schwartz, for whom she'd been named. Her grandmother could be supportive at times and act like the sweetest friend. Other times she turned cold and bitter. "Look how much you're eating! Look how much. What's wrong with you?" She also showed signs of mental instability. She was playing cards on the floor of the living room one night when she looked up from her hand and suddenly didn't recognize her own family. Another time Geraldine came home early from work and found little Alyce sitting on the stoop in the snow. She wasn't wearing a coat or underpants, only a dress. Her grandmother had put her outside, locked the door, and forgotten about her.

Alyce's father was Harry Zeoli. Her mother claimed to have married him when she was twenty-two and had the marriage annulled soon after—when Zeoli was arrested for stealing a car. The man who was largely responsible for raising Alyce was Vito Cassara, a truck driver and fix-it man who married Geraldine when Alyce was two. Vito always had a great deal of trouble finding work, but he was able to move his new family into a small brick walk-up on Ninety-eighth Street in the Canarsie neighborhood of Brooklyn, just around the corner from the Bay View housing project. He and Geraldine began having children. As Jetsunma remembers it, her mother felt best when she had a baby in the house. "If she didn't have a baby, she'd start another," she said. "It was really like that." When Alyce was three her half brother Frankie came along; he would remain close to her throughout their youth and early adulthood. Three more children followed, and Alyce was left to raise herself and look after them.

When Jetsunma remembers Vito Cassara, she mostly remembers how the electricity and gas were always being shut off in the Brooklyn house, and how Vito taught the kids to hide from bill collectors. She remembers his big fleshy nose and red face. She remembers the hollering, and the way a handprint could swell under her skin after she'd been slapped. She remembers how a bruise was blue and spongy before it became green and yellow. She and her younger brothers never could recall what they'd done to deserve punishment. Vito drank when he was worried about money.

Vito threw an ax at Frankie once, and another time Jetsunma says she watched her stepfather beat Frankie with a saw. She watched the imprint of the saw's teeth marks rise on Frankie's legs. He was five when Vito knocked him to the floor and kicked him in the head so many times that his eyes crossed and he had to be taken to the emergency room. Geraldine said he had fallen down a flight of stairs, but the doctors pressed her, trying to get her to admit that her husband had done it. She wouldn't. "She protected him," Jetsunma would say years later. "That's the one thing I hold against her the most."

Alyce liked to comfort Frankie and reassure him. Someday things will be different, she'd say. Someday, she'd say, we'll buy a big white house in the woods, and it will be beautiful and perfect and safe.

She fantasized about her real father, too. She imagined Harry Zeoli ringing the doorbell on Ninety-eighth Street. She imagined him discovering how her life was and taking her away from

Brooklyn, from the violence and ugliness, from the small house crowded with her half siblings and Vito and Geraldine and her crazy grandmother. "I used to ask my mother about my real father, and she would always paint him to be a terrible person. But I never believed it," she said. "I held out. To me, my father was a good father. . . . In fact, when I used to watch the show *Ben Casey* on TV, the star of the show was named Vince Edwards, but I learned somehow that his real name was Vincent Deoli,* and I had a fantasy for a while that he was my father and he'd changed that one letter of his last name, from a Z to a D, and that he was a great guy. I even imagined that he was really a doctor, too, and he'd come and save my life."

The family moved to Miami when Alyce was fourteen so that Vito could find work more easily; eventually he opened his own locksmith business. And it was there, in the sunny suburb of Hialeah, that Alyce discovered that other families weren't like hers. "I noticed that other people actually talked to each other without screaming," Jetsunma said. "And other families never beat each other. It was a huge awakening for me, and a tremendous relief. It meant there might be something else out there. Some other way of living for me."

In Hialeah she made friends easily and attracted strangers. . . . She had what the Tibetans would later call *ziji*, charisma, and a certain kind of energy that made people want to stare at her and spend time in her company. She did impressions, cracked hilarious jokes. Her face was pretty. Her voice was husky and kind. Her body was plump and maternal. Her goodwill was infectious. And her ability to connect was dazzling. Impatient for her new life to begin, she started pursuing boys. They tended to be druggies and dropouts—"inappropriate guys who generally weren't up to my speed," Jetsunma said. At sixteen she started craving independence. She bought a car and got a part-time job with the phone company. She began her first serious relationship with a boy. The

* According to Ephraim Katz, *The Film Encyclopedia*, 2d ed. (New York: HarperPerennial, 1994), the actor who played Ben Casey was named Vincent Zoimo, not Deoli.

next year they ran away to Georgia, planning to get married. But the law there had been changed—you had to be eighteen to marry. Alyce and her boyfriend decided to lie to their parents and claim they'd gotten married anyway. They talked about having a baby soon, too, to ensure that they be allowed to stay together.

Alyce called her mother from a pay phone in Georgia, but she found herself unable to lie. "Something she said made me trust her," Jetsunma said, "and something in her voice had made me homesick and start crying." At her mother's urging Alyce told her where she was—and within minutes Vito had called the Georgia State Troopers. "You better get to my daughter before I do," he told the police, "because I'm going to kill her."

Back in Hialeah and forbidden to see her boyfriend, Alyce retreated to her room, and a weird detachment crept over her. She felt removed from herself, then removed from her body—as if she were across the bedroom and watching herself fall apart. "It must have been near the holidays, because I had this Christmas corsage," she said, "and I remember picking this corsage up and that it suddenly wasn't a corsage anymore but my doll Mickey that I had when I was a little girl. It was a doll I had before my mother and my stepfather had gotten together. So I was holding this corsage in my arms and I was singing to it, singing to Mickey, and I was holding Mickey. And then I began throwing Mickey against the door, and pieces were falling off.

"My mother must have heard the sound of the knocking in my room, because she came in. She told me later that I was talking like a little girl, baby talk, saying words I used to say when I was little. And I told her, 'Mommy, Mommy, Mickey is broken. I don't know how to fix him. I don't know how to fix Mickey.' "

Jetsunma believes she had a "kind of breakdown," but it felt planned, like a lucid decision to lose control. The whole thing felt "contrived" and "totally honest" at the same time, she said. "Both sane and insane."

Her mother, oddly, seemed to know exactly what to do. "She became very strong and clear," Jetsunma said. "She walked me around the house and started talking to me very softly and made me warm milk. She made me feel safer. And then she put me to bed, tucking me inside the sheets like I was a baby."

The next morning Geraldine called Hialeah High School and asked whether she should send her daughter to classes or not. Alyce was acting very strange. Was there a school psychologist her daughter could see? "I wasn't acting like a baby anymore, but I was definitely still out of it," Jetsunma said. "Like I was directing myself in a movie."

A school counselor evaluated Alyce and sent her to the offices of Dr. Ronald Shellow, a psychiatrist who specialized in adolescent illness and juvenile delinquency. She began therapy with him that would last nearly three years and was paid for by the state vocational rehabilitation program. "I made some slow progress," she said, "but I don't remember very much of the following year—the year I turned eighteen. Apparently I had some rather big adventures. Later on, guys would come up to me and say, 'Hey, that was a great time we had!' and I had no idea what they were talking about."

Dr. Shellow helped Alyce make the decision to move out of her parents' house and continue school and her part-time job. She began doing her own cooking, learned how to live paycheck to paycheck. She broke up with her boyfriend but always found a new one. "I had to have a boyfriend," she said. "It gave me a sense of security, I think, and the illusion of support. Thinking back on it, I have the image of two puppies in a box. It's a comfort to them—but are they really involved in caring for each other?"

More than any boyfriend it was Dr. Shellow who got her through those years. He believed in her, made her feel good. After a certain amount of time in individual analysis, he encouraged Alyce to join a therapy group he was running. In an interview Dr. Shellow—who was given permission to discuss his treatment of Alyce—remembered her as "overweight" but "an attractive girl who took care of herself." She tended to be hysterical rather than depressive. She had sexually provocative fantasies. She told the truth. She was concerned about being "a good girl." She wrote poetry that worried her high school teachers. Her boyfriend was a loser, her stepfather was a drunk, and her mother "had her own problems—mostly with her husband."

But it was Alyce's dreams that Dr. Shellow remembered most. They were "very interesting dreams," he said. She was pregnant in most of them. And the recurring theme was that she was in the hospital, giving birth. The baby was beautiful but also "had something wrong with it." Sometimes the baby had crossed eyes or funny hair. And Alyce felt tremendous love for the baby. But in the dreams, rather than taking the baby home and keeping it for herself, she planned to give the baby to her mother—as a way finally to make her happy. "I've never had another patient give me a dream like that," said Dr. Shellow, "this fantasy of giving birth to something wonderful and it being for somebody else."

In his therapy group Alyce talked easily and candidly about her feelings; she was never withdrawn or seemed uncomfortable. She was adept at dispensing advice and quickly became involved in helping her group mates. Eventually she became more interested in helping them than in talking about herself—although it probably needs to be said that this stance allowed her to remain in control and be the center of focus. "She was always jumping in," said Dr. Shellow, "solving problems, making comments, interpreting everybody else's dreams . . . often before I had the chance to come in and say something. Essentially, she led the group. And it was always very interesting."

With each passing year the world of Alyce's childhood—the bleakness, the impotency and despair—grew fainter and fainter. By the time she was an adult, the house on Ninety-eighth Street in Canarsie literally didn't exist; it had been torn down and another small brick house built on the lot. Her mother divorced Vito Cassara, and he disappeared into legend; Alyce came to believe, or hope, or dream, that he had been sent to jail. Her real father, Harry Zeoli, would never emerge as the star of *Ben Casey*, or turn up at her door.

She moved on and stumbled upon compensations. When she was nineteen she married Jim Perry, a boyfriend from Miami. They had a baby named Ben. Opportunities to go to college never came, but she took night courses and worked as a day-care assistant and as a nanny. She got jobs in retail stores and sold clothes. After she and Perry were divorced, she moved to Asheville, North Carolina, with another boyfriend, a radiologist named Pat Mulloy.

During these years, as her own life began taking root, Alyce's contact with her old family—Geraldine and Frankie and the rest—was sporadic and difficult. They barely spoke. Alyce would sometimes find herself missing them. She'd call up and arrange a reunion. Her yearning never ceased—for a mother, for a real father, for brothers and sisters to love. She'd find herself believing again that repairs were possible, that intentions had been good, that the mistakes were forgivable, and that people could change. So periodically Alyce would find herself sitting around with her mother and half siblings, whose lives were now tortured by their own demons. During these reunions the boys would open their shirts and show the scars. Alyce would tell dark jokes, her rage funneled into disgust and vulgarity. Geraldine would smoke cigarette after cigarette, always remaining silent.

Following such an evening Alyce would feel exhausted, then overcome. She'd go to bed and cry for hours. "Tell me I'm not like them," she'd say to her husband. "Please, please, *please*. Tell me I'm not."

In Asheville she lived on the fringes of town. There were dilapidated shacks and trailers nearby and, sprinkled among them, a few nice houses that looked cared for. Alyce's small farmhouse was one of those. She owned a cow, grew her own vegetables, stoked the woodstove in the winter, and lived a relatively quiet life. After several years together she and Mulloy had a son, Christopher, and were married.

She was a housewife and a mother. There were meals to cook, groceries to shop for, dirty clothes to wash, an ordinary life. Yet, as the months, and indeed the years, passed, the more ordinary her life became, the more restless Alyce grew. It was "a profound restlessness that wasn't entirely conscious," she recalled. And by the time she was in her mid- to late twenties, "it was powerful, a dynamic force from way inside me." She had always been sedentary by nature, a bit lazy—and in recent years she had become quite overweight. Suddenly, though, she felt energized. She felt propelled toward something. *But what?*

The force felt magical, and she turned to magic for answers. A fortune-teller told her she was psychic; an astrologer told her she was important. An old tarot card reader on Coney Island told her she was originally Tibetan. Her dreams became powerful. Once asleep she was welcomed into a strange and elegant wonderland. She walked into mystical palaces and met half-human creatures. Again and again she was told she was special, she was different, she was gifted and full of wisdom and insights. Soon she began wanting to be asleep more than she wanted to be awake.

She started to meditate—as a way to enter a dream state without sleeping. She taught herself, made up things as she went along. She didn't learn until much later from the Tibetans that you are supposed to sit, not lie down. You are supposed to keep your eyes open, not shut them. At first it was just an hour a day. She would slow down, sink into a different state of consciousness. Her meditations were not simply exercises in relaxation, or strings of sounds, a mantra, repeated over and over. She preferred to be praying, and her meditations became little plays she would run inside her mind, visualizations—in which she made wishes and offerings to God. She was fascinated by the mechanics of praying, and by an ambition to devise more efficient and powerful forms of prayer. It became almost a game. On her bed in the afternoons, she imagined she was offering up parts of her body to God. First she'd offer her toes and her feet to God. The next day she would offer her knees, her legs, her hips . . . She spent hours contemplating the various parts of her body and appreciating them—how well her feet worked, how they helped her stand and walk. She thought about how attached she was to her body—how much she loved her feet, and how life would be without them. And with this in mind she would offer them, imagine cutting them off and giving them to God. Years later she'd be told this is an advanced Tibetan Buddhist practice called Chöd.

She would give anything to God, she thought, anything, if her gift might help the world become settled, happier. The deeper she went—the closer she came to the kingdom of her dreams—the closer she felt to her true self. Sunk into a trance, she always prayed for the same thing: "Make me a channel of blessings." There were hours of this, days of this, weeks of this, months of this. "Make me a channel of blessings, make me a channel of blessings . . ." The prayer became a part of her breath, a part of her consciousness. After a time she felt herself changing, as though the prayer had transformed her. Suddenly it was as if she were a faucet, and the blessings were running out of her like water, and all she had to do was turn on the tap.

She prayed for peace. She prayed for the world. She prayed for an end to suffering. She prayed for purity, for light, for clarity, for answers.

The conclusions she reached stayed with her: We have all lived before, many lifetimes—and on other planets and lost continents. Our past actions are responsible for the lives we are having now. All souls are connected, in some silent, mysterious way, through their hearts. And there isn't a God so much as a universal spirit, a primordial feeling, an energy and wisdom that is formless. It is the true nature of all things and inseparable from us.

Going to church had never much interested Alyce. She'd been baptized in the Roman Catholic Church and had often attended Dutch Reformed services with her grandmother. And while the family considered themselves Jewish, too, the only Jewish thing they did was eat bagels. But it really wasn't the religious ambivalence of her childhood that had turned Alyce off. The truth was, church seemed fake to her—rigid and shallow. She imagined if she talked about her heartfelt experiences with prayer, she might be ridiculed. Eventually, she and Pat Mulloy found a home at the Light Center—a nondenominational group that met in Black Mountain, just outside Asheville. It wasn't very organized and didn't seem much like religion. It was simply a place where the divine mysteries of life were celebrated, and where serious scientific discoveries were discussed in the same breath as outrageous New Age theories. The students were instructed to pray for the planet, for world peace, for enlightenment, to end hunger, and not for themselves. Alyce was able to talk openly about her dreams and meditations, and some of the answers she'd found. She found sympathetic listeners—people who sat down beside her, enthralled. "I was instantly a joiner," Jetsunma said of the Light Center. "And I really got mixed up with that group and was really happy to be there."

Jim Gore, who ran the center, was a lecturer and psychic who became Alyce's first spiritual mentor. He taught various meditations and practices, but the mainstay at his center was a prayer called the Light Prayer. You imagined yourself as a body of light, then visualized that light going out into the world. After attending several of his lectures, Alyce approached Gore to tell him about a dream she'd had: She was walking outside when the sky opened up over her head. A dove came down and began to circle her head. A voice said, "You are the light of the world . . . this is who you are."

Gore smiled and took Alyce's arm. "I'll tell you something I know about you," he said. "You're not like other people. You're different. Did you know that about yourself?"

In her early years at the Light Center, Alyce was encouraged by Jim Gore. He felt she was a visionary, and extraordinarily psychic. On a few occasions he referred to her as a *superbeing*—the greatest compliment he could offer. He often singled her out in classes and called on her to speak to the group. After a short time she was teaching meditation and giving private psychic readings—very much at Gore's prodding. He lauded her intuition and accurate predictions, as well as her courage to cut the niceties and head straight for the core.

Late in 1980 she gave a psychic reading to Michael Burroughs, a graduate student in religious studies at the University of Virginia who was visiting friends in Black Mountain. "I'd heard all about him before I'd met him," Jetsunma would recount later. "People were always saying, 'You gotta meet Michael Burroughs. You gotta meet him.' " He was a southerner with a slow Tennessee drawl and at twenty-five—four years younger than Alyce—seemed charming and wise beyond his years. Like Alyce, Michael had a quick mind, a mystical bent, and a rather dark sense of humor. But unlike Alyce he was well educated and accomplished—he was finishing work on his second master's degree, and made a living as a church organist and a regional lecturer of Transcendental Meditation. Alyce was still working in the day-care center, and the thought of supporting herself as a spiritual teacher seemed a remote possibility.

"Do you have a girlfriend?" she asked Michael, during his first reading.

"Not really," he said.

"Well, you are about to be involved in a terrific relationship," she said. "Boy, I wish I were going to have a relationship like that—and the woman's name is Catharine."

Michael started coming more often to Black Mountain. He encouraged Alyce, came up with ideas for how she might support herself as a teacher, suggesting she begin offering workshops and seminars. Quickly becoming close friends, they gossiped about other students they knew and about Jim Gore's recent teachings. Alyce liked the way Michael ridiculed some of the New Age practices at the Light Center—so when Gore began encouraging her to try channeling, she wanted to know what Michael thought. Alyce had tried it privately but felt embarrassed and unsure about channeling in public. When Michael visited Asheville again, would he help her?

Over the summer Alyce confided in Michael that she was considering leaving Asheville—and had dreams of starting her own prayer center. "We were both growing a little critical of the goings-on at Black Mountain," she said. "It was getting too psychic phenomena–oriented and flaky. It became too much about aura cleansing and trying to project your consciousness to different places. None of which does the world much good at all. Michael and I thought of ourselves as much more serious."

Jim Gore had also become a bit overbearing. Alyce had started to attract attention with her psychic readings—people were coming to her now, wanting help with their meditation techniques—and Gore had begun ignoring her. "He told me I was a *superbeing,*" she says, "and eventually didn't have anything to do with me." Unlike the students who were made insecure by this kind of treatment and drawn further into Gore's influence, Alyce saw through it and quietly made plans to depart.

She and Michael talked long into the night during this time about what the ideal spiritual center would be like. Alyce had grown to believe that the New Age feel-good talk was vapid, overly upbeat, and that studying psychic phenomena—although fun and entertaining—was a waste of time. People should be taught to search themselves in a deeper way, to face their intentions, to deal with their demons and commit themselves to a practice of prayer that would build compassion. Alyce felt a sense of mission and a calling as a teacher, a muse, a spiritual instigator. She had already seen how she was able to attract people to begin an examination of their lives. Michael, having been raised in the Baptist Church, understood the need for structure, rules, a sense of hierarchy and order. Together they agreed that the perfect spiritual center would be nondenominational but teach the general guidelines and scriptures that all religions hold in common. And it would emphasize "active prayer" above all else. Prayer was real, and worked. It was an acknowledgment of the oneness of all things and showed devotion to that universal spirit, to the essential nature that all things share.

It came as a shock to the students at the Light Center when Alyce announced, later in 1981, that she and Pat Mulloy were separating. The perception was that Alyce and Pat were a supportive and spiritual family—Jim Gore had called them the "First Christed family"—and meant to be together. Since they'd become close friends Michael had known that Alyce was unhappy and wasn't surprised by the news that she wanted to leave Mulloy. But what came next did surprise him. Not long after her separation Alyce confessed to Michael that she believed the two of *them* were destined to be together. In a channeling session she told him that they'd been together in many previous lifetimes—often as rulers of galaxies and unrecorded ancient civilizations on earth. Over the summer, as they grew closer, Alyce embarked on a serious diet, and by Christmastime she had dropped one hundred pounds.

Eventually Michael came to feel it was true. He and Alyce had something special together. There really wasn't anybody like Alyce . . . the way she made friends instantly, how funny she was, how warm, how smart. Her spiritual capabilities seemed endless to him, and her talent for teaching—once she'd made up her mind that she wanted to have students of her own—was incomparable. Michael even believed some of the past-life stories Alyce had told him. Why not? Who's to say those things couldn't have happened? Above all, Michael felt very strongly that her intentions were pure. She wasn't one of these self-involved flakes who populated the landscape. She believed deeply that her mission was to help people and make the world a better place. Over time he found himself unable to imagine life without her.

By the following winter they were a couple. Michael moved to Washington, D.C., to study comparative religion at American University—for his third master's degree—and Alyce drove up on weekends. To help make ends meet, and in hopes of attracting some students, Michael made arrangements for Alyce to speak informally at spiritual centers and to New Age groups. Through these events they were quickly able to find kindred spirits, even in a place as buttoned up as Washington. "They came to dinner at a group house I was living in," remembered Wib Middleton, "and she channeled afterward, which really blew us all away. And I remember when we were alone, she looked at me and said, 'I've been meeting lots of *old friends* lately.' And I felt I knew what she meant. We had a strong connection."

To mark her new life, she decided that she didn't want to be called Alyce anymore. She didn't *feel* like Alyce. She didn't even look like Alyce. She decided to start calling herself Catharine.

She got a job at Paul Harris in Mazza Galerie for a time, selling men's clothes, and Michael was playing the organ at various churches. They quickly made new friends, mostly through a network of former Light Center students living in the Washington area. Through a friend of a friend they met Eleanor Rowe, a refined intellectual—a former Russian literature professor at George Washington University—who had a fascination for metaphysics. Eleanor became a patron of sorts, a sponsor and supporter of Catharine. She hired Catharine to work as her nanny, to house-sit while she traveled over the summer. And later, convinced of Catharine's abilities as a channeler and psychic, she consulted her about a string of physical ailments that had been plaguing her. "She was a tremendously gifted healer," Eleanor said. "And I'd tried everything—acupuncturists, priests, a shaman, various yogis. I knew all kinds of big-name gurus, including Swami Muktananda. But only Catharine was able to diagnose the problem, and then fix it."

Michael played the organ at the Church of Two Worlds in Georgetown, a spiritualist congregation. He and Catharine were married there in 1983 by Rev. Reed Brown—who later ordained them at the Arlington Metaphysical Chapel as "metaphysical ministers" in his spiritual church. But Catharine worked better on her own, so Eleanor offered her house as a place where groups could gather informally for her teachings. Eleanor also began recommending Catharine's psychic consultations to friends and acquaintances. Sylvia Rivchun came for a session. Jane Perini and Shelly Nemerovsky came, too. These were something like conventional psychic readings except that it was difficult to keep Catharine interested in the mundane—and questions about jobs and houses and marriages sometimes went unanswered. She was mostly interested in a person's spiritual path, and the extent to which a person was living consciously, being ruthlessly honest, and practicing compassion. Often she would recommend meditation to a client and suggest a few techniques of her own.

You have lived many lifetimes, Catharine told people, many, many lifetimes. Look into the night sky, look up at all the stars, the millions of stars. We have all lived as many lifetimes, and we've come from places as far away.

Catharine and Michael moved into an apartment in Silver Spring—a place large enough to hold her classes in the living room. Twenty or thirty regulars sat on the floor and listened to Catharine's teachings every week. They called themselves the Center for Discovery and New Life, and within a year membership had doubled and then tripled. To accommodate the expansion Catharine and Michael moved into a one-story brick rambler in Kensington. It was a nice neighborhood of Maryland, close to Rock Creek Park, but the main feature of the Kensington house was the big basement, with its knotty pine paneling. It was an ideal place for the group to hold weekly meetings—and for Catharine to give her psychic readings more privately than in the family living room. There was a small bedroom next to the paneled basement, too, which Michael used as an office.

It was Michael's ambitions for the center, and his public relations skills, that often drew newcomers to the classes. He had even begun to arrange out-of-town speaking engagements for himself and Catharine—and they'd attracted a group of students in Lansing, Michigan. But it was Catharine's talent for teaching and connecting to students on an emotional and nonintellectual level that kept them there. At a distance they seemed like an odd couple, Catharine and Michael. They had been married less than a year. He was of medium height and slight build—weighing no more than one hundred and forty pounds. She was large framed, fairly tall, and had thirty or forty pounds on him. While she had a bawdy sense of humor and a deadpan delivery, by nature Catharine was a homebody and not entirely comfortable meeting people. Michael was more reserved on the surface. He was erudite, an academic—a person, it seemed to some, who was all brain and little heart. But he was also a natural at administration, at filling out the proper forms for tax exemption and coming up with ways the group could expand its reach.

The early students would later be regarded as very special and referred to as the First Wave. In their most heady moments they thought of themselves as something like the twelve apostles. "We were kind of a ragtag group," said Wib, "but we felt like an intimate family and like what we were doing was important." They were Wib Middleton, Eleanor Rowe, Shelly Nemerovsky, Sylvia Rivchun, and Jane Perini. There was a software engineer named David Somerville. There was Don Allen, an administrator at the U.S. Postal Service, who first came to the Kensington house in 1982 and introduced his son, Jay, to the center by giving him a private consultation with Catharine for his nineteenth birthday. Jay dropped out of James Madison University after his freshman year because he didn't want to miss Catharine's weekly teachings. "I had found the thing I was looking for and the thing that was making my life meaningful," he would recount later. "I had to pursue it."

Janice Newmark came to Catharine for a private consultation, admitted she was suicidal, and began attending classes—reinvigorated about her life. Tom Barry was a Washington-area businessman with Pentagon contacts when he first came to a class in 1983 and had a four-hour consultation with Catharine, asking her if it was possible to attain enlightenment and be an arms dealer at the same time. "The divine can do anything," Catharine told him, "but why push it?"

Karen Williams began coming regularly—she was a sound technician at NBC, a cheerful and wry-humored ex–flower child from Berkeley—and sometimes brought her NBC colleagues. Christine Cervenka was a beautiful twenty-four-year-old blonde from New Jersey who had given up on the Catholic Church—and Catharine told her she'd had a dream that she was coming. Ted and Linda Kurkowski—he was a solar energy expert, she was a management consultant—had come for private consultations with Catharine and stayed. Elizabeth Elgin was an insurance secretary when she first met Catharine, and also never looked back. The students in Michigan had become organized and devout, too—Catharine flew in once a month to teach there. Another far-flung student, a recently divorced businessman from Florida who had met Catharine in Asheville, moved to the Washington area when he learned she'd started her own center. His name was Jon Randolph. Catharine told him he'd been her student before—in ancient Egypt.

She and Michael described their center as nondenominational, but many of the members—like Wib Middleton and Jay Allen—considered themselves "metaphysical" Christians who were being taken by Catharine to a new level of spiritual understanding. Others simply felt they were studying a kind of Western mysticism. Still others just came for the wild talk of past lives and UFO's. "The man at NBC who originally introduced me to Catharine," said Karen Williams, "stopped coming to classes after the first year or so, when he figured out it was more about prayer than intergalactic travel. That's all he ever wanted, really—to be taken up in a spaceship—and somehow he thought Catharine could make that happen."

"She talked about the absolute nature of all things, and the focus was always the power of prayer and benefiting others," said Wib. "Her voice, and the way she said things, made sense to me. We were all looking for something to sink our teeth into—and she was talking about compassion and not self. At that time what was out there, in the spiritual marketplace, was very self-absorbed, about healing the self. . . . I'd done est weekends, among other things, but what really struck me—and many of us—was here was somebody who wasn't talking about self-improvement or psychic development."

Quite naturally, and also at Catharine's encouragement, students began to hook up romantically. Wib Middleton began dating Jane Perini in late 1983, Don Allen hooked up with Shelly Nemerovsky, and David Somerville fell in love with Sylvia Rivchun. "When the group would meditate together," David remembered, "I would close my eyes and become sure that Sylvia was staring at me. I could *feel* her, staring at me. And then I'd look up, and she'd just be sitting there, meditating. And her eyes were shut."

Catharine delivered her teachings in a trance state. She sat in a green velour chair, closed her eyes, and spoke in the voice of a man who called himself Jeremiah. The voice taught about the indivisible union of all things, about the emptiness of the physical world, about stewardship and caretaking of the earth and all the creatures on it. The voice was against abortion. It loved Jesus Christ. The voice was always encouraging the audience to act ethically and consciously and compassionately in the world.

Sometime in 1984 the teachings became increasingly Eastern and esoteric. Michael himself had gotten interested in Buddhism and had purchased some books on the subject. Catharine disliked taking a scholarly approach to spirituality, but she was drawn to what Michael told her about Buddhism. "He'd read something to me," she'd say later, "and I'd feel I knew what was being talked about." She quickly put the concepts into her own words. She wrote a vow that she asked her students to take, not unlike the *Bodhisattva vow*, which Tibetan Buddhists take, dedicating themselves to helping the world. She talked about "voidness" and "oneness" and the indivisibility of all things—and gave a teaching called "no-thingness"—which made the Buddhist concepts of emptiness and nonduality easily accessible to her students. That year, when she and Michael bought a new car, a blue Renault Alliance, they ordered a vanity license plate: OM AH HUM," the words for "body, speech, mind," and a Buddhist prayer.

Catharine talked about karma, too. She told her students that the United States had a "karmic pattern of compassion" that began with the founding fathers—and that Thomas Jefferson was a "wisdom being." If one was born in the United States, that compassion was one's legacy. There were prayer vigils at the Jefferson Memorial on several occasions after Catharine predicted that a tragedy was about to take place—a political figure was about to be assassinated or a negative entity in outer space was heading toward the earth in a spaceship. The group often prayed all night—and they were thrilled by their success at keeping negativity at bay. "Catharine would always proclaim afterward," said Karen Williams, "that we'd accomplished some miraculous thing."

Catharine had taught them a form of meditation called the Light Expansion Prayer, a variation of Jim Gore's prayer in Asheville. Eventually the group began a round-the-clock prayer vigil in the basement of the Kensington house—a prayer for peace, for harmony. The students came and went at all hours, praying for peace in two- to four-hour shifts.

In the fall of 1984, Catharine's prayer group was introduced to a man named Kunzang Lama, who represented a large monastery in south India. He was raising money for Tibetan refugees. Did the Center for Discovery and New Life wish to sponsor young monks in need of books and clothing and proper food? Kunzang Lama arrived at the Kensington house one rainy night with a carload of Tibetan rugs to sell and photographs of beautiful Tibetan boys in robes. Catharine's students were soon sponsoring twenty little monks, then fifty, then seventy. The rugs sold quickly.

Several months later Kunzang Lama contacted them again. The head of his monastery, Penor Rinpoche, was making his first trip to the United States. Kunsang Lama asked if their group could find a place for the rinpoche to stay. Catharine and Michael offered their house—and they organized a dinner for the lama and arranged two speaking engagements for him in suburban Maryland. Despite a burgeoning interest in Eastern religion, Michael seemed to think that Rinpoche was his last name. "I didn't really know what a Buddhist was, *much less a lama*," Catharine would say a few years later, when the reporters came, and the magazine writers, and the TV crews. "And when I imagined Tibet, my first thought was of old men and smelly rugs."

Their first inkling of Penor Rinpoche's status came when Michael and Catharine arrived at the airport to meet his plane, thinking they would be the only ones there. Instead, they found a hundred or so well-dressed Chinese swarming Penor Rinpoche's gate, holding white scarves and bouquets of flowers. Michael and Catharine looked at each other. Who could have known? They couldn't really see the lama as he emerged from the Jetway, but a sea of dark heads in front of them began bowing, then prostrating. Hands were reaching out to him, with offerings and scarves for the rinpoche to bless and return.

Catharine would later describe the moment she first laid eyes on His Holiness Drubwang Pema Norbu (Penor) Rinpoche, the eleventh throne holder of the Palyul tradition in the Nyingna lineage, as a miraculous and stunning awakening. She would tell the story many times, and on each occasion the description seemed to become more wondrous and fateful. "It was like a shampoo commercial," she liked to say. "I looked over the crowds of people and suddenly caught sight of His Holiness." He was a short and stout figure, wearing burgundy robes and heavy eyeglasses, and limping faintly as he passed the hoards of welcomers. As his face looked up into hers, Catharine says she broke down sobbing. "I felt," she says, "like I was meeting my mind."

A few hours later, after a lunch in downtown D.C. and a couple of prearranged stops and appointments, Penor Rinpoche arrived at Catharine and Michael's brick rambler in Kensington to stay for four or five days. The basement was crowded with Catherine's students, waiting to meet him. Trunk after trunk was unloaded from the car. Two mattresses were separated and put on the floor of the guest room. And after a brief speech about Buddhism, the lama retreated to his bedroom, where he kept to himself most of the following day. Catharine and Michael heard chanting, and clanking bells, coming from the room. They smelled burning cedar. One of the lama's trunks, Michael learned later, was full of books. Another held ceremonial objects. He remained closeted for hours as he practiced.

The next night, Michael and Catharine had a vegetarian meal with tofu and chamomile tea delivered to Penor Rinpoche's bedroom—assuming that Buddhists do not eat meat. After a few minutes his attendant came out.

"His Holiness wants to know what else you have to eat."

"What . . . else?"

"His Holiness says this tea tastes like hay."

"What does he like?" Catharine asked.

"Steak."

It was on the second or third day in Kensington that Penor Rinpoche became a bit more sociable and ready for sightseeing. Michael and Catharine took him to the National Zoo—they were told he loved animals—as well as the Smithsonian, the Capitol, and several of their favorite memorials. Over lunch at Thai Taste on Connecticut Avenue, the lama began asking Catharine questions about her classes. "What do you teach?" he asked through an interpreter. Catharine explained about the Light Expansion Prayer, the meditations she'd invented over the years, and her lectures on "oneness" and "voidness" and "no-thingness." Penor Rinpoche seemed particularly interested in how she'd been able to attract students. He would be happy to meet with the students individually, if they'd be interested.

"We had no idea how important he was," Jetsunma recounted years later, "or how to treat a lama. We walked in front of him. We stood over him, and sat down next to him. All of these things I would never do now—nobody would—and on the last day, we threw a barbecue in my backyard in his honor, and served him potato chips and hot dogs."

It was on the last day that Penor Rinpoche gathered Catharine and her students in the Kensington living room and made a dramatic announcement—through Kunzang Lama, acting as interpreter. Catharine had been teaching Mahayana Buddhism without any formal instruction. Penor Rinpoche attributed this miraculous ability to many lifetimes of Buddhist practice, performed at such a high level that it would always be in her mind. Michael turned to look at Catharine. Her eyes never strayed from Penor Rinpoche.

"You are all Buddhists," the venerable lama told the group. "And you are already practicing Buddhism."

He asked them to echo him as he uttered a string of words in Tibetan—words that went untranslated. "It was really like, Repeat after me," Wib remembered, "and we all did it."

Years later, after they had founded KPC—and many of Catharine's students had become ordained monks and nuns—they were still discovering what the words meant, and how their lives had been changed by them.

I dedicate myself to the liberation and salvation of all sentient beings. I offer my body, speech, and mind in order to accomplish the purpose of all sentient beings.

I will return in whatever form necessary, under extraordinary circumstances, to end suffering. Let me be born in times unpredictable, in places unknown, until all sentient beings are liberated from the cycle of death and rebirth.

Taking no thought for my comfort or safety, precious Buddha, make of me a pure and perfect instrument by which the end of suffering and death in all forms might be realized. Let me achieve perfect enlightenment for the sake of all beings. And then, by my hand and heart alone, may all beings achieve full enlightenment and perfect liberation.

I take refuge in the Lama.
I take refuge in the Buddha.
I take refuge in the Dharma.
I take refuge in the Sangha.*

* Translation of Bodhisattva and Refuge vows used at KPC, written by Jetsunma Ahkön Lhamo and approved by His Holiness Penor Rinpoche.

4.

What's a Chakra?

CLOQUET HATED REALITY BUT REALIZED IT WAS
STILL THE ONLY PLACE TO GET A GOOD STEAK.

—WOODY ALLEN

A couple weeks after Sangye's accident in November, Wib called to give me an update on the stupa building—and to announce that Jetsunma was now ready to talk to me. "She's had a lot going on," he said, his polite way of acknowledging that nearly a month had passed since I'd last bothered him about seeing her. "Building the stupa has created all kinds of obstacles." Jetsunma's back had been in spasm—and there had been many trips to the chiropractor. Her schedule had been in flux, too. Wib sounded a bit harried.

"How does lunch sound?" he asked. "Jetsunma says she needs to get out more."

She arrived at Hunter's Run, a dark palm-filled place in the center of Potomac, walking a little slowly in a tight-fitting gray suit. She looked as though she were holding her breath, or afraid to move her ribs. Apparently the chiropractor hadn't done much good. Her face looked relaxed, but puffy—like she'd just woken up.

Wib and I stood up to greet her. She smiled as she approached our table. It was a warm smile, a knowing smile, the kind of openhearted look you'd give to an old friend after a long absence. You couldn't help but like somebody who looked at you that way. As she came closer, I noticed that her dark red lipstick matched her fingernails perfectly. Her suit was not gray, as it had appeared at a distance, but a bold houndstooth, an interlocking pattern of black-and-white checks. It was the sort of snug suit, with 1940s shoulder pads and a short jacket, that called to mind a woman in a Raymond Chandler novel. Jetsunma had an air of beauty salon around her, too, of perfume and perfection. She looked like a Beverly Hills real estate agent, to tell the truth. I remember feeling a bit plain as she sat down, unadorned and uninteresting. And the table felt very small suddenly, too small.

She smiled again, and chuckled. Her front teeth both looked like they were capped. "I'm in my civvies," she said, gesturing at her suit.

Western writers used to travel to Tibet and describe the amazing feats they'd seen Buddhist lamas perform. Tibet itself was the "mystic land of the Grand lama, joint God and King of many millions," according to L. Austine Waddell, who'd made a visit to the remote mountainous country at the end of the last century.[*] The "lama-priests" were magicians and wizards, supernatural beings who had spent many lifetimes studying the nature of the mind.[†] They were psychic and telepathic—"one cannot have close contact with Tibetan lamas without discovering so many instances of it that it ceases to astonish," John Blofeld wrote in the 1960s.[‡] They could predict the day and place of their death, and make those predictions for others. They could read minds and, more important, hearts.

The Tibetans had developed mental exercises over the centuries that had given them great powers, according to the legends. The lamas walked on water and walked through walls and fire.

[*] L. Austine Waddell, *Tibetan Buddhism: With Its Mystic Cults, Symbolism and Mythology* (New York: Dover, 1972).

[†] Alexandra David-Neel, *Magic and Mystery in Tibet* (New York: Dover, 1971).

[‡] John Blofeld, *The Tantric Mysticism of Tibet: A Practical Guide to the Theory, Purpose, and Techniques of Tantric Meditation* (London: Penguin Arkana, 1970).

They could take other forms—temporarily becoming a bug, a bird sitting on a fence—and could appear in many places at the same time. Practicing *tum-mo*, they would climb into the mountains, meditating naked in subarctic temperatures, and melt thick blocks of ice. In the old books about Tibet, one reads about lamas shrinking themselves to the size of a dust speck, making objects disappear, or producing jewels in the palms of their hands. They could levitate and become invisible. They could even fly. While doing the spiritual practice of *lung-gom*, they could enter a trance state and begin "speed-walking" or "flying" for days. The lamas were said to visit each other at faraway monasteries this way, hovering over the ground and traveling at amazing speed.*

One of the Tibetan terms for these advanced beings is *tulku*. Before coming to Poolesville, I'd never heard the word. When I was growing up in California in the 1970s, the spiritual landscape seemed crowded with Eastern-style lamas and gurus and yogis and swamis—terms that were, for the most part, interchangeable. Tulku, I discovered after meeting Jetsunma, is a concept unique to Vajrayana Buddhism of Tibet, Mongolia, and Bhutan—and unheard of in Zen and the other forms of Buddhism. A tulku is an individual who has achieved a state of infinite wisdom or "realization," whose spiritual accomplishment is so great that he or she is able to transcend death and rebirth in samsara. But rather than avoid samsara and the human realm of suffering, a tulku returns again and again to help sentient beings on earth. As the renowned scholar Robert Thurman puts it, "Tulkus . . . are the Tibetan equivalent of our astronauts; heroes or heroines who have ventured to the limits of 'inner space' beyond death and through the dreamlike realms of the states in between."†

These are the little boys, or "little buddhas," that one reads about—and that the Italian film director Bernardo Bertolucci made a movie about—sometimes found in far-off places in the East or West, about the age of five, who are suspected of being the reincarnations of important lamas who have died. It turns out to

---

* W. Y. Evans-Wentz, ed., *Tibetan Yoga and Secret Doctrines* (New York: Oxford University Press, 1983).
† Robert A. F. Thurman, *Inside Tibetan Buddhism: Rituals and Symbols Revealed* (San Francisco: Collins Publishers, 1995).

be a delicate process, identifying a reincarnated tulku. A group of older lamas meditate, use their best intuitive powers and divinations, and still it isn't uncommon for several young candidates to materialize, each of them eligible to fill a vacant tulku seat, some of which come with throne-holding titles and well-off monasteries to run.

The Dalai Lama and the Panchen Lama—two of the highest-ranking tulkus and the spiritual leaders of Tibetan Buddhism—are the most famous examples of the enduring strength of this system. For centuries they've been coming back, over and over, sharing the responsibility of running Tibet. Since the fifteenth century, when the tulku system officially began, the Panchen and Dalai Lamas have had a father-son relationship and succeeded each other; one reigning lama nearing old age as the other reaches maturity. It's an efficient and self-perpetuating method, ensuring a reliable and known successor. Until recently, anyway—when the Communist Chinese, who have occupied Tibet since 1950, overruled the Dalai Lama's selection for Panchen Lama and came up with their own candidate, who, when the current Dalai Lama dies, will take over as Tibet's leader—and, presumably, be in control of his successor as well.

There are some seven hundred tulku positions in the Nyingma lineage alone, ranging from preeminent tulkus, like Penor Rinpoche, to the obscure. All these positions aren't filled at any given time. For one thing, it takes time and energy to officially *recognize* a reincarnated lama, as the process is called. But also, not all lamas die and return as people. A tulku could also wait many years, or even centuries, to return to samsara for another go at benefiting sentient beings. A tulku could wait for a particular time to return—and for a specific purpose. Some, it is said, come back as inanimate objects. A tulku could become a house or a work of art, a hospital or a new road or a bridge.

The Tibetans also believe that female tulkus are especially elusive and unlikely to reincarnate and become recognized. I had come to suspect this was an imaginative attempt to explain why there are so few women in tulku hierarchy. Consider the seventeenth-century saint Ahkön Lhamo, for instance. She spent most of her life alone in a cave meditating before founding the Palyul tradition of Tibetan Buddhism with her brother Kunzang Sherab. While Kunzang Sherab has been reborn over and over, his sister, Ahkön Lhamo, has made only one known and recorded reappearance since her cave days: His Holiness Penor Rinpoche had recognized the woman eating lunch with me as her reincarnation in 1986.

According to accounts of the first Ahkön Lhamo, she never bathed, had terrific body odor, and rarely spoke. Yet this time around here she was, sitting in a dark restaurant in Potomac, Maryland—wearing a citrus scent, coiffed hair, and a houndstooth suit, and ordering a sirloin steak salad for lunch.

"Red meat," Jetsunma said, setting her menu down and tapping on it with a perfectly enameled fingernail. "I just can't get enough."

It was a strange time to be telling her story, she said at the beginning of lunch. But it was also a perfect time. She had reached midlife and was spending a fair amount of time looking back. It wasn't true that lamas know everything, she said. And it wasn't true that their lives are simple. People thought being a lama meant you had a smooth go of things, effortless . . .

"But my life has not been easy," she said, looking at me rather seriously. "And I've asked my teachers to explain that to me. Why have I had such a hard life? This sounds like bragging, but I can match anybody's crummy childhood story. I've had students come to me and start telling me their sad tales. And I always say, I'm sorry, but I can match that. If you want to play that game, I can win."

She laughed a great deal throughout lunch—seemed ready to laugh—but not too far beneath her amiability and good cheer there was something very serious about her. And something deeply sad. As powerful and commanding as she was, Jetsunma seemed vulnerable and had a way of making you want to help her. Even sitting there next to her old student Wib, she seemed alone.

She had had weird dreams she wanted to discuss with me, she said, and unusual experiences throughout her life. There had also been much sadness, many disappointments. In Tibetan Buddhism you realize everything that happens is a result of your personal karma and past actions, "so you can't sit around and blame anybody else." Buddhism requires, more than anything else, a grueling amount of self-honesty—and she'd been having a lot of that.

"For instance, lately I've been wondering why none of my marriages has lasted," she said. "This has been the greatest disappointment of my life."

"It's over with Karl?" I asked, a little surprised. The previous Sunday he'd escorted her into the temple as usual.

Wib nodded.

"He's moved out of the house," Jetsunma said.

"He was your third husband?" I asked.

"Fourth," she said, looking over at Wib as if to double-check the number. "And the truth is, none of them, looking back, have been worth much—except for the children they've given me. I've always given out more than I got back."

"The relationship has always been so unequal," said Wib.

"None of them were really like husbands," Jetsunma said. "They were more like consorts.

"When I first meet up with a person, I see their potential and these incredible abilities. And I get so excited! I go overboard and my heart just leaps!" Jetsunma explained. "But potential is just potential—and it doesn't always come to be in this lifetime. My experience is that students in this society aren't really prepared for the role of consort. . . . Because of our culture, the norms and taboos, it forces an ordinary person and puts them in extraordinary circumstances. It puts them in the middle of their inner poisons and their spiritual potential—and that's a lot to expect of somebody.

"It's really hard to be with your teacher. A person has to work hard every day to be pure and honest, and particularly men, they have much less skill at looking inside themselves and seeing what's going on."

As our food arrived Jetsunma and Wib bowed their heads and prayed quietly over the plates. Then the three of us huddled and made plans, eating slowly. We discussed how the interviews for the book might go, how many I might need. Jetsunma suggested a few people outside of KPC who might be good to talk to—and offered the name of her former therapist in Miami. Wib suggested that I get an official phone list for the sangha, or group of practitioners at KPC, and that I should feel free to call anybody.

"That's one thing I don't have trouble with," Jetsunma said with a shrug. "Attracting students. In fact, it quite amazes my teachers—the dedication of my students and the depth of their practice." Penor Rinpoche had predicted that many more students would turn up. "They've told me to plan on building a temple to seat fifteen hundred," she said, "which is partly why we acquired the sixty-five acres of woods across the street. We need the space."

By "teachers," Jetsunma was referring mainly to Penor Rinpoche but also to Gyaltrul Rinpoche, an older, respected lama who was enjoying a comfortable life as a retired guru in Half Moon Bay, California. He was famous for his astute wisecracks and blunt delivery. He was also known for his profound teachings and respected books, as well as a Tibetan Buddhist center he had established in Ashland, Oregon. Gyaltrul Rinpoche had been advising Jetsunma—and since Gyaltrul was considered the reincarnation of Kunzang Sherab, her past-life brother, it was hard not to notice some similarities between them, a certain irreverence. The previous summer, while covering Penor Rinpoche's visit to Poolesville for *The Washington Post*, I'd had the opportunity to meet Gyaltrul Rinpoche. And when our news photographer tried to take his picture, Gyaltrul produced his own black plastic camera, which turned out to be a squirt gun, and shot water out into the crowd.

"I hope your book might be funny and compelling," Jetsunma said, "and not just another drippy spiritual book." As for her own story—the extraordinary trajectory of her life—she thought the one unsolved piece remained her abusive childhood. "I should be in the loony bin or I should be on welfare," she said. And if abusive childhoods make abusive adults, or turn people to crime, how come she wasn't a criminal? "My story is really miraculous, if you think about it," she said. "All that I've survived in this lifetime."

Jetsunma had something else to bring up, and the concern showed on her face. "I'm really hoping you can write this book without calling my mother," she said, "or my ex-husbands." She wasn't in touch with any of them, she said, nor did she feel their accounts would be reliable.

This might be hard, I said. There would be facts to check.

Jetsunma's face became completely still, and for the first time since we'd sat down her eyes were not twinkling. Her request disturbed me—and seemed impossible to honor.

I would work to be fair, I said, and not to pry, and let her tell her own story. But sometimes mothers and ex-husbands are invaluable sources—for their memories of all the details that make up a life. In the end, though, I said, I wanted to hear her account—in her words—of how she'd gone from being Alyce Zeoli, the battered girl, to Catharine Burroughs, suburban mother of two, to Jetsunma Ahkön Lhamo, the founder of the largest monastery of Tibetan Buddhist monks and nuns in America.

"It's been a little messy," she said, then chuckled.

"I'm sure it has," I said.

"And it hasn't been easy."

"It couldn't have been," I said.

"My job didn't come with a manual, you know," Jetsunma continued. "And my teachers contribute when they come here, but then they are gone—and it's up to me to do this thing that I literally don't have a clue how to do—except out of my own wisdom, if I have any. There are days when I wonder."

We talked on, mostly about the stupa and the relics, and how the potency of the monument was causing obstacles in Poolesville. "My back spasms are part of that," Jetsunma said. "But once the stupa is blessed—in a couple weeks or so—the worst part should be over."

I had many questions about how stupas are thought to work. How does a relic produce a miracle? Is a stupa thought to be a living, enlightened mind—or simply a monument that calls forth the worshiper's own enlightened mind? Do relics themselves have power over events—or only power to incite greater faith? Jetsunma began to answer these questions with elaborate explanations, then stopped in the middle of a sentence. "You realize that you've been a Buddhist before, don't you?"

I shook my head.

"Literally," she said, "you could not be asking me these kinds of questions if you hadn't practiced a great deal. It wouldn't be possible."

"I was a classical art and archaeology major in college," I said. "Temples and sacred sculptures are pretty familiar to me."

"Sorry"—Jetsunma laughed, then shared a look with Wib. "That's not what I'm talking about."

The restaurant began emptying of customers. A bartender arrived to work the cocktail hour and was wiping glasses and stacking them on shelves. Before we stood to leave, Jetsunma had something else to say. It was about her attendant Alana, and how they met.

"Some students come to Dharma and it's like letting a fish go in water. *Psheeew*, they take off. They vibe with everything. Their eyes just fill up, all their senses just fill up, and there's a certainty about them." And then, other times, Jetsunma explained, a student arrives and isn't particularly drawn to the teachings, the exotic statues of Buddhas, the maroon robes of the ordained. But that student might feel strangely drawn to Jetsunma. This was an indication of some kind of past-life connection, Jetsunma explained.

"They'll take one look at me and go, *Whoa . . . Teacher!* And they can't leave—they just can't leave me and they never will. Their connection isn't with Dharma, it's with me. . . . These are people who would never make it in a traditional Dharma center— and quite a number of my students are like that. Quite a number."

Particularly her early students, she said. "I call them the First Wave. Something magical happened when I met them. It was like their destiny to build this center with me. . . . They've seen it all," she said. "If they don't love me by now, they're never going to love me."

She and Wib looked at each other and laughed.

"This is a monumental, *an extraordinary life* that they've entered into. And it's not easy. You can come to a Dharma center—and that in itself takes a certain amount of karma—but to stay and make it work . . . *it's an exceptional life.* And it's a different life. It's a high life as opposed to an ordinary life."

She stopped for a second. "Have you met Alana?"

I shook my head.

"She reminded me recently of her first consultation with me. She walked in with her little high-heeled shoes and her little camel suit. She had no idea why she'd come to see me. She was just drawn. But when we saw each other, the connection was like—like you could hear it in the room. I really talked turkey with her, too. I told her that she was living a very ordinary life now, and if her whole life was a cloud—that's how I was visualizing it—it was a very high cloud but had roots in a lower atmosphere, and in the middle it was pinched. That pinching was a bridge. And I felt that she was coming to a closing of a certain element of her life, like the pinching of a cloud, but above her was something almost unrecognizable and almost scary.

"I told her that the day would come when she would be deeply involved in a spiritual practice. But not only that, that someday that practice would be her whole life and even her vocation and even her living. . . . Everything would come from her involvement with spirituality.

"I remember how she looked at me, and how she was thinking, *No way!* I mean, here was this lady with flaming red hair, a really big do, lots of hair and stylish and gorgeous."

She turned to Wib. "Remember how gorgeous she was?"

He nodded.

"She was a hot lady, really. A figure to die for. And our connection was like, well, it was like in the atmosphere. I remember looking at her and thinking, There you are! I know you! You're mine! . . . But there she is in her camel suit, very prim and proper. Nylon hose. She's Ms. Insurance Secretary . . . and she's got all the right things in America. A husband who's very good-looking, very nice body. He's got a nice car. She's got a nice car. She's got her nice job, and he has his nice job. They have two children—that kind of thing. It's very white fence. And here I am telling her that her life is about to change, that everything she knows as life is going to end and she's going to be transformed into this ultimately spiritual being.

"And she looked at me and said, 'I believe everything you say and I don't know why because it doesn't make any sense.' "

Then Jetsunma described how, at the end of the consultation, she was telling Alana about a blockage she was seeing in her chakras. "I can, if I meditate, I can sometimes see things on other levels—it's not a big deal—and I don't know how else to explain it to you, but anyway, I was telling her I had noticed something about her chakras, her energy centers. I was seeing this, and seeing that. And meanwhile I'm looking at her face, and she's listening really hard and her eyebrows are knitted together, and I'm going on and on, and finally I can't help wondering why her brows are knitted like that and her tongue is starting to come out of her mouth, and finally, I say, 'Do you have any questions?'

" 'Yeah,' she says. 'What's a chakra?'

"We play that part of the tape sometimes, just for the joke value."

We all laughed for a few moments, then Jetsunma sat up stiffly and hunched her shoulders. "Guys, I'm on the edge," she said. "And my back is definitely in spasm."

Five or ten minutes after we'd said good-bye, I was pulling my car around the block when I passed Jetsunma and Wib standing together on the street behind the restaurant. They were next to Wib's car—and the car door was open. But rather than getting inside, Jetsunma was motioning with her arms, gesturing passionately and looking upset. If I hadn't known them, I might have suspected they were a married couple having a row. But Wib did not look like he was saying anything. He just looked stunned.

Whatever could they be talking about? I remember thinking as I drove away. Whatever could she be saying to him? What had he done?

Part Two

The
Attendant

5.

Ani Land

NOTHING IS LOST; EVEN THE MONASTERY
SURROUNDED BY WALLS
SHEDS ITS LIGHT.

—ANTOINE DE SAINT EXUPÉRY, journal

There was no monastery, exactly, at Kunzang Palyul Choling. The ordained were sprinkled about Poolesville in group houses. Six nuns lived at Ani Farms, a simple white two-story farmhouse on an expanse of green pastureland. Another five or six nuns lived at Ani Estates, a large, beige stucco tract house in a treeless new development of homes. Most of the monks lived together, too, in a town house in nearby Darnestown. A true monastic residence was talked about—and certainly in the future plans—but money was scarce and there were other priorities. It didn't seem to make much difference. Every year, usually during a visit by an esteemed lama, or even His Holiness Penor Rinpoche himself, a few more men and women were ordained, monastery or no monastery.

A few days after my lunch with Jetsunma, I headed out to Ani Farms. For the last few days the nuns had been working into the night, trying to finish the decorative relief for the stupa—before the Stupa Man left town in eight days. Nearly all the nuns had worked on the stupa in some way or another, but I'd been told that Alana had been out to Ani Farms a great deal lately, and I was hoping finally to bump into her.

The crickets got louder as I drove down River Road and farther into the cold night. It was just a few days before Thanksgiving. The farmhouse of Ani Farms was dark and looked deserted. Nearby, a big white barn was ablaze with lights, and a nest of trucks and small import cars with the telltale FREE TIBET and KARMA HAPPENS bumper stickers were parked in an otherwise lonely pasture. As I walked closer to the lights, sliding a bit on the frozen mud, I heard the voice of Sherab Khandro rising above all other sounds. Before I could knock she opened the barn door.

"You made it!" Sherab hollered. But rather than wearing the maroon robes that I'd expected, the gigantic figure standing before me wore a faded baseball cap, maroon sweatpants, and a golden hooded sweatshirt jacket that was splashed in places with wet plaster and coffee.

"Martha?"

"*Sherab?*"

She roared with laughter, and threw her head back. "Didn't recognize me, did you? Me and the robes have parted company for the night. *I'm working.*"

With a theatrical hand gesture and raised eyebrow, she motioned me inside the barn and led the way, her big work boots clobbering the old wooden floorboards. "Look who's here!" she called out as we entered a room awash in various shades of red and gold. Eight or nine nuns, most of whom I hadn't met before, were in a cozy but well-equipped workshop, bending over various stupa projects. Some were sculpting, others were polishing molds or cleaning up. Ordinarily the barn was the headquarters of Tara Studios—sometimes known as Tara Enterprises Ltd.—Sherab's cottage business that produced plaster Buddhas and other sacred objects that were sold to New Age boutiques and Dharma centers around the country. "We bake those little Buddhas," Sherab had explained to me, "and pop them out of the molds like biscuits."

Lately orders had gone unfilled and Tara Studios had fallen behind. Sherab and her crew were consumed with stupa work. A firm called Architectural Stone, in nearby Annapolis Junction, had been commissioned to make the cement spire of the stupa—twelve rings, each smaller than the one beneath, rising skyward with a crystal ball on the top. In her studio Sherab had designed the stupa's faceplate, a three-by-three-foot low-relief of the young "treasure revealer" Migyur Dorje. With the help of some others Sherab had also sculpted vines for a garland of leaves that would form an arch around the seated Buddha.

There were younger nuns, middle-aged nuns, fat nuns and thin ones. They wore baseball caps over their short hair, cotton sweats in maroon or gold, and knit turtlenecks like Sherab's—ordered from the J. Crew catalog. They looked a bit like a weekend soccer league, or an aerobics class.

And rather than the modest traditional sort of *ani*, who, in India, is not allowed to attend monastic university or permitted to sit in the same prayer room with monks while teachings and empowerments are being given, the nuns of KPC were mostly Americans in their thirties and forties. They were worldly and educated, and not only were welcome to join their male counterparts during all teachings but generally seemed to overpower them, if only because of sheer numbers. In Poolesville there were four nuns to every monk—a phenomenon unheard of in the West or East. I had assumed that Jetsunma's girls'-girl personality—along with her wisecracks about the male-centered traditions of Tibet—had drawn all the women to KPC, but there turned out to be a more mystical and interesting explanation: The first Ahkön Lhamo was said to have had so many nuns worshiping at her cave site that the Tibetans called the mountain where she meditated Red Rocks because of the way the robes of the anis colored the hillside.

Sherab walked me from work station to work station, from nun to nun, making introductions and pointing out the stages of the work being done while her small brown dog, Corgie, trailed behind us. Ani Catharine Anastasia, a woman in her forties with a ruddy face and watery blue-green eyes, was polishing a piece of clay and seemed very much in her own world. Later on I was told she had once been a heroin addict. Next there was Ani Dawa, a trim athletic woman in her thirties with olive skin and a crisp Austrian accent. She had a power drill in her hands and a bit of a proprietary air. Ani Sophia, a blond and delicate waif who couldn't have been out of her twenties, wore a mysterious Mona Lisa smile as she waxed a clay piece of lotus vine. She was a member of a notable Poolesville family, and her mother and three sisters were also nuns at KPC; her father and one brother lived nearby on a large farm.

Each nun greeted me warmly—and with a sense of familiarity that was, at first, unsettling. "You're Jetsunma's biographer," Ani Sophia said.

"Smart move," said Dawa.

"She's writing her first book about Jetsunma," said Sherab, "and she says she's not a Buddhist!"

The room exploded in raucous laughter.

"It's true," I said. "I'm just a Buddhist sympathizer."

"You better be careful," said Dawa. "That's how it starts."

"Yeah," said Sherab, "that's what *I* used to say."

Not only was Sherab the tallest nun, and the loudest, but she was trying—with great self-deprecating displays of humility—to be in charge. She had the air of somebody who wasn't entirely comfortable being a leader but was a leader anyway, quite naturally. Part of it was her height and bearing, another part was her super-enthusiastic spirit. I'd heard a story about how she'd been working on the stupa one sweltering summer day when Jetsunma visited the woods to see the progress. "Gosh, there's nothing like working in the outdoors, under that big open sky!" Sherab had said to the lama.

"Sherab, what *aren't* you into?" Jetsunma asked her. "Taxes?"

"Not if I was getting money back!"

The children at the temple school had taken to calling her Ani Ace because Sherab often obliged them with a wicked Ace Ventura impression. But the nickname sprang from more than that. Shaving their heads had made most of the older nuns look hip and elegantly ageless—like downtown punk rockers who were still going to Laurie Anderson concerts—and made the younger ones look like they were recovering from cancer treatment. But Sherab, at six feet, with her broad shoulders, large expressive brown eyes, and small nose, looked stunningly like Jim Carrey.

She'd started Tara Studios sort of flukishly, or *spontaneously*, as a Buddhist might say—a word that suggests a certain magic and intuitive wisdom was in effect. She was still working at Bally

Fitness Clubs, selling memberships, when she became a nun in 1990. She had planned to keep working there and drawing her sixty-thousand-dollar-a-year salary. Poverty isn't part of a vow Tibetan Buddhist nuns and monks at KPC make—a number of the ordained held well-paying jobs in D.C., owned cars, traveled often to visit their families. While monks and nuns in India and elsewhere are not allowed even to handle coins or bills, Jetsunma was happy to make allowances for her monks and nuns who held real-world jobs.

Jetsunma also felt that some of the other Dharma centers in America had a tendency to attract people who weren't serious about their spiritual commitments and were just looking for a free ride. "Frankly, there are lots of deadbeats in the Dharma scene," she had said to me. She wanted to make sure that didn't happen in Poolesville. So aside from being out of debt at the time they took vows, the ordained at KPC were expected to provide for themselves financially—as well as contribute to the temple. At Jetsunma's center the ordained bought their own food, paid rent at the group houses, and gave a tithing to KPC; many of them also made a monthly offering directly to their lama.

Sherab was able to keep her hair a bit longer than the other nuns, too, and wear modest toned-down versions of her old work clothes—not her maroon robes—but ultimately she found it too difficult going back and forth between worlds. The temptations were too great. She'd smell the smoke from a cigarette and want one herself. She'd see a new sports car on the road and feel desire rise in her chest. With Jetsunma's approval she quit her job at Bally, sold her condo in Gaithersburg, and moved into a monastic dorm that existed briefly on the temple grounds. It was Jetsunma who originally suggested that Sherab look into making satsas, little Buddha reliefs, from molds and selling them. She told Sherab about a Hare Krishna center in West Virginia where similar molds were made—and suggested she call and inquire about the techniques.

The Hare Krishnas were most helpful, and after a few days of apprenticing with them, Sherab began experimenting with little nine-inch plaster stupas and small Buddhas. Late at night she worked in the bathroom of the dorm, setting up her plaster molds over the bathtub. "A giant mess," she said, "and I don't think I was very popular with the other ordained." Eventually, at Jetsunma's recommendation, Sherab began selling her stupas and Buddhas in the temple gift shop and was able to keep a portion of the money she made. And it was money she needed to live.

Some nuns had bona fide temple jobs. Dara, a young, soft-spoken nun with dark hair and a beautiful face, was the primary teacher of the elementary school the temple ran. Rinchen kept the temple running and clean. Alana and Atara were paid salaries as Jetsunma's attendants. But many nuns held jobs in the real world. Dechen—the smallest and youngest and brainiest nun—worked at a publishing house. Samten was a nurse at the National Cancer Institute, Ani Catharine Anastasia worked as a waitress in Potomac, and Alexandra was a personal assistant to a rich sangha member who lived in Georgetown. But few nuns had as good a job—or were as flush with income—as Ani Aileen. Aileen had been a sound technician for NBC for more than twenty years, a union job with regular raises. Over the years, by frugal renunci-ate living and saving her salary, she had contributed twelve hun-dred dollars a month to the temple mortgage payment, made a large monthly donation to the Lama Support Fund, and pur-chased a retreat house for Jetsunma in Sedona, Arizona.

There was optimism that Tara Studios would become a suc-cessful temple-run industry. After moving into Ani Farms in 1992, Sherab continued making her Buddhas in the basement, and then, as the business grew, she rented space in the barn next to the farmhouse. After Dawa, the young Austrian nun, became a partner in the business—investing the eighty thousand dollars re-maining in her trust fund—she and Sherab were able to offer a complete line of products made from molds. There were nine-inch stupas—painted white and filled with tiny rolled prayers. And there were Buddhas of every kind: Sakyamunis and Chenrezigs and Guru Rinpoches. There were statues of Tara, the goddess of mercy and great miracles for which Tara Studios had been named. Dawa and Sherab put together a brochure, a wholesale mail-order business was set up, and they soon began selling the plaster and resin statues, along with bumper stickers and cards, to boutiques around the country.

But like other ventures at KPC, Tara Studios had trouble making a profit, even in its peak years, when it was selling figurines and sacred objects of worship to nearly eighty boutiques. Different managers were plucked from the sangha to help Sherab with the business side of things—others were told directly by Jetsunma to volunteer—but it was difficult running an office and studio with unpaid labor. Schedules were hard to coordinate. Many of the monks and nuns were already overcommitted and had little time left for their practices. Sherab and Dawa often found themselves doing everything. There was also a problem getting spiritual people to focus on the mundane. "We're all so right-brained," Sherab said, "and maybe that was the problem."

More fundamentally, the idea behind Tara Studios wasn't all that smart. Buddha images and little stupas can be imported from China and India for a good deal less money than they could be made for in Poolesville by Sherab and Dawa. And it was this kind of overall lack of business sense that made failure a pervasive problem at KPC. Aside from the temple gift shop, which provided an average of one thousand dollars a month to the center's operating budget, all other ventures had been financial disasters. There was a typesetting business called Ani's Ink—much vaunted by Jetsunma as a "sure thing," partly because of the auspicious year of its inception—which left behind only debts and a cumbersome and obsolete typesetting machine that Rinchen was still paying off. There had been a failed attempt to start a New Age rock group called SkyDancer, which featured Jetsunma as the lead singer. "Be sure to get a good recording of SkyDancer," Sherab warned me. "On the tape I have, the music sounds awful and so does Jetsunma." The temple had produced an expensive CD of Jetsunma singing a Buddhist invocation; it also hadn't sold well.

Tom Barry, who had been a successful dealer of military weapons parts before becoming a monk and changing his name to Tashi in 1988, was the first supervisor of Tara Studios—and he was able to raise more capital for the business within the sangha. The job then passed to Don Allen, a U.S. Postal Service administrator. Don became frustrated with managing the operations and passed the torch on to another sangha member, Paul Wasserman.

When Paul didn't work out, Alana was asked to oversee things. According to Sherab, it was Alana who worked the hardest to get Tara Studios in shape financially and ready to realize a profit. Alana was shrewd, organized, and, as the right arm of Jetsunma, powerful enough to get sangha members to fulfill their obligations at the barn. She wasn't just powerful, though, she was famously chilly, sometimes harsh, and fanatically devoted to Jetsunma— something of a Mrs. Danvers character—and sangha members regarded her with great trepidation.

But in the last couple of months Alana had been called away from Tara Studios. She was needed more urgently elsewhere: Jetsunma had invented a hair care device that she wanted manufactured and sold. It was a cap with built-in gel packs that could be heated in a microwave and worn inside a terry-cloth turban. Jetsunma had big plans for the invention—she'd had a dream that she would sell millions of the caps for $14.95 each—and after Doug Sims and Tashi had raised start-up costs within the sangha, the lama hoped the business would support her so she'd no longer have to rely on receiving a temple salary. "I don't want to be paid," Jetsunma had told me, "for teaching Dharma anymore." She named her new company Ladyworks.

Sherab was in the middle of the Migyur Dorje stupa project when Tara Enterprises Ltd. fell in her lap again. The company was behind in filling orders. And it was still operating in the red. But Sherab continued to hope that things would turn around, that the right manager would show up—and that good moneymaking karma would ripen. But, just in case, once the stupa was finished, she planned to find a temp job.

"I don't need much," she said, "just enough to pay rent, pay for teachings, and afford good coffee. I'm hooked on Starbucks."

I wandered around the barn, looking at the nuns at work. I talked a bit with Dawa, then sat on the ground and played with the dog. Sherab was in a corner, painting an edge of the Migyur Dorje faceplate. And as I began to wander off again, she yelled out. "You're on the stupa diet, right?"

"I am."

"*Well, then,* as long as you're here, you might as well be accruing some merit!"

She set me up next to Ani Sophia, who showed me how to coat wax on a piece of vine decoration—so a mold could be made and eventually dozens of resin copies could be produced. I fumbled around at first but slowly settled down and got the hang of it. The work required patience, and the more I paid attention to doing a good job, the less I noticed my surroundings. The room seemed to grow very quiet. I liked working on the stupa—even a tiny part of it. I liked being there, in the barn with the nuns. I liked how strong they seemed, how focused, and how soft. I liked the way they teased me, and the way Sherab ordered me around.

Had I known these people before? Had Sherab and I been friends before—or was I, as Jetsunma had once suggested, a Buddhist practitioner over many lifetimes? I doubted all that—laughed at the notion—but it was strange how comfortable I felt in this absolutely foreign place, how quickly Poolesville felt like home. A few days before, Wib had said, "From our perspective, for someone even to hear the word *Buddha* indicates that they must have prior experience as a being who helped others. And for a person to drive up our temple driveway—and to be exposed to Tibetan Buddhism and actually engage in that—would indicate that this person has had many, many lifetimes of practicing compassion. . . . That's what we've been taught, anyway.

"And so for someone to be writing a book about Jetsunma—that person must have a strong previous connection with her, and a strong previous wish to do something like this, to write a book about her. Maybe you've even done something like this in the past. If this weren't the case, you wouldn't be writing a book at all. In my world all this goes without saying."

When I'd asked Wib if this meant that he and I had had a previous connection, he explained that he felt that over many lifetimes he had had all kinds of relationships with Jetsunma, with Alana, with Jane—and even with me. "The way a Buddhist looks at this," he said, "every person you encounter, every living thing, has been your mother and father. If you are mindful of this, it becomes hard to think of being cruel, or killing. It becomes hard even to squash a bug. If you and I were Buddhas, we would understand all this exactly. But we all know what it feels like to have an immediate connection with somebody. . . . Sometimes people walk through the door of the temple and they feel like old friends. And Jetsunma will say sometimes, 'Hello, old friend!' She can know and sense these things—but the knowing is not a describable knowing."

I knew what Wib meant, about the not-describable knowing, at least. Most of us have experienced that feeling, the sense that we belong with certain people, and belong in certain places. Even new places can feel like home. I thought about my favorite book as a teenager, *Cat's Cradle* by Kurt Vonnegut. One character, a prophet named Bokonon, says that people are lumped into a karass—a circle of souls whose lives will all intersect. There was even a little ditty to sing:

> *Oh, a sleeping drunkard*
> *Up in Central Park,*
> *And a lion-hunter*
> *In the jungle dark,*
> *And a Chinese dentist,*
> *And a British queen—*
> *All fit together*
> *In the same machine.*

I'd had this feeling before, too, when I first walked into *The Washington Post* newsroom ten years earlier, after taking a job as a news aide to Nina Hyde, the fashion editor. I didn't have much interest in fashion, really, or journalism. And I had no previous writing experience. The job paid slightly more than did the museum where I'd been working. I was just killing a year or two, I figured, before going back to study art history in graduate school. But very quickly after starting at the *Post* I felt I belonged there—felt a connection to the place and the people, and a sense of loyalty. I felt at home there, more than any other place I'd been. Before long I'd completely abandoned my career plans in art history. I loved newspaper writing, loved the excitement, the power. I loved the deadlines and seeing my byline. It wasn't until many years later that I began to realize the parts of myself that I'd buried or abandoned in order to fit into the newsroom culture—and succeed in it. Sometimes I missed the hours I used to spend in museums. I missed the quiet. I missed looking carefully at things. I missed soaking up the magnificent vagueness and subtleties of great art. Journalism had made me more outgoing, more practical, and more organized. But I was also more egotistical and less patient. Being with the Buddhists made me see how impatient I had become, and how egotistical.

What had Sherab given up? I looked at her working on the Migyur Dorje faceplate. She was scratching her nearly bald head. There was a long laundry list of vows the nuns had to take upon ordination—no killing, no lying, no stealing, no sex, no drinking, no dancing, no listening to music for pleasure. . . . Did they ever miss their old lives, or miss the lives they didn't have? The children they didn't bear, the lovers they didn't embrace? Did they ever crave a glass of wine? They were all reasonably young and seemed talented and full of life. What did a renunciate life give them to compensate for all the things sacrificed?

There were lots of reasons, I guessed, to raise a white flag and surrender interest in the material world. Aside from the well-trod pleasures of the quotidian—holidays at the beach, dance parties—you could still feel a greater need for something else entirely. You could feel a hunger and emptiness. You could be tormented by unanswered questions. Modern life leaves many people feeling insignificant and a bit lost. If you were living a spiritual life—and believed you were helping to end suffering—that could make you feel quite potent, I suppose. And while secular life has a tendency to lose its shimmer—how many dance parties, or holidays at the beach?—spiritual life is infused with supernatural events. From a spiritual perspective, the world can always seem new and wondrous, the way it felt to us as children.

As the time passed and I got better at waxing the vines, I became aware of the sounds in the room again. I heard a small tool dropping, the floorboards creaking. Conversation between the nuns started up, stopped, then started again.

One of the nuns mentioned she was cooking for Jetsunma over the weekend. "No green peppers and no oil," she said.

"It's a great honor, you know," Sherab said, walking over to me, "getting to cook for your teacher."

"Or driving her," another nun said.

"Or cleaning her house."

"Alana says things are really changing drastically for her," Sherab added, "since she's been attending Jetsunma again."

"Things really happen around your teacher," a nun said.

"Oh boy," said Dawa.

"Do they ever."

Someone asked if there was any news of David Rust, a sangha member who was dying of AIDS.

"I heard Jetsunma might be seeing him today," one nun said.

"She went."

"How did it go?"

The room fell silent.

"Alana will know," Sherab said, and turned to me. "Have you met Alana?"

"Not yet," I said.

"*Ohhhh*," a chorus of three nuns said behind me.

"You're in for a real treat!" said Dawa. And I couldn't tell, exactly, if she was being serious. A few of the other nuns were chuckling.

I thought about Jetsunma's description of Alana at lunch: incredible figure, stunning redhead, didn't know what a chakra was.

"She should be here any minute," Sherab said. "She's painting the Migyur Dorje faceplate. She's much more accomplished at fine work than I am."

I turned around to look at the faceplate of the young Migyur Dorje propped up in the corner of the barn. His unfinished face was pale, the color of gypsum and resin and whatever else the faceplate was made of. He was holding up a finger—as though he were about to say something.

"You know," Sherab said in a reverential whisper, "Alana is Jetsunma's best friend."

Alana arrived quietly. I heard only the barn door open, the creak of a floorboard, and a faint rustling of fabric. Her face was plain, Anglo-Saxon-looking, and reminded me of portraits of colonial

Americans. It was plain the way a Quaker's face would be plain, or a Puritan's. Her eyes seemed small. Her skin was very pale with light freckles. When she took off her thick wool cap, her hair was an inch long, a strawberry blond so light, and flecked with white bristles, that it looked almost pink. She took off her heavy down parka, and I was surprised by the stout body underneath, made heavier by a thick sweatshirt. The elastic in her old turtleneck was tired and her collar fell loosely around her neck. As she entered the workshop, the nuns looked up and said hello, smiled, but there was no special greeting or burst of enthusiasm.

"How is David Rust?" one of them asked quietly.

Alana smiled brightly for the first time. A network of crinkles took over her eyes, which seemed now intensely blue and sharp. As she spoke, though, there was a matter-of-factness that startled me. She didn't talk about a dying man the way you'd expect.

"Jetsunma sat on his bed and sang him the Seven Line Prayer," she said. "And she told him what a noble life he'd had."

The room became quiet. Nobody asked how long he might live—or anything else about his condition. There were no words like "what a shame" or "his poor family" or even "how sad"—the kinds of things we tend to say in moments of sympathy. Apparently what Alana had conveyed was all they needed to know.

"*That's incredible,*" Sherab finally said.

"What a lucky man."

I continued buffing wax on the clay vines. Alana walked silently over to the Migyur Dorje faceplate, picking up a paintbrush. Something had changed since she'd entered the room. A shift, a sense of heightened energy. She'd brought news of Jetsunma, and described a deathbed scene of David Rust. Looking around the room once again, I couldn't help but feel a little moved by the nuns, by their lightness and seriousness, clarity, purpose, warmth. I felt their sense of belonging to each other, to the center, to Jetsunma. Maybe I romanticized their lives. Maybe they didn't always get along this way. But I couldn't help but compare the sense of community that I felt in Poolesville with the only real sense of community I'd known for a decade: the newsroom with its endemic unhappiness. It was a place where I had belonged once, but now somehow I felt I never had.

Sherab rubbed her neck, and I could see the stiff outline of her metal back brace under her sweatshirt. I thought about how hard she had worked on the stupa, the digging, the pouring of concrete all these months. All the nuns had had a role—sewing bags of beans and rice, rolling nearly a million mantras, doing prayer shifts, cooking and cleaning for the stupa crew. In eight days the stupa would be sealed forever and blessed by the Stupa Man—and even though it wouldn't be painted until the spring, it would be officially alive.

"What's going to happen when the stupa is finished?" I asked.

"What do you mean?" said Dawa.

"Like, won't things get a little dull around here?"

Sherab laughed. "Anticlimax? Stupa withdrawal?"

I nodded.

"Definitely," she said, laughing.

Thirty seconds or more passed, then Alana spoke up. "You know what I think's going to happen when the stupa is finished?"

"What?" I asked.

"The world will change."

6.

Alana

MYSTERY IS A GREAT EMBARRASSMENT
TO THE MODERN MIND.

—FLANNERY O'CONNOR

Years ago, before Alana found her way to Poolesville, she was called Betsy Elgin. She had red hair, an aloof sort of pristine beauty, and when she was growing up in suburban Maryland she had the usual questions about life—the ones everybody thinks are appropriate for teenagers and embarrassing later on. But Betsy was not as remote, or as unfeeling, as she appeared. She just had a way of hiding her feelings. When she got pregnant her senior year of high school, she hid that, too—six months pregnant under her graduation robes and not even her parents knew. She and her boyfriend got married when they were seventeen, raised their daughter, and, four years later, they had another.

She had grown up in a Protestant household, but in her early twenties Betsy attended lectures on Buddhism. It was the sixties, and Eastern religion was in vogue. The lectures were dry, though—just lists of books to read, words to memorize. Later on, following another burst of spiritual passion, Betsy had a born-again Christian experience. A bit later she was divorced and re-married.

As she grew older, Betsy's youthful questions, and sense of wonder about life, left her. The days became ordinary. She was working as an insurance secretary, raising her two daughters, feeding her two cats, vacuuming the carpets in her suburban town house, and trying, on the side, to start her own interior decorating business. The mystical did not present itself: The strange connections between things went unnoticed. Her husband—an insurance agent, NFL football referee, bodybuilder—was utterly grounded in materiality. And if Betsy ever raised doubts about the way they were living their lives, he'd say, "Why are you even asking that question? The universe? Why are you talking about the universe?"

When Betsy was thirty-five years old, a friend told her about a psychic who lived in Silver Spring. "You pay her twenty dollars and she goes into a trance and tells you about your past lives and other crazy stuff," her friend said. It was a hoot, really—the kind of thing Betsy could have a good laugh with her girlfriends about later. "I went to see this channeler, and . . ." But when Betsy called the number she was given for the psychic, her heart was pounding. A sweet voice answered—not the old witch she had imagined—and Betsy made an appointment to see Catharine Burroughs on a weekday afternoon in the fall of 1983.

Betsy arrived at a redbrick apartment building in Silver Spring and found the first-floor apartment where Catharine Burroughs lived. Betsy had come from work, and was wearing a camel suit with matching camel-beige pumps and handbag. Her hair was bright red and down to her shoulders. Her body, even under the boxy suit, was noticeably strong and curvaceous.

A heavyset woman with a pretty face answered the door and smiled very warmly. "Oh, you're so beautiful!" she said.

"You are too!" Betsy blurted back. She looked down at Catharine's African print skirt and perfectly manicured red nails. There was an awkward pause and a fumbling for words. Betsy suddenly felt a great intimacy with this woman, which made her a little queasy.

She was led to Catharine's small living room, which, to Betsy's eye, needed decorating. Clearly this psychic wasn't making much money. "There were crates instead of furniture," she recounted, "and a lamp sitting on the floor because there was no table to put it on." Some large quartz crystals were scattered about—lending a New Age feeling.

Once she was settled, Catharine explained to Betsy what would be happening during the psychic reading. She would meditate, she said, examine Betsy's energy on various levels—the physical plane, the emotional plane, and the spiritual plane—and tell her what she saw. It was a little like a checkup, she said. Then Catharine sat back in a green velvet, overstuffed chair and closed her eyes.

"How is your marriage?" Catharine asked.

"Fine," Betsy said. "Really fine."

Catharine said nothing.

"Is your father dead?"

"No," Betsy said, getting nervous. "I mean . . . I hope not. I don't think so."

"I can see your father in your energy field," Catharine said, "but it's like somebody has taken an eraser and erased his face."

When Betsy heard that, she started to cry. "It was such a perfect description of my relationship with my father," she said later. "He was there but not there."

By the time the session was over, she had cried many times. With Catharine she felt as though she was talking with an old, dear friend, someone who knew her better than anyone else did. She had a feeling of being deeply cared for in a way she'd never experienced. Catharine had also said some incredibly nice things that made her feel incredibly good. She told Betsy that she was a "great being," a great *spiritual* being. And she said that someday—while it might seem hard to believe—Betsy's life would be completely different from what it was now. It would turn over, like a pancake. Her whole world would become spiritual.

"Is your full name Elizabeth?" she asked.

"Yes."

"Why don't you call yourself that?" Catharine asked.

"I've always been Betsy."

"The names we use are very important—and have great spiritual significance. Betsy's a cute and nice name, but . . . *Elizabeth* has nobility. And it suits you."

At the end of the session Betsy was invited to attend a Tuesday night "teaching" Catharine was giving at her apartment—every week, she explained, she gave lectures on various spiritual subjects. And when Tuesday night came Betsy returned—and this time, the place was crowded. She quietly found a spot on the floor with a cluster of Catharine's other students—and introduced herself as Elizabeth. Later, when Catharine caught sight of her, she smiled warmly, almost proudly, and invited Betsy—Elizabeth—to attend a Friday night lecture, which was reserved for the more advanced students.

On Friday, Catharine lectured about kindness and compassion. She used the phrase "developing one's Christ nature" along with other Christian language, which made Elizabeth feel comfortable with the Center for Discovery and New Life even though, as she would put it, "many of the people in my class were very strange. I mean, *way out there.* . . . I remember one night where two women were talking about this occult stuff they'd done, something involving putting candles around the room and ghosts and negative beings appearing. I was like, *What am I doing here? What am I getting into?* But Catharine always saved me. She was always very kind, and dealt with me on a level that I could understand."

Soon Elizabeth's weeks began to pivot around these evenings. And when Catharine moved her center to Kensington, Elizabeth continued to commute from Gaithersburg—sometimes to her husband's dismay.

Eventually Catharine felt that Elizabeth was ready to attend a class where the lecture was channeled—this took place every Thursday, with a group of ten or twelve students who had been with Catharine for a year already. "She was more nervous than I was," Alana said later. "She said, 'I'm warning you, it's really strange. I close my eyes and I twitch and I talk in a man's voice.' " But Elizabeth felt flattered to be invited—and she trusted Catharine. In just a few months the women had become close friends. "When you first meet your teacher," Alana explained, "there's a big rush of merit and karma coming forward—that she's helping to pull forward—and a lot can happen very quickly." Elizabeth also felt a great love for Catharine, and a sense that she had found something she'd been searching for her whole life. Their bond, she said, was like a "deep spiritual marriage." In fact, they had formed a friendship that was intense enough to threaten both their husbands and become a source of stress at home.

By early 1984, Catharine was offering two weekly classes in Kensington, each lasting about two hours. She didn't want to charge fees for her teachings, so donations were suggested. The class for newcomers, the Tuesday Class, began as a series on attachment but evolved into an exploration of Eastern philosophy. The Thursday Class was reserved for Catharine's original group of students or by invitation—because of the unusual nature of the evenings. It was on Thursdays that Catharine channeled an entity who claimed to be the Old Testament prophet Jeremiah. Actually, the voice of Jeremiah played a kind of emcee role at these sessions, introducing the students to an assortment of other entities who were speaking through Catharine and sharing their wisdom. There was Enoch. There was Santu, a high-pitched voice who said she "came in love." And there was Andor, who claimed to be the head of the Intergalactic Council.

As time passed, the class became familiar with the various personalities. When Catharine's voice turned deep and masculine, the students greeted Jeremiah like an old friend. He addressed members of the group, encouraging them, advising them, joking with them—while they sat stunned. "I remember pulling up in the car in front of the Kensington house," said Wib, "and looking over at Jane or Shelly and saying, 'How could this week be any more incredible than last week?' But it always was."

The basement of the Kensington house was stuffy and crowded with students the night Elizabeth first came to hear Catharine channel a lecture. Elizabeth carried her tape recorder and walked through yet another crowd of strangers—Catharine's core students, like Wib and Jane, Shelly and Eleanor. She found a place on the floor in front, next to the green velvet chair where Catharine would sit, close her eyes, slump as though she'd fallen asleep, then awaken in a trance. But Elizabeth didn't get a chance to meet Jeremiah that night. Instead, Catharine channeled a new entity who called herself Ms. Buddha. She spoke about the nature of love and how ceaseless prayer could really change the world.

"The whole thing was so sweet," Alana recalled. "When she came out of the channel, she was disoriented for a while. But then she looked over at me and said, 'Are you okay? Was that too strange?' "

After her introduction to the Thursday Class, Elizabeth found herself even more involved with the Center for Discovery and New Life—she spent her time after each evening in Kensington excited about the next one. She gained a reputation for being "spiritually evolved" and able to connect with Catharine in a profound way. She was also loyal. When the group began its twenty-four-hour-a-day prayer vigil, Elizabeth became the most loyal participant of all, arriving at 4:00 A.M. to take a two-hour shift before driving to work.

Elizabeth felt incredibly fortunate—blessed—to have found Catharine, or have had Catharine find her. She enjoyed the camaraderie of the group and relished her status as Catharine's confidante. The classes continued to become more dramatic. Catharine channeled yet another new entity—White Moon, a Native American spirit—and afterward nearly fainted from exhaustion. She also channeled information about herself, explaining that in a previous life she had been one of the female disciples of Christ responsible for passing down the Gnostic texts. And, in a private moment with Elizabeth, Catharine revealed that in a past life they had been romantically involved. In fact, Elizabeth had been her consort.

While Elizabeth's new spiritual life was crowded with extraordinary events and romance, her old life—particularly her marriage—seemed increasingly dead. People often talk about individuals changing in a marriage, but Elizabeth didn't feel she was changing as much as becoming more herself. Her husband had come to a few classes in the early days, but it was harder and harder to share the things she was learning with him and her young daughters. She felt pulled in two directions. A large part of her existed in the spiritual world with Catharine. A smaller part was with her family at home.

It was both sad and strange to feel so in touch with her heart, so much more compassionate about the world—to be part of a ceaseless prayer vigil—yet to have become an absentee mother.

"I was still in my tight little box," Alana recalled, "and I was not happy. I remember lying in bed thinking, Here I am in my perfect town house with my perfect little kids and my perfect little husband and everything . . . *but why do I feel so empty?*"

She wasn't exactly sure why she was joining Michael and Catharine at National Airport—they were welcoming a Tibetan lama who was arriving from India—except that Catharine had indicated that it was a good thing to do. And Elizabeth always paid attention to suggestions like this, even the smallest ones.

The center had sold rugs to raise money for some young Tibetan Buddhist monks, but Elizabeth wasn't sure what the connection was between the visiting lama and the rugs. Did he run the monastery where the monks were? Was he related to the Dalai Lama? Everything was pretty blurry. It seemed blurry to Catharine and Michael, too. If Kunzang Lama, the guy who'd gotten the students into selling the rugs, had ever mentioned that Penor Rinpoche was a big deal in India, it had been lost on all of them. Nobody seemed to know that he'd been recognized as a tulku when he was two or three, or that he'd performed a great number of miracles as a child, or that he'd fought the Chinese with guns and hand grenades to get out of Tibet in 1950.

Like the other students, Elizabeth was still reeling from recent developments in Kensington and not thinking about much of anything else. After initiating the round-the-clock prayer vigil, the group had decided to change its name. Rather than the Center for Discovery and New Life, which sounded flaky and self-centered—and the *new* in New Life was a little too close to the *new* in New Age—they would be the World Prayer Center. This name matched their sense of purpose and the feeling that they weren't about self and self-improvement—or self-work as the New Agers like to call it. The World Prayer Center was about praying and compassion. Selling the rugs had figured into their new focus, too. The group wasn't the Kensington Prayer Center. It was the *World Prayer Center*—a global place, with an agenda to pray for world peace.

Alana would later remember the first meeting of Penor Rinpoche at National Airport as undramatic. There was a crowd of

Chinese, which seemed to part for a short Gandhi-like figure. And rather than the romantic accounts that would be circulated years later—in magazine profiles and newspaper articles—about sobbing upon the sight of him, or running into his arms as in a shampoo commercial, Catharine said little at the airport as Penor Rinpoche appeared, according to Alana's account, but she did seem "very wide-eyed."

They went directly from the airport to a welcoming lunch at Mr. K's, an expensive Chinese restaurant in downtown D.C., and afterward, driving to Kensington, Catharine spoke up for the first time. "She said she couldn't believe how much the Tibetan lama was checking her out over lunch," Alana later said. Catharine seemed to feel that Penor Rinpoche had been waving a spiritual metal detector over her body. She felt a sense of invasion and, at the same time, the presence of great spiritual power. "She'd never met anybody who could do that," Alana said. "Her first instinct was to try to block it out, and then she decided, No, I'll just live with it."

Several days later Catharine called Elizabeth at work. Her name wasn't on the list of students who had signed up to meet privately with the Tibetan before he returned to India. Elizabeth said she had been busy and didn't think she had the time. "This is an opportunity," Catharine said, "and I don't think you want to pass it up." She told Elizabeth to arrive early and plan to spend a few minutes meditating before meeting with the lama. She suggested having a couple of questions ready for him.

"So I went over there, and I'm thinking, What am I going to ask him?" Alana recalled. She kept worrying about possible questions, but nothing was coming to her. "He was seeing people in the living room," she said, "and I waited downstairs to be called up. And something really bizarre happened while I was sitting there, meditating and waiting. I finally thought of a question to ask him, and then, suddenly, the answer came into my mind. When I thought of another question, it happened again. Three times. . . . It was so weird. That's when it started to dawn on me that something special was going on."

And when Elizabeth was called up to the living room, she was stunned by the appearance of Penor Rinpoche. He didn't look anything like she'd remembered. "At the airport, he looked short and fat—a little guy. But sitting on that sofa, he suddenly looked immense."

She asked him a couple of questions about her life, which he answered quickly without much interest. "I was completely me-centered at the time," she said later, "all caught up in self." But when Elizabeth asked how she could be useful in the world, he said, "In this life, you need to learn to take refuge in nothing but the three precious jewels." Then he gave her a blessing, by putting his hands on her head and blowing on the top of her head. "I remember my body was shaking, vibrating, and when he blew on me it went right through me, like a strong clear feeling," she recalled.

When Elizabeth emerged from the living room, she saw Michael. "What are the three precious jewels?" she asked.

"I'm not sure," he said, "but there's a book in the office that might explain." Downstairs she found a book, *The Door to Liberation*, and she looked up the three precious jewels. She came across something called the Refuge vow. There were three sentences, one for each precious jewel:

> *I take refuge in the Buddha.*
> *I take refuge in the Dharma.*
> *I take refuge in the Sangha.*

Catharine and Michael were anxious to hear a report from Penor Rinpoche afterward—a sense of how he felt the students were doing, and if they'd been taught properly. The rinpoche told them, unequivocally, that both Catharine and Michael had a strong connection to Mahayana Buddhism. He said that Michael had been a Buddhist scholar in prior lives. He told Catharine that she had been a Buddhist practitioner and teacher over many lifetimes. "Bodhisattvas come back again and again for the sake of sentient beings," Jetsunma remembered Penor Rinpoche saying, "and you are a great, great Bodhisattva."

"I remember hearing," Alana recalled, "that he said the very fabric of her mind was the Dharma."

Their students had "very good intention," the lama continued, but they needed to learn better technique. For one thing, they had to be taught to "dedicate their merit." This was very important. Immediately afterward Michael went down to the office and poked around in a few books trying to figure out what Penor Rinpoche was talking about. Eventually he found a Tibetan "dedication" prayer:

> *Throughout my many lives and until this moment,*
> *Whatever virtue I have accomplished,*
> *Including the merit generated by this practice,*
> *And all that I will ever attain,*
> *This I offer, for the welfare of sentient beings.*
> *May sickness, war, famine, and suffering*
> *Be decreased for every being,*
> *While their wisdom and compassion increase*
> *In this and every future life.*
> *May I clearly perceive all experiences*
> *To be as insubstantial as the dream-fabric of the night,*
> *And instantly awaken to perceive the pure display*
> *In the arising of every phenomenon.*
> *May I quickly attain Enlightenment*
> *In order to work ceaselessly*
> *For the liberation of all sentient beings.* *

The next evening Penor Rinpoche was scheduled to give another talk. About twenty-five students sat close together on chairs lined up in the Kensington living room and listened patiently. It was sometimes hard to follow the Tibetan—things were left out in the translation. But at the end of the talk the students were very clearly asked to repeat a string of words. A few of them noticed that other Tibetans in the lama's entourage seemed to be crying. "We had no clue what he was saying," Alana recalled. "It was like *gobble-dee-gook, gobble-dee-gook, gobble-dee-gook.* And we just went *gobble-dee-gook, gobble-dee-gook, gobble-dee-gook* after him."

Then the translator spoke: "You are all Buddhists now. Congratulations."

---

* Translated by Chagdüd Tulku Rinpoche.

On the last night of his visit, at the barbecue in his honor, Penor Rinpoche sat on the back porch eating hot dogs and potato chips. When Catharine noticed that he was alone she took Elizabeth aside and asked her to go sit with him. "Do I have to?" Elizabeth asked, with a laugh. "I mean, what am I going to talk to him about?"

The next morning, as the lama's trunks were being loaded into the car, Catharine and Michael felt a vague sense of relief that their normal life would return—but also a sense of sadness. They sat with him for a few minutes in the living room, hoping their warm smiles would communicate their intense feelings about him, and their appreciation for what he'd brought to their students. "Now we have a connection," Penor Rinpoche said, smiling back. "You can be a center here, *my center,* and let's see what happens."

Did His Holiness have any advice for them? Michael asked.

"To start," the lama answered, "you need to find a bigger place."

"We are already looking for a bigger place," Michael said. "But a bigger place costs money. We don't have much."

"Find a bigger place," Penor Rinpoche advised, "and the money will come."

7.

Becoming Buddhists

WILL I EVER LIVE AGAIN—AS A MOUNTAIN LION,
OR A ROOSTER, OR A HEN? A ROBIN,
OR A WREN, OR A FLY? OH, WHO AM I?

—LEONARD BERNSTEIN, *Peter Pan*

It wasn't long after the departure of His Holiness Penor Rinpoche that Catharine and Michael seriously began looking for a new center. Michael, in particular, felt an urgency to get organized—and to find a way over some very high hurdles. One was money. He kept in mind what His Holiness had said and tried to have faith that things would work out. He contacted real estate agents, talked with banks about funding, and eventually learned how a limited partnership could be formed among members of the center to raise the capital for a down payment.

A formal announcement had been made to all students, too, that Penor Rinpoche had expressed interest in staying in touch with them—and had been impressed by their "intention." Perhaps because of the need to raise money in a short time, or a desire to incite the enthusiasm for the changes ahead, there was a bit of confusion about exactly what else the Tibetan had told Catharine and Michael. Word began to trickle out that Penor Rinpoche had told Catharine that she was "a great bodhisattva." There were hints, too, that she was possibly the incarnation of a great Tibetan lama. It was Michael whose imagination seemed sparked by the news and who seemed most noticeably delighted by it. Catharine glowed when talking about Penor Rinpoche—as though her real father had finally shown up at the door—and Michael entered a time of energetic planning. If Catharine were indeed an important spiritual teacher in the Tibetan Buddhist tradition, something ought to be done about it. As he would joke many times, "Give me a sacred cow and I'll milk it."

"Michael had a catalytical effect on my life," Jetsunma said many years later. "He had an element that I was missing: *ambition.*"

It was hard for most of the twenty-five or so members of the World Prayer Center—that "ragtag group," as Wib had described them—to comprehend the enormity of Michael's dreams for them or, indeed, the predictions of Penor Rinpoche. The Tibetan holy man had seemed quite confident that the center needed to find a headquarters with space to accommodate hundreds of students at formal ceremonies and empowerments. This seemed an impossibility. The World Prayer Center had ten thousand dollars in its bank account, and with the exception of Eleanor Rowe and a few older and financially secure students, most of the members were struggling to get by.

But Catharine had taught them to believe in things that were almost unbelievable. She had told them all, in private consultations, that they were special beings, *great* beings. They had been born for a specific purpose. They had a mission beyond money. Penor Rinpoche had come and seen that.

By the middle of the summer, just six weeks after the Tibetan's visit, the search for the World Prayer Center's new location had boiled down to three choices, all in Maryland: a large Victorian house in Laurel, a former Greek Orthodox church in Bethesda, and a white colonial-style mansion with a guest cottage on the outskirts of Poolesville. Each was within a forty-five-minute drive of downtown Washington, D.C.

Feeling unable to decide, Catharine and Michael attempted to contact Penor Rinpoche for help, but the lama was traveling and temporarily unreachable. They remembered a vision that Reed

Brown, the spiritualist minister and psychic, had shared with them two years before. They would eventually settle in a spiritual center, he predicted, and it would be "a large house with white columns." This seemed to suggest the Poolesville house, which had six thin white columns in front, in a dimestore *Gone With the Wind* manner. When Penor Rinpoche was finally reached, he told Catharine and Michael to pick "the biggest place with the most trees around it." This pointed, quite decidedly, to Poolesville. The mansion sat on eight acres of grass, just off River Road, and was surrounded on all sides by trees. But the asking price was high: $880,000.

It was a muggy day in July when Catharine and Michael decided to look over the Poolesville house carefully, despite the fact that there was no foreseeable way the group could raise even a 5 percent down payment. They toured the place with the current owner, Darwin Trynor, an older gay man whose longtime lover had recently died and been buried behind the house. As Michael began to tell the story of the prayer group and Catharine's recent encounter with the visiting Tibetan lama, Trynor asked them to stay and visit over drinks. He seemed taken with Catharine in particular—her husky laugh and bawdy sense of humor—and gave her a hard time about how her long red nails perfectly matched the print of her dress. The meeting went on for hours, cocktail after cocktail, and finally ended when Trynor passed out cold on his way upstairs.

The next day he called Catharine and Michael, insisting that their prayer group buy his house. It was meant to be, he said. He could *feel* it. And he was willing to knock two hundred thousand dollars off his asking price—as long as they agreed to one condition. When Trynor died he wanted to be buried next to his partner in the backyard. But when a vote was taken among members of the World Prayer Center, it turned out Catharine was the only one who wanted to buy the big white house. "People thought it was too far away," said Jon Randolph, "and tacky."

Still nervous about making such a huge purchase with so little cash in hand, Michael arranged to have photographs of the Poolesville house faxed to Penor Rinpoche in Hong Kong, again asking for his help. His Holiness agreed to do a *Mo*, a divination procedure commonly used by Tibetan Buddhist lamas. Each lama tends to employ his own Mo techniques—usually tossing prayer beads on a cloth or throwing a pair of dice with mantras inscribed on each side. But the results of a Mo performed by an esteemed lama are considered highly reliable. Through Penor Rinpoche's attendant it was reported to Catharine and Michael that the Poolesville property looked good and they should proceed with confidence.

Quickly efforts to raise a down payment among the twenty-five regular members of the World Prayer Center began, and the six students who had the best credit histories—Ted and Linda Kurkowski, John and Catherine Windolph, Don Allen, and Karen Williams—formed a limited partnership. It was decided that all the partners, except the Windolphs, who already owned a farm nearby, would live together in the Poolesville house, along with Michael and Catharine and Catharine's two sons. Each would pay rent to the limited partnership—raising the monthly mortgage payment of nearly $7,200. With the details worked out, an offer was made and accepted. Darwin Trynor, worried that the group wouldn't be able to come up with the cash down payment of $70,000, arrived at the closing with $100,000 in a briefcase to lend them if they needed it. In October 1985 they were able to move in.

Elizabeth yearned to be closer to Catharine during these months of excitement and felt a strong pull to move to Poolesville. The center and its students seemed to be hoisting anchor and sailing off on a great adventure together, and there was a funny feeling of events compounding, of each day being filled with more hours and changes than anyone thought possible.

Walls were knocked down in the house, and downstairs two large rooms were created for teachings, in addition to a community room, where the students could eat meals together. Carpets were laid, a twelve-seater hot tub was removed from the back, and plans for Buddhist altars and other sacred decorations were made. Students who had experience doing construction were called upon to lead work crews. Wib taught David Somerville to hang drywall, and David taught Jay Allen. Richard Dykeman, one of Catharine's students in Michigan who was also a professional carpenter and builder, was asked to move to Poolesville temporarily to help with the renovations. Since there was no room in the main house, and Don Allen and his son, Jay, were living in the guest cottage, Richard pitched a tent in the nearby woods and slept there, off and on, for the next three years.

Michael quit his daytime job selling Apple II computers in Bethesda and applied himself entirely to settling into Poolesville and creating an impressive Buddhist center. He boned up on Buddhist texts, tried to figure out how other Dharma centers were run. When he bought four hundred dollars' worth of crystals at a gem and mineral show and sold them back to students for twice the price, he got the idea to open a gift shop on the premises and decided also to sell the Buddhist books that he and the other members would eventually want to read. He had extraordinary drive and energy, and focus.

Catharine was unwell a great deal of the time after moving into the Poolesville property. She suffered from phlebitis, was forced to spend weeks in bed, and had begun to gain weight again. "She was expending a tremendous amount of spiritual energy," Alana explained later. "She would be vacuuming and cleaning, cooking dinner for her family, then coming downstairs to channel for two hours. She was teaching another class and doing consultations that lasted hours. It was unbelievable. And, on top of all that, she was dealing with many students and their many needs. What a juggling act!"

Elizabeth had been suffering, too. She wanted to spend more time in Poolesville and even less time at home. She went to Catharine for advice and, in a channeled consultation with Santu, she was encouraged to divorce her husband. Her life had flip-flopped, just as Catharine had predicted two years before. Elizabeth found an apartment in Germantown and moved in with her two daughters.

It was hard for Elizabeth, those first few weeks alone in Germantown, even with Santu's blessing. Ambivalence nagged her. She felt herself going back and forth in her mind, from her husband to Catharine. She felt fragile and confused and began to see more of Catharine—leaning on her for support and advice throughout the divorce. As for Catharine, she joked that she felt a bit lost herself. Michael had become preoccupied with the new center and making some kind of official change to the practice of Buddhism. Having Elizabeth around was a joy. She was smart and had a wicked sense of humor, which she sometimes used at the expense of the other students—and at Michael's expense, too. Over the summer and fall of 1985 it became clear to everybody that Catharine and Elizabeth had grown closer than ever. "We were all jealous of Elizabeth, like crazy," said Karen Williams. "She and Catharine were so close, right away . . . and Elizabeth was so damn spiritual." But it also wasn't long before things would change again.

"Once the marriage split up, and my little box started to fall apart," Alana explained later, "everything that happened wasn't necessarily spiritual." It was hard to make all the adjustments to her new life—particularly a life in which she had no primary relationship. This caused tension in her connection with Catharine. "I was needy and compulsively fixated on her and our friendship," Alana said. "I was trying to make that replace what I had given up. I felt a need to have *something.*"

Catharine quickly saw what was happening, according to Alana, and began to pull away. The lunches together, shopping trips, and visits to the Silver Spring beauty salon abruptly ended, along with the laughs and good times. "As soon as I got needy around her, she cut it off," Alana said.

Angry and hurt, Elizabeth went out "like a junkie," she said, looking for another love relationship to fill the void in her life. She went through a period of promiscuity, becoming sexually involved with several men at the center and others outside. For nearly two years "I was either at the temple," she said, "or out on a date. It was a bit crazy." Her daughters were left alone at night. Eventually the older one moved out to live with her father. Her younger girl, just sixteen, was "close to the edge."

"I don't know what else to say," Alana said, describing those years, "except that I wasn't a good mother." In time, she would become close with her daughters again—and even become a doting grandmother. "But I'm not sure I know why things turned out so well," she said.

Aside from occasional faxes from His Holiness Penor Rinpoche, Michael and Catharine received little assistance or instruction. Michael would send lists of questions he hoped would be answered. And he and Catharine would get letters back, translated badly and rarely answering their questions. As for money, the Tibetan had none to give. His own monastery in southern India was far poorer than any middle-class American suburbanite could imagine. Penor Rinpoche had built it by himself with just ten monks, mudbrick upon mudbrick, after clearing a dense sandalwood jungle infested by cobras. At the time, he had not yet become the supreme head of the ancient Nyingma lineage, a school of Tibetan Buddhism that counts hundreds of thousands of members worldwide. He had only his approval and a vague sense of patronage to offer the World Prayer Center. But, as his new American students discovered, whenever they encountered other Tibetans in the West, the reputation of His Holiness Penor Rinpoche was unassailable. He was considered a traditionalist and a cautious conservative man. Weight and attention should be given his every word and suggestion. If he told them to start a large center in Poolesville, they should. If he told them they were already practicing Buddhism, they were.

But Michael and Catharine were hesitant to contact other Dharma centers in America. For one thing, many of the other centers were not in the same school or did not adhere to the various Palyul customs, and the differences only confused their students. Also, the Burroughses had begun the World Prayer Center their own way—and wanted to continue to expand as they saw fit. Many of the other Tibetan Buddhist centers tended to be loaded with intellectuals and, Catharine thought, elitists who bragged about how many empowerments or teachings they'd received. She wanted her center to be vital, have a broader appeal, be focused less on intellectual matters and more on action and compassion. "We're builders," she liked to say, "not academics!"

But there is more to Tibetan Buddhism than good intentions, and the builders had a lot of studying to do.

In the spring of 1986, Michael invited two Tibetan brothers, both scholars or *khenpos*, to visit from New York City and give traditional Buddhist teachings, which Catharine did not feel qualified to give. Khenpo Palden Sherab and Khenpo Tsewang Dongyal taught the students the Seven Line Prayer, a beautiful and haunting chant that is the fundamental invocation of the Nyingma school and is used to open every teaching. Later on Penor Rinpoche began sending lamas to Poolesville. Dr. Lobsang Rapgay came from Nepal to teach, and Chagdüd Tulku came from California. "We were sort of desperate to get a lineup of people who could come and teach," remembered Karen Williams. The students were taught about the Seven Nonvirtues of the Body— which, much to their dismay, forbid Tibetan Buddhists from performing oral sex or masturbating. The students were surprised to learn about the eighteen hell realms where a Tibetan Buddhist could wind up. There are hot hells, like the Black Line Hell, where one's body is cut into pieces with burning saws, or the Rounding-up and Crushing Hell, where one is thrown into a mortar of iron the size of a valley, along with millions of other beings, and where everyone is beaten with hammers and crushed to death. There are cold hells, like the Hell of Blisters, where one is tormented by blisters from the freezing temperatures, or the Hell of Burst Blisters, where one's blisters from the cold are continually bursting open. There is also the Hell of Great Lotuslike Cracks, where one's skin turns dark red and splits into sixteen pieces that are penetrated by worms and eaten.*

The students were taught *phowa*, the prayers and visualizations that are done at the time of death, in the hope of having a good rebirth. They were also taught *Vajrasattva*, a fundamental purification practice. While Catharine had taught her students various homemade meditations over the years, none were as complicated and precise as the images Buddhist practitioners are routinely expected to memorize and visualize while praying.

But there were also some striking similarities. In her "Ex-

---

* Patrul Rinpoche, *The Words of My Perfect Teacher* (Boston: Shambhala, 1998).

panded Light Practice" meditations, Catharine had taught students to imagine their bodies becoming purified by white light,
and that light slowly expanding out, to purify the universe. In the
Vajrasattva practice, as it is taught in the Nyingma tradition, one
imagines that the deity Vajrasattva is embracing his consort over
one's head. From their union "a cloud of nectar" drops onto the
crown of one's head, "falling like drops of camphor." The nectar
seeps thoroughly inside one's body and mind, and cleanses one
from the contaminated actions of the past, negative emotions, and
the afflictions of desire. It purifies "actions and afflictions which
cause all suffering," the prayer goes, and asks that "sickness, spirits, sins, obstructions, faults, infractions, and defilements of myself and all beings in the three realms be made completely clean."*

The deity and his consort dissolve into light, and become one
with the practitioner, and light rays shine out in all directions. Or,
as the text has been translated:

> *Like a sun shining in a dark place, the rays clear away all*
> *darkness and suffering, spreading first to the hells, and then*
> *to the realms of hungry ghosts, animals, humans, demi-gods*
> *and gods. The realms of all six types of living beings are*
> *purified and transformed into the eastern pure lands of*
> *Vajrasattva, called the Very Joyous.*†

By the summer of 1986, it was hard to believe it had been
only one year since the group had first met His Holiness Penor
Rinpoche. So much had changed. But the transitions had continued to leave Catharine tired, overextended, and overwhelmed—
and Penor Rinpoche was too far away to help. She was unable to
teach, stayed in bed most of the time, and, when she was finally
hospitalized for phlebitis, her weight was close to two hundred
and fifty pounds.

Frustrated and concerned, Michael called Gyaltrul Rinpoche,
who was very close to Penor Rinpoche. Michael spoke honestly

---

* Khetsun Sangpo Rinpoche, *Tantric Practice in Nying-ma* (Ithaca, N.Y.: Snow Lion,
  1982).
† Ibid.

about his wife's condition, and Gyaltrul Rinpoche suggested that Michael and Catharine come to Oregon without delay. He had heard about Catharine already, from Penor Rinpoche himself, and he was looking forward to a meeting.

The connection between Catharine and Gyaltrul Rinpoche, by all accounts, was strong and immediate. When she arrived on his doorstep—in bad health and with many questions—he interrupted a retreat, took her into his private home, encouraged her, and made her laugh. Gyaltrul Rinpoche had a full head of black hair and a huge gap-toothed smile. Unlike Penor Rinpoche, he spoke English well and was quite familiar with Western culture. Gyaltrul had recently married a willowy blond American scholar and translator, Nanci Gustafson, who had taken the Tibetan name Sangye Khandro.

Gyaltrul Rinpoche had such a lightness to his spirit—a cheerfulness and silliness—that he made misery seem impossible in his presence. He started calling Michael "Chopsticks" behind his back, because he was so thin.

"Look!" he said to Catharine one morning, as they giggled about Michael over coffee. "You've only been here two days and we're already family!"

She wanted to start a Tibetan Buddhist monastery, Catharine confessed. Some of her students had already inquired about becoming monks and nuns. And she herself was beginning to believe that she could do more, and live more peacefully, practice more deeply, if she took vows and lived as a nun. She had already imagined herself shaving her head and wearing robes. Did Gyaltrul Rinpoche think this was a good idea?

The Tibetan was impressed by her aspirations—and her drive and intention. He told Catharine that she was surely an incarnate lama, one who had taught for many lifetimes. How else could one explain her teachings, her students, the center she had built? "You're here for a reason," he told her. There was no doubt of that. "Tibet is falling, and the Dharma is going to be lost. It makes sense that some of the high lamas are being reborn here." The fact that she had been born in 1949, the year before Tibet was so violently taken over by the Chinese, seemed important to him.

He encouraged Catharine to see Penor Rinpoche in India, to

"investigate" her past-life connection to Buddhism. A lama as great as Penor Rinpoche could tell Catharine who she was, he said. And if she were to become officially recognized as an incarnate lama, it would benefit her center, her students, the monastic orders in the United States, Tibetan Buddhism in the West, and, eventually, all sentient beings.

Gyaltrul Rinpoche insisted that this was the only answer. She needed to see Penor Rinpoche again in person. But to Catharine, going to India seemed so far off, like taking a trip to Oz.

The rinpoche had another message for her as well: if Catharine didn't lose weight, she would die.

Gyaltrul Rinpoche visited Poolesville for the first time a few months later, to have a look around, to watch Catharine teach, to meet some students, and to give what is considered the essential foundation practice of Tibetan Buddhism, Ngöndro. When one becomes a Tibetan Buddhist in the Nyingma school, it is Ngöndro that one begins practicing, and, ideally, one completes Ngöndro before moving on to other teachings and other practices. Ngöndro is designed to purify the mind—to bring students to a greater understanding of their own nature so that, ultimately, they can benefit other people. In India it is common for a monk to have completed Ngöndro by the age of eight. There are four parts to the practice. The student does one hundred thousand prostrations. These are followed by one hundred thousand Vajrasattva purification mantras, one hundred thousand Mandala offerings, and one hundred thousand Guru Yoga contemplations.

Gyaltrul Rinpoche was very serious with the students at times. "Do this, and it will end suffering!" But he also made jokes: "Don't do this, and your toes will fall off!" It wasn't easy to do prostrations at first, and the students would get together and discuss their embarrassment, their awkwardness. "What if my parents walked in," Wib said, "and saw me right now?"

As you prostrate, you repeat refuge prayers—I take refuge in the Guru, I take refuge in the Buddha, I take refuge in the Dharma, I take refuge in the Sangha—and one visualizes the three jewels. But as Gyaltrul Rinpoche outlined the visualizations to the Poolesville students, they seemed impossible to follow. He read pages and pages of descriptions, but they were hard to picture. "There was something about a refuge tree, and all these Buddhas appearing in the tree," remembered Chris Cervenka, "and something else about lotus petals. . . . Later on we ordered a poster of the refuge tree to sell in the gift shop, and that made it easier."

In Poolesville the students were determined to finish Ngöndro as quickly as possible. Group sessions were held in the Dharma room twice a day so that students could do their prostrations together in sets of five hundred.

It was something like an aerobics class—people came in workout clothes and running shoes, shorts and jogging bras, headbands and wristbands. Traditionally, a Tibetan Buddhist practitioner keeps count of prostrations on the beads of a *mala*— which is like a rosary—the same way one keeps track of one's mantras. But in Poolesville, Michael and Richard Dykeman started using plastic clicker-counters, the ones that security guards use to count attendance at large events. Every prostration, another click. It was much better than having the mala swing around and hit you in the face. The other students took to the innovation, and during the sessions that was the predominant sound in the room—besides knees and elbows cracking—breathing and clicking, breathing and clicking, breathing and clicking.

Some people could do one thousand prostrations in one session, take a walk around the temple, and do another thousand that night. The weeks passed, and then the months; the entire sangha was doing prostrations. There was almost a buzz, a sense of euphoria, that came with doing long sets of them—and afterward the students talked about how alert and strong they felt. It wasn't just Catharine who was looking and feeling better. Within just a few weeks they all started feeling healthy and good. "I really felt I was changing," said one student, "and felt a change in my life. And I believed—I think we all did—that it was the beginning of something very important."

"How long have you been a Buddhist?" people would ask. And the answer was a little complicated: "I'm not sure," Elizabeth would say with a laugh. "Are we Buddhists yet?"

And it was like that for the next year or more. A sense of fumbling and bumbling along. They read books on Buddhism, watched videotapes of teachings. They recited the Seven Line Prayer over and over and over and over. They did Vajrasattva, completed prostrations, imagined the Mandala, an idealized universe, and tested out new visualizations. They tried to ask questions of visiting lamas without seeming too stupid or too American or just plain rude. Slowly it began to unfold. Slowly they saw more, understood more, and the bizarre words grew more comfortable. The exterior world of suffering was called samsara. The teachings were Dharma. They weren't a prayer group anymore; they were a sangha. Catharine wasn't Catharine, she was the guru. Their prayers were called mantras, the fruit of their actions was called karma, their faith was called devotion. There wasn't a God anymore, but Buddha nature. And they weren't praying for world peace so much, either, but the liberation of all sentient beings.

Gyaltrul Rinpoche was surprised by the enthusiasm he saw in Catharine's students. He also loved that she had attracted "normal Americans" and not just lots of "ex-hippies like the other Dharma centers." He was stunned by the notion of a twenty-four-hour prayer vigil—which continued in Poolesville. And when he was told about the episodic prayer rounders, as Catharine called them, when her students would pray together for twelve hours straight, he said, "How can you get people to do that?"

The impatience of Americans is both naïve and endearing. To the Tibetan mind, suffering is endless, forever, has no beginning and no end. It isn't something that anybody expects to solve so soon. Catharine's students seemed to believe it was possible to achieve enlightenment in one lifetime—and that the end of suffering was close at hand, not an infinite number of lifetimes away.

In the Nyingma school, lamas can choose to be celibate or not—to be ordained monks or nuns, or to marry and have children, and Gyaltrul Rinpoche had personal advice for Michael and Catharine, too. "You have started such an amazing temple," he told them one night, as they drove him and his wife around Washington, D.C. "Let me tell you something. Never get divorced. And never sleep with the students. It causes such problems in the sangha."

On that first trip to Poolesville, Gyaltrul Rinpoche also saw Catharine channeling—something Penor Rinpoche had never witnessed, or been told about. From the back of the large Dharma room, the rinpoche watched Catharine in a trance. She was sitting in her green velvet chair. She was speaking in the deep voice of Jeremiah, who briefly turned the floor over to the soft, feminine tones of Santu. "It is I, Santu," she said, "and I come in love." Gyaltrul Rinpoche watched solemnly, and respectfully, as the students began asking questions.

"That's very interesting," the Tibetan said, turning to Michael. "But there's no Jeremiah or Santu. It's all her."

Early in 1987, when Catharine was preparing for a trip to India with Michael, she called Elizabeth out of the blue. It had been nearly a year since they'd spent time alone together, and Elizabeth's commitment to the center had been flagging. Catharine said she was worried about Elizabeth, had been thinking a great deal about her. She'd had dreams, too.

"You have one foot in samsara and one foot in the Dharma," Catharine said to her, "and I think there's a good chance when I get back from India that you will be gone. And I am giving you permission to go."

Elizabeth said nothing.

"You are still young and beautiful," Catharine said, "and you think you can still find happiness out there, in the world. I know you have this spirituality inside you, and eventually you will return. It might be two weeks and it might be twenty years. But you will be back and you will say, 'Oh my God, what have I done with my life?' "

Elizabeth *was* close to leaving the center—in many ways felt she was already gone. Since Catharine had stopped being her friend, Elizabeth had become less and less interested in practicing or praying, in doing the prostrations and becoming Buddhist. It was such hard work—and without Catharine's daily attentions and encouragement, it had been nearly impossible to stay committed. But she was thrown off by Catharine's remarks about how she would return one day. Looking for guidance, she decided to do Vajrasattva practice.

"I started to do Vajrasattva," she said later. "It's a very powerful practice, a powerful purifying practice." She did it day after day, for many hours. She imagined the nectar falling into the crown of her head. She saw the rays of light flowing out in all directions. She imagined the nectar and the light cleansing her body, cleansing her spirit, and she imagined exhaling the cleansed pure breath of blessings into the world. Over and over she blew out blessings upon the world, purifying, purifying, purifying. And after a time she experienced something real, she said. Something so real and so true it was hard to put it into words. "It was like," she said, "I was seeing that all of my suffering was caused by the fact that I had already, in my heart, offered everything. . . . I saw that I was truly a nun—a nun in the true sense of the word. *Renunciation.* That I had already offered, somewhere, sometime, everything I had, and that my suffering came from my trying to take back what I had offered, as though I were trying to take back a vow."

Elizabeth went to see Catharine in her private quarters. It was days before Catharine was leaving for India. They sat down on a sofa together, and Elizabeth wasn't able to speak right away. Catharine sat quietly and waited.

"I want to become a nun," Elizabeth said. "I want to become a nun because *I am a nun.*"

Catharine began crying and kept crying. And Elizabeth started crying. They held each other for a long time. "She wasn't saying anything," Alana described later, "but she had this look on her face, like, Finally, she's figured it out."

8.

The Stupa Blessing

I took a break after my visit to Ani Farms and didn't wander out to Poolesville again until the week after Thanksgiving. I had a few unanswered questions, things that nagged me—mostly about the stupa—things that only somebody like Sangye could answer. But Sangye was still unreachable, recuperating in a cottage on the temple grounds. So I went looking for David Somerville. He worked most days in a trailer just ten yards from the Migyur Dorje stupa.

There was snow on the grass in front of the temple, but the narrow dirt road to the stupa was deep in the woods and still dry. When I reached the end it was four in the afternoon and the sky was growing dark. The stupa was gloriously tall and articulated now—with a throne or bum-pa, garlands around a faceplate, and an elegant spire. It had been finished just yesterday in a hectic rush of meritorious activity. Sherab had pulled an all-nighter in the barn, painting Migyur Dorje's robes, then hauled the faceplate to the woods in the back of a truck. David Somerville had wired the seventy-pound faceplate to his back, then climbed thirty feet up a ladder that was leaning against the stupa. Doug

Sims and a few others on the stupa crew had stood on scaffolding and fixed the faceplate to the concrete with long, tamper-proof nails, one of them having to be driven right through Migyur Dorje's head.

Just as the work was done—a crystal ball was placed on top of the spire—white fluffs of snow began falling lightly. I'd already heard via the temple grapevine how miraculous and auspicious the snowfall had been, and now the melting remnants of this good omen lay among the cedar chips.

David was working inside his trailer, and I could see him through a small window. A warm yellow light reflected on his face. When he looked up and saw me, he opened the trailer door and offered me a chair inside.

I really didn't know David, except to see him across the room at various Sunday teachings. He was tall and lean and had whole-some good looks—dark hair, light blue eyes, a white toothy Kennedy smile. He and his wife, Sylvia, were among the most re-spected lay practitioners at KPC, and two of Jetsunma's earliest students, but they seemed to exist largely beyond the beehive atmosphere at the temple. They dutifully attended the teachings and prayer shifts, and their three young daughters attended the fledgling grammar school, Pema Choling, but otherwise the Somervilles managed to keep a low profile. If Jetsunma herself hadn't urged me on several occasions to see David with any ques-tions I had about the stupa, I might not have met him. And Wib, as her emissary, often echoed her advice. "Ask David Somerville that question," he would say, or "David would know about that. David has a pretty complete understanding of how a stupa works."

When I once told Wib that I'd spoken to Doug Sims about the stupa, too, and that he'd been very helpful—remembering dates and details, and walking me through the building process step by step—he received this news with surprise. *"Doug?"*

"He's really been great," I said.

"Really? There's probably other better people, like David or Sangye . . ."

When I explained that Doug had the sort of mind that made my work much easier, in that he actually remembered, in a quite orderly and linear fashion, how the stupa had been *built*, it seemed to provide further evidence of Doug's failings. "Oh yeah." Wib laughed. "His mind works like that."

In contrast, David was thought to possess what was called a *subtle mind*. This meant that his mind was clear, sensitive, and operating at a profound level of understanding. Doug's mind—and my own, I had to guess—was pedestrian and tuned to surface. We suffered from something I hadn't quite figured out yet, called *Ordinary View*. At KPC, I had recently come to learn, everybody had a rap. And once you had a rap, it couldn't be refigured unless by Jetsunma. Wib was seen as sweet but a bit dopey—and at times deluded—while his wife, Jane Perini, was considered nearly perfect. "She gives the teachings when Jetsunma is away," I was told several times before I realized the magnitude of the compliment. Sherab was thought to be something of a work in progress, a little like the young Maria in *The Sound of Music*. Eleanor Rowe, whose younger son was a monk at KPC, was a moneybags—always mentioned as "an important contributor." Ani Aileen was blunt and generous and "Gyaltrul Rinpoche's favorite ani in America." Alana was clearly a terrifying force within the sangha, a kind of Mother Superior figure, and students spoke about her with careful neutrality or the backhanded compliment "Underneath *all that*, she's a softy." Talking about fellow sangha members in this way wasn't gossip, or considered harmful. It was simply the passing along of lama wisdom. If one could come to see situations and people the way Jetsunma did, one would be that much closer to enlightenment.

Along these lines a number of the children at the temple were singled out for their good "qualities." I was told by several people that Wib and Jane's oldest daughter, Tara, was "thought to be very special" and "possibly a young tulku"—and I wondered how her little sister felt about not being as special. The older daughter of Rick and Chris Finney, a composed and beautiful red-haired girl named Eleanore, had been detected as clearly important—I'd heard that several visiting Tibetans had eyed her and whispered comments to Jetsunma. There was also Jetsunma's daughter,

Atira, a precocious and sweet-natured seven-year-old. "This monastery won't die when I do. Someone will take my place," Jetsunma had said during one interview, when I asked what would happen to KPC after she was gone. "There are some children here with very special qualities. . . . One I'd give the job to right now."

Among the ordained community there was also a sense of hierarchy—and reputations that some monks and nuns had trouble shaking. The spiritual world was in many ways as brutal as the newsroom I came from. Tall and elegant Ani Alexandra was once criticized by Jetsunma at a large sangha meeting for "floating on the surface" and "not connecting," I had been told—afterward she received subtle and not so subtle insinuations from her fellow Buddhists that she was superficial. Another nun had been told by Jetsunma that she liked feeling important. Ani Dechen had a long history of changing raps, particularly for a nun so young. At seventeen, when she first came to Poolesville to study, Jetsunma had proclaimed Dechen "delicate" and a "hothouse flower" and told sangha members that she needed extra care and feeding. Several years later Jetsunma revealed that she thought Dechen was "insecure" and had become "an approval seeker"—which prompted the sangha to be a bit tough on her. Still later, when Dechen seemed rebellious—had trouble paying her rent and fulfilling her obligations at Tara Studios—Jetsunma simply declared her "a brat," which was where her rap was in the winter of 1995, when I met her. There was also one young monk who was discovered to own several *Playboy* magazines—a breakage of a celibacy vow—but I'd been told that his "addiction to masturbation" had been cured by Jetsunma. How she did this, though, was a mystery.

Cruel or not, the monastery continued to thrive—and occasionally the monks or nuns overcame their raps, by sheer hard work and perseverance. Sangye was one. Ani Rene, the daughter of devout Quakers, was another. They stood out from their peers and were seen by all as *very pure*: honest, subtle, unencumbered by neurosis and egotism. They exuded integrity and clarity of purpose. They both happened also to be good "practitioners," which meant they were accomplished at meditation.

In general, one's ability to perform the daily prayers and traditional meditations of Tibetan Buddhism—or what is referred to sometimes at other Dharma centers as "the quality of one's practice"—was downplayed at KPC. Part of this was Jetsunma's distrust of dry intellectual achievement and her preference for outgoing, outdoorsy students who liked to build things. But a larger part of her bias was the result of the nature of her teachings. As in Zen and other forms of Buddhism, the Tibetans believe there are many paths to enlightenment and realization—enough to suit any kind of student. Lamas instruct and guide students, and give them practices tailor-made for their needs. Each center has its own style, and each teacher has his or her own leanings.

The path that was emphasized in Poolesville was called Guru Yoga—which is sometimes called Deity Yoga or Deity Generation. It is a practice designed to train the mind and heart of a student to see the lama as a living Buddha and ultimately to become one with him or her. It is thought that devotion to one's lama alone can bring about enlightenment. To prepare one's mind for the practice, the lama is visualized in space and time, and the lama's special qualities—pureness, perfection, primordial wisdom—are contemplated, and the student must feel a strong desire to achieve whatever the lama has to teach. There are long visualizations and recitations and prayers that follow, but without complete faith in the lama, and belief in the lama's buddhahood, there is no benefit.

Jetsunma seemed naturally able to instill devotion and had attracted loyal students—an ability that had greatly impressed Penor Rinpoche—so it seemed fitting to the Tibetans that she would emphasize the Guru Yoga practice at her center. It is essentially an uncomplicated practice, too, simple ideas, one general concept, which is applied verbally and visually. At other Dharma centers Guru Yoga is often considered one of many fundamental practices leading to more advanced work. But in Poolesville, Guru Yoga and the path of devotion was the predominant philosophy. Jetsunma taught that by surrendering to a higher power, in this case surrendering completely to her as the Guru, one could achieve happiness and compassion. She acknowledged, of course, other routes, far more esoteric practices or high teachings—that are popular among an elite crowd of American Buddhists—but Jetsunma had always felt these would be off-putting to many of her students and too inaccessible to appeal to a broader spectrum of Americans. She felt there was a snobbism at the other centers, and a sense of competitiveness about how advanced their practices were. She often reminded her students that becoming "heart-centered" and "kind" is ultimately the goal of Buddhist teachings and that the simplest Tibetan Buddhist prayer, *Om Mani Padme Hum*, is known to bring about enlightenment.

"Many of my students wouldn't make it at a conventional Dharma center," Jetsunma had said, and the more I came to know about her temple, the more accurate this assessment seemed. The truth was, a number of her students had trouble practicing at all. It was often repeated how Tom Barry, or Tashi, a big bear of a monk who was a longtime student of Jetsunma, had stood up at a sangha meeting in the early days and said he was still "new to Buddhism" and couldn't "practice worth a damn," but he knew that when he died Jetsunma would take care of him. Sherab admitted similar feelings. "The connection I feel is really with *her*," she had said to me. "I hate to admit this, but I'm very weak in my sit-down meditation process . . . and if you took Jetsunma out of the equation and stuck another Dharma teacher in there, it just wouldn't be the same for me."

Alana was another self-described "bad practitioner." In the ten years since she had taken the Bodhisattva vow, she had not yet completed the initial phase of Ngöndro—the one hundred thousand prostrations. She saw her job as Jetsunma's attendant as a higher calling and a far more profound practice of Buddhism than repeating mantras and meditating. "The way I see it," she once said to me, "I can stay at home and visualize Tara above my head, or I can go to work and see the real Tara every day."

Inside the heated trailer David sat down on an office chair with casters and rolled back and forth on the linoleum. He propped his work boots upon a box. Lately he'd started thinking he might take the trailer farther down in the woods—where it would be out of sight—and keep running his own construction business there. After six months in the woods, and making his business calls from the trailer, he wasn't sure he wanted to leave.

Looking out the small trailer window, I could see why. The stupa was magnificent. The concrete was gray-green, the color of a rainy day. At the very top the crystal ball was resting on a crescent moon shape. The crystal was meant to represent the sun, and the empty, clear mind, as well as purity, and soft light, and something called nondual suchness. In the spring there was a plan to gold-leaf the surface of the stupa—an expensive and time-consuming job, as David described it. I winced at the thought. Gold seemed a bit garish . . . it also seemed, I had to confess, a very Jetsunma touch.

"I have a question to ask," I said to David. "You seem to be the expert on matters related to all things stupa."

"Fine." He laughed. "Fire away."

"Why did Sangye fall?"

David leaned back in his chair and grew more serious. This was exactly the sort of question that Buddhists seem to enjoy pondering, if they feel qualified. "From one point of view," he said, "we were told that when Sangye fell it ripened a lot of negative karma in a fairly benign way. He's still walking six weeks later. And he could be a quadriplegic right now. Look at Christopher Reeve, *he just fell off a horse.*"

I nodded and remembered how one of the nuns at Tara Studios had referred to Reeve this same way, using the exact phrasing. *Just fell off a horse . . .*

"So from this point of view," David continued, "it's wonderful that Sangye ripened all that karma, all that negative karma."

This was what confused me. "He fell because of the ripening of his negative karma?" I asked. "Not because of obstacles trying to prevent him from building the stupa?"

David thought for a moment. "In order to get a correct answer to that, you should probably ask Jetsunma," he said. "But from my understanding, it's probably a little of both. You can't really separate these things out. The sangha is the body of the lama, and so, yes, of course, we are individuals, yet the body functions as one. So to say it was Sangye's individual karma would not be correct. You'd have to say it was a combination of his karma and then, perhaps, a little bit of, you know, *obstacles.*"

I nodded again. *Obstacles.* The Tibetan Buddhists never talked about bad luck or bad planning or bad timing. There seemed to be only . . . obstacles.

"People sometimes will do things, even unintentionally, that ripen karma and purify karma for a group of people," David said. "You might not even be aware that you were doing something to cause negative karma to ripen—or that helps the sangha or all sentient beings. Who knows?"

This intrigued me. It seemed an unconventional concept, and something I hadn't read about in the Buddhism books. "So Sangye's fall helped everybody at the center?"

"Quite possibly," David said.

"And possibly helped all sentient beings?"

"That is what I've been told," David said.

Outside the trailer we heard a shuffling of feet. A loud knock rattled the thin metal of the door. David jumped up, pulled the door open. A strange hooded figure was standing before us.

The elusive Sangye Dorje had come out to circumambulate the stupa and had seen the lights in the trailer. As he stood at the door, I could see that he was wearing two hoods—a brown jacket with a hood over a maroon hooded sweatshirt. And when he pushed them back, the face that emerged was sweet and young, ruddy-cheeked and clean.

"Hey," he said. "Is there an extra chair?"

"You want to join us?" David asked, sort of incredulously.

"Is that okay?" Sangye said. "I can wait outside."

"No," I blurted out. *"Please stay."*

The monk was wearing soft-soled suede work boots and walked with great care and a certain rigidity. He leaned on a tall, stainless-steel cane that was bent into a crook at the end and covered in black rubber. David brought him a chair, and Sangye sat down very slowly—a cartoon of Buddhist mindfulness, except that, instead of living in the moment, he was obviously just in pain.

As he took off his brown jacket and unzipped his sweatshirt, a chest brace became visible; it covered his torso from collarbone to hips. At first I thought a blue thunderbolt had been painted on the front, but Sangye told me that it was a Tibetan *phurba,* a ritual dagger that symbolically pierces through delusion and negative demonic spirits. And underneath the phurba, in gold letters, the words SUPER MONK had been painted—the handiwork of Sherab Khandro.

"We were just talking about you," David said.

Sangye raised his eyebrows.

"And why you fell," I said.

Sangye paused for a few moments. "Negative karma that ripened," he said. "Jetsunma told me personally that it requires a tremendous amount of merit to get to the point where you are working on a stupa—and you spend merit to get the chance to work on one."

"I thought you received merit by working on a stupa," I said, "not spent it."

"It's like," Sangye explained, "if you had ten thousand dollars and invested it wisely. Then you could have one million dollars in fifty years. But in the meantime, you'd be poor. And that's why, immediately after the construction of a stupa, you've spent most of your merit and the period afterward can be very difficult."

David shifted in his chair.

Sangye finished his thought. "Right after we finished the thirty-six-footer in the parking lot—in 1988—the whole crew of us, four of us who worked on it daily, had a very hard time," he said. "The other two monks eventually left the sangha. Ani Rene also had some difficulties. . . ."

"David, you did a lot of work on the other big stupa, too," Sangye said, turning to his friend. "I can't speak for you . . ."

"I don't know, really," David said. He looked a little stunned.

"Maybe it was too long ago for you to remember," Sangye said.

"Yeah, maybe," David said, then paused, as if to plumb his memory some more. "We've had some rocky times. Sure. The whole sangha's had problems," he said. There was another extraordinarily long pause. "That's interesting. The impact is supposed to be *immediate*? I didn't know that."

"You spend all your merit," Sangye explained, "but then every day that the stupa's functioning, and people are walking around it, the merit is coming back to you. And if it's up a thousand years from now, that's merit increasing and increasing, every day. We'll be reaping benefits in future lives, and it won't stop until this stupa breaks down."

David looked out the small window. The twilight sky was darkening to a deep blue. He rolled his office chair around. "I have faith in Jetsunma," he said finally. And he turned to me. "I don't know how familiar you are with how you die and go into the bardo and whatnot, and I'm convinced that Jetsunma is going to be there for me and pull me through the bardo—and in a very positive way. And as a matter of fact, after Sangye fell, I stayed up one night thinking I should get a life insurance policy—*maybe I was next*—but then I thought, I don't need that. Jetsunma isn't going to let me fall. I'm the only one left. And that faith . . . who knows how it works, even from a simple psychological perspective. Maybe if I really believe that I am not going to fall, I won't. But I think there's more to it than that."

"That's why we have teachers around," said Sangye, "to take care of things like that."

"Especially," said David, "when you are dealing with a stupa that's so potent."

The morning of the stupa blessing, the hot sunshine came and went, along with a very cold breeze. The snow piles were shrinking on the ground, and the grass in front of the big white temple facade was green again. Chimes tinkled in some far-off tree. And inside the warm foyer of the temple, I heard muffled singsong chants coming from the prayer room.

The ordained had been up since dawn. Fresh water had been poured into hundreds of offering bowls on the altars in the prayer room, the candles had been replaced and lit, the incense sticks renewed. A wooden platform had been taken out to the woods and set up for the lamas, with chairs and a small table. Flowers and candles had been laid at the base of the stupa, and a corn wreath placed in the center. There was a cabbage plant, several poinsettias, and chrysanthemums. There were pieces of fruit—apples and oranges mostly—and peacock feathers, crystals, precious stones, sprigs of boxwood. Doug Sims had been out at sunrise with more cedar chips, hundreds of pounds, and spread them in a circle around the bottom of the monument, to dry up the ground and keep people from slipping as they circumambulated. But more than that, cedar would purify the place and prepare it for sacred activity.

Wib had been busy on the phones, talking to the media—and he had already called me. Jetsunma had woken up that morning with a broken tooth. She did a practice, Wib told me, then left with Alana for the dentist's office.

As I was throwing my coat over the top of a crowded coatrack and taking off my shoes, Rinchen passed me on her way into the prayer room and gave me a hug hello. "Coming in?" she asked, holding the door a bit ajar. "Not yet," I said. A few moments later Sherab passed by, too. "Did you hear about Jetsunma?" she asked.

"Her tooth?"

"Hopefully, it's the last obstacle that she has to absorb."

Sherab walked through the prayer room doors, and her maroon robes seemed to vanish inside the dark maroon cave. Through the little glass windows in the doors, I could see Tulku Rigdzin Pema—the Stupa Man—sitting on a large throne. There were bright colors and fabrics glowing around him. His small mouth and pencil-thin mustache moved ever so slightly. His eyes were open, but he followed no text. He was leading the group in the Noble Light Rays practice, the one he had done hundreds of thousands of times, perhaps a million times, in order to become a Stupa Man. It is a practice to purify and remove obstacles. It creates a clear space for blessings to occur.

He moved his arms, made a gesture with his hands called a mudra. His arms were long and spindly. His skin was golden brown. Most of Jetsunma's students were on the floor, sitting on soft pillows and little back-support chairs that looked like something you'd take to the beach. There was a glut of figures in maroon who blended into the colors of the room. I saw the back of Wib's white mane. I saw the long blond braid of his wife, Jane, nearby. The Somervilles were there, Doug and Shelly Sims, Eleanor Rowe . . . about fifty or sixty people in all. Jamyang, the Stupa Man's attendant, was speaking. The group chanted, prayed. Drums went *tat-a-tat-tat*. The Stupa Man held up a large brass bell and rang it several times. Even from outside I could smell the cedar and mint rising from the burning incense. The prayers converged and then separated into distinct strains.

I stood in the warm foyer for the longest time. The praying went on, the chanting. I watched through the windows. I felt pulled inside, to become a part of the room. Something true was happening there—inside the prayer room—but it also seemed far off and vaguely ridiculous. I wanted to go inside, but an awkward feeling kept rising in me.

Sherab's beautiful, deep voice was rising, leading the prayers. She was an *umze*, a chant leader.

How do spiritual people do it? The confusion, the conflicting worldviews, believing in things that make no sense, really, and telling yourself that they do. Faith came in waves for me, and I wasn't good at enduring the lean times. For me, it had always been more comfortable to remain a fence sitter, a nonjoiner, a perpetual admirer from afar. Still, there I was—standing in the foyer with my shoes off. Something had drawn me, something I wanted. At the same time there was something there that kept me outside, too, something I didn't trust.

Several TV cameras were set up and waiting for the ceremony to start when I arrived at the stupa site. I watched two reporters struggle with equipment and notebooks, and locate a young American monk named Konchog Norbu, who was their press contact. The blessing of the stupa was a solemn occasion, as solemn as anything I'd seen the students in Poolesville do. Riding in a truck earlier, some nuns and I had spotted Sangye limping along the road with his cane, on his way to the ceremony. Sherab gunned the accelerator and pretended to be aiming for Sangye as the other nuns whooped and rolled the truck windows down.

"Oh. Is it okay to laugh?" one of the nuns asked.

"It's *always* okay," Sherab said. But once we had arrived at the stupa, the smiles left their faces and the nuns seemed purposeful and intense—even as they stood waiting for the prayers to begin. The stupa was believed to bring more benefit to the whole world than ladling a thousand cups of hot soup to the homeless, or finding a cure for cancer.

The smell of cedar was everywhere. Large green boughs of it had been cut down, set up in piles, and ignited. The greener and fresher the cedar, the more it smoked.

It was so solemn and so quiet I could still hear the two creeks nearby, and the squawking of the crows in the trees. I stood with Sherab and Wib, and watched the sangha slowly assemble— about seventy or eighty members. The monk named Jon Randolph arrived, with his long face and wry eyes. Kamil, the monk from the Virgin Islands, gently dropped off some fruit at the base of the stupa. As I scanned the gathering crowd, I realized that I was slowly coming to know many of them. I knew some of their stories already. And in the months to come I would hear more.

Three chairs had been set up, for Sangye and two other sangha members who had recently injured themselves. One of them, it turned out, was Karl Jones—Jetsunma's current husband and consort, a handsome young redhead who was wearing a cowboy hat and a long, dashing Australian outback coat. He had broken his foot several weeks ago, I'd been told, while angrily kicking a piece of furniture in Jetsunma's house. The story interested me, since I'd read somewhere that the Buddha said you could burn aeons of precious good karma accumulation in one moment of intense anger. The last chair was for Jetsunma's younger son, Christopher, a beautiful boy with a head of dark curly hair, who was wearing jeans and a camouflage-print jacket. He had dropped a concrete brick on his toe while working on the stupa. Sangye sat down next to them, with his cane between his thighs.

A blue Toyota Tercel pulled up to the stupa site. Behind the wheel I could see Alana in robes and sunglasses. Her face looked ghostly in the glare of the windshield, and tired. Jetsunma emerged, wearing a black leather jacket with many zippers, black high-top boots, and black gloves. She was holding a string of red prayer beads and looked very thin, as thin as I'd ever seen her. Her face looked beautiful, too, not puffy, as it often did. Her makeup had been perfectly applied. She floated over to Konchog and the TV cameras.

One reporter sidled up to her after Konchog had arranged an introduction. "People will come here, why?" he asked her.

"I think for hope," she said. She squinted in the sunlight and brushed a strand of hair away with her fingernail. She seemed perfectly nonchalant about the TV camera hovering just inches from the side of her face. "As Buddhists, we pray that if people are hungry, that we would be food. We pray that we could be a bridge for travelers or a shelter for those who are in need. And this stupa provides for us a way to offer to the world a place of pilgrimage and a blessing."

Big bundles of incense sticks were burned at the foot of the stupa, and, as the ceremony began, the ordained put on another layer of robes, a bright golden cotton, that are reserved for formal occasions.

Sherab struggled with the heavy cotton, and I helped her put the robes on—then worried that I wasn't supposed to touch them. "What are these for?" I asked her. "I've forgotten what it's called, exactly," she whispered, "but the yellow robes represent another level of vow."

There was a card table in front of the Stupa Man. On it were photographs, images to be blessed. There were little *tormas,* or colored clay ritual cakes, set on a plate as offerings. Three crystals sat, with the bright sunlight hitting them, next to a round mirror. Tulku Rigdzin Pema sat down wearing golden robes and sunglasses, and brown rubber-soled shoes.

After the Seven Line Prayer began, Jamyang brought the ritual objects for the Stupa Man to bless. The tulku held everything with a white scarf. There was a dorje, a little lightning bolt. There was a little gray-silverish bum-pa, a little ritual vase with a spout and a spray of peacock feathers coming out the top. The Stupa Man poured oil onto a plate. A long strand of five-colored string was held up between the tulku and the stupa. "That's something like a telephone line," Wib explained from behind me. "It symbolizes a connection between them."

A bowl of warm dry rice was passed. It was yellow and flecked with tiny filaments of crimson saffron. We took handfuls of the rice and began tossing it in the direction of the stupa, as though it were a bride embarking on her honeymoon. The entire crowd began chanting now, out loud, the lyrical and lilting Seven Line Prayer. Jetsunma was wearing a cordless body mic, and you could hear her voice above the rest.

> *Hung orgyen yul gi nub jyang tsham*
> On the northwest border of the country of Urgyen
> *Pema gesar dong po la*
> In the pollen heart of a lotus
> *Ya tshen chhog gi ngo drub nyey*
> Marvelous in the perfection of your attainment
> *Pema jyung nye zhey su drag*
> You are known as the Lotus Born
> *Khor du khadro mang poi kor*
> And are surrounded by your circle of many dakinis.
> *Khyed kyi jey su dag drub kyi*
> Following you, I will practice.
> *Jyin gyi lob chhir sheg su sol*
> I pray that you will come to confer your blessings.

> *Guru Pedma Siddhi Hum*
> *Oh Ah Hum Vajra Guru Padma Siddhi Hum*

An owl flew low over the crowd. The smell of saffron grew thick and soft in the sunlight. Steam rose from the mounds of melting snow. Jetsunma stepped down from the wooden platform and began circumambulating the stupa, the cedar chips crunching under her boots. After she'd made several passes, the crowd began to follow her, began walking around and around, their heads bowed, their faces serious. It was a blur of gold cotton and maroon—maroon parkas, maroon knit caps, maroon chenille scarves and wool turtlenecks. I stepped down to join them.

The Buddhist scriptures describe the benefits of circumambulating stupas—and decorating them with offerings of gold, flowers, incense, and devotion. You honor the seeds of enlightenment by doing this and the seeds of enlightenment within yourself. Circumambulate a stupa and, according to the sutras, you are promised a long life, good health, mindfulness, clear perception, and intelligence. You are promised a radiant appearance, too, freedom from greed, joy in giving, enjoyment of life, strength, perseverance, self-discipline, profound understanding, great renown. Devote your spare moments to walking around a stupa and the benefits come in this lifetime and in lifetimes to come. It is written that you will dwell happily in the womb in your next incarnation, receive a beautiful body, be born easily, and drink happily at the breast.

Once the ceremony was over, the crowd began to talk among themselves. "Did you see that owl?" somebody asked.

"The owl . . ."

"Incredible."

"Did you see the rainbow in the sky earlier?"

"Really, a rainbow?"

"Amazing."

Jetsunma grabbed the edges of her black leather jacket and pulled it tighter around her as she walked to the car, then turned, suddenly, to face the crowd. "I can't remember a day this happy, ever," she called out. Alana smiled and opened the car door for her lama, then got behind the wheel again and they were gone.

9.

Who's Ever Heard of Ahkön Lhamo?

FOR OUR ANCESTORS, DREAMS,
HALLUCINATIONS, REVELATIONS, AND
COCK-AND-BULL STORIES
WERE INEXTRICABLY MIXED WITH FACTS.

—WILLIAM JAMES, *The Varieties of Religious Experience*

There was great fanfare and rejoicing when the Poolesville students sent their lama off to India for the first time, in February 1987. There was a feeling of restless anticipation, too. They'd been told that Catharine was an important reincarnation—possibly something called a tulku—and Penor Rinpoche had agreed to look into the matter and discuss it with her.

Just before leaving for India Catharine arranged fifteen-minute private meetings with each student, the kind of one-on-one face time most of them hadn't gotten in a long while. She and Michael could be gone as long as two or three months—and Catharine was concerned that the group might disintegrate. She tried to say things that would encourage a sense of commitment in her absence. Again and again she told students that she loved them and reminded them that they were "great" beings. Many students came forward at this time, as Elizabeth Elgin had, to formally announce a wish to be ordained.

Elizabeth hadn't spoken to her fellow students about what had transpired during her private meeting with Catharine—that she'd declared herself a nun—but several had seen her leaving Catharine's rooms in the temple that day. Elizabeth's eyes looked red and swollen from crying, but her face, they noticed, seemed smooth, relaxed. She had a glow that could only be described as beatific. "She never looked more beautiful than that day," said one sangha member, "and word got out pretty quickly that something miraculous had happened between her and Catharine." In recent months the two women hadn't spent much time together. But in the days leading up to the India trip, they seemed again inseparable. Michael and Catharine were full of wonder themselves, and intense curiosity. Gyaltrul Rinpoche had told them that Catharine was surely a tulku, a reincarnated *somebody*. But who? "Get a name," Gyaltrul Rinpoche had instructed Catharine before she left. "Be sure to ask His Holiness to give you a name."

Catharine and Michael were accompanied to Kennedy Airport, in New York, by Ted and Linda Kurkowski—to help them check in, get their baggage handled, and pay hundreds of dollars in extra freight. The Burroughses traveled with eight large suitcases on rollers and several carry-ons. A few women in the sangha had gotten together and made dozens of *chubas*—Tibetan robes that wrap around the body—for Catharine to wear and a number of happi coats out of silk. The students had raised the money to pay for Catharine and Michael's entire trip overseas and handed Michael an envelope with ten thousand dollars in cash—to buy statues for the temple, and for offerings. They had purchased new clothes for Catharine and a number of exquisite and unusual gems and crystals, a mala made from ten-millimeter lapis lazuli beads, and one piece of clear quartz the size of a fist to give to Penor Rinpoche and other Tibetan dignitaries. Among the eight pieces of luggage was one reserved for Catharine's toiletries—including her blow dryer and hairbrushes, her hair conditioners and sprays, a few months' supply of Lee Press-On Nails and Estée Lauder makeup.

Jane Perini was left in charge of the Monday night teachings in Catharine's absence. In the Dharma room one afternoon,

Catharine was overheard giving Jane this piece of advice: "If you aren't getting people's attention, do what I do: make up a crisis."

It was a hard trip, starting with a twenty-hour flight on Air India. After arriving in Bombay, Catharine and Michael checked into a Holiday Inn and kept trying to reach Penor Rinpoche at his remote location in Bylakuppe by telephone, but they weren't able to get through. Eventually, after they reached Bangalore, a monk named Pema Dorje turned up and hired two taxis to take the Burroughses to the monastery in the south: one taxi for them, another for their luggage. It was a seven-hour ride from Bangalore to Bylakuppe, on bad dusty roads in a car with intermittent air-conditioning. They had come to India at the hottest time of year, in one-hundred-degree heat and 100 percent humidity. It was also the end of Losar, the Tibetan New Year, a chaotic time of non-stop festivals, dances, teachings, performances, and demonstrations, celebrating the two weeks of miracles once performed by Sakyamuni Buddha.

They were greeted warmly by Penor Rinpoche when the taxis arrived at Palyul Namdroling, his large monastery compound in Bylakuppe, but they were surprised by the lack of modern conveniences. There was no air-conditioning in any part of the monastery, including Penor Rinpoche's small mudbrick house. Electricity came only once a day. There was no hot water, either, and, in keeping with Buddhist respect for all living things, pest control was out of the question. There were untouched beehives everywhere, and monks walking through swarms of bees without a thought. After a couple of weeks in the guest hostel, Catharine's legs were raw and swollen with sores from bedbugs.

Their days were spent at teachings, given by the old and venerable Dilgo Khyentse Rinpoche, a lumbering giant of a Tibetan— nearly seven feet tall—who had to be supported while he walked to and from his throne. Once inside the large dark temple, the lama read so slowly into his microphone that three weeks of teachings and empowerments went on for three months. Hoping to make an auspicious connection with the ancient lama—who

had recently become the head of the Nyingma lineage—
Catharine and Michael took him the large, perfectly clear quartz
crystal, and the lapis lazuli mala, as an offering. They were
thrilled when they learned, secondhand, that their gifts had been
a huge hit. And they were told over and over how delighted
Khyentse Rinpoche was to see them. But the lama was there to
give teachings, not to make new American friends or recognize
tulkus, and all morning, all afternoon, throngs of students came
to hear him. There were yogis and lamas, a thousand monks or
more, scores of tulkus, and a sea of lay practitioners from all over
the globe wearing their best clothes. Khyentse Rinpoche's microphone was wrapped in a white silk scarf or *kata*, and his words
were broadcast by loudspeakers to an overflow crowd sitting on
the temple grounds. Everywhere Catharine and Michael looked
there were hundreds of people meditating, visualizing, and recit-
ing mantras—and at the day's end a tally of mantras accumulated by practitioners was made public on a scoreboard.

Days passed this way, then weeks. Catharine and Michael sat
respectfully in an area roped off for Westerners, right behind
Khyentse Rinpoche's throne. It was an impressive temple, and
over the years Penor Rinpoche had been criticized by other Tibetans for its opulence. Inside the magnificent space with a fifty-
foot ceiling were huge pillars painted turquoise and red and
seating for three hundred. The walls were painted with Buddhist
deities and smothered with statues, altarpieces, enormous burning incense sticks, and brocaded fabrics in rich reds and gold.
Catharine and Michael were the only Americans in attendance
but for one lone fellow, a student of Sai Baba, a Hindu lama who
was famous for being able to make ashes fall out of thin air.

At night they grew restless. How long would the teachings
continue? When would the recognition come? There was a feeling
of endlessness, of a visit without a plan and a loss of control. Loud
thighbone horns began sounding at four in the morning to wake
the monks, and huge drums were pounded. The food was another
thing entirely. They were fed a diet of rice and dhal—a yellow, liq-
uidy paste made from overcooked lentil beans and curry. Occasionally there were a few vegetables, boiled cabbage or potatoes,
and bits of gristly meat. But Bylakuppe wasn't a rich place, and

there were thousands of monks to feed. As for venturing outside the compound, the neighboring town of Kushalnagar at the time was just a series of mud huts, with no stove or restaurant.

Each evening Michael would recap the day's events into a tape recorder he'd brought, and each week he'd send a ninety-minute tape back home to Poolesville. At the Monday night meetings the tapes were played for the students—with some listening in by speakerphone from home. There were descriptions of the hoards in the streets of Bombay, the dirt, the starving people. There were accounts of Penor Rinpoche's monastery. After a tape was played in which Michael mentioned that Catharine was having trouble sleeping—that her bed was on the ground and bug infested—the sangha sent two inflatable air mattresses. On other tapes Catharine expressed concern that some students wouldn't hang on, continue being Buddhists, if she died in India or never returned.

Michael reported that the Tibetans in Bylakuppe called Catharine Jetsun-droma, which is the Tibetan name for the goddess Tara. It was quite an honor, actually. One night she channeled Jeremiah for them, and the Tibetans seemed to enjoy it.

Eventually, Michael decided to pay a visit to Penor Rinpoche, to ask about Catharine's recognition. So far the lama had been utterly silent on the subject—and hadn't asked to see Catharine privately to discuss it. Everyday after lunch Penor Rinpoche received visitors. They would line up outside his small cottage holding katas, usually asking for a blessing or a name for a baby.

Michael joined the line one day and waited his turn. Once inside he found himself among cages of singing birds and large aquariums of fish. His Holiness sat near a picture window looking out on papaya trees and a lush garden. His attendants and other lamas sat on the floor around him. An aluminum lawn chair with woven plastic strips was brought out for Michael. Penor Rinpoche seemed glad to see him—and offered Michael some coffee.

As they drank together Penor Rinpoche smiled and nodded his head. But he left the questions to Michael. After mentioning the teachings and expressing how he and Catharine were enjoying Bylakuppe, Michael tiptoed up to the subject of Catharine's possible tulku status. He wanted to be respectful and tried to keep a lid on his impatience. Would the recognition be taking place? Penor Rinpoche's responses were evasive and vague. Michael grew worried. He didn't understand the Tibetan tradition of the broad hint, a lama's way of communicating indirectly. And he didn't know that being too direct is considered unsubtle and insulting. "I remember telling you at dinner in Maryland that she had obviously been a serious practitioner in the past," Penor Rinpoche said.

"Has this matter been investigated?" Michael asked.

Penor Rinpoche pursed his lips, looked down at his lap, and the subject was changed.

After a couple of weeks Michael returned and asked again about Catharine's recognition and if the lama could give her a name. This time he told the lama that students back home were growing anxious and confused. He and Catharine were more than happy to be patient, he said, but the students in Poolesville needed to hear what Penor Rinpoche had to say. Michael held letters the students had sent requesting information about Catharine's recognition and begging to be told who she was. Again Penor Rinpoche changed the subject. "It's too soon for recognitions," he said.

On Michael's third visit Penor Rinpoche seemed noticeably irritated when the subject was raised. And he grumbled in Tibetan to his interpreter, a scholar named Khenpo Tsewang Gyatso. The two Tibetans talked for a while, then Khenpo told Michael that Penor Rinpoche had very much hoped to delay the recognition until the following month—when he would be able to travel to Nepal with Catharine and give her a Bodhisattva name on an auspicious date. He had wanted to make the announcement at the great Stupa of Bouddha, the holiest place in the world. Once there he planned to present a "recognition" letter to Catharine. This would have been the most auspicious way to proceed—and would have resulted in fewer obstacles. But because of Michael's insistent pressuring, and the demands of the students in Poolesville, Penor Rinpoche had decided to delay no further.

Within a day or two Penor Rinpoche called Catharine and Michael into his rooms and presented them with two scrolls, which proclaimed Catharine Burroughs the official reincarnation

THE BUDDHA FROM BROOKLYN • 135

of Ahkön Lhamo. They were told that Ahkön Lhamo was a saint, a woman, a student of Migyur Dorje, and one of the founders of the Palyul tradition—a lineage within the Nyingma school—which Penor Rinpoche had headed for decades. "If people need to know how you can teach, you show them this," the rinpoche said to Catharine.

Penor Rinpoche said he felt a strong connection to Ahkön Lhamo. As a young boy in the Palyul monastery in Eastern Tibet, he had held the human skull or *karpala* of Ahkön Lhamo many times and prayed that someday he would find her incarnation. Since her life in the seventeenth century, she had not been re-born—or at least hadn't been recognized. But now, Penor Rinpoche said, he felt that his prayers had been answered. The brother of Ahkön Lhamo, Kunzang Sherab, had been recognized a handful of times, and his modern-day incarnation was Gyaltrul Rinpoche—his trusted friend and ally in the West. Gyaltrul Rinpoche and Catharine were past-life brother and sister, which ex-plained the immediate connection between them.

Catharine smiled, her eyes full of wonder. Michael sat solemnly by, making mental notes of the conversation. It was use-less to complain and rude to communicate even the slightest hint of disappointment. But who was Ahkön Lhamo? Truthfully, he was a bit puzzled by the news. In time he and Catharine would learn that not many Tibetan Buddhists outside the Palyul tradi-tion had even heard of Ahkön Lhamo. And in time Catharine made jokes about wishing she'd been recognized as a more impor-tant historic figure—Yeshe Tsogyal, for example, one of Guru Rinpoche's primary consorts. In a great number of Catharine's past-life dreams and memories, she had been an exalted person-age. She was a ruler of ancient kingdoms, a traveler from splendid faraway galaxies. She'd told her students in early teachings that she had known Jesus Christ and been by his side as he died.

But in a way the Ahkön Lhamo recognition was a relief—something Catharine and Michael came to understand in time. Catharine didn't speak or read Tibetan and had virtually no for-mal training in Tibetan Buddhism. Had she been recognized as a terton—a higher level of tulku—there might have been pressure on her to perform, to live up to a splashy lineage. As Ahkön

Lhamo she would be freer to find her own way. With no other Ahkön Lhamo rebirths that anyone knew about, there was very little to live up to.

As Catharine had predicted, the unity of her students in Poolesville began deteriorating in her absence. They had held up well the first weeks she and Michael had been away, but arguments and anxiety had taken over in the second month. A number of students felt lost without her and were bogged down by the day-to-day operations of the temple. Until Michael left nobody could have guessed how much he did: the water-offering bowls he cleaned and filled, the candles he lit, the orders he placed for the gift shop. Money was also a problem. In order to make the mortgage payments several students had maxed out their credit cards and gotten cash advances. But the problems were mostly emotional. The students had grown dependent on Catharine, and her absence made them aware of a loss they'd been feeling over the last year as she'd receded. "She had been so accessible before. It had been so intimate—like a family," said Jon Randolph. "There was a feeling that we were all in this thing together. And it was changing. It was very pronounced. We were the students. She was the teacher."

Catharine wasn't their friend anymore—she was their lama. And this was really beginning to sink in. There was more talk than ever, suddenly, about ordination. It was a way of making a commitment to Catharine for life and perhaps another way of becoming close to her.

Elizabeth spent her days working on a huge project. Before leaving Catharine had called upon certain students to help build a retreat center on the temple grounds. It would be a place where visiting lamas and their entourages could stay during teachings and, at other times, a residence for students on retreat, who could pay to rent rooms at fairly cheap rates. There was a stable next to the temple building, and during April and May of 1987, a crew of students began converting it into a two-story dormitory. There was a central hallway on each floor and small bedrooms along either side. There was also some talk—among students who had decided to become ordained—that it might someday become a monastery residence, where Catharine's monks and nuns could live in truly monastic style.

Jay Allen was working on the project, and David Somerville and Richard Dykeman—who was still living in a tent in the woods across River Road. Also working on the stable conversion was a guy who appeared from another Buddhist center; everybody called him Bucko. And the minute they met, he and Elizabeth began to fight.

"He irritated me so much," Alana said. "I guess I took one look at him and *knew.*" What began as a feud became a flirtation and developed into a relationship. "It seemed so cool," Alana said. "We would practice together—Ngöndro—and it was all so *very Dharma.* I thought, Isn't this fun, isn't this great: I'm in love and we're both into the Dharma together."

Students recalled how Bucko and Elizabeth would talk dreamily about their past lives together and how they were doing "practice together"—assuming they meant they were attempting Karma Mudra, the famous Tantric lama-consort sex practices. Alana doesn't remember telling anybody at the temple that she planned eventually to become a nun, but word seems to have slipped out anyway, and other students came to their own conclusions about her relationship with Bucko. "Like most everybody, I guess, I assumed it was a big last fling before ordination," said Karen Williams. "What did I know? I was just an ex–flower child from Berkeley. A little fling never bothered me. . . . Otherwise, they were a weird match—and on a major ego trip. They talked about how they were going to practice together and change the world."

By the time Penor Rinpoche began his series of empowerments—preparing her for "recognition"—Catharine wasn't feeling particularly well and Michael had come down with dysentery and lost close to thirty pounds. The monsoon season had begun, and the ground had turned to mud. The monks at Namdroling threw blankets down for Catharine to walk over, so the leeches wouldn't attach themselves to her on her way to Penor Rinpoche's cottage.

Some of the teachings and initiations were confusing, too—and Khenpo Tsewang Gyatso's translations were hard to follow. Catharine and Michael had received some of these empowerments or *wangs* already from Gyaltrul Rinpoche in Poolesville, but there were new ones mixed in. This is the Nyingma way of doing things. Each of the four schools of Tibetan Buddhism has its own style. Teachings in the Kagyu lineage are a little like joining the Marines—tough going, with hard-core lamas who emphasize three-year retreats. The Sakya lineage has a very formal, slow, gentle style of teaching. The Nyingma, the oldest lineage (*Nyingma* means "ancient ones"), has a style that is sometimes called flying in space. The Nyingma lamas give their students every possible kind of teaching—high, low, esoteric, and basic—in no particular order. It is up to the student to sort things out, to figure out how to complete Ngöndro, to meditate, and, it is hoped, to develop *inner qualities.* The Nyingmas hold firmly to the idea that the Buddha seed is in all of us, and if you give enough people enough teachings, eventually the Dharma will take root.

The Gelukpas are the reform branch—created in the seventeenth century in response to decay and corruption that had descended upon the other three lineages. The Gelukpas' style is the antithesis of the Nyingmas': orderly, emphasizing academics and proper preparation for higher teachings. The historic petty rivalry still exists between them. The Dalai Lama is a Gelukpa, and while he is the titular head of Tibetan Buddhism, the four schools are fiercely independent and his authority is vague and indirect. He is a universally respected spiritual leader and teacher. But his word is not law.

Catharine felt greater comfort in Bylakuppe following her recognition, as though a mission had been accomplished. She felt more relaxed around Penor Rinpoche, too, and began drinking butter tea with him in the afternoon. She wore her chuba and took to the new practices she was learning. But it wasn't easy. The heat was unabated, and the bugs continued to be a problem. Eventually Catharine's phlebitis came back—and prevented her from doing *tsa-lung,* the physically demanding Tibetan-style yoga. As the weeks dragged on she started feeling more and more homesick—missing her family and her students. She had heard that her younger son, Christopher, had pierced his ear and changed his name. While she wasn't sure what awaited her in Maryland, she was anxious to leave. But before that could happen she and Michael were supposed to accompany Penor Rinpoche on an auspicious trip to Nepal and, later, Tibet.

Nobody had talked to her about how to be a tulku—or what a tulku is, really. She had little idea what the future would bring in the way of official enthronement and the ordination of her students. Nobody had given Catharine advice about how to run a Tibetan Buddhist center, either. It was assumed she already knew that—once consecrated, her center in Poolesville would be the largest Nyingma center in the United States. But Penor Rinpoche did say that giving her a center, and the recognition as Ahkön Lhamo, would inspire Westerners and women in particular. He had asked for nothing from them—not money or a formal financial arrangement of any kind. He had only one concern. That they practice, and practice well.

In Nepal, Catharine was disturbed by a phone conversation she'd had with Jane Perini, who told her about the affair between Elizabeth and Bucko. The truth was, both Catharine and Michael were exhausted—and not getting along. It had been nearly four months of nonstop heat and humidity, of empowerments and translators, of eating rice and dhal. It wasn't until later that Catharine realized the hot butter tea she was drinking with the Tibetan every afternoon was also making her sick. In Nepal, she abruptly decided to cancel plans for Tibet and go home. They had stayed in India an auspicious number of days: one hundred and eight, the number of beads on a mala.

There were other reasons to leave Nepal early, at the risk of disappointing her Tibetan teachers. Catharine had woken up one morning worried that Elizabeth had left her "mindstream." She began circumambulating the Great Stupa of Bouddha—and repeating Elizabeth's name. She called Jane and told her to tell Elizabeth that she must end the affair. "I see great negativity coming," Catharine said. "Negative karma. And I'm not sure how to stop it."

Later Catharine told Elizabeth that she could see the karma ripening, like the tip of an iceberg rising above the ocean. "We can see maybe the surface of the ocean, the tip of the iceberg," Alana recounted. "But the wisdom mind can see what's under the ocean—and she was seeing miles and miles of deep, deep pockets of negativity."

A few skeptical members of the sangha suspected that Catharine was simply made jealous by Elizabeth's affair. At first Catharine told Elizabeth that she had broken a "samaya of the heart" by having the affair with Bucko. A *samaya* is a pledge of devotion to a teacher. Later on Catharine said that Elizabeth had taken a "deep vow" to her, which had been broken by her affair. Later still the story was amended again. "I thought I was having my last fling before becoming a nun," said Alana, "but what I didn't realize was, at the time of telling Catharine about my plans to become a nun . . . that I had already, in a way, taken vows. And by being with this man, I was breaking them."

The seriousness of the situation became apparent to Elizabeth just a month after Catharine and Michael had returned from India. Elizabeth had moved into a group house in Gaithersburg—jokingly called the Nunnery, since so many of its occupants had decided to become renunciates—and one morning she tried to get out of bed and fell suddenly to the floor. The next thing she remembered was being in the hospital. She had a tumor, she was told: a meningioma, the size of an orange, on the surface of her brain.

When the doctors told Elizabeth that the tumor had been growing slowly for ten years, Catharine announced this was impossible. "If it had been there," she told Elizabeth, "I would have seen it. This has occurred much more spontaneously than that."

"The Tibetans call it *rangjung*," said Alana. "A car spontaneously appearing out of a rock, or Adolf Hitler was a spontaneous appearance of evil."

Elizabeth was told she needed surgery in three days, and while she waited, Catharine had her move out of the Nunnery and into her lama's private quarters, where Catharine nursed her, prayed for her, and brought her meals. Among her students Catharine was also organizing a vigil. She employed a device she'd used back in the Kensington days—having all students called at home and told to join the sangha for a night of collective prayer. The morning that Elizabeth entered George Washington Hospital, eighty or ninety students were gathered in the prayer room. They opened with the Seven Line Prayer, followed by group chanting, group prostrations, then prayer and meditation. It went on for twenty-four hours.

"I only have two memories of the hospital," Alana said. "I remember feeling held in a kind of vibration of prayer, really feeling everybody praying and really kind of floating and being held and feeling okay, like I was going to be okay. It was strange. I felt the prayers like a hum, like a vibration."

When she woke up she was told her tumor had been removed. It was pronounced benign.

Catharine came to visit Elizabeth in the hospital and was startled to see her head covered in surgical gauze. There were tubes running into the bandages, and her eyebrows had been shaved off. When Catharine reached for Elizabeth's hand, her eyes flickered open.

"Do you know who you are?" Catharine asked her.

Elizabeth looked up. "I'm a Buddhist," she said.

10

Can a Woman Be a Rinpoche?

Talk of ordination dominated the spare moments of temple life following Catharine and Michael's trip to India. And it was the rare student who did not, at some point or another, imagine himself or herself in robes. The announcement had been made: Penor Rinpoche would be coming to Poolesville the following summer. He would be giving a long series of empowerments, consecrating the temple, officially enthroning Catharine, and ordaining the first group of her students. On Monday nights Catharine gave teachings and talked passionately about creating a monastery. To her closest students she indicated that she hoped eventually to join the nuns and take vows herself. Michael, she said, was considering becoming a monk. It wasn't long before word of this development leaked out.

"Taking robes," as it was called, seemed an easy decision for some. Ani Rene, or Deborah Larrabee, as she was known at the time, was certain she wanted a renunciate life. Catherine Windolph and three of her daughters had also come forward. Janice Newmark had talked to Catherine before the trip to India and learned that ordination was the right thing for her. Michelle Grissom—even though she was only twenty and had never lived away from home—cut her hair short and started wearing burgundy in preparation for ordination. Two years before, in her first private consultation, Catharine had told her, "I predict you'll want to be an ani! And you'll be a light in the darkness."

Elizabeth Elgin had made her decision, of course, and was living permanently in the main temple building following her surgery. Catharine wrote her long, encouraging letters and frequently dropped in on her old friend. "My mind felt so different at that time," Alana recalled. "The world appeared like Jell-O—as though it were clear, very clear—like you could pass through anything if you wanted." She had been purified, Catharine told her—and she was sensing "how a purified mind feels after years and years of practice." Struck by seizures on occasion, Elizabeth was not allowed to drive or to leave the temple grounds without Catharine's permission—an arrangement that continued for a year. "My karma was so funky still," Alana said, "I needed the protection."

For most others, though, the decision to become ordained—or not—was far more wobbly and tortured. After one married couple went to Catharine, saying they were thinking about separating in order to become ordained, word went out that all married students, particularly those with families, should stay married and not consider ordination. This left the single, unattached students wondering, What does Catharine think we should do? Chris Cervenka spent hours praying, wondering whether to become a nun. Karen Tokarz and Holly Heiss were famously undecided and seemed to change their minds each week. Many students wrote to Catharine asking for guidance. Jay Allen had written to her asking if he should take ordination, and Catharine said no. Jay had been a monk in so many previous lives, she told him, that it was unnecessary this time around. Others heard nothing from her, and wondered what *that* meant.

"I felt that some students needed the refuge of the vows," Jetsunma recalled later, "and the strongly defined boundaries—particularly students who had alcoholic backgrounds or who were drug abusers. The vows would take them farther from the realms that were really hurting them."

The solarium in the back of the temple became an informal meeting place where students drank tea and coffee and discussed ordination—what the vows entail, what the lifestyle would bring them, and the future. "Some people started avoiding the solarium, just to avoid the conversation," said one student. Others were drawn there, hoping to hear a bit of news that might help them make up their minds. Or hoping to run into Catharine.

"I was always trying to find out what she wanted me to do," said Jon Randolph, "what she thought was best for me. . . . But she remained studiously aloof. She wouldn't give any indication. So I tried to intuit what she wanted. And it was kind of crazy: Why wasn't I deciding myself? Why did I care so much what she thought? It was my decision, right? But I had that much respect for her sense of what was good for me, and what was good for everybody around her. So I kept looking for some kind of hint."

It was a blessing, and a relief of sorts, to be singled out for monastic life. Karen Williams was walking downstairs to breakfast in the temple one morning when Catharine pulled her aside. "I think it's about time you thought about ordination," she said. And later that day Karen cut her shoulder-length hair and began accepting a decision that had been made for her.

Catharine was a little less direct with her student Roger Hill. Roger had come to Poolesville from the Virgin Islands two years before—just for a visit—after hearing tapes of Catharine's teachings. On St. Thomas, where he had three children, an ex-wife, and a job as a schoolteacher, he'd tested several churches and spiritual avenues, but none of them had stuck. He'd always felt a hunger, a yearning, to connect with something greater. And in Poolesville he seemed to find what had been missing in his life. He moved to Maryland, became an active member of the World Prayer Center, welcomed the transition to Buddhism, and, after Catharine and Michael's trip to India, fell in love with another sangha member. The couple hadn't had much time together before Roger heard, secondhand, that Catharine objected to the relationship. When he wrote to her trying to explain his reasons for the involvement and why it was a positive thing, Catharine returned his letter with a handwritten response at the top. "The arrogance of this letter!" she wrote. "I can't really condone this relationship!"

Although he felt ambivalent, Roger quit the relationship immediately. "It was hard to adjust to having a guru so involved in my personal life," he said. "But after a while I began to see something else. I hadn't come to Poolesville to have a romantic relationship. I came for the path, the teachings. And my whole life had been looking for this path to practice. And it suddenly became crystal clear: the most expedient path and best path was to become ordained."

When the news leaked out, through various channels, that Catharine had been advised against becoming a nun, none of those committed to ordination seemed deterred. The students assumed that this directive had come from Gyaltrul Rinpoche, or even Penor Rinpoche himself. But it was Michael, in the end, who tried very persistently to convince Catharine to stay married to him. Her center would be more attractive to Americans, he argued, if she were an accessible Western woman with Western ways—not an off-putting renunciate with a shaved head. She shouldn't give up her love of Motown records or her weekly manicure, her shopping expeditions, he argued, or her enthusiastic sex life. She was a Brooklyn girl, sometimes loud and outspoken, maybe a bit garish. Indeed, her Westernness should be emphasized. She was a new breed, a pioneer. And she should be out in the world. In time Catharine would come to believe Michael was right. "In my heart, I feel like a nun," she said, but there was a larger purpose to serve: She was going to lead her American sangha on a crucial mission to create a place for Tibetan Buddhism to flourish in America.

"The future of Dharma in the West is riding on us," she told her students. "Each one of you represents an aspect of Western life, a flaw, a downfall, that needs to be overcome. Pride, arrogance, laziness, dependency. . . . If this center does not succeed, and if I don't succeed, the teachings of Buddha will never take root here."

In the headlong rush to fulfill Catharine's ambitions and consider ordination, there was a palpable anxiety around Poolesville during the fall and winter of 1987. Financially, things continued to be unstable. Sangha members were still paying off Catharine and

Michael's India trip, and, meanwhile, in anticipation of Penor Rinpoche's visit, new projects and costly renovations were being talked about. The temple itself had been refinanced—after the property had been appraised at one million dollars—to fund renovations and to help raise the capital for a one-hundred-thousand-dollar crystal collection from Brazil.

When students seemed concerned about finances, the cost of the crystals, and Catharine's strange disregard for money, they were told that they lacked insight and wisdom. They had Ordinary View and ordinary minds, while their gifted teacher was able to see far into the future. If it weren't for her vision, would there be a temple in Poolesville at all? "Catharine doesn't really get into limitations, and [issues like] money," said Jon Randolph. "She really doesn't compute it. But everybody else does—and usually we get stalled on it to the point where we can't even function. We become paralyzed and everything seems impossible."

Something else was beginning to strain the atmosphere in Poolesville at this time, too. Catharine and Michael seemed unhappy together, and a sense of uneasiness trickled down from their marriage to the sangha. Catharine wasn't feeling well most of the time—even after the difficult India trip she was seriously overweight. "She was always sick," said Karen Williams, "and always in bed." The students were told that they lacked merit, and this had affected Catharine's health. They were just calling themselves Buddhists; they weren't practicing deeply enough. "There was a feeling in the sangha that when we became Buddhists that we had suddenly become better people," said Eleanor Rowe. "Catharine complained that her students were acting like they'd just furnished their houses with nicer rugs. That being Buddhists enhanced us in superficial ways, that we felt *more special.*"

Catharine didn't want her students feeling special, or better. This wasn't the point of Buddhism, she said. It is a path designed to diminish the ego, not enhance it. "You don't acquire, you offer," said Eleanor. "You are always giving back, letting go. And examining your motivation and examining your mind to see what's going on, to see if you're grabbing—or having any hatred or anger."

The Tibetan Buddhist lessons on impermanence were useful at this time. Nothing remains the same, the students were reminded, and one must stay fluid and flexible. One's anchor should be planted deeply in the teachings and one's devotion to the lama. The ripples above in samsara—and the tidal shifts of emotion and worry about material things like money—are as constant as the weather changes, and as insignificant.

While the students were prodded toward greater self-examination—and to complete the four phases of Ngöndro—Catharine enrolled in a weight-loss program at a clinic in Northern Virginia and embarked on a strict diet. She slowly began to slim down and feel better, and as she did she became more consumed than ever with temple renovations and improvements to prepare for Penor Rinpoche's arrival. The grounds needed landscaping. The grass needed seeding—and somebody had better start mowing it regularly. She wanted two new altarpieces, dedicated to the goddess Tara and Sakyamuni Buddha—with elaborate sculptures of the deities, hand-sewn altar covers, and matching rice and water-offering bowls. She wanted the seventy crystals in the temple collection moved to more auspicious locations, and spotlit with overhead lights and cylinders on the floor. She also thought it was time to build a stupa. What was a Tibetan Buddhist center without one?

Most of her students had never seen a stupa except in photographs and knew even less about how to build one. But Catharine had been inspired by them in Bylakuppe and Nepal and felt strongly that they provided a focus for practice and offered potent blessings to practitioners. She chose the site of her temple's first stupa—next to the guest cottage where Penor Rinpoche would be staying. As for stupa builders, Catharine didn't wait for volunteers. Students were told, very specifically, that the lama expected them to pull their weight—and much merit could be accumulated by working on temple projects, especially building a stupa. Building a stupa was an investment for the future, and the builders would reap benefits for many lifetimes to come.

By early 1988, six months before the Tibetan's visit, every sangha member was involved in some sort of elaborate temple renovation—whether they had the time or not. Orders came through Michael in most cases. Increasingly reclusive, Catharine left the day-to-day operations of the temple to her husband as a kind of managing director. And it was the beginning of what some members came to call the Catharine Says syndrome. When Michael delivered news, it was always a little unclear exactly what Catharine's wishes were. Michael had a tendency to put a weird spin on the messages he delivered. "It always came down to, what did she *really* say?" said Karen Williams. "And what did she *really* mean?"

Jay Allen had been working for weeks on the new Sakyamuni altarpiece and had just finished nailing the altar into place when Catharine happened to appear in the prayer room. "Why is that altar on *that* wall?" she asked, startled.

"Michael said you wanted it there," Jay answered.

"*No!*" she shrieked. "*Michael got it wrong!* I wanted the Sakyamuni altarpiece on *that* wall," she said, pointing to the far south wall. "And the main altar goes there!"

Stunned into silence, Jay and the other students in the prayer room at the time quickly began plans for switching the Sakyamuni altarpiece. It would require weeks of work, they figured—several days alone pulling out the hundreds of nails Jay had just hammered in. It was an expensive alteration, too, requiring the purchase of more wood. While it might have been natural to blame Michael for the mistake, within minutes a new understanding of events came to roost in the students' minds. There was a great lesson behind the mix-up—a lesson that Catharine and Michael had perhaps devised for their benefit. It was a lesson about obedience and Correct View, and learning to follow their spiritual teacher without resistance. And rather than anger or upset about switching the altarpieces, another mood prevailed.

Stories about the great Tibetan saint Milarepa and his harsh teacher, Marpa, began to circulate. Marpa, the founder of the Kagyul lineage in the eleventh century, treated Milarepa like a slave and was forever driving him crazy with nonsensical requests. He ordered Milarepa to build towers, then tear them down, then build them again.

Marpa seemed cruel and sadistic, and at times Milarepa was near suicide.* Eventually, though, the abused student was said to

* Patrul Rinpoche, *The Words of My Perfect Teacher* (Boston: Shambhala, 1998).

have received the greatest Tibetan teachings available and, along the way, invaluable lessons in diligence, determination, surrender, and devotion. "We even started calling it the Milarepa Altar Incident," Karen Williams said. "And the altar was moved without a qualm."

She could have kept her name, Catharine Burroughs, of course. She'd only had it five or six years. But both she and Michael felt it was important that she adopt a new name to signal the changes in her life. Very briefly she called herself Pema Khandro, a name given to her when she took Refuge vows with Gyaltrul Rinpoche. Later, after a few other experiments, she opted for Ahkön Lhamo, the Refuge name Penor Rinpoche had given her. It would mark her passage to a place of prominence in Tibetan Buddhism and be a reminder of her recognition. But Ahkön Lhamo *what?* Other lamas use honorifics before or after their Tibetan names. They are rinpoches, tulkus, khenpos. How was this decided? In India, at the time of Catharine's official recognition, Michael had asked Penor Rinpoche, "What do we call her now?"

"Call her whatever you want," Penor Rinpoche said.

"She's a reincarnated lama?"

"Yes."

"But is she a rinpoche?"

"Whatever you like," Penor Rinpoche said, dismissively. "It's not my concern. Call her what you want."

He didn't explain to Michael that in Tibet and India a recognition doesn't come with a title. The title is granted by popular decision. A boy who was discovered as a reincarnated lama would often be called by his birth name—no title or mention of his tulku status—years later, in acknowledgment of many good works and teachings, of achievements made in this lifetime, he might be called rinpoche by his students and fellow lamas. As in the military, or royalty, there is a hierarchy of titles—although not quite so specifically delineated. There are all kinds of rinpoches, just as there are all kinds of generals. And in Tibetan Buddhism it is always thought best to play down status and titles. Others might greet a lama and call him "rinpoche" as a demonstration of respect and recognition of spiritual accomplishment, but when referring to oneself, or putting one's name in print, a humble title is more appropriate. Penor Rinpoche, for instance, is actually a *drubwang*, one of Tibetan Buddhism's highest titles, but he chose to be called rinpoche, a more modest epithet. At his monastery in India he was called simply Penor Rinpoche. Americans felt the need to inflate this to His Holiness—which is more commonly used when addressing the Dalai Lama.

Michael, however, toiled in ignorance of Tibetan custom. When he heard Penor Rinpoche say, "Call her whatever you want" and "It's not my concern," he didn't know enough about Tibetans to study those words for subtle hints and innuendo, for signs of underlying advice. Michael simply assumed that he was free to choose any title for Catharine, and, in a way, he was.

At first the students in Poolesville were told to call their teacher Tulku Ahkön Lhamo, but it wasn't long before they decided that was just too hard to say all day long. Another trial balloon went up. How about Ahkön Lhamo Rinpoche? Michael ordered stationery printed with the new title, but it didn't sound right to him. Most of the rinpoches he'd met were men. Could a woman be a rinpoche? The students began to make lighthearted jokes about it.

"Why couldn't we call her rinpo-chelle?"

"How about rinpochette?"

"Or rinpo*chess*?"

Michael asked a few sangha members who had been studying Tibetan if there were other options. In particular he inquired about the title Jetsun. The Dalai Lama's sister was referred to as Jetsun. And in Bylakuppe there had been a dignified old nun staying in the monastery guesthouse who was highly revered. People addressed her as Jetsunma. The name seemed more fitting, and more feminine, than rinpoche. It was a high title, too—a little splashy, not unlike Catharine herself. The new title and spiritual name finally were announced: She was Jetsunma Ahkön Lhamo and would be referred to as Jetsunma for short.

"I remember Michael running around and correcting us all," said Alana. "If we called her Catharine, if we called her Rinpoche. . . . 'She's *Jetsunma*,' he'd say. 'Jetsun-ma. Jetsun-ma. Jet-sun-ma. Let's all get used to it.' "

More important than a name or title, though, was that the students have a complete understanding of what a tulku is. It wasn't a common expression in America, and, even among Buddhists, it is only a Tibetan tradition. At Penor Rinpoche's monastery there were a great many tulkus, but that wasn't something that Catharine and Michael emphasized. Westerners tend to have a disregard for other cultures and non-Western religious practices. The center in Poolesville would never flourish if Americans couldn't see the uniqueness of Jetsunma Ahkön Lhamo or if they had doubts about the spiritual accomplishment and perfection of tulkus.

The conventional definition of a tulku is an enlightened being who has evolved beyond the cycle of death and rebirth but chosen to return to the human realm—to dwell again in samsara—as a way to help sentient beings. Michael pushed the point further and, perhaps with the best intentions, explained to students that all tulkus are "living Buddhas," which is not the usually held view. Tulkus are magical, brilliant, powerful, and all-knowing, he told them, adding that Jesus Christ was in fact a tulku.

"Jetsunma is Buddha," Elizabeth often repeated to other students. "The very definition of tulku *means* an enlightened Buddha."

"We were taught that she was a tulku, and that tulkus were the most magnificent things in the world," said Richard Dyke-man. "Tulkus walked on water, did miraculous things. That they incarnated for us, not for themselves. It wasn't until much later that I learned differently."

Along with Catharine's name change, and the instruction on the meaning of the word *tulku*, came a greater insistence on Correct View and formal displays of devotion. At other Dharma centers in the United States and India, students tended to prostrate to their teachers before receiving formal empowerments. But it was announced during a channeled teaching—Jeremiah still communicated with the students on special occasions—Jetsunma's students needed to do prostrations before their guru upon first sight of her every day.

These prostrations were not for Jetsunma, it was explained. The students bowed to her for their own benefit. It was simply a way to begin instilling Correct View, which would lead to greater devotion, which would lead to enlightenment. Prostrating was a sure way to reverse the Western tendencies of pride and arrogance. In India students automatically held their teachers in higher regard. In America this had to be taught.

It was also suggested, in a more subtle manner, that students should consider giving their teacher private cash offerings as a way to receive special blessings.

11.

Hog-Tied

FAITH AND PHILOSOPHY ARE AIR,
BUT EVENTS ARE BRASS.

—HERMAN MELVILLE

The entire sangha waited at National Airport for Penor Rinpoche's flight to arrive for his second tour of Maryland. But a thunderstorm had arrived first and caused delays. The students sank into the plastic chairs near the gate, watching the rain sheeting down beyond the windows as the flowers they'd brought began to wither. Their spirits did not droop, however. Jetsunma had reminded them that the bad weather was just another sign of the potency of His Holiness. The local gods in the skies above Washington were making a great show of noise and lightning.

When he stepped off the plane, though, Penor Rinpoche didn't appear pleased by the auspicious weather. His face seemed tight and grim. There were sixteen young monks trailing after him, as well as two attendants. And soon enough sixty or seventy of Jetsunma's students were lined up to greet him and offer their white katas for his blessing. They were surprised that His Holiness seemed a bit impatient with their scarves, their most humble prostrations, and all their grateful emotion. "He was like a short, stubby storm cloud himself," said one student, "and seemed to be gritting his teeth."

Only a few students had remained at the temple to light the smoke pots—the boughs of fresh cedar set up along the entrance to the property. And when the rains washed out the chalk drawings of the Eight Auspicious Emblems that had taken hours to sketch on the cement driveway, they were redrawn in time for the lama's dramatic arrival. The temple had rented a black limousine for him, and he rode with Jetsunma and Michael and with Gyaltrul Rinpoche, who had flown in that day from Oregon. Behind them a big burgundy-colored van had been rented for the monks.

The sun came out during the drive, the kind of sunlight that causes windshields to glare. Strange mushroom-shaped clouds appeared overhead. It was hot and harsh, and the light struck River Road with such intensity that steam began to rise. Several cars of students raced ahead in order to line the driveway to greet the lama. The smoke pots were set on fire. Baskets full of rose petals were passed from hand to hand and tossed at the lama's limousine.

His Holiness, in spite of the long flight and the delays—and that apparently grumpy mood—didn't go straight to bed. He went into the temple, to the throne that had been prepared for him. His monks scrambled to assemble the large Tibetan horns they had packed. Opening prayers were chanted, horns were blown, more flowers were produced, and after the brief ceremony and remarks, the lama retreated to his white cottage and wasn't heard from until the next day.

His entourage of young monks, however, was impossible to miss. They were loud and playful. One grabbed a skateboard belonging to Jetsunma's younger son and was seen descending the hill of the parking lot all the way to the retreat center. The rest of his colleagues began unpacking their things with great jocularity. "Who speaks English?" they were asked by a sangha member, trying to help out. All the monks pointed to the one young man who spoke none, then exploded into hysterics.

Most of Penor Rinpoche's monks were seventeen and eighteen years old. The sound of their boisterous laughter was heard each night in the newly built retreat center, where they were staying. And in the morning they were sometimes hard to rouse. Back in India monks were not allowed to sleep past 5:00 or 6:00 A.M.

"Don't let the sun shine up your *shung-lam* [ass]" is how the Tibetan expression goes. But in Poolesville the boys slept and slept. And when they weren't sleeping they were often misbehaving. It was explained later that Penor Rinpoche had brought only the naughtiest monks with him, boys he was worried about leaving behind.

The Poolesville students could barely contain their joy at Penor Rinpoche's arrival. He brought an exotic world with him, a quiet feeling of great wisdom and solidity, the assurance of spiritual patronage. It was as though the Wizard of Oz had showed up at the door. For months the students had been taught that it was an enormous blessing just to set eyes on His Holiness. If he singled out a student for conversation, or any form of contact, it was a sign of a student's good karma. Serving him in any way—cooking, cleaning, driving—was a great opportunity and a chance to accrue merit. It wasn't long before a subtle sort of competition began. Who would drive him? Who would cook his dinner, arrange the flowers on his throne, wash and prepare the bowl of fresh fruit in his cottage? Who would clean his bathroom or vacuum the carpet in his bedroom?

In India students saved pieces of hair and nail clippings of a lama to carry inside a *gau* or box or to wear in pouches around their necks. Students in Poolesville had already begun saving Jetsunma's discarded acrylic fingernails, and Elizabeth, who accompanied Jetsunma to the beauty salon, saved tufts of her cut hair. Even a discarded toilet seat from Jetsunma's house had been rescued and saved by her students as a precious relic. These relics were potent charms, it was believed, protecting students from disease and accidents, negativity and demons. Now the Poolesville students began to focus on Penor Rinpoche's bodily detritus. Would it be possible to score a lock of his hair? A piece of his fingernail? A cuticle clipping?

The excitement about His Holiness's proximity went hand in hand with nervousness and insecurity. Even Jetsunma and Michael seemed to succumb to the jitters. Students were reminded about the proper way to tie a chuba skirt and grilled about deportment.

They were told to make a display of humility when addressing His Holiness, and to do prostrations upon first seeing him in the morning. It had been easy to be in the presence of Penor Rinpoche before he had become a divinity in their eyes. Now, for many of the students, it was difficult to be physically close to him or even stand in the same room. "We were trying to do everything right," recalled Karen Williams. "And suddenly, I think Jetsunma was under a great deal of pressure to get her students in shape and the temple in shape. It was everything from how to wear a chuba correctly, and the zen, and how to practice correctly . . . it was all *form*, as the Buddhists would say. Before the teachings were all about heart and compassion. And we lost that, the first couple years. We were all trying so hard to be Buddhists and not embarrass Jetsunma in front of her teachers."

"I remember feeling stunned by His Holiness," said another student, who would eventually become ordained, "and instantly sorry that I had spent so much time sewing altar covers instead of finishing Ngöndro. When he started giving us the teachings, I felt unready for them. My mind was still gliding on the surface and not properly prepared."

The pace had been unrelenting over the last six months, and the temple projects still hadn't been completed. Even as His Holiness began to give his teachings, the twelve-week cycle of empowerments called the Rinchen Ter Dzod—never before given in the West—a group of female students were still sewing silk ruffles for the prayer room, redecorating the altars. A large new throne for Jetsunma was being built. And a crew of six students was desperately working to finish the temple's first stupa—even though Gyaltrul Rinpoche had tried several times to discourage Jetsunma from building it. "It's too ambitious!" he said. "You'll make mistakes!"

And indeed, some dramatic blunders were made. To begin with, Tom Barry had accidentally run over the stupa's ancient relics with a bulldozer and ground them irretrievably into the dirt. When Jetsunma learned what had happened, she called Tom into the temple rooms and in front of a circle of stunned sangha members screamed insults at him for fifteen minutes—explaining later that it was an effort to "purify his karma." Just about the time that Penor Rinpoche and Gyaltrul Rinpoche had arrived with replacement relics—and to reconsecrate the land where the original ones had been so inauspiciously obliterated, the Poolesville crew learned that they had made a serious miscalculation in design. The cavity of the stupa—the hollow chambers around the relics—had been made unnecessarily large. After His Holiness told them these chambers had to be filled to the brim with offerings, and not left partially empty, it cost thousands of dollars to buy more rice and beans.

Meanwhile, most of the students still hadn't completed Ngöndro—even though Penor Rinpoche had urged them to do so before his arrival. "Jetsunma told us there was more virtue in building than in doing your own practice," one student recalled. "She taught that there was even an element of selfishness in practice—it was something you did just for you." And when the teachings began, the students who were involved in stupa building and altar decoration had trouble finding time to attend them. It wasn't uncommon for Penor Rinpoche to look up and see only half the sangha in attendance, sometimes fewer.

There were gentle jokes about Jetsunma during these months. She was Marpa, a slave driver. Or she was, behind her back, Our Lady of Perpetual Motion. But mostly, from her perch above the fray, she kept her students in perpetual motion. She seemed to know instinctively what they needed—and how to heighten their devotion to her and the center. "It was organized chaos," said one student. "But it felt so good, it was like a drug." The more they poured themselves into working and building, sewing altar covers, mixing concrete, painting her throne, the more they'd feel a part of the temple, part of a family, and part of her. And when Penor Rinpoche praised the amazing growth of the Poolesville center—as, indeed, he did—the feeling of accomplishment was the entire sangha's to share. And so, as they worked, slaved, prayed, contemplated ordination, and tried desperately to finish Ngöndro—the one hundred thousand prostrations, mantras, offerings, and visualizations—their feeling of fullness grew, and the sense that their lives had meaning.

Only three years before, when Penor Rinpoche had first visited Maryland, they'd been members of a small and undistinguished New Age group, a handful of people praying for peace in a suburban basement. Now they were about to christen their large, luxurious temple Kunzang Odsal Palyul Changchub Choling—the Fully Awakened Dharma Continent of Absolute Clear Light.

They had credibility and patronage, and were on the verge of establishing a monastery. There were twenty students wishing to be ordained. Jetsunma continued to collect new names, and soon the tally came to twenty-two, then twenty-three, then twenty-four. Holly Heiss and Karen Tokarz had both decided to become nuns. And although he had loudly declared he had absolutely no interest in being a monk, Richard Dykeman—the construction worker from Michigan—while carrying an air conditioner out of Jetsunma's private quarters one day, told her he'd decided to take robes. "Why have you changed your mind?" she asked.

"Well, I can't sing," he said, referring to the monk's vow to never sing or dance for pleasure.

Jetsunma laughed. "And you sure can't dance worth a shit, either."

"Yeah," said Richard, "exactly what I was thinking."

"I guess," his lama said, "you might as well, then."

For some, the pull toward ordination was irresistible. For others, it came quietly, a strong and subtle force. What did they hope to gain? What were they about to lose? Students who had decided against ordination watched with relief—and envy—as the twenty-seven brave souls stood waiting their turn in the temple foyer, with shaved heads and malas, with eagerness and dread, numbness and shot nerves, about to take the vows. "Give me the hopeless," Jetsunma begged Penor Rinpoche. "Give me the ones who would never enter the path, give me the hardest to train."

At first Penor Rinpoche had been cautious about ordaining Americans. In the history of Tibetan Buddhism in the West, no American monk or nun had remained ordained or "kept robes." Americans tended to view the vows as fluid and temporary, as though a year or two as an ordained monk was akin to a spiritual Outward Bound experience. So when Penor Rinpoche came to

Poolesville in 1988, he warned his new tulku that if she wanted him to begin ordaining her students in the Nyingma and Palyul traditions, Jetsunma herself had better make sure it was going to stick. And if her students took vows, they had better keep them.

Penor Rinpoche held nightly meetings that summer for those who had been accepted for ordination. The teachings were meant to prepare them for ordination on a mystical and spiritual level, but he had other methods of preparation, too. Previously the members of the sangha in Poolesville had seen Penor Rinpoche only as a beneficent Buddha. But during those long August and September nights, they witnessed his wrathful side. Before teachings began, there was a hazing. Penor Rinpoche would lay into them, yelling in Tibetan, pounding the desktop of his throne.

"Why are you doing this?" he'd shout in Tibetan. "You think taking vows will make me happy? It won't. . . . You think it will make Sakyamuni Buddha happy? He's already enlightened. He doesn't need you." The prospective monks and nuns were asked to write him letters saying they would never give their robes back. When a timid woman from another Dharma center sent a letter asking if it was really true she could never give back her robes, Penor Rinpoche exploded in a rage.

Holding the letter above his head, pounding a table with his fist, his brown face turning dark red, he shouted, "How dare you ask this! Do you have to keep the vows forever? Yes, you do!"

Later that night Jetsunma asked Elizabeth to gather the ordination students for an emergency meeting. Elizabeth rounded them up in the garden behind the temple's prayer room. They stood in a half circle, waiting for a long time for their teacher to come.

Jetsunma appeared suddenly, walking quickly. She was carrying a baseball bat in her right hand. "Who wrote that letter?" she screamed. "Who?"

There was a moment of quiet. One monk was shaking visibly. Richard Dykeman said he was feeling sick to his stomach, and his hands were clenching. He hadn't realized yet that Jetsunma's baseball bat was plastic—a Wiffle bat—and not wood. Finally, the timid woman stepped forward. "I wrote the letter to His Holiness," she said.

"You aren't my student," Jetsunma said. "And if you were, I was going to beat you into a bloody pulp! This is still a very bad beginning, for all of you—to upset the mind of this wonderful lama with stupid questions. . . . Well, let me answer those questions again. These are vows you do not break. *These are vows you do not break.* If there is anyone here who thinks that these are vows that they can break—or that these are robes they can give back—I want you to back out of this ordination immediately."

In Buddhism there are ten basic vows. The first four vows—or root precepts—are considered very serious: no killing, no stealing, no sexual misconduct, no lying. These are followed by six vows—or branch precepts—that are less serious: no intoxicants (alcohol or recreational drugs, et cetera); no singing or dancing or playing music; no wearing of perfume or ornaments to beautify the body; no sitting on a high or expensive bed; no eating after midday; no touching money.

While the first seven precepts seem pretty straightforward—and the ordained in Poolesville held to them very strictly—the writings of the Vietnamese Buddhist monk Thich Nhat Hanh are sometimes used in Western monasteries to interpret the eighth. The precept against sitting on "a high or expensive bed" is really a rule against the desiring of luxury or any luxury item. And the ninth and tenth—not eating after midday, not touching money—which, if literally understood, would be nearly impossible to keep at KPC—are considered to be precepts against gluttony and the accumulation of wealth.

There are two steps to becoming fully ordained. At one's first ordination a pledge—the Getsul vow—is taken to follow the ten precepts. Usually one or two years later, when one's ordination is completed, the list of precepts grows to thirty-six prohibitions:*

1. Taking a human life
2. Killing an animal or insect

---

* This list is taken from a handbook called "Preparing for Ordination: Reflections for Westerners Considering Monastic Ordination in the Tibetan Buddhist Tradition," edited by Bhikshuni Thubten Chodron (produced by *Life as a Western Buddhist Nun*).

3. For selfish reasons, doing an action that might incidentally cause the death of an animal or insect and not caring about it (cutting grass, digging ditches)

4. While doing something for others, causing an animal or insect to die and not caring about it (splashing water where an insect might live)

5. Sexual intercourse

6. Stealing or borrowing things and not returning them (includes not paying taxes when required)

7. Claiming to have spiritual powers that one does not have

8. Accusing another ordained of transgressing a root precept when he or she has not

9. Insinuating that a monk or nun has transgressed a root precept when he or she has not

10. Causing disharmony among the sangha through untrue slander or taking sides in an argument

11. Supporting someone who has caused disharmony in the sangha

12. Making untruthful complaints and remarks that could undermine laypeople's faith in the sangha

13. Telling lies

14. Criticizing a storekeeper in the monastery of giving more to some and less to others when this is not the case

15. Insinuating that the storekeeper of the monastery has given more to some, less to others when this is not the case

16. Claiming that a fellow monastic gave a teaching in return for a little food when this isn't the case

17. Criticizing a monk or nun for transgressing a precept in the second group when this is not the case

18. Abandoning the training or rejecting the good advice of a fellow monk or nun

19. Covering vegetables with rice, or covering rice with vegetables

20. Taking intoxicants

21. Singing with self-attachment or for nonsensical reasons

22. Dancing with self-attachment or for nonsensical reasons

23. Playing music with self-attachment or for nonsensical reasons

24. Wearing ornaments
25. Wearing jewelry
26. Wearing perfumes
27. Wearing a mala like jewelry, wearing flower garlands
28. Sitting on an expensive throne
29. Sitting on an expensive bed
30. Sitting on a high throne
31. Sitting on a high bed
32. Eating after midday (exceptions: if one is ill, one is traveling, or one cannot meditate properly without food)
33. Touching gold, silver, or precious jewels, including money
34. Wearing laypeople's clothing and ornaments, or letting one's hair grow long
35. Not wearing the robes of a Buddhist monastic
36. Disrespecting or not following the guidance of one's ordination master

Monastic life is designed to allow for a deep and committed practice of Buddhism. The lifestyle is meant to undermine attachment—to family, to material things, to pleasure. The core of all these qualities is considered to be compassion. If a monk or nun develops enough compassion for others, and an understanding of the unseparateness or oneness of all living things—the nondual, as Buddhists call it—then following the precepts will make so much sense it will happen naturally and without great effort.

And by living according to the precepts a monk or nun is supposed to become ethical and trustworthy—and therefore stronger and more confident. The ordained are asked to focus on the development of four special qualities: When harmed they are asked to try not to respond by harming others. When made angry they are asked not to react with anger. When insulted or criticized they try not to respond with insult or criticism. When someone abuses or beats them they try not to retaliate.

Just before ordination there was a sense of foreboding and strange occurrences in Poolesville. A deer was seen timidly approaching the new stupa and walking around it three times. An enormous black snake was seen at the site, too, slithering in a circle. Upstairs in the temple, Karen Williams opened her closet door one morning and a swarm of bees floated out on a gust of wind. Later on, a rattlesnake was found on the second floor, too, wound around the base of a coffee table.

Students talked about rangjung, the self-arising happenings, evil in the air . . . like Elizabeth's brain tumor. It was true, they were told: Obstacles would come during ordination, and karma would quickly ripen, because of the intensity of the empowerments being transmitted, the vows being taken, and the great merit being accrued. Students were told to work hard, be careful, and do extra practices. "Everybody was on edge, nervous as heck," recalled Karen Williams. "All of us who were about to be ordained . . . our stuff was coming up, and we were so busy and tired and stressed out. Working our jobs, building a stupa, doing practice, finishing Ngöndro . . . and then there was the deer, the snake, the swarm of bees."

The young monks in Penor Rinpoche's entourage seemed particularly bothered by some of the bizarre events and gossiped about KPC among themselves. The man cooking for them, an American Buddhist who had been hired for the visit, had become certain after a few weeks in Poolesville that Jetsunma and Michael were running a cult, not a Tibetan Buddhist temple—and several of the young monks secretly began agreeing with him. One monk, Pema, kept pulling two young nuns in training aside, teasingly whispering, "Danger! Danger!"

"What?"

"Cut. Cut."

"Cut what?"

"Cut!"

"You're worried I'm going to cut myself?"

When they figured out that Pema was saying *cult*, they laughed. "Oh, you've just been talking to the cook again."

The ceremony was private, and the doors to the Dharma room were shut. Even Jetsunma was not allowed to attend the ordination of her students—having never been ordained herself. Penor

Rinpoche sat on his throne, presiding, and three students entered at a time. Altogether, there were twenty-three women and four men. They'd been prepped by the Khenpo brothers, who flew down from New York to answer questions, and by Gyaltrul Rinpoche, who'd offered a few pieces of advice about renunciate life. And they'd been prepped by Ani Marilyn, a respected older American nun from another center.

"Why do you want to become a nun?" Ani Marilyn had grilled Michelle Grissom, the waif whose mother had been a longtime student of Jetsunma's. Ani Marilyn seemed concerned that Michelle was too immature to make the decision wisely. "You're so young! You're only twenty! Are you sure you're doing the right thing?"

"I want to help sentient beings," Michelle answered, a bit automatically. Beyond this she really didn't have the words for her feelings about ordination. She had always wanted to be a nun—that was all she knew. Later, the word came down from Jetsunma, through Elizabeth: "The decision to become ordained is between you and Guru Rinpoche, and it is nobody else's business if they ask."

Part of ordination involves taking vows and donning the robes. But before all that there's a list of important questions to be answered. Penor Rinpoche asked these questions in Tibetan, and they were promptly translated by Ani Marilyn. Elizabeth Elgin was in the first group of women to be ordained, along with Deborah Larrabee and Karen Williams—and when their ordination was finished, Elizabeth pulled some of the remaining would-be nuns aside to brief them on the secret ceremony. In particular, she was worried about Michelle and two of the young Windolph sisters. They were only twenty, twenty-one, and twenty-two, respectively. "We were told no matter how strange the questions were, just answer them," recalled Michelle. Some of these questions were quite practical: One needed to be over fifteen years of age, not in financial debt, not a thief or a spy, and not mentally ill. Some were philosophical: One needed to believe in the karmic law of cause and effect and not hold non-Buddhist beliefs. Some were quite unusual: One had to say that one wasn't an animal or a spirit, or had committed matricide or patricide. Other questions were stranger still.

No explanations were provided. The novices were told just to nod their heads and respond to each question by saying *"La med,"* which in Tibetan means "No, I am not."

The three girls stood facing Penor Rinpoche with Ani Marilyn nearby. They ran through a list of twelve or thirteen questions, then:

"One is not a hermaphrodite," Ani Marilyn said, very seriously.

"La med."

"One is not a eunuch."

Michelle held back a giggle. *"La med."*

"One is not crippled."

"La med."

They continued, with great seriousness, through thirty-eight such questions. One had to claim that one wasn't from the lowest caste—wasn't a blacksmith or fisherman or an albino. One wasn't from "the Northern Continent." And then:

"One has not changed one's sex three times."

Michelle giggled openly—and one of the Windolph girls joined her. Penor Rinpoche's face remained unresponsive, then stern. The last question wasn't so funny, but in some ways it was the oddest of all.

"One does not resemble a person born from another world or continent."

"La med."

But, as Americans, they did, of course. They resembled people from another continent—and in fact they were.

Jetsunma waited in the temple foyer, greeting the nuns and monks as they emerged from the Dharma room in their new yellow robes. There were hugs and red eyes, some laughing. "I remember we were told not to show emotion during the ceremony," said Alana, "so I cried a lot afterward . . . and felt an overwhelming deep joy. It's a very powerful experience, and something inside you does change." Jetsunma called her nuns and monks by their new names. Students of Tibetan Buddhism often receive a spiritual name after taking refuge or receiving an empowerment—and new ordination names are given out, too. But at most

Dharma centers in the West, Tibetan names are rarely used. In Poolesville, though, many of the students seemed eager to follow the example of their lama and use a new name as a way to signal a change of self—and another way to make a break with old ways, old habits, and old attachments.

Janice Newmark became Rinchen. Michelle Grissom became Zomchi—and later Dechen. Catherine Windolph became Samla. Jan Hoge became Palchen. Tom Barry became Tashi.

Some didn't want Tibetan names. Roger Hill asked for a new name—but he wanted something vaguely Western that was chosen by Jetsunma. She renamed him Kamil. Some of the nuns, too, didn't like the prospect of carrying a Tibetan name and asked Jetsunma to give them a Western name. Deborah Larrabee became Rene. Angela Windolph became Sophia. Vicky Windolph became Ella. Karen Tokarz became Dara. And, for several reasons, Jetsunma was partial to the *ah* sound. It is a sacred sound to the Tibetans and was emblazoned inside the karpala of the first Ahkön Lhamo. To help her give *A-* names to her students, Michael bought a baby-naming book and made a list of names beginning with *A* for a group of special nuns. Karen Williams became Aileen. Diane Johnson became Alexandra. Maria Windolph became Arene. Judith Kreitemeyer became Ariana. Holly Heiss became Atara. And Elizabeth Elgin became Alana.

In the foyer after ordination, they gathered in their stiff robes and newly shaved heads. They shared a plainness now, and freshness, a spiritual beauty. They felt a sense of unity and oneness. And, looking into the eyes of their lama as she greeted them, they felt her boundless, unconditional love, they felt they caught a glimpse of Buddha. They had been nuns and monks before—many of them believed—in previous incarnations. And Jetsunma had been their teacher. It was an ancient connection, now renewed. But they weren't just renunciates and dedicated to the Dharma. "We were told," said one, "that we had married Jetsunma, in a way. And now we were hers forever."

People seem to remember little about September 24, 1988, but for the blaring of horns, the crashing of cymbals, the endless pounding of drums. The Dharma room was hot and crowded. Jetsunma Ahkön Lhamo's enthronement was a long and serious affair. So serious that when Gyaltrul Rinpoche tried to break the heavy mood by throwing a pillow at a newspaper reporter covering the event, everyone followed Penor Rinpoche's example and refused to laugh. The newly ordained were feeling quite strange in their huge yellow robes and emotionally drained. As they watched from the floor of the Dharma room, the exotic grandeur of the day was overpowered by exhaustion. "We all felt rearranged," said Alana, "and afterward it was like remembering a dream."

Several of the newly ordained, along with a handful of sangha members, had been up all night preparing the temple, cleaning, setting up buffet tables, arranging the trays of food for the *tsog*, or offering. Still others had labored over a last-minute painting of Jetsunma's new throne—the sangha's gift to their lama in honor of her enthronement. Jetsunma herself had been up most of the night, too, worried that she wouldn't be able to blow a conch shell horn properly—for the next day's ceremony—and practicing until her lips were swollen.

A crown had been brought from India for Jetsunma—it was large and heavy, made of copper and painted. At the beginning of the ceremony, a few monks from Penor Rinpoche's retinue tried to tie the crown on Jetsunma's head, but it wouldn't sit right on top of her thick mane, and the ties kept getting caught in her hair. She smiled good-naturedly, and a bit nervously. Penor Rinpoche sensed her embarrassment and said, "We don't usually have to put crowns on hair like that." A TV camera trained on her face belonged to one of Ani Aileen's colleagues from NBC, and others from local TV stations crowded together off to the side. *The New York Times* ran an article the next day. *The Washington Post* would later run a photograph of Jetsunma under her awkward crown.

A multicolored string was stretched between Jetsunma's throne and Penor Rinpoche's to signify the connection between them. Elaborate offerings were described by the Tibetan, and Jetsunma was instructed to visualize them. The sangha sat silently with katas, and at the end of Jetsunma's visualization they were instructed to approach her, one by one, and drop their white scarves at the base of her throne. At almost all other Tibetan Buddhist ceremonies, a student hands one of these white scarves to a lama and the lama gives it back, putting the kata around the student's neck. It represents a blessing the lama gives to a student—and the scarf is usually returned. But in this ceremony the students left their scarves with Jetsunma until there was a large pile of white scarves, like a mound of snow. Blessings to her, from her students. Blessings upon blessings upon blessings. Some sangha members cried when they saw the pile. There was their beloved Jetsunma, her face round, her eyes warm, her mouth closed and holding in some emotion.

Later on there was lama dancing, a Tibetan tradition in which monks dance to horns and drums in ceremonial costumes and giant masks—a sacred ritual dance, the only kind a monk is allowed to do. There were prayers, too, of course, and a huge spread of food outside. Lights had been mounted on wires above the grass. And as the hours went on, the emotion in Jetsunma's face, which had been so poignant at times during the ceremony, began to drain away. "She just looked stunned," said one nun.

And perhaps she was. The summer of 1988 had been exhilarating but difficult, and Jetsunma hadn't been protected from hard times. She wasn't herself that summer. She seemed preoccupied. "She'd been a nobody her whole life," said Richard Dykeman, "and now she was going to be somebody. She was going to be acknowledged in front of the whole world. She was desperate, and I sensed that desperateness in her."

For the first time since her childhood Jetsunma found herself governed by others, worrying about pleasing others, and subjected to male authority. Michael had always been pliable, willing, cooperative—almost too much so. But Penor Rinpoche was another story. Repeatedly it seemed he had tried to humiliate Jetsunma during his visit. He had asked the ordained to circumambulate the entire temple grounds every afternoon—the custom at his monastery in India—and for some reason he'd made Jetsunma walk at the end of a line. She'd tried so hard to condition her students to be respectful of her and devout. Why did she have to walk at the end of the line? At times she worried that His Holiness was trying to break her, dominate her—or perhaps he didn't like her. He seemed critical. He seemed very gruff. And he didn't refer to her as Jetsunma—only Ahkön Lhamo.

Gyaltrul Rinpoche had also been critical of her during the weeks leading up to her enthronement. In the past he'd been so upbeat, so goofy and supportive. Now he seemed more difficult, almost as though on behalf of His Holiness. He'd been horrified to learn from Kunzang Lama, one of Penor Rinpoche's attendants, that electric bug zappers were being used on temple grounds. "But we're Buddhists! We can't kill!" he'd said. Jetsunma had prayer flags put next to the zappers—as a way to offset the bad karma from killing the insects—but one night it was discovered that the electric cord had been cut.

Gyaltrul Rinpoche had yelled at Jetsunma one day, when she had arrived two hours late for an event and kept people waiting. "How dare you make anybody wait two hours for you!" he shouted. "Why don't you come down a notch! You're too arrogant and proud! You need some humility!"

On another occasion he said, "You think this throne is a privilege, but it's not. It's a prison. The whole world will be watching you!"

When *The Washington Post* ran a story by staff reporter Don Oldenburg in which Jetsunma was referred to as a living Buddha, it was Penor Rinpoche who became enraged. He ordered the students out of the Dharma room the morning the article appeared and locked the doors. Sitting on his throne, in front of Gyaltrul Rinpoche and a few others, he shouted at Jetsunma. "Are you teaching your students that you are Buddha?"

Jetsunma shook her head.

"You think because you are a tulku that you are enlightened?"

She shook her head again, and her eyes filled with tears.

"There isn't anybody enlightened within one hundred miles of this place!" the lama said. "Including me and Gyaltrul Rinpoche. Are you telling me that you are enlightened and we're not? *That you have more realizations than we do?* Then I'm going to leave. You don't need me here. Because if you are enlightened, you don't need anybody!"

"His face was red," Jetsunma recalled years later, "and his temples were throbbing, and he said, 'How could you disappoint me this way?' "

Michael jumped in. "This is my fault," he tried to interject. "There's been a misunderstanding." But Penor Rinpoche ignored him and turned to Jetsunma again.

"If you ever call yourself a living Buddha, it would be a serious mistake!" he said. "This is incorrect view; your students will go to Vajra Hell, and if you continue this sort of thing, I'll never come back!"

Jetsunma and Michael told the lama that he had misunderstood the newspaper article. Jetsunma hadn't referred to herself as a living Buddha, somebody else had. And the reporter had clearly misinterpreted the remark. "I cried and cried and cried," Jetsunma remembered. "Don't ever claim to be enlightened!" Penor Rinpoche told her. "You are not enlightened! None of us should claim this! Even the Dalai Lama doesn't say he's enlightened!"

Afterward, Jetsunma shared some of her difficulties with her students. "Teachers will test you," she said. "You wouldn't believe how much." She shook her head, and her students were sympathetic. They had felt tested, too, in the last few months. Penor Rinpoche had accused her of arrogance, she told them, and made her feel "young and raw and vulnerable. I was crying and sobbing," she said, "and he threatened to leave and all this horrible stuff." She told the students that His Holiness had "purified obstacles" from her life with his wrath. But later on she threw herself at Gyaltrul Rinpoche's feet in distress. "Oh, don't worry," he had told her. "Sometimes lamas will test you. . . . What he said—all those things—they aren't true, are they?"

"You know," Jetsunma assured him, "they aren't."

The worst of the storm passed in time, but it never seemed entirely over. The tiptoeing and confusion continued. At dinner one night Penor Rinpoche looked up from the table and said to his new tulku, "How did you get that title, *Jetsunma*? It's higher than mine."

Michael and Jetsunma froze and shot each other an embarrassed look.

"Should we not use it?" she asked.

Penor Rinpoche looked at his lap.

"Should we call her something else?" Michael asked.

Finally, Penor Rinpoche shrugged his shoulders and said, "Well, it's *your* karma."

Others might have heard the not so subtle suggestion buried beneath the shrug. Others might have run out and changed their names immediately—to avoid causing conflict, to avoid making trouble, to avoid being controversial. Indeed, something more humble and less flashy might have been more appropriate. But Ahkön Lhamo kept the title Jetsunma, and in time it became her—and belonged to her—an emblem of her aspirations and achievements, her ambition and unrest, too. The Tibetans never stopped asking about it, but eventually even they became resigned and philosophical.

"How do you feel?" Ani Aileen asked her guru the day after enthronement.

Jetsunma sighed a very long sigh. "Hog-tied," she said. "I feel hog-tied."

Part Three

The
Consorts

12.

Dinner with Jetsunma

It was a few weeks after the stupa blessing in December—and nearly Christmas—when I went to take Jetsunma to dinner. She lived in a converted barn that had been built for her by the students in 1993. It was tucked behind the temple in a place that seemed secluded although it really wasn't. Strangely enough, in all the months I'd been coming out to Poolesville, I had never noticed the building or even been too curious about it. Jetsunma had become such a mysterious figure to me—a phantom—that it didn't seem possible she lived anywhere but on some majestic hilltop, far from ordinary life.

I pulled up to her house and shut off the headlights. The large brownish building was decorated with white Christmas lights and two big stars on the roof. Some colored lights had been draped over the bushes.

Her older son, Ben, answered the door, and invited me in. Like his younger half brother, Christopher, he was tall and beautiful and had a confident air. He was in his midtwenties, and his hair was short and black and slicked down with some kind of shiny gel. He wore tight jeans and an earring in one of his ears. "Jetsunma is upstairs getting ready," he said. "She said to tell you she'd be down soon." As he disappeared around a corner, I took my coat off and dropped into an overstuffed sofa in the living room.

It was a cozy space, a comfortable cave of brown tones and soft velveteen and wall-to-wall carpeting. A large Christmas tree stood off to the side, with twinkling lights and wrapped presents underneath. In her students' homes the walls often displayed colorful mandalas, maps of Buddhas in their perfect universes, and on the tabletops there were little seated Sakyamunis and Amitabhas. But Jetsunma seemed to have created at least one Buddha-free zone.

I realized I was nervous. I had always prided myself on my ability to remain calm as a journalist, but I'd found myself a bit unhinged by Jetsunma lately. Since our lunch at Hunter's Run in the fall, she'd met me in the Dharma room a few times for interviews, and I'd seen her at ceremonies and teachings. Yet despite her continual warmth and friendliness to me, I'd noticed as the months had passed and I learned more about her, that, rather than feeling closer to her and more comfortable, I grew less so. For one thing, I always worried that I wasn't being respectful enough. Her students seemed so kind and thoughtful, and moved gracefully through the temple rooms, and when they began bowing before Jetsunma as she walked by, or prostrating themselves on the floor—even her children prostrated to her every morning—it felt strange to be the only one in the room who was not bowing, or prostrating, or offering her scarves. Others had revealed they felt awkward around her, too.

"We used to be friends and, like, went to dinner and *stuff*," Sherab had said to me about Jetsunma. "We really enjoyed each other's company. But once I became her student, I had trouble. I had terrible tulku trouble. I got neurotic, bitten by the protocol bug or something. How do I act? What do I do now? That can happen to you in this place. It's a mind thing. Your mind gets tight and reactive. Instead of being like, *Ahhh, tulku, a wonderful presence of enlightenment in the world, enthroned in my heart,* I was like a rabbit in the headlights."

"What you see, when you see Jetsunma," said Alana, "is simply a reflection of your own mind. That's what a tulku is, a reflection, a perfectly clear mirror."

Or a hall of mirrors. I felt increasingly lost in Jetsunma's company and unsure of myself. Sherab was right. It was a feeling of tightness and mental constriction. There was also a feeling of impotency. Talking to her students over the past months, and hearing their testimonials of devotion, had had a bizarre effect on me. Rather than seeming like some beneficent goddess of mercy—the woman who was leading Westerners out of the wilderness—Jetsunma was quickly becoming something of a monster in my eyes. She seemed to dwell like Count Dracula, or Kurtz in *Apocalypse Now*, in an eccentric kingdom of her own creation where the rules of conventional society didn't apply. She communicated with entities nobody else could see. She traveled to galaxies no telescope had yet found. She spoke in spirits' voices. She made predictions based on dreams. She looked up at the sky, at rainbows and mushroom-shaped clouds, and said they were messages from the universe. One could make a list of these things or put them to paper—as I would have to do one day—and nothing would add up, nothing could be proven. Perhaps it was all smoke and mirrors, hocus-pocus, the shenanigans of a great con.

But there were facts, and as they began emerging from the haze around Jetsunma—separating from the myths, past lives, dreams, and other uncertain ephemera—I remained just as fascinated by her. She had a lunatic determination, a sense of mission. What drove her? Why are some people born with the ability—or imagination and confidence—to invest themselves so completely in the unseen world? All of her channeling, psychic consultations, predictions, and spiritual exorcisms. Little by little she had built something tangible from the invisible. "A teacher calls her students to her," Alana had once told me—and indeed they had come, drawn to Jetsunma as though she had her own gravitational force. Once they were in her orbit, she pushed them, pressed them. She changed them. They paid more attention to their health, their conduct, their morals, their *character.* She had them praying in shifts that went on twenty-four hours a day. She had them building altars, cleaning offering bowls, pouring concrete, and prostrating one hundred thousand times to complete the first phase of Ngöndro.

The students said they were practicing Tibetan Buddhism, but how many times had they saved the planet from space invaders? How many negative entities had been pacified? Their endeavors seemed laughable—or insane—but when I spoke to Jetsunma or heard her give a teaching, there seemed to be no more reasonable, practical person alive.

Afraid that my judgment was skewed, I'd even dragged my skeptical boyfriend out to Poolesville one Sunday to hear Jetsunma teach. He sat rapt through a two-hour teaching. "Oh, there's no question about it," he said later. "All those Americans with shaved heads and robes running around trying to be Tibetan are annoying, but she's got it—whatever it is. She's incredible."

Tibetan Buddhists believe that everybody has a mandala or universe—circles of activity and energy and perception. There is an outer mandala or display, which is one's appearance or apparent everyday reality. There is an inner mandala, one's quality of mind, one's energy and relative nature. And one's secret mandala relates to an ultimate reality or truth—it is very simple and direct but also the most difficult to comprehend. I wondered what Penor Rinpoche saw when he looked at Jetsunma. Does wisdom itself have an energy that could be seen when she walked into a room?

And what had drawn him to her little brick rambler in Kensington ten years before, on his first trip to America, and then caused him to proclaim her a tulku? It had been an unusual step for a conservative man like Penor Rinpoche to take, and a controversial one. Jetsunma was the first Western woman to become a tulku in the male-centered religion of Tibetan Buddhism. "His Holiness has said that he meets tulkus in India quite often," Alana had told me. "But he doesn't recognize them. They aren't ready yet." Wib had suggested something similar. "There are probably bodhisattvas all over, and we just don't know it. Some poets, rock musicians, philosophers . . . who knows? They don't all become teachers and set up monasteries."

I heard footsteps and looked up. Jetsunma was standing by

the door with her daughter, Atira. The girl was seven and had the same wavy dark hair as Jetsunma, but her skin was paler and dotted with light freckles. She seemed, as Alyce Zeoli must have at her age, precocious and self-assured. Jetsunma and I hugged hello, and we discussed the Christmas tree. "Were you surprised I had one?" Jetsunma asked. "As a Buddhist, it's just hard to know what to put on top."

"A star?"

"Doesn't really belong there anymore," she said.

"An angel?"

"*Nahhh . . .*" She scrunched up her nose and made a face. "That wouldn't work, either." She bent down, looked into Atira's eyes, and said good night, then walked over to a closet in the hall and pulled out a long black leather coat. It was then that I noticed she was wearing a blue-gray knit suit—with baggy trousers and a long jacket—which was strikingly similar to the one I was wearing. And when I looked down at her feet, I saw she had on the exact pair of thick-soled brown Doc Marten boots that I had worn. A perfect mirror.

"Hey! I knew we were sisters," she said. "We've got the same Docs!"

By the time we walked to my car, it had begun to rain lightly. And I wondered aloud if this was a good sign. "It could be," Jetsunma said, "and, according to my astrological chart, I have a very auspicious meeting with a woman today. *That has to be you.*"

The dinner, like every encounter with Jetsunma, had been an enormous hassle to arrange. Her private phone number had remained private, and her calendar seemed crowded with mysterious events. For a woman who rarely left the temple grounds, except to visit the acupuncturist, the chiropractor, the homeopath or hairstylist, she was awfully busy. Wib still called regularly, to ask how things were going and brief me on new developments at the temple. As soon as the stupa had been blessed, Jetsunma had gotten her students into high gear again. There were so many changes, it was hard to keep up.

Lately Wib kept mentioning something called the Mandarava

recognition, so I asked about it. The year before, 1994, a Tibetan terton named Kusum Lingpa had visited the temple and apparently been so impressed with Jetsunma that quite out of the blue he'd declared her a reincarnation of Mandarava, a consort of Guru Rinpoche or Padmasambhava, the Indian saint responsible for bringing Buddhism to Tibet. Kusum Lingpa was a funny guy, unpredictable and intense, and something of a crazy yogi. Being a terton, or treasure revealer, meant that Kusum Lingpa was capable of uncovering the hidden wisdom of early masters—and the teachings came to him as revelations, often arising spontaneously into his mind. One of these revelations came in the form of a poem to Jetsunma, which Kusum Lingpa wrote upon arriving on the temple grounds in Poolesville. In the poem he referred to her as an *emanation* of Mandarava.

An emanation is a bit different from a strict reincarnation of a person. There are actually several ways of being a tulku, and various methods of being reborn. A great lama sometimes returns to earth with exactly the same personality intact—with similar tastes and attitudes and talents. Other times a great lama simply lends "blessings" to a person—and passes along a few traits or *qualities*—this was the kind of tulku Jetsunma was, Penor Rinpoche eventually told me in an interview. To be blessed in such a way makes you a blessing tulku. And then there are emanations. Wib explained to me that it is possible for tulkus to spread out their qualities and become reborn as several people at once; each one of these is considered an emanation.

Even though it had been a year since Kusum Lingpa's visit, his revelation was only now having an impact on Jetsunma, according to Wib. She had just gotten used to the idea of being Ahkön Lhamo, and now the news of this second recognition—even though it had not come from as revered a source as Penor Rinpoche, and it hadn't been roundly accepted or confirmed within Tibetan Buddhist circles—was just beginning to sink in. She felt it held an important clue to her identity. "She's been considering this recognition a great deal, lately," he told me, "just sitting with this news a bit more deeply."

I looked up Mandarava in my reference books and found her

easily. She was a very glamorous figure on the Tibetan Buddhist stage and loomed much larger than Ahkön Lhamo, who didn't seem to be mentioned in any of the books I'd found. Mandarava was "a peerless princess" from the kingdom of Zahor, "who could find no partner worthy of her beauty and intellect," according to one nineteenth-century scholar.* She was sixteen when she met the great Padmasambhava and became determined to become his disciple. In protest the king of Zahor had his daughter thrown into a pit of thorns and had Padmasambhava burned alive on a pyre of sandalwood. When the king came to inspect the damage, he found that the fire had become a clear lake. And in the middle of the lake, sitting on an open lotus flower, were Padmasambhava and his consort, looking "cool and fresh."†

The couple moved to a cave in Nepal called Maratika, practiced the yoga of longevity and achieved immortality. Later in her life Mandarava became renowned as a single mother, the queen of *siddhas*, or saints, and had numerous followers.

In light of her meditations on the meaning of the Mandarava recognition, Jetsunma was now considering a second trip to India in the spring of 1996. Wib told me that she wanted to visit with His Holiness, of course, but, more important, she planned to make a pilgrimage to the pit where Mandarava's father had thrown her. She wanted to visit Maratika Cave, too—even though it was in a remote location that required a three-day backpacking trip with sherpa guides. Wib explained that by returning to these places where she had dwelt in a past life, Jetsunma would be able to "connect with Mandarava's mindstream," as he put it, and feel Mandarava's spirit much more alive inside her. He added that Jetsunma hoped I'd join her—a prospect that both excited me and filled me with a strange dread.

"We're already beginning to do a little fund-raising for the trip," Wib said, and I sighed inwardly. I wondered how the temple

---

* L. Austine Waddell, *Tibetan Buddhism: With Its Mystic Cults, Symbolism and Mythology* (New York: Dover, 1972).
† Yeshe Tsogyal, *The Lotus-Born: The Life Story of Padmasambhava* (Boston: Shambhala, 1993).

stayed afloat. When I expressed sympathy to Wib—assuming he'd be pushed to find the donors—I was surprised to discover that he wasn't worried about how to pay for the India trip, or even how to pay the mortgage.

"Ladyworks is the thing I'm focusing on now."

"Ladyworks?"

Ladyworks was the other subject that Wib had tended to bring up in recent weeks. Sometimes I found the conversational shift from Mandarava's pit to Jetsunma's invention of a hair-conditioning gel cap a bit dizzying, but I had grown used to—and looked forward to—just this sort of wild twist in our talks. Wib and I had become friends over the months, and he knew that I counted on him to keep me informed. The Ladyworks business needed a boost of two to three hundred thousand dollars in order to "get it off the ground," he confessed. I found this amount staggering. Where on earth would it come from? I was fascinated by how the students at KPC, with Jetsunma's guidance and blessing, were always expanding beyond their means and getting further into debt. Meanwhile, the stupa was still in need of landscaping, benches, and an asphalt road. Not to mention the gold leaf.

I suspected that Eleanor Rowe would be hit up for capital, but there had to be others on the sidelines willing to hand over their extra cash. Wasn't it one thing to give money to support a Buddhist temple and another thing entirely to give it to a fledging hair care business? The hair-conditioning cap was already for sale in the Sharper Image catalog for one hundred dollars—I'd sent one to my mother for Christmas—but Wib said if the temple were going to make any money on the invention, it needed to be selling them directly by mail order. He sounded a bit beleaguered, and tired, when he talked about it, despite his efforts to seem upbeat.

"You can't sit around worrying about money," he said. "Money has always been our problem—not our problem, our *challenge*." Buddhists like to be positive. "And it looks like we have to make a second infomercial."

"You've made an infomercial?" I asked.

"Yeah, and it had some incredible testimonials in it, but it hasn't tested well."

"And you're making another?"

"We're still deciding whether Jetsunma will be in this one or not."

"Jetsunma? She's *in the infomercial?*"

"That hasn't been decided yet."

"Not a good idea, if you ask me," I blurted, unable to contain myself.

"Really?" Wib sounded surprised by my reaction. "There was some thinking that it would be a blessing for people just to see her on TV and make a connection."

We wrangled about this for several minutes. This phenomenon of *making a connection* seemed to be a Tibetan Buddhist favorite, but it was something I had never fully appreciated. Wherever Jetsunma went, whatever Jetsunma did—even the most routine errands and banal encounters—was thought to bring benefit to the world. If people saw her on TV, they might make a connection with her that would allow them, somehow, to meet her in a future life and step onto "the path." Frankly, just proselytizing seemed simpler. But Buddhists don't believe in applications of direct pressure.

Connection or not, it seemed a low bow to marketing and commercialism for a spiritual leader to be selling a hair care product in an infomercial on TV. But this point of view didn't get anywhere with Wib. He kept raising the benefits of her appearance—and how the infomercial guy at a production company in Northern Virginia seemed to think Jetsunma was telegenic—until I got the distinct feeling that Jetsunma herself was pushing for it.

Wib was full of good intentions, but I began to suspect one could be too full of them. He seemed foggy, and lacking in critical judgment. There are a number of places where Tibetan Buddhism and conventional wisdom will never meet, and, when forced to choose between the two, Wib stuck with the Tibetan Buddhist perspective until the bitter end. To Wib's way of thinking, every single action of Jetsunma was a manifestation of goodness. All her ideas and intentions were above reproach. She was a pure being, a living Buddha. Whatever decisions she made were unassailable.

"Well," I said, finally, "if she wants to be in the infomercial, you can't really argue with her, can you?"

"It's not a matter of whether she *wants* to be in it," he explained. "It's what she decides will be of the most benefit. Selling the hair-conditioning caps may have nothing to do with it."

As for dinner with Jetsunma, it continued to hang in the air for another week or so. The date was moved twice, because of her health. And deciding on the location required more phone calls. "She likes sushi, Thai, and Italian food," Wib told me. "And sometimes she likes to sit in the bar and have a drink before dinner." It was finally decided that we would go to the Normandy Farm Inn, a large country French restaurant in Potomac.

"Pick her up at her house at seven," Wib called to remind me, the day before. "And be on time."

The atmosphere inside Normandy Farm Inn seemed flat next to the presence of Jetsunma herself. It was a comfortable old shoe of a restaurant, the kind of spot that Potomac families went to on the night the country club didn't serve dinner. I was pretty sure that Jetsunma's long black leather coat was the only one that had been checked at the door. And that she was the only tulku in the room.

We sat down at a table and ordered a couple of glasses of Merlot. We chitchatted a bit, about the book, how my interviews were going, and which of her students I'd talked to. I was entirely free to talk to any of them—if the student was willing—and Jetsunma always seemed to enjoy hearing about which ones I'd chosen to see and what I thought. When some names came up, she was critical. It always felt a little like gossiping.

When I said I'd liked talking to Sangye Dorje about the stupa, she beamed proudly. When I mentioned that I'd enjoyed getting to know Alana—and observed that the students seemed afraid of her—Jetsunma smiled again. "And they should be!" And when I said that I'd really come to like Sherab most of all, Jetsunma almost couldn't contain her joy. "She's great, isn't she? We used to be really good friends. Did you know that?"

I nodded that I did.

"How we got together is a pretty incredible story."

I wasn't sure I knew the details, I said. But I was going to be seeing Sherab in a couple days and I'd ask.

"I miss her company so much," Jetsunma said. "You know, I can't really hang out with the nuns. For one thing, there's all these things they can't do . . ." She lifted her wineglass and shrugged. "And it wouldn't be fair for me to talk personally with them, like girlfriends."

After we ordered the same thing for dinner—filet mignon—Jetsunma produced an envelope from her purse. She had brought old family pictures for me to look over. There was a picture of her in Brooklyn as a very young girl, sitting on Santa's lap. In another snapshot she was wearing a funny Easter hat and her dress had a tiny bow tie. There were pictures of her mother, Geraldine. "I always thought she looked like Loretta Young," Jetsunma said.

I thought of Brooklyn and the other stories she had told me about: the cigarette burns and bruises, the way she had described how skin turns spongy after a beating, and the red turns to black, then green, and finally yellow. I looked down at the pictures scattered next to my elbow. I looked at the little girl on Santa's lap. Her wide-set, dark eyes had the same twinkle, the same wisdom, and the same sadness as the eyes of the woman across the table from me. It was impossible to imagine how someone could hit her.

"You look like Atira here," I said, tapping on one photo.

"People always say that," she said—then paused. "But you knew that Atira isn't my natural daughter?"

"No," I said, a bit embarrassed.

"Do you know who Ani Catharine Anastasia is?"

Catharine Anastasia was one of the nuns I'd met that night at Tara Studios, working on the stupa garlands. I remembered she was a quiet woman with a plump face and watery blue-green eyes. I suddenly recalled the story I'd heard about her.

"Former drug addict? Homeless? Lived under a bridge?"

Jetsunma nodded and began to explain that before Catharine Anastasia became a nun her name was Jalee. She was single, had been off drugs for a while, and had been coming to Poolesville for nearly two years for teachings. In the fall of 1987 she came to see Jetsunma privately to say that she was pregnant. Her former boyfriend was the father, but they had no plans to marry.

Jetsunma was very happy for Jalee at first, she said. "Oh that's wonderful, just wonderful," Jetsunma told her.

But Jalee didn't seem too excited. "No, it's not," she said. Jetsunma thought she could understand why Jalee might be hesitant to become a mother. "She'd come so far—really, it was unbelievable how well she was doing," Jetsunma said to me. "Maybe being a mother was one thing too much." She told Jalee that she should make arrangements to give the baby up for adoption. Again, Jalee didn't seem too excited. She felt if she gave birth to a baby, Jetsunma said, "she'd have to keep it.

"I told her," Jetsunma recalled, " 'Maybe you should keep it then.' "

But Jalee shook her head, according to Jetsunma. " 'I'd rather have an abortion,' she said.

"So I told her," Jetsunma continued, " 'Look, I don't favor abortion. I could never kill something that grew in my body. To quote a comedian I heard on Comedy Central, If a shoe came out it would still be mine. I could literally never do that.' "

Jalee still seemed unconvinced, Jetsunma said. "Look," Jetsunma told her, "to a Buddhist a human rebirth is very precious. And this child may have used up all its merit just for a chance to be born. Don't you think this child needs a chance? If not with you, then a chance with someone else? It earned this."

Jalee remained quiet. "She couldn't give up a baby," Jetsunma said to me at dinner, "but she was able to have an abortion. This just didn't make sense to me. So finally, I had to get kind of heavy with her. I said, 'Look, it's like this: Terminate this child's life—kill this unborn child—*and I cannot be your teacher anymore.*' "

This had some impact. Her choice, as Jetsunma put it to me, "was now between what was convenient for her and me being her teacher. Well, she chose me. And she went ahead and arranged for the baby to be adopted through an agency."

As Jetsunma remembered it, in March 1988, when Jalee gave birth to a girl, Jetsunma went to the hospital to bless the infant before she was given up to the new parents. "So I went to bless this baby," she said, "thinking that was my lamalike duty—and I take the baby, hold her up, and I get ready to bless her. She was ten pounds and two ounces. She had these beautiful round cheeks, this little apple head. She was beautiful, *just beautiful.* And the minute I saw her, *I knew she was a Buddhist.*"

Jetsunma pounded on the dinner table between us. "I knew it! I mean, to the depth of my being, I knew this child had practiced Dharma. I knew it! To the *depth of my being*, I knew it!

"So I said to Jalee, 'Look, I don't know how to tell you this, but *we can't let her go.*' "

Jalee was stunned. "What? You're kidding," she said.

"I'm not. This kid has very strong karma with the path. She needs to practice. It's her right to practice."

While Jalee tried to wangle out of her adoption deal, Jetsunma went back to the temple and called a sangha meeting to ask if any of the students would be willing to take the baby. Several parents came forward—Wib and Jane, Ted and Linda Kurkowski, Bob and Carol Colacurcio. "I also put my name on the list," said Jetsunma. "I thought, Well, I could afford another child, and I could raise her in the Dharma. I'm motherly, and I'd take in every lonely baby if I could. I'm just like that. But . . . frankly, I wasn't all that excited about it."

The next day Jetsunma went back to the hospital with the list of names. "You would take her?" Jalee said, shocked.

"Yeah, I think so," Jetsunma said. "But it's your decision."

The baby was brought in again, to be fed, and Jalee told the nurses to hand her to Jetsunma. "And it was something out of a movie. I mean, they hand her to me, and this baby just opens her eyes and looks right dead up at me, which newborns never do. She looks up at me, and I am locked into her eyes. I'm locked into her. And it's like nothing could have broken that bond. I don't know how to really explain it to you . . .

"But I looked into her eyes and I immediately start crying," Jetsunma said. "And I said to Jalee, 'My God! This is my daughter! This is my daughter!' I was so happy, and I couldn't believe it, and I said to Jalee, 'Forget that list—I'm taking her!' I'm like, This is an executive decision! She's mine! And I told Jalee that she would always be a part of this baby's life. She could watch over her. She could see for herself that she was happy and well fed and well cared for. 'She won't want for anything, I promise you,' I told her. 'She will be raised as I would raise a child. . . . And Jalee was just crying and crying, beside herself with happiness."

After Jetsunma finished her story, I sat quietly for a moment, eating my dinner. They left their husbands, left their homes. They asked her where to live, whom to marry. They gave her their children to bless, and name. They gave her money, their time, their devotion. Once they turned toward her, nothing was ever the same. Jalee gave her a baby and then became a nun the next summer, shaved her head and took the vows and changed her name . . . the way the others did, scores of them. And never looked back. At the time it never seemed like Buddhism was pulling them, or Dharma, the teachings. It was her, all her. But what was the difference?

Did they worship her? *Worship* is not really a word that Buddhists use. They talk instead about devotion and Correct View. Wib had told me a story about himself once that spelled this out pretty clearly. In 1988 he had sent Jetsunma a letter—a routine self-appraisal that students did several times a year. In the letter he confessed that he hadn't been a good student lately. He felt that he'd been screwing up. He'd had some anger in his heart—and felt he had broken *samaya*, his pledge of loyalty to her, several times. He was stunned when Jetsunma responded with a note saying that Wib was "very tough to teach" and she didn't feel up to the job—that maybe he should "consider" studying with Gyaltrul Rinpoche in Oregon.

"She put it so kindly," Wib said, "but I was devastated. Really. And I immediately took her letter and went to the temple. And I remember that Jetsunma was sitting on a swing and holding Atira, and I was so devastated, my knees buckled. I just begged her and begged her. *'Please, please, tell me what I can do. Please be my teacher.'* " Distraught, he began crawling toward her on the grass and sobbing. To spare her the intensity of his emotion, Wib said he finally went away to compose himself.

Wib told me that Jetsunma was very kind to him afterward and took him back as a student. There was a proper way to treat one's teacher, she told him, a way to hold a lama in one's heart. And it led to enlightenment. Wib's response had been appropriate, she told him, and he shouldn't feel ashamed or humiliated. "She said it was such a good sign, such a good response—a sign of deep devotion to her," said Wib. Through the years Jetsunma had often told rooms of students the story about Wib crawling on the grass and begging her to be his teacher. "I'm glad," said Wib, "that other students have learned from it."

It was hard to know what to think when I heard that story. And it was hard to know what to think when I had lunch with Ani Catharine Anastasia one day, to ask for her account of giving up Atira to her lama. Huge tears began dropping from her eyes as she revealed how hard it had been, and how much, still, she ached about what she had lost when she lost her daughter.

Even more painful, it seemed, was the fact that Jetsunma's version of what transpired between them is not how Catharine Anastasia remembers it. The nun wanted to explain, very carefully, that she was thrilled to give her baby to Jetsunma to raise—it was a great blessing to make this kind of offering to your guru—but she would have been happy to raise Atira herself. "It's true that I didn't want a baby at the time. I didn't think I could provide financially for it—and I mistakenly believed it would prevent me from pursuing the path. Little did I know it *was* my path."

When Catharine Anastasia met with Jetsunma to tell her she was pregnant, she sought only guidance. She does not remember insisting on having an abortion. She remembers asking, "Should I keep this baby or put it up for adoption?" She also wondered if Jetsunma could "somehow magically pray the baby to its next life and make it okay to have an abortion."

I asked Catharine Anastasia how she reconciles herself with this misunderstanding. "I just do," she said. "There is really only one version of this story. Whatever Jetsunma told you is the real version. It's the only one that matters. Whatever I remember is just my experience, and only my experience."

People outside the temple had often asked me what I thought of Jetsunma. My friends and family and colleagues in journalism all seemed very interested. "Do you think she's *the real thing?*" a newspaper editor once pointedly asked.

"How would I know?" I answered. "The only thing that counts is that somebody came along—one of the most revered lamas in Tibetan Buddhism—and said that she is."

And later, when I learned there was a debate within the Tibetan Buddhist community about whether tulkus are divine beings, and incapable of corruption, I continued to feel the same way. It wasn't up to me, a journalist, to decide if Alyce Zeoli was really the reincarnation of Ahkön Lhamo or Mandarava. It wasn't up to me to decide if she had truly been at Christ's side when he died or once ruled civilizations on distant galaxies. Nor did it matter to me then whether she could, as she claimed, follow students into the bardo at the time of death and help them to "transfer their consciousness" to an auspicious rebirth—or directly to Amitabha's Pure Land and enlightenment. These matters were solely the concern of her students and the venerable elders of Tibetan Buddhism, I decided. It was Penor Rinpoche who protected her from criticism—and kept her in her job. And, presumably, if something went awry it was Penor Rinpoche she'd have to answer to. He'd elbow her along in the proper way. He'd be tough on her, wrathful and gruff—the way he was during the summer of her enthronement.

But what if she just decided to stop listening to him? Who would she answer to then?

On our ride back to the temple, the rain clouds sat so low in the sky, and it was so dark, that I could barely see the road. I drove slowly and carefully. There is nothing quite like driving Jetsunma around on a dark road at night. I wondered what kind of horrible rebirth awaited me if I accidentally killed her.

As lightning flashed, the pavement ahead was suddenly illuminated. The only thing visible was the carcass of a dead deer by the side of the road, its neck twisted backward. When Jetsunma saw it she began murmuring prayers.

Dinner had gone on for three hours—each story more amazing than the next—until the large room at the Normandy Farm Inn had emptied out and Jetsunma and I were the only ones left, huddled like two shipwreck survivors clutching a tiny floating dinner table. The time alone with her, as Wib had predicted, was intense—as though five weeks had been crammed into one sitting. Exhausted, we asked for one more pour of coffee and stumbled toward the door. She was less scary when she got tired—sweeter and more human.

"I feel like I've been a chatterbox," she said on the way home. "That's what you were supposed to do," I said.

"Before coming, I was thinking a lot about my family," she said. Normally she didn't like talking about her life too much, she said. It made her sad. She and her mother hadn't spoken in several years. Every time she had felt like calling her, she'd concluded that it was better not to. "I have never stopped missing my mother—or missing having a mother," she said. "That's a hole that just never gets filled up, probably in all of us." She paused for a long time. "I may not have a mother anymore," she said, "or a father, or my old family, but I have the stupa and I have Gyaltrul Rinpoche, who is the reincarnation of Kunzang Sherab, my brother when I was Ahkön Lhamo. *My old brother.* He's like my family. He took me into his house for days when I wasn't well, and he cooked for me and we ate together and laughed together, like a family. And I've got His Holiness Penor Rinpoche, who gave me the Migyur Dorje relics. He's like my family. . . . And while, in one way, it looks like I have nothing," she said, "from another perspective I am the richest woman on earth, surrounded by family at the deepest place where I live."

We were quiet for a while. There were sounds of thunder, and the rain became an impenetrable wall of dancing water. It seemed as though the world had closed down around us, as it had at the restaurant. As though Jetsunma and I were the only people alive. "I've heard you might be coming to India with us," she said, "and that makes me very happy." She asked if I'd been told of the Mandarava recognition. I said that I had.

"Lately I've been having the most incredible memories of Guru Rinpoche's cave," she said. "It's very dark, and I have a memory of standing behind him and I am combing his hair with my nails. And there's dirt and twigs in his hair—and I remember cupping my hands to my face afterward and smelling him, smelling this wonderful smell of Guru Rinpoche."

I smiled and nodded. It was hard to know what to say.

When we pulled into the temple compound and I saw the white columns of the main building, I felt tremendous relief. The night was over. Soon I'd be alone in my own car again. But then I realized something—which seemed quite dire at the time: *Jetsunma had no umbrella.* How was she going to get inside her house? Was it my responsibility to keep her dry? What would Wib do? What would Alana do? One of the Buddhist books I'd read said that if one stepped unknowingly on even the shadow of a realized lama one would be sent to Vajra Hell. I had been surprised to learn there was such a place.

At the end of her driveway we said good-bye. "It's raining pretty hard," I said. "Can I walk you to the door with my umbrella?"

"Oh, that's not necessary," she replied, opening the car door. "My students are always treating me like that. Like if I get a little rain on me, I'll melt." And then she vanished in the dark.

13.

Correct View

A COURAGEOUS DISCIPLE, ARMORED WITH THE DETER-
MINATION NEVER TO DISPLEASE HIS TEACHER EVEN AT
THE COST OF HIS LIFE, SO STABLE-MINDED THAT HE IS
NEVER SHAKEN BY IMMEDIATE CIRCUMSTANCES, WHO
SERVES HIS TEACHER WITHOUT CARING FOR HIS OWN
HEALTH OR SURVIVAL AND OBEYS HIS EVERY COMMAND
WITHOUT SPARING HIMSELF AT ALL—SUCH A PERSON
WILL BE LIBERATED SIMPLY THROUGH HIS DEVOTION.

—PATRUL RINPOCHE, *The Words of My Perfect Teacher*

The Tibetans packed up their horns and drums and bells and departed for Bylakuppe soon after the Poolesville temple was consecrated and its lama enthroned. The students escorted Penor
Rinpoche and his monks to the airport and saw them off—with
flowers and white scarves and wet cheeks—but with tremendous
relief, too. His Holiness, as much as they loved him, was both a
blessing and a bit of a pain. Once he was gone there was no longer
an entourage to feed every day, or ceremonies to attend, or
thrones to paint, or canopies to hang. The previous year's unrelenting pace vanished, too, and for a few months an atmosphere
of calm and a sense of accomplishment took over the temple. Six
men had become monks and were just getting used to wearing
skirts. Nineteen women had become nuns and kept feeling the
tops of their heads, where their hair used to be. Jetsunma had
been enthroned. And Michael tended to crow a bit about how well
things had gone.

Jetsunma looked ahead and became passionate about new
building projects across River Road. The group expanded the tem-

ple's property to include sixty-five acres of woods there, and Jetsunma decided it would one day be the seat of Dharma in the West. A fabulous new temple would be built, and a monastery large enough for hundreds of monks. Jetsunma talked about starting a *shedra*, too, a monastic university to which scholars would come from all over the world to teach. There would be gardens and pathways, prayer wheels, prayer flags, and stupas. She wasn't concerned about the money all these things would cost. It was an important step into the future. "Don't you see?" she told them, "this opportunity is something you've prayed for over many lifetimes."

Each monk and nun was charged $300 a month rent to live in the retreat center where Penor Rinpoche's monks had been staying—to raise an additional $4,500 a month. Wouldn't the ordained feel good about having their rent money going to the temple and helping to pay for the land across the street?

Very quickly the arrangements were made—and fourteen new monks and nuns moved into the small dormitory-style bedrooms that ran down the sides of a central hallway. There were two twin beds in each room, a closet on one end, a sloping ceiling on the other. The monks—Kamil and Tashi and Jon Randolph among them—were on the bottom floor and shared a bathroom. And nuns—Dechen, Dara, Atara, Rene, Alexandra, Catharine Anastasia, and Alana, and several others—shared the second-floor bedrooms and a large bathroom with two shower stalls, two sinks, and two toilets.

The quarters were cramped, the meals they cooked for each other weren't good, and the conditions didn't seem very conducive to compassionate activity. "Too many chickens in the henhouse" was how Jetsunma would later describe it. Looking back, not many of the ordained said they enjoyed living there. In the common area, on the floor with the monks, there was a small kitchen and a large farm table for eating. Alana, who had become the "elder nun" and de facto leader of the ordained almost immediately upon ordination, was famous for leaving little notes everywhere, reminding the younger monks and nuns to pick up after themselves. ("Don't leave dishes in the sink!" and "Your mother doesn't live here!")

The mornings were the most hectic. The monks and nuns waited to use the showers and toilets, rushing to get ready for work. And the phone was always ringing. Parents were calling, and bosses, and Dharma friends. Now that so many of the ordained were concentrated on the temple grounds, the lay practitioners in the sangha tended to think of them as on-call custodians of the temple. When a lay member couldn't make a prayer shift in the middle of the night, the retreat center phone would ring. When the lay member forgot to close up and clean the Sakyamuni altar in the evening—three hundred water bowls to be emptied and wiped—the retreat center phone would ring.

Life in the retreat center was trying. "It was miserable," said one nun. "Not our finest hour," recalled another. Others have slightly fonder memories. "We did have lots of laughs," said Dechen. Alana remembered being newly divorced, newly Buddhist, newly ordained, and confined to temple grounds unless Jetsunma permitted her to leave—because her karma was still causing obstacles. "Really, someone remembers the retreat center fondly? To me it seemed like hell." But there were good times, surely . . . like the night Jetsunma woke everybody up after a snowstorm—went upstairs, banged on all the nuns' doors—then ran outside, waiting to hit them with snowballs when they came out. The only problem was, nobody was allowed to throw a snowball back.

Or were they? This was part of their ongoing education as Tibetan Buddhists: What was the proper way to treat a lama—particularly one so feisty and headstrong and given to wisecracks? If you went by the Tibetan Buddhist books, there weren't just rules about how to bow and prostrate properly, there were rules within rules, and thousands of pages of text to follow. One shouldn't step on her shadow, or tread on the earth where she had stepped. One shouldn't walk in front of her, or too far behind. When she stood up in a room, so must everyone else. And when she asked something of a student, the proper response was to thank her for the opportunity to serve her.* "If you bring your ordinary mind to a situation or person," the students were told, "your experience will always be ordinary."

* Patrul Rinpoche, *The Words of My Perfect Teacher* (Boston: Shambhala, 1998).

Even so, the students continued to be ordinary and have ordinary experiences with Jetsunma. And they still leaned on her for assistance with the most ordinary decisions in their lives. "I'm embarrassed by all the things she had to put up with," said Jon Randolph, "all the petty questions. She put up with it for years." They wrote and they called her, asking about which diet to go on, which car to buy, which flight to take home at Christmas, which colors to wear. Very early one morning Michael had picked up the phone and heard a student's voice on the line.

"Jetsunma, you have to take this call," he said.

"I haven't had my coffee yet."

"It's just too unbelievable," he said. "It's just too great."

What was the question that only Jetsunma could answer? *"Is whole wheat really better than white bread?"* It wouldn't become any easier as time passed. Even Jetsunma's most devoted students would sometimes feel like failures. And ultimately some students would leave. Being a Buddhist wasn't easy in America. One had to surrender to Jetsunma—completely—and somehow remain conscious while it was happening.

In the back of one's mind there were often little whispers, voices saying things one didn't want to hear. You were being stupid, foolish . . . wasting your life. As the Tibetan lamas liked to say, "The chief American characteristic is doubt."

At first it seemed okay with Jetsunma that Richard Dykeman didn't want to live in the retreat center. He and another monk lived across the street in tents and seemed quite happy to be there. Richard liked the distance it gave him from the Ordained Hotel, as he called it, where it was always noisy and chaotic. And it was less obvious when he skipped the sangha meetings and read science fiction books in his car with a flashlight instead. The weird group thing around Jetsunma bothered him. The fawning and groveling, the whining and the need to get her attention. That wasn't Correct View. That was sycophancy, Richard thought. And when he went to the sangha meetings, he always felt like an outcast, "I was always *big dumb Richard*," he would recall. And he felt he had a reputation, undeserved, for flirting with women at the center.

Richard thought of himself as a maverick and not as spiritually naïve as the other ordained. He'd traveled the world, been a member of two Eastern-style cults, and been a student of a wild assortment of yogis and gurus. He'd met Jetsunma in 1985, when she came to speak to a Unity Church group he belonged to in Lansing, Michigan—and he'd felt intensely attracted to her. He felt her charisma but wasn't drawn in by it. "I didn't care about charisma," he said, "because I'd seen all kinds of charismatic people." But Jetsunma had something else. "She was magnificent, wonderful. A pure, pure teacher. She really opened up my mind and let me see the truth about myself."

Not long afterward—along with a handful of other students from the Michigan center—he moved to Maryland to be closer to her. "Her mothering juices were so intense," he said, "everybody wanted to be around and drink them up." He had helped renovate the temple building, build the retreat center, and work on the stupa. And in 1988 he'd become a monk. As for Correct View, he felt inspired by Jetsunma and respected her, but he didn't think it was smart to follow her advice about everything.

He was with two other monks in the woods one day clearing paths, when a group of nuns approached them, very excited. They said that Jetsunma had just revealed she'd had a dream: The sangha was going to build a hundred-foot statue of Amitabha Buddha on the land across the street.

"They came running up, all out of breath," recalled Richard. " 'The statue! The statue!' . . . Their eyes were flashing, and they were animated. 'We're going to build a one-hundred-foot statue of Amitabha! It's going to be so wonderful!' "

The three monks stood with their arms folded. "The nuns were all in a tizzy," said Richard. "*The Queen Bee had spoken.* And here we were—me and two other monks—the people whose backbreaking sweat and broken bones this statue was going to be built on."

"Oh really, do you have a plan?" one monk said.

"A plan?" asked a nun.

"Where's the road going to come from?" asked Richard.

"Where are we going to get the money?" asked the first monk.

The third monk said, "Do you have any idea how deep the

foundation is going to have to be to support a hundred-foot statue? Do we need permits? It could be an obstruction for airplanes."

The nuns started crying. "It broke their hearts," recalled Richard. "That was the thing I was always trying to expose, when I was there. Whenever Jetsunma tried to whip her flock into a frenzy, they would lose all touch with reality. And Jetsunma never seemed to care if you had to ruin your life to accomplish her ambitions. It was for the good of all beings. . . . But nobody ever dared say no to her."

Not long afterward Richard was informed that Jetsunma wanted him to move immediately into the retreat center. He was creating "bachelor energy," she said, on the property across the street. And that energy was drifting over to the temple grounds and affecting the other ordained. In a sangha meeting the monks and nuns were also told that Richard was "rebellious" and "needed to be confronted." It was for his own benefit—and ultimate enlightenment—that he learn Correct View.

Good-natured Kamil agreed to corner Richard in the back of the retreat center. "Richard," he said, "some of us want to talk to you."

Richard stood there, looking at Kamil's face. And he looked at the faces of the other ordained who had gathered in the room. "They were all trying so hard to be good little boys and girls," he thought. They had their list of rules about Correct View. And they were desperately trying to become enlightened to benefit sentient beings.

"Suddenly the futility of the place overwhelmed me," he said. "I knew beyond a shadow of a doubt that I had made a bad decision to be there. I was looking at them—they were so concerned and politically correct. We'd been told if you leave Poolesville and Jetsunma, you go to Vajra Hell. Have you ever read up on Vajra Hell? You are crushed and burned and chopped up over and over again, it repeats. You are there for eternity. I mean it. You leave her and you go down."

It was days, perhaps a week, before the other monks and nuns in the retreat center realized that Richard was gone for good. "I'd suspected all along it was a cult," he would say years later, "but somehow I was still sucked in." He never said a word to anyone. He just walked out the door, down the driveway, out to River Road, and was never seen again. Pretty soon it was like he had never been there. The sangha had a way of continuing, moving on, and forgetting the casualties left behind.

Correct View was . . . so hard. It required vigilance and patience. How many more students might leave? Gyaltrul Rinpoche eventually offered Michael some advice: The more ordinary Jetsunma appeared to her students, and the more involved she was in ordinary life, the harder time her students would have learning Correct View. And if they didn't learn Correct View, they'd never learn devotion, and if they didn't learn devotion, they wouldn't become liberated. The Tibetan told Jetsunma that she shouldn't be concerned with household duties—cooking and cleaning and grocery shopping. These should be done for her by students. It was also time for her to have an attendant. "Make yourself more rare," Gyaltrul Rinpoche told Jetsunma. "You've spent enough time with the students already."

Indeed, as time passed and Gyaltrul Rinpoche's advice was followed—as the students began taking turns cooking dinner for Jetsunma, and as Alana became her official attendant—it got a little easier for the sangha to see their lama as superhuman. And as Jetsunma became an even more remote figure at the temple— breezing into the Dharma room on Wednesday nights and Sunday mornings to give a teaching, then quickly breezing out—it became a little easier again. If students missed seeing her, the walls of the temple were full of her pictures, which they could study. Eventually little prayer cards with Jetsunma on them were printed up and sold in the gift shop. The students began to buy them, fix them to home altars, and put them on the dashboards of their cars. It was considered a blessing simply to see her face.

But what about someone who didn't need to look at a little prayer card? Someone who saw Jetsunma's real face every day? What about a student who had once been an intimate friend, a glorious consort in a past life, but had now become her servant?

People weren't jealous of Alana's proximity as much as they

were afraid. The students were careful around Alana and watched what they said. And Alana didn't cry, as she had in the past, because she felt the envy of other students. She cried because of how difficult her life had become, and how impossible Correct View was to maintain. She was no longer the guru's best friend. She was now doing her dishes, washing her clothes, and cleaning her toilet. Out in the sangha she was known as the enforcer of Correct View. But in her own room Alana knew the truth: Some days she was so angry about being a servant, and torn, and full of doubts, that she fantasized about storming out the door.

"It was difficult, the first few years, to see her in very ordinary circumstances," said Alana. "It had an effect on me, and it was dangerous. . . . And I would have these terrible thoughts about her, and her family. *Just horrible.* And then she would complain about the food I'd fixed or something—saying the salad wasn't fluffy enough—in my mind, I'd say, *Bitch!*"

Alana would always struggle with Correct View. The years would pass, her status would rise and fall—sometimes she was Jetsunma's best friend, sometimes she wasn't—she would keep going. But what about the others who were close to Jetsunma? The ones who saw her in ordinary life?

What about the man who had seen her floss her teeth, pig out at dinner, and diet the next day? The man who had kissed her, made love to her? Was he a student, too—and subject to the same conditions? When it came to a husband, which view was the correct one?

Life in Poolesville had grown difficult for Michael since India, and his own place at the temple had become less certain. Since the trip to India and his wife's recognition as a lama, Michael's own footing and sense of worth had slipped. Like Alana, he had experienced a slow but dramatic shift in his relationship with Jetsunma. Once he had felt sharing and equality in his marriage. He had felt valued. But increasingly his ideas were dismissed, his advice overridden, his protests considered improper. Jetsunma made fun of him—for being skinny, for being short. She told him he was a Buddhist in his head but not his heart. As if to compensate for the status and love that he felt he'd lost, Michael became devoted to Atira, his adopted daughter. While Jetsunma had been unwell with phlebitis, and felt saddled with great responsibilities, it was Michael who spent most of his days with the baby, who bathed her, dressed her, fed her, and put her to bed every night. "I'm a fat, middle-aged woman who's already raised her babies," Jetsunma used to joke. "Atira is Michael's."

He had once thought of himself as Jetsunma's partner and manager—almost as though she was a performer—but now she seemed to be largely managing herself. She'd grown more confident in her position as lama, and it was hard to make suggestions—everything had to be sugarcoated, every appeal had to be slightly deferential. Michael felt her distance, and he felt her growing contempt for him—and for her students. At dinner she would imitate them, make jokes about them. And every week there were messages that she wanted Michael to deliver to the sangha—suggestions, criticisms, commands. As her spear-carrier and go-between, he was sent to communicate Jetsunma's wishes, and more and more her wishes seemed critical.

As for Correct View, how could he maintain it? She was the woman he had married—with the same mood swings, the same days of depression and fogginess, the same struggle with obesity—but now these couldn't be considered as the manifestations of any psychological condition or even indications that she wasn't truly happy as a guru. Since she was pure she had no stuff, no baggage, no unconscious, no negative karma. Her depression and illnesses were attributed to external causes: the sangha had little merit, the sangha wasn't devoted enough. More and more lately, Jetsunma had begun to blame the problems at the temple on Michael and *his* karma. Since Jetsunma was perfect, any trouble that might arise could not possibly be her doing.

Michael felt enormous resentment that was now inappropriate to express. He had anger not unlike Alana's. Once people had looked up to him, asked for his advice. Once he'd felt good about himself—his knowledge, his academic accomplishments, his own insights into Buddhism. Now these were only things for which his wife derided him. His role at the temple was fixed as her subordinate. There was no subject that he could know more about than she, and no decision that she couldn't veto. In the years leading up to her enthronement Michael had happily given Jetsunma more and more power in their relationship, but he had always retained some of his own. Now everything was different.

As for his job conveying Jetsunma's messages to the sangha, it gave him power but did not make him popular. The students had begun to feel that Michael enjoyed delivering harsh news. He had a sense of superiority. He seemed eager for people to be afraid of him. "Michael put things out in Jetsunma's name, repeated things she'd said about certain students," Aileen recalled, "and it's true, Jetsunma does whack people sometimes, and it's so dead-on it can be brutal. But when she does it, she's enlightened and it isn't judgmental. But when Michael repeated it, it didn't seem that way. And it bred judgment."

And because the pronouncement came from Michael, it was always hard to know what Jetsunma had really meant—every word he uttered would be analyzed for hours. It was hard to trust Jetsunma's messenger—or even like him. Nearly every student at one time or another came to feel the brunt of his anger.

"He played people and played games," Sangye Dorje eventually recounted. "One of the most effective ways of doing that is to be pleasant sometimes. And he went through phases. There were times when he was genuinely okay. He ran into problems when he had the most power. Jetsunma would give him a lot of power, and then she'd rip it from him. You got the feeling she was putting him through a process whereby he could realize his own poisons and his own negativity so he could overcome them, look at them, and acknowledge them."

And as Jetsunma had become a huge beneficent figure in their imaginations—Michael, by comparison, seemed diminished. It was hard for people to accept him playing second fiddle to his wife, and it made him feel vulnerable to criticism, threats, and insurrections. Michael became famous for making late-night calls, for chewing students out, for having attitude and being unnecessarily negative, for scaring people and making them feel bad. "He had an edge," said Aileen. "Living in the temple together, he was always on my case about something—and worried I was going to steal his wife."

"He did not have—or appear to have—many good qualities," said Sangye Dorje. "One of the things that I've struggled with and really tried to understand was why Jetsunma was ever with him in the first place."

"Sometimes it's hard to understand her relationships," Wib said, "but I've always thought it was because she's programmed to help people, and when she sees a need, she fills it."

"What did she see in him?" Jon Randolph asked. "I never knew."

But who, in her students' eyes, would have been good enough for Jetsunma?

14

Bally's Holiday Spa

WE WANT TO PROVE TO OURSELVES THAT WE
ARE LOVERS ON THE GRAND SCALE, TRAGIC HEROES;
NOT JUST ORDINARY PRIVATES IN THE HUGE ARMY
OF THE BEREAVED, SLOGGING ALONG AND
MAKING THE BEST OF A BAD JOB.

—C. S. Lewis, *A Grief Observed*

Late in 1989, Jetsunma was heading into Bally's Holiday Spa in
Bethesda one night, with Michael by her side, when she first laid
eyes on Teri Milwee. Even from behind the counter Teri exuded a
jaded good cheer. The associate manager of the health club had
her big feet up on the front desk—and her arms folded behind her
head. Her voice boomed out enthusiastically as she greeted the
Burroughses and asked to see their membership cards. When she
noticed that Michael had a cheaper membership than Jetsunma's,
Teri immediately offered to get it upgraded. There was an em-
ployee contest at Bally's for signing up new memberships, and Teri
wanted to win it.

Teri stood up. At six feet tall she towered over Michael and had
the lean, strong body of a triathlete. She was androgenously ap-
pealing. She bounced with energy, and the mascara was very
thick on her lashes.

"Come by the office later," she said in a deep voice, keeping
Michael's card. "I'll see about an upgrade. I mean, don't you want
a membership that's as good as your wife's?"

When Michael and Jetsunma dropped by Teri's office later on, they talked about their plans for getting Jetsunma in shape. She was convinced that she needed an exercise regime. She was sluggish and uninspired—and heavy—and had just turned forty in October. She told Teri that she wanted to change the way she looked, start bodybuilding and getting strong. "Of course, I'll never look as good as you do," she said. "But I can try."

When the couple told Teri that they "ran a Buddhist center out on River Road," they didn't mention Jetsunma's status within the religion. Teri didn't seem particularly interested in any case. "I was like, fine, fine," she recalled. "I'm an assistant manager at Bally's. You run a Buddhist center. It just didn't sink in."

But Teri felt a connection to Jetsunma—and an attraction. There was something in her dark eyes, her warmth. She had a sense of understanding, of knowing, that Teri kept thinking about. Jetsunma had really paid attention to Teri, really listened to her, really looked at her, and Teri had found it immensely flattering. Teri offered to help Jetsunma put together a workout program and gave the lama her phone number. When Jetsunma called the next day to set up an appointment to see Teri at the club, Teri was thrilled. She devised a regime in which Jetsunma would be lifting weights on the Nautilus machines and on the Universal gym equipment, then doing StairMaster and other floor work and cardiovascular stuff. Even though Jetsunma was out of shape, Teri was stunned by the amount of weight she could lift.

"We clicked, something clicked," Teri said. The two women became friends—very quickly, very close. "I remember looking at her," said Teri, "looking at her eyes, and going, Oh God, she can see right through me. I'm not sure exactly when it happened, but she hooked me, fast and tight, pulled me in and stuck me in her hip pocket."

Teri told Jetsunma about her life—that after years of doing drugs, and dealing drugs, and indiscriminate bisexual sex, she had entered a rehab program in Northern Virginia. Seven years later, at thirty, she had settled into a steady relationship with a well-off professional woman and was happy. Teri admitted to Jetsunma that she had dreams of being rich herself and going into business. She had gotten some motivational tapes of Tony Robbins—and had been inspired by them. She was making sixty thousand dollars a year at Bally's but had plans for investments and real estate ventures.

Jetsunma was caring, and full of advice. She seemed touched by Teri's generosity and spirit, and the story of her life. Two weeks after they met, she gave Teri a large, emerald-cut garnet ring. "Wear this always," Jetsunma told her, "it will protect you and bring you blessings." Teri found herself studying the ring all the time. She couldn't stop holding it between her fingers. And she couldn't stop thinking about Jetsunma.

"I saw her as beautiful and loving and everything I'd want in a companion," Teri said. "And when I met her, I began to see how much was really missing in my life." Teri didn't want to allow herself to hope for too much. She lived in a world where it was still largely socially unacceptable to be a lesbian.

Knowing how much Teri wanted to win the contest at Bally's, Jetsunma brought her sons into the club to sign up for memberships. She brought monks and nuns, too, and made an announcement at a sangha meeting about a wonderful personal trainer she'd found. She wanted her students to think more about their bodies, and their health, and living longer—so they'd have time to practice, more time to help more sentient beings. Pretty soon Teri was joking that she'd signed up most of the Tibetan Buddhists in Montgomery County. At night she would catch the nuns before their workouts and ask them questions about Jetsunma and the temple. Why were they nuns? How did they decide? "I never thought about being ordained myself," she said later, "but I was so curious about who this woman was and how she had such an influence."

Jetsunma persisted in her transformation. As she lost weight she began wearing sexier clothes—and started working out in tank tops and in thongs worn over Lycra bodysuits. "She really turned herself into the sort of woman who would attract me," said Teri. "Really put on the chicken suit and danced." One night Jetsunma asked Teri out for dinner, and when the restaurant where they were supposed to meet turned out to be closed, she brought Teri back to her rooms at the temple, where the relationship became, as Teri later described it, "very personal."

After that, Jetsunma asked Michael to give her some privacy—space to be with Teri. The personal trainer was meeting up with the Dharma, Jetsunma felt certain. "She's about as interested in Buddhism as the man in the moon!" Michael exclaimed. As he grew more jealous and difficult, Jetsunma told Michael she was sympathetic and suggested that he place a personal ad in *Washingtonian* magazine to help him find someone special for himself. She and Teri became inseparable soon afterward—talking on the phone every day, going out to parties, shopping, and spending the night together at the temple. In one month Teri's life had completely changed. She moved out of her girlfriend's house, bought a condo in Gaithersburg, and started making friends in Poolesville. "I just turned around and walked away from someone I thought I wanted to marry," she said. "I just moved out. In the span of a month."

She began coming to the temple on Wednesday nights and Sundays to hear Jetsunma speak—and liked sitting in the front row. "I felt like I'd come home," she said, "like I knew these people, like this is where I belonged."

Sangha members took an interest in Jetsunma's new best friend and talked about all the attention their lama seemed to be showering on Teri. Clearly she was trying to hook Teri to the path. "Skillful, very skillful," they'd say. While Buddhists aren't really supposed to proselytize, lamas are known to be very crafty, and they use all kinds of techniques—flattery, promises, even lies—to expose a student to the Dharma. And it is thought to be an enormous blessing if a lama chooses to have sex with you. But the students in Poolesville thought Teri was just Jetsunma's new friend. "It was amazing to watch," said one nun. "When they were together," said another, "there was always a lot of energy in the room."

People were happy to see Jetsunma losing weight so quickly and feeling so good again. For nearly two years she'd been a recluse. Now she was going out at night, meeting Teri's friends, drinking and dancing. And in the afternoons she and Teri were often seen laughing together, their hands full of shopping bags. Jetsunma was buying new clothes to go with her new figure. And she had convinced Teri to change her style, too, to wear more feminine clothes. Only a few members of the sangha suspected they might be lovers. "They seemed like best friends," another student would say years later. "And if it was more than that, then people assumed that Jetsunma was entitled to have any kind of relationship she wanted."

Not Michael, though. He'd grown increasingly nervous. It wasn't long before he guessed Teri and his wife had fallen in love.

"You said you were just bringing her to the path," he said to Jetsunma one night. "But you're having a love affair."

"I can't help it," Jetsunma replied, "if I'm enthusiastic about my work."

But the affair kept going on. Winter turned to spring, and Michael's frustration became hard to contain. Desperate for some help—and some semblance of an authority figure in Tibetan Buddhism to rein in his wife—he called Gyaltrul Rinpoche in Oregon and told him what was happening: Jetsunma was involved with a woman who had become a student. Gyaltrul Rinpoche, who felt strongly that it was a mistake for teachers to sleep with their students, offered to put a stop to the affair when he came to Poolesville in April 1990 to give a tsa-lung teaching. But when the lama came, Michael was stunned to see him being kind and supportive to Jetsunma and appeasing her. One night, while in the kitchen putting a bedtime bottle together for Atira, Michael overheard the two lamas talking on the other side of a partition.

"I don't know what to do about Michael," Jetsunma said. "He doesn't have Correct View."

"What? That big-ego guy? You don't need him," Gyaltrul Rinpoche replied. "Get rid of him."

Later, when Michael confessed to Gyaltrul Rinpoche that he was unhappy in his marriage, the lama said: "What is happiness anyway? The most important thing is to bring the Dharma to the West."

Jetsunma seemed to struggle for the next few weeks—not able to get rid of Michael, as had been suggested, or to give up Teri. But by May, Michael had come to suspect that Jetsunma was trying to precipitate his leaving. While driving to the beach on a family vacation to celebrate his thirty-seventh birthday, she revealed that she had invited Teri to come along.

"I thought we would go out tonight for your birthday," Jetsunma said, "and tomorrow night I'll go out with Teri."

Hurt and furious, Michael endured the weekend—and receiving a note from Teri: "Michael, thanks for sharing." But after another week or two he was gone—first moving into David and Sylvia Somerville's basement, then finding Tibetan Buddhist friends outside the Poolesville sangha to put him up. Every night he returned to the temple to read to Atira and put her to bed. He wrote Penor Rinpoche, hoping for some advice from the man he considered to be his root guru. He received a letter back telling him that his separation from Jetsunma was "definitely karmic" and that Michael should begin doing a great deal of practice to try to reverse things. Michael also wrote up a résumé and found work as a substitute teacher. It was his first job in the outside world in eight years.

With Michael gone, Alana became Jetsunma's go-between and private secretary—in addition to personal attendant. She moved into the temple building, began delivering Jetsunma's messages to the sangha, and answered the growing number of questions about Michael with such finesse that nobody except the Somervilles really knew that the couple had separated. "Jetsunma just seemed very happy, and Teri seemed very happy," said one student, "and Michael was just an afterthought." And while Alana and Michael hadn't gotten along in recent years, and had often butted heads on the subject of Jetsunma's relationship with her former personal trainer, they were in silent sympathy. Alana was overcome with jealousy, too. "When Jetsunma is hooking a student like that, it's very intense," she said of her guru's affair with Teri. "And seeing them together reminded me of how Jetsunma had hooked me to the path—the drinking and going shopping together." The beach trip, which had been such a turning point for Michael, had also made Alana enormously uncomfortable. "So imagine," she said, "I'm a new nun and I'm watching Jetsunma have this grand time with her new playmate and I'm home scrubbing the toilets. It was very painful. And I had no compassion rising in my mind, only pride and arrogance."

In time Alana came to view Jetsunma's attentions to Teri as part of her job as guru and found a way to live with it. Michael never could. "It all came to a head over Teri," said Alana. "Michael just couldn't see Jetsunma's small window of karmic opportunity to bring a student to the path. All he could feel was threatened."

Over the fall, the rumors about Michael and Jetsunma escalated and the white noise of gossip around the temple grew louder. Michael's job "on the outside" surprised people. But he was still seen coming to put Atira to bed. By Thanksgiving the sangha was officially told that their lama and her husband were separating. It was explained that Michael had "obstacles rising" and "great negativity," not to mention dramatic problems with Correct View. They were told, in whispers and asides, that Michael had not been a proper and deserving mate to their guru—and the students found themselves feeling protective. When they were told that he had stolen money out of an account and was asking the sangha to pay him a salary for the rest of his life—both of which he later denied—they were dumbfounded. It seemed to them that Michael was even worse off karmically than they could have supposed. Eventually it was suggested to the students that any contact with Michael could be dangerous, that a conversation with him would poison their minds.

Jetsunma was the one who filed for divorce. "It wasn't like I kicked him out, exactly," she said. "But I told him that he could stay here so long as he stopped influencing my other students and talking badly about me. Michael has a very brittle, fragile ego. I left him, and . . . lots of people could see why. He was kind of a rat."

They'd spent nearly a decade together, though, marked by incredible expansion and transformation of their prayer group and wild, magical moments. She had been singled out as a reincarnated saint. He'd been branded a supernatural heel. In the end their divorce was remarkably ordinary. Michael charged Jetsunma with adultery and alleged that she kept money hidden in secret bank accounts—cash she'd received as offerings—under the name of one of her nuns. Jetsunma denied there were hidden accounts. Their lawyers bickered over the usual assortment of ordinary things: money, possessions, credit card debt, and the custody of their daughter, Atira. As settlement Michael was given twenty-five hundred dollars in cash and a large crystal ball. By Jetsunma's decree he was never allowed to see his daughter again. The adoption papers had not been processed, it turned out, and Ani Catharine Anastasia was more than happy to give Jetsunma sole custody of her child. Legally Michael had no daughter. It was a loss he'd never overcome.

Just as suddenly as she had begun her involvement with Teri, Jetsunma ended it. "We've had fun playing," she told Teri, "but now I've got to buckle down and get back to work." Jetsunma stopped seeing her, talking to her, and returning her phone calls. Devastated, Teri began calling Alana to ask her to explain. "She was so heartbroken," said Alana. "She knew she wasn't going to be Jetsunma's consort in this culture, but she still had that ache. When you are close to Jetsunma, the love is so pure and strong and so unconditional. Who wouldn't want to be in on that?"

Eventually Jetsunma asked Alana to talk to Teri about the true nature of their relationship. Teri needed to realize that it wasn't a romance, it was work. It was about the Dharma, and about sentient beings. She needed to come to see Jetsunma as her teacher and not her love object. "It was very healing for me to be able to talk with her about it," said Alana. "Because I'd been through it so many times."

And at Christmas of 1990—one year after meeting Jetsunma in the lobby of the Bally's Holiday Spa—Teri Milwee was ordained as a Tibetan Buddhist nun. Her hair was shorn. She donned the burgundy robes. She received a new name, Sherab Khandro, and became the loudest, funniest, and most physically fit nun in Poolesville. When news of this development reached Gyaltrul Rinpoche in Oregon, he responded in unlamalike amazement. "Nooooo," he said incredulously to Jetsunma over the phone. "She's become an ani? *How do you do it?*"

"Rinpoche," she said, "I guess I just know how to pick 'em."

15.

Sometimes Your Heart
Has to Be Broken

HE KNEW ALL THE DETAILS OF TIBETAN, CHINESE, MA-
HAYANA, HINAYANA, JAPANESE AND EVEN BURMESE
BUDDHISM BUT I WARNED HIM AT ONCE I DIDN'T GIVE
A GODDAMN ABOUT THE MYTHOLOGY AND ALL THE
NAMES AND NATIONAL FLAVORS OF BUDDHISM, BUT
WAS JUST INTERESTED IN THE FIRST OF SAKYAMUNI'S
FOUR NOBLE TRUTHS, *ALL LIFE IS SUFFERING.*

—Jack Kerouac, *The Dharma Bums*

It was bitter cold on the night I drove out to see Sherab at Ani
Farms. The snow was hard on the ground, and hot steam rose like
breath from the hood of my car. The white farmhouse was dark
when I got there, except for one lone light in an upstairs window.
A piece of paper was pinned to the front door: "Martha—If no one
answers—please come in. My room is at the top of the stairs at the
front of the house. S.K."

Upstairs in her small room, Sherab's long body was stretched
out on a twin bed. She was wearing maroon sweats and propped
up against a red corduroy backrest. Her face seemed colorless and
tired. After months of toiling night and day on the stupa, her back
had finally given out, and the diagnosis was in: two slipped verte-
brae. She'd been in bed for three weeks already, since the blessing
ceremony, and showed no sign of recovery.

"It could be worse." She chuckled. "It's one thing to fall apart
paying the rent—and another thing to burn out making a stupa."

I sat down in a chair next to her bed, and we caught up. I told

Sherab about my recent dinner with Jetsunma and the invitation to accompany her to India. "Oh, my God, I hope you're going to go," she said, her eyes growing large. I said that I was planning to. Was Sherab? "No, there's just no way I could afford it." The news made me sad. The trip had become quite elaborate—pilgrimages to the pit, the cave site, and two weeks with Penor Rinpoche at Namdroling. The cost was $3,500 per person for airfare, food, and lodging for five weeks—and very few of the ordained had that kind of extra cash. From what I could gather, it was mostly well-off lay practitioners who were going to India with Jetsunma. The head count was up to twenty or twenty-five, according to Wib.

Sherab held a heating pad against her back while we talked, and played with the electrical cord. A bottle of water was on the floor by the bed with two tangerines, a large bottle of aspirin, and a big foam neck brace that I assumed Sherab was supposed to be wearing at all times. She seemed subdued—for her. She fidgeted, as though she couldn't get comfortable. I reached over to hand her a small tape recorder that I had brought, and once we started the interview, she kept gesturing with it, swinging it around, like a lounge singer with a cordless mic. "I'm far too gung-ho sometimes," she said. "In the past, when I worked on projects, I've gotten sick and couldn't stay with it. So this time I tried to be really smart about myself. I was careful, took vitamins, did warm-up exercises and stretches before work, and tried not to overdo it. And I made it through . . . and then I fell apart."

I was surprised to see a tiny refrigerator in one corner of the room and a small coffeemaker on top of it. I had imagined that "monastic life" was more communal—not a situation where you made coffee alone in your room. An altar was beside the bed, too. Sherab's own. The ordained all had personal altars for practicing in their rooms, whereas in the houses of the lay practitioners I visited, there tended to be one altar set up in a spare bedroom that the entire family shared. Sherab's altar had a little gold stupa on it, and a Buddha, and seven glass bowls for rice and water. A larger offering bowl was full of nuts.

Pinned to the walls of the small room were several photographs of Jetsunma, most of them in the five-by-seven-inch range. Near the bed, surrounded by red matting, a letter of some kind had been framed under glass—along with a picture of Sherab and Jetsunma standing next to each other and smiling. I stood to get a closer look.

"That was taken on the day I got ordained," she said, pulling a thick down comforter up around her.

"That's exactly what I wanted to talk to you about," I said.

Sherab looked up at the ceiling fan as though searching for the right way to tell the story—so I'd understand, so I could see it the way she did. "I'd be embarrassed and ashamed to tell the story of my life," she said finally. "There are things that I have done, places I've been, that just make me very sad. And ways of being and treating myself . . . that have been just horrible."

I began to say something reassuring, but she continued. "But everything has changed from knowing her, and from following her lead."

Her childhood had not been happy. She began to drink in seventh grade, about the time her parents were divorced. When she was twelve or thirteen, it wasn't rare for her to be falling-down drunk on weekends. "I wouldn't want to say anything to hurt my parents now," she said, "but I felt lost. I felt a lack of love in my life, and that was painful for me as a child. So there was always an empty ache."

She began taking drugs—pot, cocaine, a little LSD—in high school and also took to selling them. "I always had an entrepreneurial side," she said. After graduation her mother kicked her out of the house because, as Sherab put it, "I was lying, stealing, and impossible to control. She was exasperated." After moving to Southern California, where her father was living and had remarried, she enrolled in Palomar Community College but didn't really enjoy the courses. She had few friends but got pregnant twice that year and had two abortions. She felt neglected and isolated. "I would sit upstairs in my bedroom, in this very nice little space they had given me, and all this material stuff that my father and stepmother had given me, but I didn't need any of it. I just needed someone to love me. And I needed someone to help me. I needed to connect with someone in my heart—and it wasn't happening. I would sit up there and drink ten shots of Wild Turkey and listen to Black Sabbath and take some bong hits and go walk around the block and come back and nobody would notice there was anything wrong with me. Give me a break. I was an eighteen-year-old girl . . . and screaming for help."

When her father had to relocate for his work, he left Teri in charge of a condominium and a car in San Diego, expecting that she'd find a roommate to help with rent and continue going to college. "I had no life skills at that point," she said. "I had the emotional stability of a twelve-year-old. I couldn't balance a checkbook and didn't have a credit card. I just couldn't take care of myself. And I was lonely. I remember a loneliness that used to wrack my bones, and I would lay in the middle of the floor in my house and just cry. *I was so lonely.* It was this deep, aching thing. And I started drinking more, and I stopped going to school. I quit my job and got another one at a factory, where I met some really wild people."

Her car engine blew up because she didn't know to put oil and water in it. She never got a roommate, never sent her father rent. She just took more drugs. Her father tried to send her back to Northern Virginia, but Teri refused to go. She drifted around the San Diego area for the next four years, living in Escondido, Vista, and other beach towns as a semivagrant, an addict who sometimes had sex in exchange for drugs and dinner. Her friends were prostitutes, drug dealers, a transvestite named Jerry, and a former Marine. Her hair was long and wavy and sun-bleached, she said, and she wandered around in bars at night in low-rider pants, halter tops, and bare feet. She wore stacks of cheap bracelets and piles of rings, and covered her face in thick, Mexican-style makeup—white eye shadow, heavy mascara.

"Some stories I'll never tell," she said. "But I did become an intravenous drug user, and tried all kinds of things—heroin, a long stint with synthetic morphine, and another long stint on crystal meth." Loaded on Quaaludes one night and drinking, she was arrested for inciting a riot and resisting arrest, and spent two nights in jail. She shared a cell with a woman who had been arrested for carving the word *snitch* into another woman's forehead.

She dated both men and women—and "just connected better

with women," she said. During these years there were "many, many relationships" and never any money. She lived in a camper van. She lived on somebody's sofa. Her friends were in and out of prison. "There was a period of real destitution. . . . I was homeless and unemployed for a period of time—I didn't own a pair of shoes—and I learned how to scam off the Marines at Camp Pendleton, hitchhiking rides, getting them to buy me dinner or drugs, then hopping the fence and ditching them."

At twenty-three she hit bottom. She returned to her sister's house and got into a drug treatment program. She kept clean by exercising faithfully and soon began competing in triathlons. She began working at Bally's, first as a personal trainer, then as an assistant manager, then in corporate relations. She fell in love with work, with making money, with buying things, and self-improvement. She bought Nightingale-Conant tapes and took Tony Robbins courses by mail. And she had dreams of becoming rich. "I had a nice car, a silver Ford Probe with the license plate 4EVRFIT. I was involved with a woman who had money. I had a closet of Ann Taylor and Ellen Tracy suits. I was making it, man." She was thirty when she met Jetsunma and fell in love. "But it was love in an ordinary I'm-in-love sort of way," she said. "It was the only thing I understood at the time—the only way I would have of connecting to her."

At first her interest in Tibetan Buddhism was only a manifestation of wanting to please Jetsunma and become more a part of her world. She began going to teachings and classes, and was eventually asked by Jetsunma to serve on a new board of managers at the temple called the Troubleshooters. Her job was fundraising and finding ways to bring new students to the temple. "People were so nice to me," she said, "and I felt I really belonged there. It felt like home." She found herself strangely drawn to the ordained and began making friends with them. But she still never consciously considered ordination herself. She was young and successful, into making it big and looking good.

"Even in the beginning," she said, "these weird thoughts of being ordained would come into my mind, like I would be driving down the road, and all of a sudden I'd see myself with a shaved head and in those robes. I'd freak out! I'd have to pull over to the side of the road. *No, no! Okay, wait . . . This is a natural thought. Any young woman who saw all these bald women in these drab clothes would have a fear . . . this could happen to you.* It was a natural fear—that's what I told myself. It doesn't have to happen. It doesn't have to happen!"

In the fall of 1990, when Jetsunma stopped seeing her, Teri was "devastated." She wrote her letters, but they went unanswered. She called but never got through. She had also noticed—along with the other students—that Jetsunma seemed to be spending a great deal of time with Jay Allen, a young male student. "Imagine meeting someone who can love the way Buddha can love," Sherab said. "Even as friends, she was so available, and it was so wonderful. And when that changed . . . I was heartbroken. I thought, I can't leave! I belong here!"

She called Alana, trying to understand what had happened. "Is our friendship ending?" Teri asked. Alana told her that she wasn't seeing things properly. The relationship wasn't a friendship and wasn't romantic. "It's not like that," she said. "The relationship you have with Jetsunma is a relationship between a student and a teacher."

But Teri wasn't sure. It had felt like love. It hadn't felt like school. "I remember riding my bike to the temple from my condo in Gaithersburg to do some work on the land. I was riding like a mad person. My pain and upset and rage was coming out in that bike ride. I was just sobbing and sobbing. . . . I was crying oceans, oceans of tears. And when I got out to the land to work, Jetsunma was there, too, working, mixing concrete with her hands. And she just smiled sweetly at me. She knew what I was going through. And she knew I had to go through it. The moment required a broken heart. It required an opportunity to break some of these things inside me down. The pain had to be strong enough to get me to look at the world a different way—and consider a different possibility."

At the end of November, on Teri's birthday, a lama called Yantang Tulku arrived from India to give a monthlong series of empowerments called the Ratna Lingpa and the Nyingthig Yabshi. The teachings were advanced—and it was considered controversial to give them to students who had not yet completed Ngön-

218 • MARTHA SHERRILL

dro—but Jetsunma communicated through Alana that Teri was ready to receive them, something that made an impression on the rest of the sangha. "She must really have the merit to receive that kind of blessing," said Alana.

Teri changed her schedule at Bally's to attend the empowerments and for the first time felt her mind turning toward the Dharma. The presence of Yantang Tulku was having an impact on all the students. He was an old and noble lama—who had been imprisoned and tortured for many years by the Chinese. The bones of his feet had been broken, and there were burn marks all over his body. When he spoke of it, he told the Poolesville students that anger had never once risen in his mind while he was held captive. He understood that the Chinese had been held sway by their own negative actions and couldn't help themselves. Teri thought about how minor her problems seemed in comparison, and how much she wanted to be like him.

"I remember we were creating prayer wheels for the land across the street," she said, "and I was sitting in the prayer room rolling up these huge rolls of mantras that were going in the prayer wheels and thinking, What can I do, what can I do? How can I contribute? . . . And it was at that point that this image came to me, appeared in my mind. I suddenly saw myself standing in robes and a bald head, and next to me, Jetsunma was looking up at me and really smiling.

"I remember feeling disoriented," said Sherab, "like I was in a spin, in a big swoosh of feeling. Disoriented from my broken heart, disoriented from my reaction to all the teachings, and watching all these ordained at the empowerments and thinking how beautiful they seemed to me. . . . I kept walking into the solarium and noticing a picture on the wall of all the early students in Poolesville before they'd become ordained. And Alana was sitting in the front row with her long, red hair, and I remember looking at that picture and not seeing Alana but seeing myself there. And it startled me. I remember thinking, My path was going to be similar to Alana's. And thinking, Oh my gosh! I'm going to become a nun!

"And I remember feeling at that point, huh, *maybe that's possible.* I didn't freak out. I had a very relaxed sort of feeling—almost an acceptance. . . . Jetsunma had opened up a huge ancient yearning in me, and, suddenly, the thought of a simple one-on-one relationship seemed very small."

In two years, she figured, she would be able to consider ordination. She would remain at Bally's, pay off her debts, save some money . . .

Only a week later Alana left a message on Teri's voice mail saying that Jetsunma wanted to see her. It had been three months since she'd heard from Jetsunma, or been alone with her. Teri felt nervous about seeing her—"like my mind was tight."

"What's going on with you?" Jetsunma asked her.

"I don't know," Teri said. "You tell me."

"No," Jetsunma said. "You have to own it."

They talked for ninety minutes—about the Ratna Lingpa teachings, and Yantang Tulku's miraculous visit to Poolesville. They talked about the student-teacher relationship. Jetsunma told Teri that she missed being with her and still really loved her. "We hugged and cried," Teri said, "but I never said anything about ordination."

"Now I have something to tell you," Jetsunma said.

"I think I know," Teri said.

"What?"

"You're with Jay Allen now."

"How did you know?" Jetsunma asked.

The next day Teri wrote a letter to Jetsunma saying she was having thoughts of being ordained. "I had written her a million letters, well, maybe not a million, since we'd met. And this was the first time she wrote back." It was Jetsunma's response that was on Sherab's wall, held under glass next to the picture of the two of them smiling.

Dear Sherab,

I was so glad to receive your letter. It was the clearest and most honest and real I've ever had from you. You're changing. I am happy at your thoughts of ordination. It is the purest offering, the most pristine method. Believe it or not, you would do well as a renunciate. You would be greatly blessed and your offering would produce a crop of merit and virtue sufficient to dispel the confusion. . . . In such a life are all the causes that remove the very suffering you have endured ever since you were a child. I pray endlessly that your confusion ends and your mind turns completely to its three precious jewels. I love you and want you to stop hurting. It's all I've ever wanted for you. If our relationship produces such beauty, such great benefit, then in my heart I will always think of it as perfect love.

Please keep thinking of the suffering of beings even if your mind returns to your own needs. Eventually love will be blooming like a child inside you and you will someday see it is your true face. I have always known it to be so.

I hold you close and pray for you always.

> In the Dharma,
> Jetsunma

"I started sobbing and sobbing when I got her letter to me," said Sherab. "It was just so beautiful. *Perfect love.* I looked all my life for that. And that's what I was trying to find when she and I met."

Alana was sent to talk to Teri again—Jetsunma wanted her to know that it was all right for her to take vows with Yantang Tulku and continue to work at Bally's Fitness. She didn't have to wear robes all the time. She could wear modest clothes to work, keep her hair short but not too styled, wear modest earrings and makeup . . . and if Teri wanted, she could take *genyen* vows, the lay practitioner's vows, which are somewhat easier to abide by than the vows of the ordained. Rather than celibacy, one vows not to commit adultery. And rather than abstaining from alcohol, one vows not to become inebriated. "I became really excited by that," said Sherab.

The next morning Teri got up very early to do some work on the land across the street. It was around eight when a sangha member found her in the woods. "They're looking for you, Teri."

"What?"

"They're looking for you at the temple, Teri. The tulku is ready for you to take your vows."

She crawled up on the back of a tractor and was driven to the temple, where the tulku was waiting. "I'm in my jeans and T-shirt. My hair's flying. I go to the temple, pull off my work boots. I'm taken up to Yantang Tulku's bedroom—where he was sitting up in bed. And I go in, sit on the floor of his room, and he chanted a bunch of Tibetan rights on me and stuff. The khenpo made translations. And Yantang Tulku was saying all this stuff and throwing rice on me, and I was saying, *I do, I do* . . . thinking I'm taking the layperson's vows."

After leaving the tulku's bedroom Teri heard that Jetsunma wanted to see her. "So I went upstairs to her room, and she was brushing her teeth or something—and on the table in her room was a set of robes and a gold blouse and belt. And she said, 'So when are you going to get your hair cut short?'

" 'I'll see if I can get an appointment today,' I said.

" 'And these,' she said, pointing to the robes, 'are for you.' "

They were Jetsunma's own robes. "It was right there," said Sherab, "right at that moment that I became a nun.

"After I took my vows and put on those robes, I felt I had landed from an incredibly long flight," she said. "Like a huge weight had been lifted off my shoulders."

The house had begun to stir during our long talk, and after Sherab and I had talked for almost two hours, Rinchen knocked on the door to say that dinner was about to be served.

"Dinner?" Sherab asked, as though she were surprised.

"Dinner," said Rinchen, softly.

"Are you telling me to come?" Sherab asked.

Rinchen nodded. I hadn't planned on eating at Ani Farms. "I have dinner at home," I said to Sherab. "But I don't want to be rude."

"No," said Sherab, "I think they've planned on you."

Downstairs there was a central dining room, a kitchen, and a living room with a large television in the corner. Sherab put on her neck brace while giving me a slow tour of the sparsely furnished house. "In terms of *feng shui*, the far left-hand corner is the money corner," she explained. "So that's where you put your large electronic equipment or plants." There were also stacks of videotapes in the feng shui corner. The ordained weren't allowed to listen to music, but they had amassed and shared a large library of movies. The boxes indicated a certain affinity for action pictures, sci-fi, and ribald comedies. *Ace Ventura* and *Dumb and Dumber* were part of the collection and several taped broadcasts of the British sitcom *Absolutely Fabulous. La Femme Nikita* was out of the box and had just been watched. A favorite, it turned out, of Ani Sherab.

The dining room was dimly lit, and the table was set for six—the five nuns who lived at Ani Farms and me. Slowly the nuns began collecting around the table, and I was offered a chair. Aside from Sherab in her sweats, all the others wore robes. There was Alexandra, a tall thin woman with a long, aristocratic face, who had cooked the dinner—jambalaya, a spinach salad, and home-baked bread. Rinchen sat down on one side of me, with her gentle demeanor and glowing smile. Palchen, an older nun with thick eyeglasses, sat at the far right-hand corner of the table.

A nun named Dechen sat directly across from me. I remember wondering how old she was, because she didn't look much over twenty. She was small and thin, birdlike. Her features were delicate, and her skin was so fine and clear and healthy that it looked airbrushed. Her glasses seemed clownishly large for her face—the glasses of someone who cared nothing about appearances. After our introduction she served herself food, looked down at her plate, and said nothing else.

Behind Dechen, on the wall over her head, was a movie poster–sized photograph of Jetsunma. It was the same photo used on the cover of the *Invocation* CD that was sold in the temple gift shop. Jetsunma's face was in profile. Her hair was long and curly and soft. She was hugging herself and looking off in the distance—with her back turned slightly away.

Perfect love. As much as I respected Sherab, it sounded like the title of a pop song. It seemed hard to imagine that Sherab, or any of the nuns, could love Jetsunma in such an uncomplicated way—or that Jetsunma could love them back in such a way. And I couldn't help but wonder, Was *perfect love* what Sherab and Jetsunma truly had? Love without fear? Love without ambivalence?

Another thing kept running through my head. *The burden lifted.* After she'd been ordained, Sherab said, she had felt "an incredible weight had been lifted off my shoulders." What was that weight exactly? What was the burden that she was now spared? Other nuns and monks had said similar things to me. It seemed as though an enormous burden of self—the weight of will, of ego—had been lifted from these men and women. Once upon a time Sherab had been alone, running her own show, and feeling "so lonely" and "lost." She saw herself as separate and apart from other people. Buddhism teaches that one's sense of self and one's separateness are an illusion, one of the many illusions of samsara. The self does not truly exist. The ego is all bluster and bravado—because in the end it promotes and protects something that isn't actually there: You.

"We talked about my days as a personal trainer," Sherab told the other nuns at the table. She was sharing the highlights of the interview. "And I was telling Martha about my Ford Probe with the license plate 4EVRFIT . . . *Forever fit*—can you imagine the audacity?"

"And then," said Palchen, "you ran up against impermanence."

"Exactly," said Alexandra.

"Impermanence," said Sherab, "and Jetsunma Ahkön Lhamo."

Sherab mentioned that she'd talked about her ordination—and "the decision" surrounding it. The nuns all tittered a bit, and I realized, finally, that none of them thought of ordination as a decision. It was more intuitive and karmic and cosmic than that. "My sister cried," Sherab said. "I didn't tell my mother for six months, and my father couldn't accept it for years."

"None of our mothers was happy," said Alexandra.

"My mother didn't mind," said Rinchen.

"Or mine." Palchen laughed.

"Well," said Sherab, "*dead* mothers tend to be pretty neutral about it."

I looked around the dinner table and wondered what each of them had given up to be there—what their old lives, and old *selves*, had been like. "There's a few of us who like to sit around and talk about how in love with Jetsunma we are," Sherab had told me. I looked up at the poster behind Dechen's head. Jetsunma with her back turned toward the nuns. A funny feeling began to creep up on me. Suddenly, instead of a table of warm friendly gentle souls—as I had always seen them—they began to seem like uncomfortable actors rehearsing a play. There was a certain carefulness, which as a journalist I was used to and had come to expect with most subjects, but not the Buddhists. Had it been there all along and I hadn't seen it?

Dechen remained silent, and I kept watching her face. Each time Sherab would say something and dominate the table, Dechen would pause, look up at her, then return to her dinner, with absolutely no change in expression.

"Jetsunma's personally invited Martha to India," Sherab said. The table was quiet.

"I hope you're going," Rinchen said.

"I'm planning on it," I said.

The table was quiet again. "Are any of you going?" I asked. There was another moment of silence.

"I would give anything to go," said Sherab, "but I don't see how. It's pretty expensive." The other nuns nodded.

The telephone rang. Dechen jumped up nervously to answer it. She dashed around the corner to the kitchen and stood there for a long time talking quietly—in a steady high-pitched and precise voice, the sort of voice you'd imagine a librarian would have, or an English professor. She laughed, a helium giggle, and then became serious again. The minutes passed. Her plate of jambalaya remained uneaten.

Sherab caught me looking into the kitchen. "Dechen's our resident teenager," she said. And when I looked around the table, all of the nuns were nodding.

Driving home, I thought how Ani Farms wasn't as I had imagined it. There was something dispiriting about the room—the dim lighting, the periods of silence, the nodding nuns. It was weird how Dechen never spoke or smiled—then disappeared for a phone call. And rising over this bleak scene was the marquee-sized poster of Jetsunma. I kept seeing her face in half profile, and her back turned. She seemed to be looming over the table, hovering over our heads, and listening to our every word. It was haunting and troubling . . . in fact, there were just too many pictures of Jetsunma, period. I wondered if this was simply a cultural divide between East and West—I thought about all those Mao posters in China years ago. Or was this the sign of something else?

It was one thing to have paintings of Buddha or Jesus, it seemed to me. They were dead—and not, as far as I knew, making pronouncements from the grave. They were not telling followers who to marry, or naming children, or fund-raising. A living God is harder to accept.

I thought about Sherab's story. It seemed worth noting that she hadn't talked about ordination openly until she'd gotten the word, officially, that Jetsunma had taken another student as a consort. I wondered if she had held out hope, and if becoming a nun wasn't just a way to cope with the news—and remain by Jetsunma's side.

"Are you still in love with her?" I had asked.

"I'm totally in love with her," Sherab had replied, without a moment of hesitation. "I love her style, her appearance. I love her sense of humor, her earthiness. I love the way she loves me. I love the way she loves other students. I love what has happened in my life as a result of knowing her—she means everything to me, really. There's a part of me that knows there are people in the world who wouldn't approve of that. . . . Oh, Sherab's been brainwashed, she's been carried down the road by this charismatic woman. But I can't give you one example of when she's led me astray. I just can't. Every time, even if it's been something that has been painful for me to deal with, it has made me richer and stronger and fuller. . . . And what's wrong with having a little leadership?"

Could romantic love be so easily transformed into something deeper and more profound—and then lead to something beyond devotion to one's lama, devotion to all living things? That's the way it is supposed to work. One surrenders to one's lama and makes the first steps toward a surrender of self. When one learns to love the lama purely, then one can learn to love oneself—and all beings—in a pure way. But the very first step concerned me: the methods a lama uses to lure students to the path. *Skillful means* is a vague concept. It allows lamas to behave very badly, from a conventional perspective, do almost anything, in order to bring students to the Dharma. Tibetan Buddhists don't believe in door-to-door marketing like the Mormons, or getting on TV like the fundamentalist Christians, but, apparently, they believe it is okay to trick some people into becoming students. Was this manipulation or kindness? Wasn't it possible that Jetsunma had simply used the ruse of skillful means to get Sherab into bed? If what Jetsunma was doing was skillful means, then it wasn't adultery. If it was skillful means, then it meant sentient beings benefited. If it was skillful means, then all of Sherab's heartbreak and misery had served a wonderful purpose, had made the world a better place—and Sherab a better person. If you bought this Tibetan Buddhist concept, then you bought that the capacity for enlightenment justifies all means. It meant that a lama could lie, cheat, be cruel, kill—and it would result in benefiting all sentient beings. Who was keeping score except the lama?

16.

The Sangye Era

BEING A HUSBAND IS A WHOLE-TIME JOB.
THAT IS WHY SO MANY HUSBANDS FAIL.

—Arnold Bennett

Jay Allen was spending lots of time across the street in the woods, clearing land with some of the monks that autumn of 1990, when Jetsunma started looking at him differently. Suddenly, it seemed, she had come out of hibernation. She was thinner, happier, and stronger—people said that at Bally's Holiday Spa she was pushing more weight than any of her monks. She was even working on the land, pouring concrete and hauling tree stumps. And she seemed to be noticing Jay. She was asking him questions and giving him a hard time about his clothes. He was twenty-six but still had a sloppy teenage way about him. Sometimes he went a few days without shaving. Sometimes his T-shirts looked a little worn out and wrinkled. His straight brown hair got stringy and stuck to his forehead. But he wasn't the sort of guy who cared. Mainly, he was into practice—meditating, praying, and finishing Ngöndro. And in 1987 he'd sold his motorcycle to buy himself some time to do it. He had once sat down on a cushion in the prayer room and announced, "I'm not leaving this room until I achieve enlightenment." Besides Tibetan Buddhism and his devotion to Jetsunma, his great love in life was watching football on TV and going to Washington Redskins games with his dad.

The two of them—Don and Jay Allen—had been students of Jetsunma since the early Kensington days. It was she who had told Jay that he didn't need to go to college. Ever since the Poolesville property had been purchased in 1985, the Allens had lived in a small white guest cottage on the temple grounds. Don was an administrator at the U.S. Postal Service, and Jay was working for a construction company started by one of the monks, but more than anything he liked working on the temple, building altars and stupas. He'd decided against becoming a monk in 1988 after Jetsunma told him he'd been one in so many previous lifetimes it was unnecessary this time around. Anyway, he wanted to get married someday and have a family—but so far no serious girlfriends had turned up. It was hard to connect with somebody who didn't get Poolesville, and had no exposure to Dharma or Jetsunma. So the world in which Jay had become an adult was a rather limited place. But it was also a sweet place, and an awfully kind place. And increasingly, since Michael Burroughs had departed, it had become the kind of place where anything could happen.

Jay fell very hard and very fast once Jetsunma cranked up the heat. He was a boyish twenty-six. She was a seasoned forty-one— and feeling adventurous and liberated from her unfortunate marriage. She swooped in with all the charisma and intensity he could bear. By the time Yantang Tulku had left, a month later, Jay was hers and she was his. It was a blessing, a fabulous mystical blessing. His ship had come in. In every moment with her, every touch of her skin, every kiss . . . there were blessings and more blessings, twenty-four hours a day of blessings. Before he knew it she had given him a new name, to indicate his new blessed status: Sangye Dorje. And for a man who seemed in a rush to be enlightened, this was thought to be the quickest path: consort to the lama.

Nobody in Poolesville really knew what was happening, except maybe Alana or Ariana or Atara, Jetsunma's team of attendants. Just as some of the aspects of her relationship with Teri Milwee were never discussed openly with the sangha, the beginning of Jetsunma's romance with Jay was kept quiet. And so it seemed to some that one day Jetsunma was married and the next Michael had trouble with Correct View and was gone. It seemed that one day Teri and Jetsunma were best friends, and suddenly they weren't.

It was the dawning of a new age in Poolesville. Jetsunma had a new body, a new boyfriend, and an entirely new feeling about her. She had been on a buying spree for new clothes. The amount she had been making—$24,000 net a year—had been combined with Michael's old salary of $12,000 and gave her personal spending ability a bit of a boost. She was gravitating away from the confining color of burgundy and heavy fabrics to light floral prints and short, frilly dresses. There were wisecracks at the time—the sorts of cracks she loved—about how eventually she was going to wind up with Richard Gere, a practicing Tibetan Buddhist. One night at a sangha party, wearing a particularly low-cut dress, she said, "Yeah, when Richard Gere finally comes here, I'm going to wear one of these."

The students felt liberated, too, free from the tyrannical presence of Michael and the tense environment that they'd come to blame on him. In the Sangye era the mood was happier, younger, more positive, and more energetic. Sangye was sweet and gentle—and said to be very pure. Eventually Jetsunma would tell them that Sangye's merit alone had saved the center from collapse. This revelation that merit could be shared had a flip side: The merit or lack of merit of one member of the sangha could negatively affect the whole. It was a one-bad-apple kind of theory, which was why Michael, it was explained thoughtfully, was such a dangerous presence, a man of such demonically low merit that the entire group had been sinking with him. Once word got around that Jetsunma and Sangye wanted to marry, but Michael was still refusing to grant her a divorce, the level of rancor toward him increased. "We wanted to get married," Sangye said. "And we were going to get married, but Michael was not willing to budge. . . . It was a fight. And it was ugly. He really turned ugly after he left. But then, again, part of the reason he left was because he was already ugly."

Nobody questioned why all the photographs of Michael—and, at the same time, photos of Jetsunma from her heavier days—had been removed from the temple walls.

The mood in Poolesville continued toward a kind of breathy exhilaration during these months, aided, oddly enough, by the Persian Gulf War. Jetsunma explained that she had seen this conflict brewing for six or seven years—in fact, the big world peace vigil that she had held in 1984 had largely been meant to "lessen the negativity in the Middle East." The effects of that vigil were now being realized, she said, and preventing the war from escalating into mass destruction and bloodshed. But there was more praying to do.

It had been a long time since they'd come together and prayed around the clock, perhaps not since Alana's brain tumor. The Gulf War reminded the old-timers of the Kensington days: the sense of purpose, the light-headedness that comes with intensive prayer. Since they had become Tibetan Buddhists, it was as though their main focus had been to build. Everything had been about doing things correctly—not about saving the world. "We were like the military," said one nun. "We had been training for this for years—and were really excited to use what we'd learned. We were ready to roll."

Things seemed cozy in the sangha in those days. Their lama was happily occupied with a new love. Walking outside the main temple building to their prayer shifts, students would sometimes turn to look in the windows of Jetsunma's living room and see her with Sangye, snuggling in front of the television and laughing. Even Sherab thought they made a perfect couple and started calling them Mr. and Mrs. Cuddles. Atira still called out for Michael in the middle of the night, but she was turning three and growing attached to Sangye. A few people thought it was a little too soon, but she had already started calling him Daddy.

There was no official wedding, but the ordained hosted a party for Jetsunma and Sangye—a Consort Engagement Party it was called—at Ani Estates, where a group of nuns lived. Sangye arrived in an outfit that Jetsunma had picked out for him, new black pants and a black-and-red shirt. His hair was styled and gelled. He'd even shaved. The couple exchanged rings. The ordained had been told by Alana that it was a lifelong dream of Jetsunma to go to Hawaii—and that it would be extremely auspicious for the monastic community to send their lama and her new consort there. So the monks and nuns raised the money among them and presented Jetsunma and Sangye with an engagement gift: a Hawaiian honeymoon, all expenses paid.

It wasn't unusual for Jetsunma to pay special attention to the pregnant women in her sangha and to fuss over new babies. She was "motherly," as she would say. And she seemed genuinely to love children. She always came to the hospital to see the new babies and bless them. She had named nearly all the children born to her students. It is an Eastern tradition, and thought to be auspicious and smart—bringing good luck to the child—to have a lama bless the baby and give it a name. Outside Penor Rinpoche's house in India in the afternoons there was sometimes a line of parents holding babies.

But it was unusual how much Jetsunma had begun to fuss over one child in the sangha. Earlier in the year she had taken an interest in the pregnancy of one of her longtime students, Chris Cervenka, who had married and become Chris Finney. She summoned Chris and her husband to her house to discuss the coming baby. Chris was a Teutonic blond with an angel face—a good twelve years younger than Jetsunma—who had been a student of hers since the Kensington days and had once seriously considered ordination. In all the seven years she had studied with Jetsunma, Chris had never been summoned to her lama's house. In fact, she had attended hours of teachings inside the stuffy basement in Kensington, had happily made the shift to Poolesville, and Tibetan Buddhism, and had married a man she met at the center—Rick Finney was a journalist and an editor of Tibetan texts—but she had never been a part of the lama's inner circle. She had never been close to Jetsunma or Michael. When special classes were held for the gifted sangha members, Chris had never been included. But she liked it that way. She worked in the gift shop, enjoyed the praying, the community life, the togetherness, had many good friends among the ordained. And she'd always had the vague feeling that proximity to Jetsunma wasn't necessarily a good thing.

"I've had a very clear dream about your baby—the kind of dream I've learned to trust," Jetsunma told Chris and Rick. Chris was six or seven months pregnant. "Your baby is a very special tulku. I'm not going to tell you who he is, and I don't want you to even speculate about it, but you'd be amazed. And I can't wait to tell my teachers that he's back!" Later on the whispering began; some even hinted that Jetsunma believed the Finneys' baby to be the reincarnation of Dudjom Rinpoche, a previous head of the Nyingma school. He had died in the south of France four years before.

Technically, only very high lamas, like Penor Rinpoche and the Dalai Lama, make claims about another lama's rebirth. And it was unusual for Jetsunma to make this sort of claim. Rebirth and recognitions are tricky things, and usually the work of a group of lamas. But the more Rick thought about it—and he couldn't help thinking about it—he felt it was possible that Jetsunma had the ability to know what she was talking about. If it was true, and Jetsunma was right, it was a great, great blessing. According to Tibetan Buddhism, people die and wander lost and helpless in the bardo for ten to sixteen weeks before they are led—by the force of their karma—to various rebirths.* They can go to hell realms and ghost realms. They can reincarnate as insects and rats. A human rebirth is the most precious, and requires tremendous merit. But when lamas—particularly an enlightened being like Dudjom Rinpoche—die, their mindstreams remain in a pure realm until the time is right or the perfect parental situation comes along.

One thing seemed clear: For Dudjom Rinpoche to be reborn in Poolesville would reflect well on Rick and Chris, on Jetsunma, and on the sangha as a whole. It would also be an international event. What would become of their baby? Would the Tibetans want to raise him? Or Jetsunma?

In March 1991, when Chris gave birth, Jetsunma seemed shocked to hear that the baby was a girl and not a boy, as she had

---

* Sogyal Rinpoche, *The Tibetan Book of Living and Dying* (San Francisco: Harper San Francisco, 1992).

predicted. "Have you done anything to change the situation? Have you been fighting?" she asked Chris and Rick in the hospital. She believed that the sex of a baby could change in the womb as a result of disturbances in the emotional field. "Well," said Jetsunma, "*something* has occurred to make the baby change its sex." She held the baby, looked her in the eyes, and gave her the name Eleanore Victoria.

Only a few days later Alana called the Finneys at home. She told them that Jetsunma was very upset. Since seeing their baby she'd had a dream that the Finneys "wrapped Eleanore up in a blanket and took her away from me." Rick assured Alana that this would never happen—and the dream prompted him to have a will written, singling out Jetsunma, or a trusted student of her choosing, to become Eleanore's legal guardian in case something should happen to Rick and Chris. As for the baby's status as a tulku, when Eleanore was about a month old, she was examined in the prayer room by Jetsunma, who announced to her parents afterward: "I think we're in luck!"

The interest in Eleanore continued to escalate as the months went by. For one thing, the child was lovely—with brilliant red hair and an unusually confident gaze. Jetsunma often asked to hold her and sometimes took her into her own quarters to admire her alone. She had made a point of showing her to various visiting lamas—Choje Rinpoche, Gyaltrul Rinpoche, and Ngagchang Yeshe—apparently for their approval. Once Jetsunma bent down to the little girl, who was just beginning to toddle around, and said, "Oh, I had a dream that you were living with me!" Then Jetsunma turned to an attendant and said, "Of course, it might be too early for that, since she's still nursing." Another time, when Rick was bragging a bit about his daughter's seemingly remarkable qualities, Alana looked at him with her cool, impenetrable face and said, "Will you give her to us?" Even though Alana would later claim she'd been joking, Rick had trouble believing her.

Eventually the proprietary feeling that Jetsunma seemed to have about Eleanore began troubling the Finneys rather than flattering them. For one thing, Jetsunma seemed often to question their parenting abilities. When Eleanore was two months old and suffering from a bad reaction to a DPT shot, Jetsunma became furious that Rick and Chris had chosen to have their daughter immunized. Their carelessness, she shrieked, had surely harmed Eleanore's delicate *chi*, or energy flow.

It seemed that Jetsunma's low opinion of the Finneys' parenting was infectious. Instead of getting praise for having such a sweet and lovely child, Chris and Rick felt criticized by sangha members—as though people didn't believe they quite deserved to be raising the reincarnated Dudjom Rinpoche themselves. They began feeling nervous and wondering what was being said behind their backs. Word had clearly reached certain members of the Poolesville community that Jetsunma doubted they were raising their child correctly. They were told they were too protective of Eleanore. They held her too much and spent too much time with her. "Put that baby down, for heaven's sake!" one sangha member said huffily to them one afternoon during a teaching. Another time Rick was scolded, "You shouldn't be so attached to Eleanore! You'll only have to let her go in the end." "In Tibet, people weren't so possessive and territorial toward their children," one of Jetsunma's close confidantes told them.

Rick began to feel uncomfortable in Poolesville. In his darkest moments he grew convinced that it wasn't Tibetan Buddhism, but something far more homegrown, useless, and certainly not heading anybody toward enlightenment, that was being practiced there. Why was there so much whispering? Why was Jetsunma meddling in their lives? Rick began to worry constantly about his daughter and wife. And about the next baby they had on the way. But he kept quiet and kept his head low. He could see that Chris still believed deeply in Jetsunma and the center. He hoped it would be only a matter of time before she, too, would see things differently.

Jetsunma had left for Hawaii seeming happy with her new consort, full of hopes for the future. On their return to Maryland she and Sangye stopped in Oregon to visit Gyaltrul Rinpoche, and she was upbeat, even making jokes about Sangye's ability in bed. Once back in Poolesville, though, her mood dropped considerably. She had horrible dreams. She dreamed that all her makeup was removed from her face and all the polish from her nails. She dreamed that she was being stripped down and other realms were calling her. All the masks of samsara were being taken from her—the facades and trickery that she used to lure students to the path. She told Sangye that the dreams meant she was going to die soon.

Overcome, Sangye and Alana begged Jetsunma to give them a session with Jeremiah—just one more time—to see what he thought they might do to prevent her death. Afterward, in the Dharma room, the sangha was gathered to hear the outcome of the meeting. Indeed, their lama was close to death, they learned. But not a death as much as "a moving on." She was taking off her fingernails and makeup and getting ready for her next incarnation. The students were stunned by the news, and many sat with tears in their eyes.

Alana jumped in when the pitch became emotional. "There's hope. We have a chance to save her. We could have lost her, but we still have a chance to keep her."

Jeremiah had told Alana and Sangye that the students in Poolesville had very low merit—in fact, their merit had totally run out. The only thing holding the center together was the combined good karma of Sangye and Alana. And since the students were causing the obstacles, the students must try to turn the situation around.

The solution: Eight more stupas needed to be built on the land across the street by Jetsunma's birthday in October. There must be a "stupa garden" within the next six months in order to save Jetsunma's life.

It was during the summer of the stupa garden project that a new student, Karl Jones, appeared in Poolesville. He was tall, had a pale romantic presence, had been raised in Ireland and spoke with a faint brogue, and was barely out of his teens. He liked music and liked to think of himself as a composer. He was smart and artistic, too, if not a bit spacey. And he threw himself into the stupa garden project as though it was a matter of life and death. Which it was, of course.

When Khenpo Tsewang Gyatso arrived in Poolesville that summer, the students took to him immediately. The respected scholar was sweet and open, and his English was much better than that of the other Tibetans who'd come around. But it was Karl, in particular, who gravitated toward Khenpo, following him around like a puppy dog. Unlike most new students—who tried hard to fit in with the sangha—Karl never bothered about making friends and being popular. He was a loner and only called attention to himself by being critical. He openly expressed disbelief that more students weren't taking time to study with Khenpo and attend his teachings. He was also critical of the old-timers, the First Wave, for not appreciating Jetsunma enough and for lacking proper devotion. She was a *dakini*, a sky walker, a female wisdom being. Nobody seemed to treat her properly. Before long Jetsunma herself was spending time alone with Karl and singling him out at her teachings.

"When Karl first came," Jetsunma would say later, "he felt he had an instant awareness of a connection with me. He showed potential for a lot of strength and devotion."

In the autumn, when the eight stupas in the stupa garden were completed, Karl took genyen vows for lay practitioners with Khenpo Tsewang.

They hadn't been together quite one year when Sangye began struggling as Jetsunma's consort. There was love, and lots of sex and very sweet good times—but Correct View had been hard to maintain. For one thing, the inequity in the relationship was very difficult for Sangye. "It was hard to figure out what she needed," he would say later. "Part of serving [as a consort] is knowing what her needs are and trying to meet them as they come up—really serving her in a subtle, effective way, functioning almost like a clairvoyant, knowing her needs before they are even obvious. There aren't many people who could handle that relationship. . . .

"If you really believe that Jetsunma is who she said she is— and who the rinpoches say she is, and who His Holiness said she is—you have to accept that she is going to live an extraordinary and unusual life," Sangye said. "And she will have extraordinary obligations and needs."

One night at a sangha meeting, while Sangye sat on the floor of the Dharma room, he said he had a confession to make: "I have failed as a consort." The problem was, he had fallen in love with Jetsunma in an extremely ordinary way. He had fallen in love with

Jetsunma as a woman, just a woman. He had become attached—in a selfish, possessive, ego-clinging way. And it had become impossible to see her anymore as guru.

Sangye apologized to the sangha for "letting Jetsunma down" and for "letting the sangha down." He appeared to be in real pain and great remorse. Alana sat next to him nodding. "The heat is hot when you're that close to the guru," he said later. "Your stuff comes up very, very quickly, out of the blue, and you realize your mind isn't as stable as you thought. Shockingly unstable . . .

"I mean," he said, "your pride comes up. Your pride is confronted regularly, just as a man. I mean, she's the boss. And I can deal with an even relationship—man-woman—on equal grounds. I can deal with that. But to have the woman above me, that's hard. *Really hard.* And that's the way it has to be if you are married to your guru. You have to be okay with that. But it's difficult to deal with and not feel emasculated. . . . You have to be very strong."

Jetsunma decided that Sangye needed to get away from Poolesville for a while, and away from the suffocating atmosphere of temple life. He had yearned to do an intensive retreat, but at KPC there had always been another building to renovate or stupa to build.

India. That was where he should go, Jetsunma decided. He could study, and practice, and consider his position as consort. He could recapture his old unselfish, ungrasping view of Jetsunma. And so, in the spring of 1992, Sangye left Poolesville to do a four-month retreat at Penor Rinpoche's monastery in Bylakuppe. Jetsunma even packed his bags.

Over dinner in New Delhi, he confessed to a fellow traveler that his goal for the retreat was to recapture Correct View and get over his conflict about the guru-student relationship. There were land mines wherever he walked, but he was determined to get through them and to see Jetsunma as a teacher again, and not as his wife.

Karl Jones had been described as "very special" all along. He had gotten Jetsunma's attention because of his devotion and musical ability—and quite definitely because of the way he looked. In the winter and spring of 1992, she spent a great deal of time with him, talking about Dharma and their other common interests. She'd always wanted to be a singer, she told Karl. So when he started writing sacred music for Jetsunma, and looked at her with great devotion—the kind of pure devotion that Sangye no longer seemed capable of—she realized that he was a man who could serve her properly. "I work best in collaboration," she said later. And she encouraged Karl to collaborate with her.

Quickly they formed a singing group called SkyDancer—with other members of the ordained community and lay sangha— which was dedicated to "promoting compassionate living through musical creations," as the brochures for their concerts would say. Karl seemed to love the way Jetsunma sounded when she sang and only praised her abilities, even though, as one student would later note, "nobody had the guts to tell Jetsunma when she was singing flat, which was about all the time."

It was May 1992, and Sangye hadn't been gone a month, when Karl stood up before a packed crowd at a sangha meeting one night and made his own very personal confession: He felt sincerely and profoundly that Jetsunma's salary was too low. He was appalled that the sangha treated her so poorly. "It came out of the blue," Wib would recount later, "and seemed to spring spontaneously from a sincere place of devotion."

Jetsunma had the same responsibilities that a president or a CEO of a corporation had, Karl told them. The students sat hushed. So many details and responsibilities were falling to Jetsunma now. She had to run the center, teach, practice. She had to answer questions, and letters and calls. The sangha was growing. The center was growing, and quickly becoming a place for Dharma to flourish in the West. And what about all the sentient beings she was helping? How do you put a price on that? How can you?

Some of Jetsunma's oldest students were surprised. They realized—although Karl probably didn't—that she had just received quite an increase in salary after Michael left. The health benefits for her family were paid for by the temple. She had food that was offered to her by students, and groceries that were purchased every week by the temple. Her living expenses were paid for. She had a full-time attendant, a nanny, all paid for. What was there left for her to buy?

Karl seemed nearly overcome with devotion. Tears filled his eyes. His pitch continued. Jetsunma had special needs, and great health concerns. Lamas were known to absorb all the negativity around them and keep their students safe from disease. They had to take extra good care of themselves. Yet here they were, giving her a small amount and treating her like the most ordinary of persons. They were in the company of Buddha, *a living Buddha,* and only offering her the most meager salary—nothing like Michael Jordan was getting to play for the Bulls, nothing like Lee Iacocca got to run Chrysler.

The night became emotional, as though Karl's passion, so touching and tender, so well expressed in his faint Irish brogue, had infected the crowd. Emotional speech after emotional speech—declarations of love and worship—followed. They had Buddha right there, in their midst, in Poolesville! God only knew what would happen to them if she ceased to be in their lives.

To their way of thinking, Jetsunma's value to them, and to all sentient beings, was inestimable. And once this issue had been raised it was nearly impossible to dismiss. How could they not pay her what she was worth? "If we woke up tomorrow and spiritual value became the coin of the realm," Wib said later, "she'd be Bill Gates."

The students who had been with Jetsunma since Kensington began to feel a bit sheepish—and ashamed. Maybe they had taken her for granted. Somehow only a new student, Karl, could see that. Let's double it! Whatever she's getting now, let's double it! But ultimately they did better than that: They decided to give Jetsunma a hundred thousand dollars a year—free and clear of taxes.

Three months later, when Sangye returned from India—and learned that Karl Jones had given back his genyen robes and grown out his hair and was engaged to marry Jetsunma—he was stunned. And heartbroken. "I never stood a chance," he said.

There was a fever of devotion that summer and fall, as though Karl had set the sangha on fire. There had never been a student so devoted, so sincere, so openhearted. He made everybody else look tight and ungenerous. At a Wednesday night teaching, Jetsunma told a roomful of students that Karl had made her come alive again, rescued her, pulled her out of a slump and made her excited about being a lama again. In past lives Karl had made potent wishing prayers to be with her—and with those prayers he had saved Jetsunma and saved the temple.

She went around the room and told her students their faults—the things she'd felt about them for years and hadn't said. "You *aren't* great beings," she told them. "I told you that just to get your attention. The only way you'd listen to me was to appeal to your egos. But it was a lie."

Karl had come, out of the blue, and made them all see how much she was to them, how much they needed her. And how far they still had to go.

The Dharma room was thick with devotion the night the vote was taken to increase the lama's salary, but not many sangha members who were present that night knew the specifics of the financial situation at the temple. They didn't know how much money came in, where it went, or even how decisions were routinely made. In the early days Michael had looked after the finances, and David Somerville had kept the books. After Michael's departure there was still no formal or elected board of directors, only a small roster of students whom Jetsunma would appoint to help run things. Sometimes she referred to these students as the Board; she later renamed them the Troubleshooters, then the Pilot Committee, still later the Transition Team, and then the KPC Finance Committee. But no matter what Jetsunma chose to call it, the duty required unflappable nerves and an enormous amount of Correct View. Bills were paid at the last minute, and creditors were always calling. The mortgages—on the temple and the land across the street—had been close to foreclosure several times. Since its inception KPC had never operated within its means nor obeyed ordinary rules of fiscal caution.

Jetsunma didn't seem to believe in caution. She believed in expansion, aspiration, prayer, and a positive attitude. If things weren't working out, it was usually because they weren't dreaming big enough. Time and time again when things looked the darkest, she would envision something even grander, more daring—a new stupa, a school for the children, or a feasibility study on building a KPC waste treatment facility—in anticipation of the new temple, monastery, retreat center, university, and hospice. And the Troubleshooters would somehow have to find a way to pay for it.

But the Troubleshooters had their weaknesses. Sherab "curled up in a ball" on her bed and cried rather than make the cold calls and fund-raising pitches that were expected of her during her first year as a member of the Troubleshooters—despite the fact that she'd been in sales. Wib, who had years of experience in marketing—selling corporate jets, telephone systems, pricey vitamins—had many dark nights of the soul looking after the temple finances. Money was sometimes raised for one thing and spent on another, a robbing-Peter-to-pay-Paul approach that didn't bother some board members as much as it did Wib. "Things were always by the seat of our pants," he said. "As Bob Colacurcio used to say, 'Our feet planted firmly in midair.' " In 1992, Tashi Barry was asked by Jetsunma to manage things. And while Tashi enjoyed the proximity to Jetsunma, it was a job that he grew to dislike. "I was always delegating money issues to other people because it was always so gut-wrenching and upsetting and difficult to deal with personally and emotionally," he said. "We were always on the brink of collapse and foreclosure, and that was hard to live with."

The books had always been generally unavailable to the sangha—largely because of the temple's embarrassed circumstances. The students had big dreams and had come to see themselves a certain way: They were custodians of the planet, bringing Dharma to the West. The meagerness of the account balances would have reflected a reality that didn't agree with their sense of purpose. Money was ordinary. Their mission wasn't. And to open the books after 1992, the year Jetsunma's salary was raised to one hundred thousand dollars a year, would have revealed the enormous burden that decision placed on the temple budget. Her salary was now one half of the total operating expenses.

The temple raised the ticket prices to empowerments and retreats—teachings that were often free at other Dharma centers around the country. The suggested "tithing" amount rose that year, to three hundred dollars a person per month and six hundred per family. But, aside from Eleanor Rowe and Bob Colacurcio, there weren't many students who actually gave that much. People just did what they could afford. Many of the ordained had already given over their savings and retirement accounts to the temple and didn't make enough in their jobs to tithe large sums.

But Jetsunma's dream of building a colossal statue of Amitabha, the Buddha of limitless light, which had been just an ongoing and much kicked-about notion until 1992, now became quite adamant. A model was commissioned. A site was discussed. And to raise money for the project, four sangha members—Wib, Bob Colacurcio, Linda Kurkowski, and Jon Randolph—were sent to Taiwan. The Taiwanese were thought to feel a special connection to Amitabha, unlike Americans, who were unable to see the value of building such a statue. Penor Rinpoche helped arrange for Jetsunma's students to spend three months at a monastery in Taipei, but the foursome returned only partially successful. They had raised nearly a hundred thousand dollars. But the estimate for the statue was five times that amount.

Jetsunma had originally wanted a hundred-foot statue, then, after some students with construction and engineering backgrounds got to her, the size was reduced to seventy-five feet. It was difficult to tell Jetsunma no—not just because she was a determined person but because of her divine status. "You could say no," recounted Tashi. "You *could*. But I never did. Others, like Don Allen and Bob Colacurcio, would worry that some decision was irresponsible, but I never went along with that. My sense was, This is the Buddha saying we need to build a statue, and we just need to do that, no matter what it looks like. And in the past it has always worked. We've always come through and built what we needed to."

In the early days, after Penor Rinpoche had prophesied that they would need a large temple—large enough for fifteen hundred—the students had assumed this expansion would happen effortlessly. And when the rinpoche returned in 1988 to give the Rinchen Ter Dzod empowerments, Jetsunma had told her students to expect standing-room-only attendance. But the crowds hadn't come—and Jetsunma declared it was time to get better organized and do more outreach. Wib was assigned the job of drawing new people out to Poolesville, particularly on Sundays, when the teachings were more accessible. Jetsunma specifically wanted to attract prosperous yuppies and professionals, not the "poverty mentality types," as she called them, who had been circling around the temple for years. And pretty soon Wib began to deliver them. "I'm not sure how he did it," said one nun, "but suddenly there were all these new faces every Sunday—and they were always well dressed, seemed prosperous."

Indeed, a new crowd of people and students had begun gravitating to KPC in the early 1990s, particularly as the teachings of the Dalai Lama became more popular and the political issues surrounding Tibet became more well known. Bob Denmark, a successful accountant in Bethesda, was one of the new faces. Another, Bonnie Taylor, was a psychologist and social worker who had spent years searching for a spiritual home and felt she'd found it, finally, in Poolesville.

Another new face was Kathy Coon. From an old Yankee family with money, she was already a practicing Tibetan Buddhist when she wandered into the Poolesville center. But Kathy's first impressions weren't particularly positive. "The students seemed so self-absorbed and self-important," she would say later. "And Jetsunma seemed so unlike my own teacher—who was such a steady, humble reflection of affection."

But as the years passed, and Kathy felt more starved for a connection with the Dharma and a Tibetan Buddhist environment, she spent time at KPC and eventually came to believe that Jetsunma was an "incredibly powerful teacher" and became "accepting of her." She thought the sangha seemed "corporate" and too well dressed—"all the other Buddhist crowds I'd been around were scraggly and soft," she said—and she'd felt "shy" at first, hadn't known how to contribute or feel special. After she gave her first lump of money, though, in 1992, from a trust fund left by her mother, Kathy discovered she had found a way to make friends. Even members of Jetsunma's inner circle came to know her name. Like Bob Denmark and Bonnie Taylor, who were also prosperous

new students, Kathy started getting invitations to special teachings—and pleas, often urgent, to make more offerings. The new
students had no idea about Jetsunma's salary, or that its doubling
had caused financial stress. But the years passed, the center
seemed increasingly desperate for money, and Denmark, Taylor,
and Coon each became more involved, giving KPC more of their
time and money. "I responded to their desperation," Kathy said,
"and also, I wanted to cut through to my own clutching. I had my
own worries about being too attached to money." Giving it away
was supposed to help with that.

With her divorce from Michael about to go through, and plans for
a wedding to Karl in the works, Jetsunma began reflecting upon
the hard road behind her. The divorce had been ugly, and had
taken a toll emotionally. She found herself concerned about the
legacy of bitterness that she felt Michael had left in Poolesville. She
wanted her marriage to Karl to heal the sangha and take the group
in new directions. And just as she felt it was important for her to reflect on the previous ten years, and the end of her marriage, she
felt it was important for the students to have a forum to dispel
"negativity" and their hostility toward Michael. She had divorced
Michael. Now it was time for the sangha to divorce him, too.

Newer students would not have been told about the special
meetings held to discuss Michael. The inner circle was always
careful to protect newcomers from the darker side of the center—
and the things they would not be able to comprehend correctly.
Older sangha members were invited by phone to attend one of
three meetings—held in private homes—where students planned
to discuss their feelings about Michael and vent honestly, in a sort
of group therapy style. They read aloud from nasty letters they
had received from him. They repeated the put-downs and criticisms that he had delivered. They shared how Michael had made
them feel small and unimportant. He paraded his power, they
said, and insinuated hurtful things in Jetsunma's name. Several
sangha members had stories that lasted more than an hour.

"We all started to share our experience of him," Alana said,
"and nobody, *nobody*, was sorry he had left. Isn't that sad? I had

had a terrible time with him, but I thought all along it was just me. He was a powerful person and ran everything—the temple, the office, everything—and he wielded that power. He delivered messages to students, the way I do now, but he made people feel really, really badly."

Once Jetsunma got wind of how deeply people felt, she decided to organize one more event: an all-sangha Divorce Party, where students could speak their piece and say good-bye and good riddance to Michael Burroughs once and for all. Several students who heard about the party at the Wednesday night teaching made the decision not to attend. They said they were sick, or had to work, or had to stay home with the kids. "I knew what it was going to be about," said one nun, "and it wasn't for me."

The Divorce Party was held in the community room, and a table of food was spread out, along with a big bowl of a strong tequila punch for the lay practitioners. Eighty to one hundred students turned up, took a drink of punch or a shooter of straight tequila, and before long the room took on a cocktail party–like atmosphere, with Jetsunma the presiding presence, sitting off to one side with Karl.

On a chair in the middle of the room, an effigy of Michael had been set up. It looked something like a mummy, a piece of cloth bundled up and tightly wrapped with cords. And it had one special feature: a banana had been attached to the cloth to represent Michael's penis.

One by one, as the party got rolling, students were encouraged to vent. Many of them had come with prepared remarks, with toasts, gags, and long stories. There were great cheers and applause, and the students began holding their drinks high in the air and shouting. As the night wore on people grew louder and more drunken—at one point all joining in a raucous singing of "Nowhere Man." As a person Michael was really a washout, the stories insinuated, and Jetsunma was well rid of him.

Alana arrived at the party with a gag knife stuck in her back and said, "Michael, you were my friend and then you stabbed me in the back." Ayla Meurer, one of Jetsunma's students who had moved from Michigan to be near her, addressed the effigy and complained about how Michael had caused her to suffer. Jetsunma shouted out, "Ayla, you can still walk a line! You aren't drunk enough!" Another student approached the dummy and began a satirical account of Michael's actions—claiming that he had "cross-dressed in front of small children"—and the crowd went wild.

The effigy of Michael was propped up in a chair closer to Jetsunma, so that she could watch while students walked up and stabbed it with their knives and forks. A line of six or seven students formed, including one nun in her robes who did a timid dance up to the body and very delicately stabbed it.

Reactions to the event were mixed, despite the hilarity and sense of raucous fun. Several Tibetans who were visiting Poolesville at the time returned to India with stories of the party and seemed perplexed and vaguely horrified. Rick Finney, already very doubtful of the goings-on at KPC, was reminded of the "Two Minutes Hate" in George Orwell's *1984.* He felt sickened by the proceedings, particularly the sight of a nun stabbing at Michael's effigy. Many others remembered having a good time and feeling exhilarated afterward. "It was done in the spirit of a roast," said one student, "except that the person being roasted wasn't there." Alana would later describe it as "necessary."

Jetsunma herself read from a list of grievances against Michael that was three pages long. She told about having a vision of starting a prayer center many years ago—and about how she'd made intense prayers that this vision come true. She had things she wanted to accomplish, and a big center to build. In answer to her prayers, she said, she met this demon. His name was Michael. The audience cheered.

Then she approached the dummy and said, "Michael, you look funny. Something's wrong here." Jetsunma made a fist and then punched it into the banana, smashing it flat. "That's more like it!" The room exploded in cheers.

At the night's end Jetsunma ordered that the effigy be thrown into the driveway in front of the temple, so everybody would have to drive over Michael on their way home. The bound cloth sat on the blacktop as the cars passed over it with their bighearted bumper stickers: PRACTICE RANDOM KINDNESS AND SENSELESS ACTS OF

BEAUTY. Then a sangha member, drunk and carried away, stood over the flattened cloth and urinated on it.

Jetsunma was going to be married again, and with this decision came a whole new look and wardrobe. Her clothes were becoming increasingly hip and young. The frilly, superfeminine look gave way to black leather jackets and boots, and jeans as tight as she could zip up. Her shopping excursions to nearby malls, and into Washington, D.C., became legendary during this time, but she relied for the most part on ordering clothes from catalogs, and every week boxes arrived for her from Victoria's Secret and Bloomingdale's and Saks Fifth Avenue.

Rather than being dismayed by this apparently unspiritual activity, Jetsunma's nuns seemed proud of her. To them there wasn't anything unspiritual about Jetsunma, and her desires never sprang from ordinary emotions like vanity or lust, only from the compulsion to end the suffering of all sentient beings. And if Jetsunma's personal needs seemed to have increased since she had gotten together with Karl, it was only another opportunity for her students to exercise their devotion.

One of the great devotional stories of this time that circulated among the sangha was about Alana and the coat. One afternoon the attendant heard Jetsunma complain that she'd purchased a coat from a catalog—and had been promised immediate delivery—but the garment had been delayed and was now apparently lost in delivery. Alana hated seeing Jetsunma upset or unhappy. She made a few calls. When she learned that the coat was stranded in a Chicago warehouse, and most likely wouldn't arrive in Poolesville for another eight to ten days, she flew to Chicago, took a cab to the shipping warehouse, located Jetsunma's coat, and came home with it that day.

There were other stories about clothes. Once Jetsunma saw a pair of carved wooden clogs in a mail-order catalog that were very expensive, and a collection was taken up among the ordained to help her buy them. She didn't want them for herself, Alana explained. Jetsunma needed to buy the clogs so that a particular person in the ordering department at the catalog company would see her name on an order sheet—and that would create the cause for this person to meet Jetsunma in a future life.

In the years that followed, this would become the explanation for Jetsunma's apparently liberal spending habits. She bought dresses not because she desired them but because she needed to "make a connection" with the designer. She used her credit card so billing clerks and Visa and MasterCard representatives could meet her in a future life and find the Dharma. "This is how compassionate she is," Aileen said. "She isn't interested in money, or clothes. She only buys all those things so that she can wear them once or twice and then give them away—and the people who wear them afterward are able to make a connection with her."

When Jetsunma and Karl married in 1993, at the auspicious beginning of the year, it was done outside at the white stupa, under a huge blue sky. Jetsunma performed the service herself. And since there is no such thing as a traditional Tibetan Buddhist wedding ceremony, she made it up, from beginning to end. She held up a double-sided mirror between herself and Karl, and talked about the nature of mind. When they married it was "primordial wisdom" marrying, she said, and then the mirror was passed around and each member of the sangha was to look into it. A chalice was filled with wine, meant to represent "the nectar of bliss and emptiness," and passed around for all to sip from. Jetsunma wore a tight black top and a floor-length full skirt of tiny patches of multicolored silk, which had been made for her by a "sewing team" of students. During the ceremony she handed out a pincushion and a needle with a strand of burgundy thread to each guest. With this wedding, she said, she was "stitching the sangha up," and when they went home she wanted them to sew the thread into a piece of clothing, as a way to remember this day and their own participation in the sangha's "healing."

She had another gift for each of the guests—laminated prayer cards with her picture on one side and her long life prayer written by Penor Rinpoche on the other.

The mood was jubilant, and there was a palpable sweetness between Jetsunma and Karl. The students had come to trust that the marriage was a good thing because they trusted Jetsunma. Most of them felt they didn't really know Karl well. He was never a go-between as Michael had been. That job was now Alana's. He was not the benevolent and lovable and pure Sangye Dorje, either. Karl had kept to himself, focused his attentions on Jetsunma. "I've never really been able to talk to him," said one monk. "Nobody *gets* Karl but Jetsunma," said Alana. Most others agreed.

More than anything, Karl seemed very young. Jetsunma was forty-three when she married him, and Karl was twenty-three. The Tibetans in particular seemed fascinated by the age difference and would ask students over and over, How old is he? She had never intended to marry a man so young, Jetsunma eventually explained. They were together because of a "long-standing karmic connection." It was Karl who was supposed to be Jetsunma's consort and by her side during the building of the Poolesville center, she said. But because of an unfortunate turn of events in the bardo, where he had lingered too long, Karl had been born twenty years late, in 1969 instead of 1949. It was Karl's fault that he was so young. And it was something that Jetsunma would have to live with.

Jetsunma called her old consort Sangye into her rooms just a week after her wedding festivities. She felt it was time to talk. In the months since his return from India, and his discovery that she had taken up with Karl, he had moved off temple grounds and become a caretaker on a nearby farm.

"I want to talk to you about ordination," Jetsunma said to him.

He shook his head. "I'm not going to do that."

She reminded him that being the consort of a powerful lama was a tremendous blessing. "And the best way to keep the blessing intact," she said, "is to become celibate and never involved with ordinary women again."

Sangye had known it was a blessing to be a consort, but he hadn't heard this other part—about becoming celibate to keep it.

"This blessing is very important," Jetsunma said. It might be more potent than any of the stupas he could build or all the hours of sit-down practice he could accomplish.

Sangye felt sure of his decision. Even if it was the fastest path to enlightenment, he didn't want to be a monk. He was only twenty-nine. He didn't want to give up sex or the prospect of having a family. And he didn't want to give up drinking and listening to music. He was sure about not becoming ordained. But he could feel Jetsunma working on him sometimes. "Psychically, she was bearing down on me," he said. "I mean, I could really feel it—and I was irritated by it."

Eight months later a highly revered Tibetan master, Jigmey Phuntsok, arrived in Poolesville to ordain a new crop of monks and nuns. About a week before the Tibetan was due, Sangye began experiencing a great deal of discomfort—tension, insomnia, frustration. Jetsunma's mind was pressing into his. She was working on him, he said later, she was trying to get him ordained.

He began visualizing Jetsunma in front of him one night. And he yelled at her. "Jetsunma! Hear me! I am not going to take ordination!"

The next morning when he awoke, Sangye felt a sense of quiet relief. He felt calm, too, for the first time in many months. Something else had happened: He had changed his mind.

Why? How? He had faith in Jetsunma, he explained later. "Why would she make me miserable for the rest of my life? Even if it were the best thing, the quickest path, she wouldn't want to make me miserable, would she? So I had faith in her, that she knew best." It was a faith shared by all of the KPC ordained and one they all believed would be unshakable.

Part Four

The
Nun

17.

Whisperland

PENETRATING SO MANY SECRETS, WE CEASE
TO BELIEVE IN THE UNKNOWABLE.
BUT THERE IT SITS, NONETHELESS,
CALMLY LICKING ITS CHOPS.

—H. L. MENCKEN

Like two of the monks and three of the other nuns in Poolesville, Dechen had been a student of Jetsunma since she was young. She was the smallest nun, and the youngest. She was just five foot one and weighed eighty-seven pounds. Her shoes were size four. When she bought regular clothes, she shopped in the children's section. She had pretty features, large brown eyes and smooth skin and a wide toothy smile, but she kept herself mousy and invisible, smaller than life. She was shy, modest. She liked to sew. She liked to read. Before she'd become ordained, she'd liked playing the piano. She had taught herself. Dechen was a virgin and just twenty when she became ordained in 1988—that long, hot summer when His Holiness was yelling every night.

Dechen's mother, Ayla Meurer, was divorced and working in Michigan as a sales representative for McGraw-Hill when she met Catharine and Michael Burroughs in late 1984. Ayla was a kind woman, a loving woman, but busy and overcommitted. Her spiritual pursuits and daily involvement in est seminars took up much of her spare time and passion. Her two children, Kyle and Michelle (as Dechen used to be called), were left alone a great

deal—and often fed themselves dinner at night. When Catharine
Burroughs entered their lives as Ayla's new spiritual teacher—
coming to Michigan once a month to give lectures—things began
to change for the better. Catharine seemed genuinely interested in
the children and tried to connect them to a growing family of her
other students, in both Michigan and Maryland. And when the
Center for Discovery and New Life turned toward Tibetan Buddhism in 1986, both of Ayla's children were enthusiastic con-
verts. In 1987 the family relocated to Maryland—as had Richard
Dykeman, Bob and Carol Colacurcio, and several other Michigan
students—and joined the KPC mission to help bring the Dharma
to the West.

While Dechen could remember her life before Jetsunma—
nights alone with her brother while her mother was at church
and est seminars—she couldn't imagine her life without her.
Dechen's devotion to Jetsunma was unquestioned. And when Jetsunma told her in a private consultation in 1987 that her mother
was the source of her spiritual and emotional problems—that
Dechen and Ayla had been involved with each other in a troubled
way over many lifetimes—she believed her. When Jetsunma told
her to move out of her mother's house and live with another
sangha member, Dechen did. When Jetsunma suggested her
father wasn't the best influence in her life, Dechen stopped calling
him. When Jetsunma told her that she shouldn't worry about
going to college—because eventually there was going to be a
monastic university in Poolesville and a three-year retreat center—Dechen felt sure this must be true. And when Jetsunma told
her that she had trouble with "needing approval" and described
her as a "hothouse flower," Dechen came to think of herself that
way, as rare and delicate and not a strong person. Several years
later, when Jetsunma revised her opinion of Dechen and publicly
called her a brat, Dechen had to admit that she did act rebellious
and bratty sometimes. To Dechen, there wasn't anything Jetsunma had ever uttered that wasn't true or a promise she hadn't
kept.

At first Dechen had taken the ordination name Penor Rinpoche had given her in 1988: Zomchi. But later, when Jetsunma

complained that Zomchi sounded like "donkey," she was given a new name, Dechen, pronounced *DAY*-chin. It means "great bliss."

She lived in the retreat center after taking vows and held various outside jobs over the years, as a receptionist, a secretary, and a systems tester for a computer programmer. For a while she drove a lunch wagon that sold meals to construction workers all over Potomac. When she pulled up in the van, the men yelled, "Hey, it's the flying nun!"

For many years her first thought every morning was of Jetsunma and the temple in Poolesville, and of her fellow sangha members there. She drove to work playing a tape of Jetsunma's teaching. When she met new people, she made a point of discussing the temple with them, told them funny ani stories—about Aileen or Sherab and tried to leave them with a positive impression of Jetsunma and the Dharma. Kunzang Palyul Choling was her entire life and intertwined with everything else. She had wanted to be a Tibetan Buddhist nun from the moment she had heard there was such a thing, when she was seventeen, and she wanted to devote her life to ending suffering and praying for the world and doing no harm. Coming home from work, like most other members, she got out her mala and said prayers as she drove.

She had a good mind, and her memory—an important quality for a Tibetan Buddhist practitioner—was astounding. In school she had always tested well, but her grades were often poor because of a lack of discipline. She excelled, however, at Tibetan Buddhist practice. It engaged and nourished her. While practicing she was able to recall even the most intricate details of a long visualization in proper order without effort. At first students tend to learn the visualizations quite generally; with more practice they are taught to add more details. Each detail carries great meaning and has its own blessing or benefit. So the more details you can remember, the more blessings received. It bothered Dechen sometimes that she hadn't gone to college—it felt like, not a *mistake* exactly, but perhaps Jetsunma hadn't understood Dechen completely. Was that possible? To feel more challenged mentally, Dechen began studying Tibetan in 1990—with Rick Finney or with visiting Tibetan lamas and khenpos. She liked academic work, but this, as well as a few other things about Dechen's personality, seemed to rub Alana the wrong way. Because of this, living in the retreat center wasn't easy. Alana complained that Dechen read instead of doing her chores, and that she was behind on her rent. Once Alana complained so bitterly about a pair of black sneakers that Dechen wore with her robes—black was a "demonic" color, Alana told her—that Jetsunma got sick of hearing about it and bought Dechen a new pair of shoes herself.

And it was Jetsunma who suggested that Dechen go to India to study at Penor Rinpoche's monastery in 1992, when the nun had told her in a private consultation that she wanted a career as a translator of Tibetan texts. It was at Namdroling that Dechen first encountered monastery life outside Poolesville. She was surprised by how different things were there. After she was paired with a seventh-year shedra student to help her study Tibetan, she was free and on her own. Nobody complained if she didn't pick up her clothes. Nobody cared if she read too much. "I was left alone to study—and it was startling to realize that this was not just acceptable, it was respected." The main focus of the monastery was its shedra, or university, and an atmosphere of scholarship and learning prevailed. By comparison, KPC seemed like a place where only group activities were highlighted. It was a small, insular village where everybody knew your business. The emphasis was on not knowledge and study but emotion. "Everyone was supposed to talk about what was on their minds, and reveal things," she said, "and people invaded your mind and thoughts and privacy."

In this new freer environment Dechen came under the spell of a charming young Tibetan monk who was thought to be a tulku. He had come with Penor Rinpoche to Poolesville for Jetsunma's enthronement in 1988, and he had been as naughty and rebellious as the other young monks. Now, four years later, he was more mature but still a bit of a troublemaker. Dechen liked his personality. And she was impressed by his tulku status. "I believed what Jetsunma had always said, that tulkus could do no harm," she said.

He was a monk, but the young tulku seemed interested in Dechen and flirted with her. She found herself flattered by this, and while she had brushed away the advances of many other young Tibetans in Bylakuppe, she did not brush this one away. He was an enlightened being, and, Dechen said to herself, he could do no harm. When he told her it was okay to swim in a nearby pond with him and some other monks, she believed he was telling the truth. And on an overnight trip to Bangalore, when the young tulku told Dechen that it was okay for her to share a hotel room with him and some other monks, she also believed him. And when he said that she should sleep with him in one bed, while the remaining monks shared another, she did. "He was a tulku," she told herself, "and it was okay." Once the lights were out he whispered to her, "Ani, don't tell anybody." And he rolled over on top of her in the dark and began kissing her. And then he made love to her.

"What's going to be the result of this?" she asked him, after it was over.

"I have no mistake," he said. *"But you have mistake."* Dechen left the bed and closed herself in the bathroom. Panicked, she began laughing uncontrollably. She had broken a root vow—sexual intercourse. The nonvirtue she had created could cause great harm. "I felt I had sent millions of sentient beings to the lower realms because of my broken vow. . . . And I thought, like Alana, I was going to get brain cancer and die on the spot."

The next morning, against the wishes of the young tulku, she called the temple in Poolesville. Rinchen answered the phone and told her that Jetsunma was at the beach. The next day Dechen was able to get through to Alana and eventually have a conversation with her guru. Dechen expected she would be thrown out of KPC for her actions, but, instead, Jetsunma seemed sympathetic. "This is a *violation* on his part," Jetsunma said. She seemed careful not to use the word *rape*. She instructed Dechen to discuss the incident with Khenpo Tsewang Gyatso, the head of the shedra at Namdroling, and use the word *violation*—and when she did Khenpo was very kind but troubled by the fact that Dechen had called Poolesville already. This meant he would be forced to tell Penor Rinpoche what had happened, and the repercussions for the young tulku would be very grave. The tulku had been brought there as a young boy because he had been difficult to raise. Over the years Khenpo had taken a fatherly attitude toward him and had hoped to look after him until he grew up. But he had guessed right. After he told Penor Rinpoche what had happened, the young tulku was sent away. Dechen felt partly responsible, but she didn't know what else to do. Was *violation* too harsh a description for what had happened? It was true: she had flirted. She had encouraged him. Dechen felt overwhelmed. Everything seemed unclear. She wanted to go home suddenly, very badly. Before she left Khenpo said, "Tell no one what happened."

In Poolesville, Jetsunma was very comforting to Dechen. It was agreed that what had happened to her in India would remain largely a secret, but in order to purify the negative karma that had been generated by a breakage of the celibacy vow, Jetsunma told Dechen to temporarily give back her robes and enter solitary retreat. First in an upstairs temple room, later in a bedroom in her mother's house, she began doing Vajrasattva, the purification practice, sixteen hours a day. There was an early morning session, then breakfast, a late morning session, then a rest, followed by an afternoon and an evening session. She did not leave her bedroom for five months. Her mother brought meals to the door.

"It's a confessional practice," Dechen said. "At the beginning of Vajrasattva, you are taught to examine everything, leave no stone unturned. You bare all your worst things, while doing prostrations and the mantra. There's nothing like Vajrasattva to make you feel like the lowest. Later on, you are purified and it's very gentle."

During the retreat Dechen completed eight hundred thousand Vajrasattvas; eventually she finished one million. The numbers aren't as important as the method—which is called the four powers or the four potencies. The first potency is recognizing that you have done something wrong, the second is remorse, the third is confession, and the fourth is the promise never to do it again. But after five months Dechen begged to be let out. She had gotten to the part of the practice where she needed to examine her relationship with the guru, and she found that she couldn't. It was very strange. "You have to be very honest and accept responsibility," she recounted later. "And you see things you don't like. When I saw things I didn't like about Jetsunma, I wanted to stop."

Even after she had returned to regular life, had retaken her ordination vows and moved into Ani Farms, Dechen found she had difficulty understanding exactly what the nature of her relationship with Jetsunma was—and what a tulku really was. There was a discrepancy between what was taught in Poolesville and what was written in the Tibetan texts. In the traditional book on Ngöndro, it said that if a lama told a student to do something wrong—or, as the Tibetan Buddhists say, *nonvirtuous*—the student would still suffer the karmic consequences of that act, regardless of having been instructed to do it. Dechen began to wonder. Why would a text even suggest that a tulku could cause harm if tulkus were perfect?

It was the summer of 1995 when he arrived in Poolesville—a man who can only be called the Monk.* He came to meet Penor Rinpoche and to receive the Nam Chu empowerments and teachings, then stayed for a while. It was a rare opportunity to take these teachings in America, and the Monk arrived with great hopes that, at long last, he might have found a monastery to call home. He had lived at many Dharma centers. He was an American, a famous practitioner, a former rock musician who had become a monk more than a decade before, learned Tibetan, read Tibetan, and done three-year retreats, a rare accomplishment in the West. He was so tall that he towered over little Dechen—and he was so homely that she found him almost adorable. He was very traditional. He was excruciatingly honest. He was never out of his robes. He slept on the floor. And when he looked at Dechen—as they began to work on some translations together— he saw something that the others in Poolesville had missed. He didn't see an insecure approval junkie or a hothouse flower or a brat. When the Monk looked at Dechen, he saw how refined her beauty was, and how refined her mind was. She was smarter than any of them, he told her. The clarity of her mind and her ability to translate Tibetan would surely surpass his in no time.

* He spoke with the author under the condition that his name not be used in these accounts.

They began driving to the Library of Congress together to work on texts. And in the car they would talk. The Monk had a chronic health problem and was often unwell. Dechen found herself worrying about him and wondering if he was being taken care of properly, if he had enough to eat and the right medication. She also began to think about how she might get him to stay in Poolesville permanently, instead of wandering from Dharma center to Dharma center. Why was he always wandering around? She respected him, admired him, and liked the way he treated her. She never wanted him to leave.

As her friendship with the Monk grew, she found herself having a harder and harder time at Ani Farms, where she had been living for a year and a half. The nuns were always on her case about something—her messy room, the hours she spent on the phone. "If I left a book bag on the stairs, that was a huge problem," Dechen said. Her domestic habits, she was told, were affecting the "energy of the house." She didn't enjoy sitting around, the way they did, psychoanalyzing students who weren't present, and she felt she had become the subject of the psychoanalyzing with greater frequency. It was true that the other nuns discussed her when she wasn't there. As Sherab would explain several years later, "I think it was difficult for her because a real maturation process had not taken place . . . she seemed to need people's attention and approval. And she was always trying to act like a big girl, but she wasn't. There was a lot of door slamming and curling up like a ball on her bed and not coming out of her room."

About two or three months after they had become friends, Dechen became more open with the Monk about Ani Farms. It was hard being a nun, and having a job, and living in a group house where nobody seemed to like her. Over the summer all the ordained had gathered at Ani Estates and been asked to sign a paper that released KPC from the responsibility of taking care of them in sickness or old age. When Dechen signed the paper, she felt as though she were "signing away" her life. What kind of monastery was this? She had dreams of renunciate life, but why bother being a nun if you weren't going to have time to practice or go on retreats? Signing this legal document seemed like the death knell: Dechen would have to work as a secretary for the rest of her days, come home to Ani Farms and do housework and temple jobs, have the other nuns griping about her book bags on the stairs, and try to fit in practice somewhere. Apparently Dechen wasn't the only one who was upset—when the papers were collected by Tashi at the end of the meeting, one of the monks had returned his document unsigned with "fuck you" written across the top.

Dechen had given up a secretarial job to attend the month-long Nam Chu empowerments. She had saved some money but was living off a dwindling supply. A month after the empowerments were over, she still hadn't found a new job, hadn't even tried, and in August her rent check to Palchen—whose name was on the lease—bounced. In September her rent went unpaid again, and the atmosphere in the group house grew icy and bitter. The household held an emotional meeting in September 1995 at which Dechen and Sonam, another young nun at the house who owed money, were informed that their debts were "intolerable" and "anti-Buddhist." They were both expected to find part-time jobs to repay their debts. Alana had suggested that Dechen get a job at McDonald's and that Sonam find something at 7-Eleven.

One night soon after the household meeting, Dechen woke up and saw that the lights in Sonam's room were on and the furniture was gone. She heard a window closing and the front door pulled open. When Dechen went downstairs to investigate, she found Sonam sitting in the front seat of a large airport shuttle van, which was taking her and all of her belongings away.

Dechen was devastated that Sonam was leaving. Sonam was one of the few people she got along with. And Dechen was stunned that Sonam would sneak off in the middle of the night. It wasn't a good thing to leave that way—or to leave at all. Without the protection of Jetsunma, she could get sick, suffer obstacles, wind up in Vajra Hell. But looking at Sonam's determined face and her halo of stubby red hair, it didn't seem the right time to say any of that. Dechen could see that Sonam just wanted to be left alone.

"I guess you won't be coming to any more meetings," Dechen said.

"No, I guess not," Sonam said.

Sonam left her bed, a lamp, and a phone. Dechen was never sure why. She left her car, too, and arranged to rent it out to another nun as a way to pay off her debts to Ani Farms. She never came back to Poolesville. Her departure was unimaginable to Dechen—and it left her even lonelier. Sonam had been her only friend, except for the Monk.

As she grew more miserable, Dechen confided further in the Monk—mostly on the phone. In the past her complaints about Poolesville had been minor, that the nuns seemed to be micromanaged by Alana while the monks were left alone. But she found when she became braver, and started to talk more generally about the temple and how it was run, her friendship with the Monk began to blossom. And he took her into his confidence. He had his own concerns about monastic life in Poolesville. It was weird how the monks all had jobs, went to work during the day, and came home and watched *The Simpsons* on TV, and how Rinchen always seemed to be watching soap operas in the temple office. The building of the Migyur Dorje stupa was a fine thing—the prayer room was full of bags of rice and beans and cedar chips—but it seemed the students were geared only to building and painting and sewing. There were very few really strong, sit-down practitioners in the traditional Tibetan Buddhist sense. The Monk liked many of the students and had a good feeling about them, but they seemed to be racing around on the outside and stagnant inside. "Normally you go through lots of upheavals and changes in a Tibetan Buddhist community," he said. "You change or you leave." He found himself questioning: "Are these people progressing?"

He felt that Dechen needed to know that other Dharma centers in the country weren't anything like this—weren't run like Poolesville and didn't feel like Poolesville. In fact, there was something a little creepy about KPC.

Dechen always defended the temple and her fellow ordained. This was a new kind of Dharma center, she said, and the students were pioneers. Why should it be like anywhere else?

Little by little, as they grew closer, the Monk revealed that he had questions about Jetsunma, too. She didn't act like other Dharma teachers and tulkus, he told Dechen. Her actions were so far off the map that it was hard to explain them. Why didn't she

direct her students' devotion away from her and toward the teachings, the way the other lamas did? It was natural for students to fall
in love with their teachers during an initial "honeymoon phase,"
but why had Jetsunma allowed them to worship her in such an
overboard way? She might be the real thing, a true bodhisattva—
the Monk was always willing to entertain that possibility because
he believed in Penor Rinpoche and Gyaltrul Rinpoche—but her
teachings were untraditional. They were often tinged with New
Age thinking, and Jetsunma made bizarre claims.

It was highly unusual, for one thing, that she promised to
meet up with students in the bardo. And it was unheard of that
she or any of her students would claim that Jetsunma was a
ninth-level or tenth-level bodhisattva, a profoundly realized
being—because Mandarava was supposed to be. "To speak of
one's spiritual attainments is to lose them," the Monk told
Dechen. As for her past-life memories and knowledge of the past
lives of her students—even if they were real—they would ordinarily be kept to herself. No other lama he'd ever known talked
this way. The Dalai Lama had often joked that he couldn't remember things that happened last month, let alone in another lifetime.

But even stranger was the emphasis on money. At the other
Dharma centers it was discussed one day a year, usually around
tax time—and students were never browbeaten about giving. The
Monk had been upstairs in the temple office over the summer and
found a printout of the budget. Did Dechen know how much
money Jetsunma received every month? Close to ten thousand
dollars in cash. Tax-free. Dechen was stunned by the amount.
"She has all kinds of expenses," Dechen said at first. The Monk
wouldn't hear of it. This was an unheard of amount for a lama to
be paid, he told her. Penor Rinpoche owned just his clothes. Gyaltrul Rinpoche lived very simply. Tibetans in general are frugal and
financially cautious people. They don't have lifestyles that include
huge wardrobes and beach vacations. And whatever money they
get, they give to their Dharma centers. In India, Penor Rinpoche
raised money to support and feed thousands of monks and nuns.
He provided for them, not the other way around.

The Monk remembered how, at the Nam Chu, he'd been told
by Wib that the sangha had given Jetsunma the same amount of

money as Penor Rinpoche—twelve thousand dollars—even though she hadn't been teaching. Didn't anybody know that His Holiness was supposed to get more than she did, or the entire offering? And traditionally an offering made to a lama for a teaching was immediately given back to the center, not kept. Where did all Jetsunma's money go?

As more time passed the Monk made another revelation to Dechen. Did she know that Jetsunma was shopping around for a new consort? That Karl was on the outs? Dechen hadn't known anything about this, except that Karl had told her once that Jetsunma had slugged him one day—so hard that he was knocked over a piece of furniture. And that Gyaltrul Rinpoche had told him that being beaten by Jetsunma was a "great, great blessing."

"New consort? Who?"

The Monk believed that Jetsunma had shown an interest in him. One day, in front of many students, she had walked right up to the Monk and kissed him flush on the mouth. She had praised his translations and told him she wanted him to stay and teach. A number of times he had felt her eyeing him—putting out a certain seductive vibe. And one of her attendants had come to him, asking if the Monk could personally give Jetsunma the Dream Yoga practices and other high Tantric teachings. Since she hadn't done the requisite retreats and purifications, he had refused.

The funny thing was, while the Monk wasn't interested in Jetsunma he did seem interested in Dechen. He always found ways to tell her that she was special—delicate and subtle and intelligent and aware. He showered her with praise. "I had never been treated so well by anybody," she would say later, "and nobody had ever said the things he did to me."

In late October, over the phone, the Monk admitted that he was falling in love with her.

"I know," Dechen said.

They were quiet for a while. "You aren't going to leave me now, are you?" she asked.

"I should," he said. "I should break this off."

"I have nobody left but you," Dechen said. "Sonam's gone . . ."

She had no romantic feelings for him, she told him. He seemed to accept this, and Dechen was sure the subject would never come up again. It was a crush, she told herself. It was fleeting. And he had been a monk for so long that he surely knew how to deal with these things. But on Dechen's birthday in November, the Monk took her to dinner in Bethesda and to see *Carrington*, an Emma Thompson movie about a celibate love affair between two Bloomsbury bohemians. Before the movie he handed Dechen a poem that he had written for her. She read it and was stunned. It was romantic, emotional, and very physical. "It had a lot of imagery," she said, "and was a praise of every part of me."

She reread the poem in her bedroom, later that night, then crumpled it up and threw it in the trash. The next morning she fished it out again and flattened it. And she called him.

"You can't do this, you're a monk," she told him.

"I thought you'd never call me again," he said.

"I shouldn't," she said, "and don't write any more poems."

"Okay."

They were driving home from the Library of Congress one night in the car, and after a tender conversation they began to kiss. "It was stupid of me, but I didn't see it coming," said Dechen. They pulled the car over to the side of the road and continued their embrace. The Monk told Dechen that he loved her. He wanted to marry her. He wanted to take her away from Poolesville. Dechen grew quiet, and the Monk drove her home.

The next morning she felt once again that her friendship with the Monk had to end. But almost as soon as she'd decided that, she called him. They had to be friends. Who else did she have? Also, she felt herself on the verge of something. Was it love? She began to allow the Monk's fantasies to bloom inside her. She began imagining the possibility of not being ordained, of marrying him and living side by side, two lay practitioners of Tibetan Buddhism. "And he told me about all these other Dharma centers we could visit," she said. "But I still didn't really want to be anywhere but Poolesville."

Just a few nights later, a stranger came to Ani Farms, a journalist who was writing a book about Jetsunma. Most everybody had heard about the book, and there'd been some tittering in a meeting about it. The sangha had been wondering when the rest of the world would begin to recognize Jetsunma and the miraculous work she had been doing for years.

The night I came to the farmhouse, Rinchen knocked on Dechen's door and told her to come to dinner. *Dinner?* Usually the nuns didn't eat meals together, and lately they hadn't been speaking to Dechen, much less allowing her to eat out of the general food supply, since she was not contributing her share of money. When Dechen said she wasn't coming to dinner, Rinchen explained she had no choice.

The dining room was dark, and Dechen felt odd and uncomfortable. She sat down across from me, as she would recount two years later, and witnessed the unfolding scene. She remembered noticing that I had long dark hair and was almost as tall as Sherab. She remembered that Sherab and I acted like kindred spirits. We were comfortable with each other, made jokes, and seemed like old friends. We had been up in Sherab's room talking for hours, too. Dechen remembered how the other nuns nodded their heads—and acted like they had dinner together every night. It wasn't an act, really. Dechen understood how it was. When outsiders came you wanted things to seem a certain way.

Dechen was thankful when the phone rang and it turned out to be for her. She stood in the kitchen for the remainder of the meal and talked with the Monk while her dinner grew cold. Finally I left.

They were always talking on the phone in those days, and the Monk was always saying that he wouldn't leave Poolesville without her. Ordained or not, she couldn't remain in that place, he said. She needed to find another Dharma center where her talents would be appreciated and understood and she'd be left alone to practice and do three-year retreats. A healthy place. A good place. But he had to admit to himself—when he thought of the Dharma in the West and his own experiences—there were few if any good places.

There was Tibetan Buddhism, and the actual teachings of Buddha, and there were people, human beings, and all their accompanying needs and habits. There was Tibetan Buddhism, and there was a system that was employed to teach it. That system wasn't Tibetan Buddhism. And the politics within that system weren't Tibetan Buddhism. And the Tibetan tulku system wasn't Buddhism, either. It was just another system, created by people. Democracy had no place in it. Someday things would be different, he told Dechen. But probably they wouldn't live to see it.

Dechen found herself pondering the Monk's words and wondered if he was right. She also wondered if he was telling the truth about wanting to marry her. Down deep, she didn't believe him. And when she searched through her own feelings, she decided that she didn't love him. She didn't feel sexually attracted to him. But she felt it was possible that over time they could make a life together built around the Dharma and grow to love each other. And she might be able to practice more that way than as a nun at Ani Farms.

She decided to test him, and herself.

The Monk went to New York for a few days, and he called her from the train on his way back. Dechen told him that she would drive into Washington, D.C., and meet him at the station—even though the city was shut down in a snowstorm. The Monk was surprised and seemed to have a sense of what the meeting was about. At the train station they were reserved in their greeting, but each knew what was coming next. Dechen had already gotten them a room in a D.C. hotel. They checked into a one-hundred-dollar-a-night room in their burgundy robes.

The next morning Dechen sat on the edge of the bed and looked at the Monk. He looked very sad. And she felt sad, too. She didn't want to give up her robes. And she felt strongly that he didn't, either.

"I don't want to give up my robes," she said.

"I know," said the Monk.

"And I don't think you want to, either."

"Really?"

"You seem sad."

"Yeah," he said, sighing. "It's hard."

"Yeah."

There was silence for a while between them, but not for long. They had grown into each other's lives, become best friends. They had much in common, felt on the same wavelength. And what they had together, they found they could not give up.

Not long afterward Dechen told him that she wanted to go to Jetsunma and confess. This was the only proper thing to do.

"Jetsunma? No fucking way," the Monk said.

"How about Gyaltrul Rinpoche? He's coming at the end of the month."

"Maybe. Let's talk about it later."

She had learned, when she had broken her vows before, that if one confesses to a breakage—rather than being discovered—the offense, the bad karma that had been generated, is rectifiable, or, as the Buddhists say, purifiable. The Monk insisted that this wasn't necessarily so. Essentially, they had just touched bodies and kissed. He had read the rules very carefully, and this wasn't a "root vow breakage"; it was considered less serious, a "branch" or "remainder vow breakage." He had been very careful when they'd been together and had not entered any orifice of her body. Their breakages were only as serious as masturbating, he told Dechen. And because the root vows of ordination were not broken, they were not technically required to confess. It had been wrong, and unwise, he admitted, but they had been careful.

The Tibetan custom, he told her, is to handle these lesser infractions privately. You pick yourself up, do purification practices, and go on. And in his lineage of Tibetan Buddhism, this is true. But the Monk also knew that in Dechen's—the Nyingma school—it is not. He told Dechen that, technically, it would take a jury of five monks who had held robes as long as the Monk had to weigh in on the situation. But there were no such monks in America.

He and Dechen went over and over the same ground. It became the daily argument—with Dechen pushing him to talk about it again. The Monk claimed to know what was in the texts and how things were done traditionally. Dechen knew only what had happened to her before, in India, and how important it seemed that she had come forward on her own. But the days passed, and the argument between them went on.

18.

What a Lucky Child

WHERE THERE IS NO BELIEF IN THE SOUL,
THERE IS VERY LITTLE DRAMA.

—FLANNERY O'CONNOR

At the end of the year Gyaltrul Rinpoche came to Poolesville, but he never heard a confession from the Monk or Dechen. At first the Monk had agreed with Dechen—they should go together to see the old Tibetan. But later he changed his mind. It would have been hard to see Gyaltrul Rinpoche in any case. He hadn't come to Maryland to see students as much as to minister to Jetsunma. In phone conversations she had told him that she had been down lately, feeling at sea. There was so much work to be done still. And she feared that her marriage to Karl was ending and wanted Gyaltrul Rinpoche's advice.

The lama arrived around Christmas but soon after became very sick with a stomach virus. He stayed downstairs, in his quarters of the temple, and saw nobody. When Jetsunma came down with the same flu, Alana explained at a sangha meeting that the merit of the students must be awfully low to have caused such illness. What was causing this low merit?

Dechen sat in her chair and began to worry. Later she asked the Monk again to show her the texts that said they didn't need to go to the lama and explain what happened. "Just do some confession on your own and Vajrasattva," he told her. "There's no need to go to anybody."

After Gyaltrul Rinpoche's departure there were two sangha meetings to discuss the fallout from his visit and new developments at the temple. They were held on separate evenings. The ordained met in the prayer room and the lay practitioners in the larger Dharma room. As was usually the case, only a small circle of students who were close to Jetsunma had any idea of what was coming. Gyaltrul Rinpoche's visit was heard about secondhand, in whispers, if you were the sort who listened to the whispers or were around the temple enough to notice changes.

The white noise around the temple in those days was mostly about Karl. He'd had an unhappy look on his face all year. While the inner circle had known that Jetsunma's relationship with Karl had been stormy for months, that he had been living at the monks' house in Poolesville over the summer, the split between the lama and her consort was just now going public. As usual, before an actual announcement was made, Alana had been a subtle conduit for leaks that helped the students adjust. "Gyatrul Rinpoche pointed to Karl and said, 'You! Get back in robes!' " she told a few members of the sangha in passing. "He told Jetsunma that Karl didn't belong in her house anymore, but he didn't belong with the lay practitioners either. He is a strange case, neither fish nor fowl."

Neither fish nor fowl. This had certainly been the sangha's impression, too. Nobody knew what to make of the young man Jetsunma had taken as her fourth husband—fifth, if you counted Sangye. Karl had always been a mystery to them, an unknown force inside Jetsunma's house, although more like no force at all. He rarely spoke to sangha members aside from a mumble. And, increasingly, he had looked glum or brooding.

Alana had told several close students that Jetsunma felt very bad about the ending of her marriage. Karl was young—way too young—and hadn't known how to treat her. Jetsunma had asked Gyaltrul Rinpoche why she'd been married so many times and why things never worked out. "You were damaged as a child," he had explained. "Give yourself a break. This is your compassion. It's like you can't help yourself. You see a bird with a broken wing, and you just go for it, you want to save it. Look at Michael. Spiritually, isn't he better off?"

"Well, yes," Jetsunma said.

"Look at Sangye Dorje. He's a geylong monk now. Isn't he better off?"

"Yes."

"Karl—is he better?"

"Well, yeah."

"So shut up!" Gyaltrul Rinpoche said, with a chuckle.

"But I just go from one to the other?" Jetsunma asked. "Is this what my life is going to look like?"

"So what?" Gyaltrul Rinpoche asked her. "They're all better off, aren't they?"

"That makes me sound like some kind of machine."

"Well, you are," Gyaltrul Rinpoche said. "Why do you want to be like other women? Can they liberate beings? Take all these feelings, and meditate on the emptiness of them, the emptiness of everything including feelings. You have these feelings because this is your display—but they aren't really anything. And, yes, you are a machine."

Chris Finney got a phone call from Sylvia Somerville, one of her closest friends at the temple, telling her about a special meeting to be held following Gyaltrul Rinpoche's departure. From the urgency and seriousness in Sylvia's voice, Chris quickly guessed that the meeting wasn't open to all sangha members. It was one of *those* meetings, the dark meetings, the laundry-airing meetings. Over the years she had seen new students pulled out of the Dharma room and told—gently and kindly—that it wasn't really appropriate for them to be present.

Lately Chris had been avoiding the meetings in Poolesville. She had two daughters now, and life was busier. Also, a shift had taken place inside her. She wasn't sure whether it was her and Rick, and what they'd been going through, or whether the place itself had changed. Chris kept her doubts about KPC to herself.

She had found it easier simply not to raise the subject. And when anything about the temple came up, Rick seemed careful not to say too much.

Fortunately, the attention paid to the Finneys' older daughter, Eleanore, now four years old, had died down. This might have been because a young boy had been found to be the rebirth of Dudjom Rinpoche, which would rule out little red-haired Eleanore as his reincarnation. But the Finneys felt that the meddling had continued. Over the summer, during Penor Rinpoche's visit, Rick had not attended teachings. He had looked after the couple's daughters instead. Chris was sitting on the front porch of the temple one afternoon, talking with Alana and Atara, when the two attendants began discussing Rick. "He really doesn't get it, does he?" one of them said. Chris didn't know what to say and felt defensive.

A few days later Rick was approached by Atara, who said she had a message from Jetsunma. They stood on the porch for a few seconds; then Atara pulled him into the temple foyer. "Rick," she said, "Jetsunma is deeply concerned. If you don't pay more attention to your involvement here, when you die you're going to go further and further down, and your daughters will go further and further up. And you'll never see them again."

When Rick relayed the conversation to Chris, she grew concerned. She felt strongly that it was Rick's business where he practiced and whether he accepted Jetsunma as his root guru or main teacher—but she also knew that sometimes couples at KPC were encouraged to separate. What would she do if she had to make a choice?

Rick had been a student of Tibetan Buddhism for more than two decades already—in his twenties he had studied with Geshe Lobsang Tharchin, and later he had spent six years as a student of Chögyam Trungpa Rinpoche, a gifted Tibetan lama who died in 1987. And Rick felt that he had seen what havoc a brilliant but self-destructive tulku could produce. Trungpa Rinpoche, although Rick admired him greatly, was a terrible drunk who lived a rather posh upper-class English lifestyle, and, albeit married, he slept with a large circle of students.

And although Rick felt strongly committed to the Dharma, in the past years he had given up on KPC. It was one thing to put up with some bad behavior from a real tulku and a qualified Dharma teacher, but Rick had come to suspect that Jetsunma wasn't even that. He had tried to keep his views to himself, and hidden from Chris, but suddenly, it seemed, Jetsunma had gotten bolder in her meddling. If it was no longer okay with Jetsunma that Rick wasn't taking the teachings in Poolesville, he worried that very soon it wasn't going to be okay that Chris was married to him. He also couldn't help but worry that Chris would leave him and take the girls with her.

With his wife's approval Rick decided to write a letter directly to Jetsunma—hoping to clear up a misunderstanding about his lack of involvement at the center. He tried to be direct and honest and not disrespectful. He explained that he was supportive of Chris's involvement in Poolesville, but he had made a decision to hold another teacher of his, Khenpo Konchog Gyaltsen, as his root guru.

He addressed the unresolved questions about Eleanore, too. On several occasions in 1991 and 1992, it had seemed to Rick that Jetsunma had wanted custody of her. Jetsunma herself had joked about wanting to raise her. Alana had asked Rick, "Will you give her to us?" Rick took the hints of a lama and her attendant seriously. And he felt he needed to tell Jetsunma that, rather than pleased by these attentions, he and Chris had felt harassed.

He enclosed a twenty-dollar bill with the letter and gave it to Atara. Rick and Chris had heard many times that if you wrote to Jetsunma it was appropriate to put some cash in the envelope. "We were told if there wasn't an offering in the letter—as a pro forma thing," said Rick, "that she wouldn't even consider it."

Months would pass before the Finneys heard a reply. And as Chris waited, she felt a change in herself, a new feeling. Having a doubt about one's lama, or about the Dharma, according to the Buddhist texts, has serious repercussions. Chris thought if she doubted, she would lose her way, lose the Dharma. And she would lose her friends, her social life, her spiritual life. What would she have then? "In the past, I had thought that if I examined some of this," she said later, "I would almost disappear—like I physically couldn't keep integrated anymore."

Chris worried about her samaya with Jetsunma. In Tibetan Buddhism a student makes a deep and lifelong vow to honor, respect, and obey the root guru, in exchange for the transmissions of wisdom and empowerments to come. A broken samaya is a broken pledge of devotion, a dishonoring of the guru, a dishonoring of one's true nature, making further spiritual transmissions problematic. Early on Michael Burroughs had put a punitive Christian spin on the concept by telling students that a broken samaya could result in Vajra Hell—a bad rebirth.

The students were supposed to train themselves to have utter faith in Jetsunma—as blind as possible. But the doubts were unstoppable for Chris that summer, like a bad taste she couldn't get out of her mouth. She suddenly remembered episodes that she had long since buried: the time that she had cried inside the temple and been told to leave the grounds because her emotions were "damaging" the crystals. She remembered how she'd been "Vajra-commanded" by Jetsunma to work at Tara Studios, even though she was pregnant and became allergic to some of the chemical compounds being used there. Why hadn't Jetsunma been able to foresee this?

Then she caught herself. She tried to see things another way—to go around the mountain, as Jetsunma always taught, and see it from a different perspective. Chris remembered all the high lamas who had visited the beautiful temple rooms in Poolesville. The Tibetans were always so taken with the look of the place, with the appearance, and with the warmth of the students with big smiles and profuse bowing and humility. The lamas seemed almost misty-eyed when they came to Poolesville, as though the best of Tibet had been re-created there. Chris trusted their reactions—and wanted to keep trusting them. Penor Rinpoche, she kept telling herself, couldn't be wrong. Could he?

Doubt was like a disease, or a weed, or an infestation. Chris remembered hearing Alana describe how she struggled with her own doubts. She used to say that one small kernel of doubt that lasted one moment could result in your leaving Poolesville six months later. Chris had watched Bob Colacurcio go through some bouts of it, and seen the strain on his face. She'd thought she'd seen it on Wib's face, too. But they had wrestled their doubts and come back even stronger. There was almost a sense of exhilaration that came with wrestling doubts and winning the fight. Rick had been told by Jane Perini once, "If you distrust her, you distrust your own enlightened mind."

Maybe that was all this was. Chris doubted herself—and therefore doubted Jetsunma.

In late September, after three months of waiting, Rick received a phone call from Atara saying that Jetsunma had read his letter. Her response to him was in his file folder in the solarium—where messages were left for students. Rick drove immediately to the temple, sat in the pew in the foyer, and opened Jetsunma's note. The handwriting was sloppy, an angry scrawl. Jetsunma seemed to have been outraged by his letter to her. *I don't know what Alana meant by what she said, why don't you ask Alana?* her note said, according to Rick's recollection. *I can't believe how many statements made by my students are attributed to me. . . . How self-important! How arrogant! How ungrateful! I won't even address the other questions.* She also returned the twenty-dollar bill. *Here's your twenty. I don't want your money,* Rick read at the bottom of the last page. *Give it to the stupa fund.*

Things were even worse than he'd thought. Rick looked at the note again, at the handwriting. "She's a total psycho," he said to himself. After a few days Atara approached Chris to ask if she and Rick had gotten Jetsunma's response. "Yes, we did," Chris said.

"What are you going to do?" Atara asked.

"I don't know what I'm going to do about the letter," Chris told her. "I haven't decided."

But lately when Chris did Guru Yoga practice in the evenings, instead of imagining Jetsunma over her head as the guru, she imagined the substantial and beneficent figure of Penor Rinpoche. Suddenly her mind became much calmer.

It was a cold night in January—and four months since Rick had received Jetsunma's note—when Chris arrived a bit early at the temple for the special meeting. She was alone. Rick was home with the girls. Chris took her shoes off in the foyer and left her coat on top of a crowded rack. The Dharma room was packed already, and Chris found a cushion and took a place on the floor near Sylvia Somerville.

Alana was standing in her robes in front of sixty or so students. Chris looked around and realized they weren't all old-timers—there were some fairly new faces in the crowd. Chris was surprised. And she wondered how some of them would react. Alana began by discussing Gyaltrul Rinpoche's visit over Christmas. The sangha needed to know that the Tibetan's illness was surely the result of the students' karma, their low merit.

It was unlike her, but Chris found herself arguing with Alana in her mind. "Bullshit! We just built a stupa! Just the biggest, grandest thing ever. And it wasn't hastily done. It was done in all the right ways!" If there was truth to this merit business, Chris was thinking, then this calculation wasn't right.

Alana moved to the main thrust of the meeting. Significant changes were taking place in Jetsunma's life. Chris noticed that Karl was on a cushion in the front row, at Alana's feet.

Jetsunma was concerned that the students didn't realize how much she had suffered in her marriage to Karl, it was reported. Jetsunma had heard of people complaining, Poor Karl, poor Karl, and she felt that some students seemed sympathetic to him. But it was time for the students to become aware of a few things—to help them realize what Jetsunma had been going through these last two years. Karl was immature. He had bad role models for relationships. And while he had been sent through a Twelve-Step program and psychotherapy to help clear up some of these bad habits, he still was unthinking and inconsiderate, and continued to treat Jetsunma very badly. Alana recounted how one night Karl was watching TV with the family when Jetsunma began to feel sick. She went to the bathroom and began vomiting, and Karl kept watching TV—he never came to see how Jetsunma was.

Chris could hear several students gasp in horror.

"Karl's ego needs to be cut down," Alana said. "He doesn't seem to realize what he has. And he seems to think he can dominate her!" It was up to the sangha to break him, "like a wild mustang," Alana said. "Karl needs to be reminded who the lama is around here."

Chris had a hard time looking at Karl. His head was down, and he was staring at the floor. She saw the back of his neck and his profile. He was twenty-five years old but suddenly looked much younger.

She looked around the room—at all the people with whom she'd cast her lot for so many years. They appeared to be taking in this attack on Karl as though it were a new teaching, the latest instruction. And nothing seemed odd to them about it. "Each and every one of us has to take it upon ourselves—whenever we see him doing something that isn't right—to break him," Alana continued. There were many Wendys in Poolesville, she told the crowd, the types who liked to help out Peter Pan and might feel compelled to take Karl under their wings. They should not do this.

Chris found her mind racing. Had she been blind all these years? How many moments of insensitivity had she witnessed? How many misguided lessons in compassion? She couldn't believe that the spiritual center where she had spent so much of her life, and where she had uttered so many prayers, had so many dear friends, allowed this. "They were just nodding their heads like zombies," she said.

The room opened up for comments, and people talked about Karl angrily. They were disappointed that he was treating Jetsunma so poorly. One after another students spoke. Chris watched as Wib and Jane said their piece. "We're just so clueless, all of us," Wib said. "We don't understand what a blessing Jetsunma is. And here Karl is, with the emanation of Tara, and he's not treating her appropriately."

Palchen said, "People come into the gift shop and inquire about Jetsunma's marriage. What do I say to them?"

"If you were doing Guru Yoga properly," Alana said sharply, "you wouldn't have to ask that question."

Other people were ordinary and needed to keep vows and live more conventionally, Alana said. It was important to remember that Jetsunma was not ordinary and wouldn't be living ordinarily. "I know that some of you have been commenting on Jetsunma's sex life," she said, "and the number of partners she's had . . . and seem to have judgment about that." She paused and looked around the room, as if singling out a few students with her eyes. "She should be able to have as many partners as she wants, and nobody should bat an eye," Alana said. "And just because Jetsunma is married didn't mean she couldn't have others. That is the nature of a consort relationship. It isn't necessarily exclusive. . . .

"Whatever she does, you should accept it unconditionally," Alana said. "You should be prepared to have that kind of devotion to a lama. And, ideally, if you saw a dakini walk down the road and cut the head off a sweet infant child, your only thought should be, *Oh, what a lucky child.*"

Chris waited a few moments, then rose. She stepped through the crowd to the door. Out in the foyer she felt suddenly better. It was going to be easy to walk out, she told herself. Very easy. She reached for her coat and quickly slipped on her shoes. How could she have missed so many obvious signs for so many years? How could she have lived that way—paying so little attention to the truth? There were two Poolesvilles. There was the one she allowed herself to see and the one that was hidden, the one she had never wanted to face. She could hear Alana's voice still, inside the Dharma room. The attendant had switched tacks and was asking the sangha for devotional stories—wanted to hear people talk about what a difference Jetsunma had made in their lives. There didn't seem to be any immediate volunteers.

Rinchen stepped into the foyer from the solarium and smiled at Chris. "I'll have that brochure done soon," Chris told her—referring to an unfinished temple project she had been working on. What version of the night's events would Rinchen be telling herself in the future? How would this night look to them, all of them, when they thought back on it? Would they even remember it? When she got outside Chris turned around to look at the facade of the temple again. She took in the whole place suddenly, all of it, the large white porch and huge columns, the roof and the sides. It was as though she had never really seen it before. Her ears were ringing, the way one's ears ring after a concert, and she could still

THE BUDDHA FROM BROOKLYN • 279

hear the talking inside, and Alana's voice, and the students mouthing their stifled words of devotion.

She took in a breath, then exhaled. "I will never come here again," she said to herself. "Ever."

The next morning she left a voice mail for Jane Perini. "Based on what I heard at that meeting last night, I won't be able to be a member here anymore," Chris said. Soon afterward she got a call from Sylvia Somerville. "I can't believe you're leaving," Sylvia said. "You've been there right along with us, since the beginning. I feel like we're climbing a mountain together and you just let go of the rope. We were making progress going up the mountain. . . . We're going up and now you're going to fall."

When Chris heard that—about going up the mountain and the rope being cut—she didn't imagine herself falling. She felt herself rising, flying, *soaring.*

"Can I ask something?" Sylvia said.

"Yes."

"Would it be easier to stay if you weren't married?"

"No," Chris said. "It wouldn't be easier."

The phone rang a lot after that, but Chris didn't answer it. She didn't want to talk to Alana, or hear about her broken samaya, or anybody's explanations, or one more thing about Jetsunma's compassion, ever. She knew what she knew—and nobody was going to try to take it away from her again.

The meeting for the ordained about Karl hadn't bothered Dechen too much. It felt like many meetings she'd been to before. She was more troubled by a chilly phone call she'd received from Alana soon afterward. Alana was exasperated that four months had passed since the Ani Farms household meeting and Dechen still hadn't gotten a part-time job. From what Alana had heard, all Dechen was doing these days was translating Tibetan texts with the Monk and Khenpo Tsewang Gyatso. That would have to stop.

"You are no longer permitted to translate until you have gotten a job," Alana told her, "and have begun to make payments on the money you owe Palchen."

Dechen saw the Monk later that day and immediately began complaining. "This is ridiculous," she said. "How can they do this? How can Alana have so much control over my life?" As she drove the Monk to a doctor's appointment, he urged her once again to find another Dharma center. Afterward they found themselves sitting in the parking lot of the Safeway in Darnestown for six hours, talking about KPC and the way it was run. Recently it had been discovered that Sonam had gone to Tashi Choling, Gyaltrul Rinpoche's center in Oregon. Wouldn't Dechen be happier there? There were many centers, lots of places where she could be an ani and not be told where to live or how to spend her time. Dechen was too upset to think about it, so upset and rebellious that she suggested to the Monk that they find another hotel where they could be alone together. So they did.

Alana called again, a week later. "We need to meet with you," she said, "to discuss some things. *Some problems.*"

"A meeting?" Dechen felt a twist in her stomach.

"Yes, Dechen. *A meeting.* On Saturday morning at ten o'clock."

Dechen felt her heart pounding. She felt certain that Alana knew about her and the Monk. "What problems?" she asked, her voice becoming tight and dry.

"We need to talk about Palchen and the money you owe her," Alana said.

"*Oh, that,*" Dechen said. "Okay."

She was still shaking when the phone rang again a few moments later. "I heard something in your voice just now," Alana asked her. "*Did you break your vows?*"

19

The Great Blessing

YOU HAVE TO SEE THROUGH THE LUSTER
OF ALL THE THINGS YOU PLAY WITH.
YOU HAVE TO TAKE THE INNER POSTURE
OF LEAVING THE PARTY.

—JETSUNMA AHKÖN LHAMO

Dechen borrowed her mother's white minivan the next morning and drove to the town house in Darnestown where the Monk was living with five other monks. She parked on the street and went inside. "I'm going to see Khenpo," she told the Monk, "and I think you should come, too."

On the drive together there were long periods of silence. When directly confronted on the phone, Dechen had told Alana about the affair. And when Dechen insisted that she had not "broken her vows"—meaning her root vows—Alana had accused her of obnoxious hairsplitting. "You were together alone on a bed in a hotel, *and you say you didn't break your vows?*" There were several rounds of this until Alana simply said, "I can't talk to you anymore," and hung up. Dechen then called the Monk and told him what happened.

"You told *Alana?*" he said, in horror.

But later that night Alana called again to say that a meeting with Khenpo Tsewang Gyatso had been scheduled for noon the following day and that Jetsunma would see her in the evening.

Nobody had suggested that Dechen bring the Monk along. That was her idea.

The drive to the temple seemed very long, and dreadful. Now she saw that it was a mistake not to have confessed. This was the worst possible outcome—to be found out by Alana and dragged before Khenpo, the venerable Tibetan scholar. She had memories of India, of having gone before the very same man once before with news like this. The irony staggered her.

Dechen and the Monk walked inside the temple together and found Khenpo upstairs, in a suite of rooms he always used when visiting. He ushered them inside and sat down on a purple sofa in his bedroom. Khenpo was a short man with a small mustache and a perfectly round head. He was younger than most Tibetan scholars—still in his fifties—and while he seemed easygoing and simple, he was also known for having one of the best minds in the Nyingma school. There didn't seem to be an esoteric point that he couldn't elucidate or a question he didn't have an answer for. More than anyone, the Monk had been awestruck by Khenpo's intellect and wisdom, by his subtlety and clarity. The Monk had hoped to stay by Khenpo's side and keep working on translations with the scholar. As a teacher he was revered in both the United States and India, where he ran the monastery in Bylakuppe and the large university as well. For the last couple of years he'd been coming with greater frequency to Poolesville to give teachings and instruction. For a while now the Monk had suspected that Khenpo's trips to KPC were designed to keep Penor Rinpoche informed of the students' progress there, and—in light of some of the New Age overtones to Jetsunma's teachings—make sure that her students were also offered something more traditional.

Dechen sat at Khenpo's feet. The Monk sat farther behind, in a display of great humility and modesty. Khenpo seemed to want no further details—he'd already heard enough from either Jetsunma or Alana—and launched immediately into an angry diatribe. His face looked pained.

"How could you do this?" he said to the Monk. "You've been a monk for twelve years! . . . You may have some realization, but without moral discipline *you have nothing.*"

"And you!" he said to Dechen. "You knew! You knew you needed to confess!" She looked back at the Monk. He said nothing.

Khenpo explained that it was true: their root vows had not been broken. They had broken a branch vow, which would now remain forever broken. But he was clearly appalled. "The hiding! The secrecy!" If they had come forward and confessed, the negative karma could have been purified. But because they didn't come forward and were found out after a confrontation, the vow would forever be broken, and forever unpurified.

Dechen listened very hard for instructions and advice from Khenpo during the twenty-minute meeting. "Do Vajrasattva practices," he finally said, but he didn't suggest an amount. They could try to purify the karma, but, basically, "Nothing can be done at this point."

Driving home, Dechen said, "I won't say I told you so."

"Good," said the Monk. They said nothing else.

Dechen didn't mention the meeting she had scheduled that evening with Jetsunma. She assumed it would be one on one, and assumed she'd be reamed out. The Monk came from another school of Tibetan Buddhism, and it wasn't really Jetsunma's place to reprimand him. He had already pondered this himself. Technically, Khenpo was the only person in Poolesville—besides perhaps Alana—who should ever know what had happened between the Monk and Dechen. When vows were broken it was a private matter. If it became public it would be an insult to Khenpo, suggesting that his advice alone wasn't enough—and showing a lack of respect for his ability to handle the situation properly.

Still, the Monk had a bad feeling about this vow breakage. He had a feeling it wasn't going to remain a private matter. Jetsunma didn't seem to care about doing things in a traditional way. And Poolesville wasn't like the other Dharma centers; it didn't feel like the other Dharma centers. It was the kind of place where anything could happen.

After she dropped the Monk at the town house, Dechen began the drive back to her mother's. She felt small behind the wheel of the lumbering minivan, and the burgundy robes felt heavy on her skin, a demanding weight that engulfed her small body. She drove on Quince Orchard Road and began thinking about whether she should remain in Poolesville. But she worried. If she couldn't make it as a nun at Kunzang Palyul Choling, the largest concentration of Tibetan Buddhist nuns in America, where could she?

The sky was dark, the color of fresh wet concrete. It was about two o'clock on the afternoon of February 9, 1996. She made the left-hand turn onto Longdraft Road and never noticed the small beige car in the oncoming lane. It was going fifty miles per hour. When the two vehicles collided, the minivan was totaled. So was the other car—its front end was flattened up to the windshield.

Dechen was dizzy when she squeezed out of the minivan, and she brushed the broken glass off her robes. She stepped over to the small beige car. "Are you okay? Are you okay?" she asked. The driver was a middle-aged blond woman in a business suit. She looked dazed. "I can't really feel my leg," the driver said. Dechen stood next to the car and worried—until other cars began to stop and their drivers told Dechen to get back into the minivan. Her face was covered in blood. When the paramedics came, they put her in a neck brace and carried her to the ambulance, where the driver of the other car was already stretched out. Together they were taken to Shady Grove Hospital in Gaithersburg. The driver of the car had a sprained leg and a bruise on her shoulder. Dechen had lacerations of the face and head from the broken windshield glass—she had forgotten to wear a seat belt—and after receiving fourteen stitches and being given Vicodin for pain, she was told that she was still in shock and needed to rest.

Sherab and Dawa arrived at the hospital—they'd driven by Quince Orchard Road and recognized the crushed white minivan as Ayla Meurer's. At first the two nuns assumed that Ayla had been in an accident, but once they realized that it was Dechen who'd been driving—and that she was going to be okay—both nuns turned critical. "How could you get in a car accident?" they asked her. It was more evidence of the negative karma that Dechen had been accumulating lately. They immediately called Alana from Dawa's cell phone. Dawa spoke with Alana for a moment, then handed the phone to Dechen.

Alana's voice was cold and stern. "Don't think that this means you can get out of tonight's meeting," she said quickly. "Jetsunma says *you aren't hurt that badly.*"

By the time Ayla arrived at the hospital, her daughter was being released. As they drove, Dechen felt her shame and despair drifting into numbness. Scattered around her face and short, dark hair were shaved marks and cuts, and the thread of the stitches. "I already heard that you're fine," Ayla said, "so I can say that I'm really mad at you. How could you break your vows?"

Ayla handed Dechen a folded bundle of yellow robes—the robes the ordained wore for ceremonial and special occasions. She'd been called by Alana and instructed to get her daughter at the hospital, give her the yellow robes, and take her directly to Ani Estates. There was going to be a meeting. In the car with her mother, Dechen stared straight ahead at the road. A meeting. She felt nothing. She never got hysterical when unexpected things happened like this. Her reaction was always delayed. And, anyway, the last thing she was going to do was cry.

"You know," Ayla said as she dropped Dechen off, "you're in serious trouble."

It was about four-thirty when Dechen arrived at Ani Estates, the large, beige stucco-and-wood tract house on Spates Hill Road where five nuns—Dawa, Dara, Aileen, Alana, and Dorje—lived. Dechen walked into the house alone and saw that activity had already begun. Several nuns were in the kitchen washing large offering bowls. Atara was standing in the middle of the living room, repeating Jetsunma's instructions. "Jetsunma says there should be chairs lined up in here, like this," she was saying. "And Jetsunma says there should be an offering out for the ordained"—so pretzels and chips and other refreshments were to be set out. The table in the dining room was to be removed, "and under here," where the dining room table was, "Jetsunma says there should be two chairs."

Dechen had been inside the house many times, for all kinds of reasons. She'd come frequently to borrow movies there from Aileen's video library. She'd exercised on the Health Rider. She'd helped with some Tibetan translations there. She'd even lived there for a week once, when she had no other place to live—and she had cleaned the house to make money. When Jetsunma and Sangye got together, their Consort Engagement Party had been there. And over the summer Dechen had attended the meeting of the ordained at Ani Estates where everyone was asked to sign a paper relieving the temple of any responsibility for taking care of them. But never had Dechen—one of the mousiest of the nuns—been the center of any attention like this. She sat on the floor in the corner and watched the preparations. She watched Atara stage-direct and everybody follow her orders. She noticed that the vertical blinds were drawn.

The house grew darker as night fell. As the monks and nuns began to trickle in, it was clear most of them had very little idea of why they had been called to Ani Estates. The meeting was mandatory for all ordained. Only Sangye Dorje—later admitting that he had a sense of what might transpire—quickly volunteered to take the prayer shift and remain at the temple. As the rest of the nuns and monks arrived, they saw a table of food and began picking at the snacks. Dechen had moved to a spot on the carpeted stairs that overlooked the room and tried to keep her head down. She was feeling a bit woozy. She kept touching the stitches on the top of her head, and it was weird that they didn't hurt. One cut on the left side of her face kept tickling her. She overheard whispers among the monks—they were always the most clueless. "What's going on? Do you know?"

The Monk was among the last to arrive. He came with Konchog and was told to sit away from Dechen until the meeting began and not to speak with her. He sat on the floor in the front hallway and furtively looked up to the stairs, trying to catch Dechen's eye. She only looked away.

Then Atara led them to the dining room and told them to sit on the chairs under the lights. Dechen found herself looking around the room, and at the monks and nuns in the chairs lined up facing her. One by one she looked at their faces. She had known many of them a decade, since she was seventeen. She had sat beside them, prayed beside them, learned to prostrate beside them, been ordained beside them. It felt like they'd been through the wars together. They'd followed the voice of Jeremiah, made the move to Poolesville, enthroned their lama, watched Michael's leaving, built the stupa garden, and seen Jetsunma marry Karl. They'd done all-night prayer rounders together, floated through the exquisitely beautiful White Tara retreat and the amazing Rinchen Ter Dzod, and sat together through last summer's Nam Chu empowerments. They'd kept a twenty-four-hour prayer vigil going, without a break, since it started in the dark basement of the little brick house in Kensington ten years before.

Here was the largest collection of Tibetan Buddhist monks and nuns in America. They were kind people, good people. Dechen admired so many of them, for wanting to dedicate their lives to something good, for building such a beautiful Dharma center. For trying to live by their ideals.

A broken vow wasn't a small matter. The results would be profound and long-lasting. The bad karma would spill inevitably into the path of everyone in Poolesville and create obstacles. It would cause ripples that would produce more suffering. Dechen and the Monk had not just betrayed themselves and their own Buddha nature but defied the guru and hurt the entire sangha. Why hadn't Dechen been able to see that all along? Why hadn't she come forward months ago?

Most of the lights in the house were dimmed. And the lights in the living room were shut off. Only the lights over Dechen and the Monk were kept brightly lit. Alana was wearing burgundy robes and stood in the dining room before her fellow ordained.

"There has been a vow breakage," she said.

The room became utterly quiet. "Nobody is ever to speak of what happens here tonight. And remember, everything you see is compassionate activity." Alana looked squarely at the Monk. "You are not to speak—*either of you*—or defend yourselves in any way."

Some headlights flashed behind the windowpane in the front door. Dechen saw that Jetsunma had arrived. The front door flew open, and the room of ordained rose to their feet. Jetsunma quickly pulled off her black overcoat in the foyer and tossed it to Atara. Underneath she was dressed entirely in black, too—black wool and black leather.

"You fool!" she shouted at the Monk, as she ran toward him, then struck him hard on the head with her open hand. The Monk lost his footing and staggered momentarily. When his balance was regained, he realized that his wire-rimmed glasses had been knocked to the floor and he couldn't see.

Jetsunma studied him briefly. With his glasses off the Monk looked like a mole—soft and blind. "Sit down!" she yelled. The Monk and Dechen began to drop onto the seats of their chairs, and Jetsunma yelled again. "No! Sit on the floor! You don't deserve to sit on the same level as these other ordained!"

Dechen sat on her knees. The Monk sat cross-legged on the ground, with the large lights swinging overhead. "I brought you into our hearts!" Jetsunma yelled at him, then bent down to punch the Monk again hard on the side of the face. "We took you into our homes! And this is how you repay our kindness? I should throw you through that sliding glass door but *you don't have the merit.*"

The ordained were quiet, barely moving in their chairs. Dechen looked out into the living room; in the shadows she could see the outlines of a few nuns who were holding their stomachs. One monk had his hand over his mouth.

"This is a stain on all of us—and has harmed all ordained forever," Jetsunma yelled, continuing to punctuate her comments with blows to the Monk's head. "This has shortened my life, the lives of our sangha, and made it harder for all future ordained to keep their vows. And it's shortened their lives as well. They worked so hard to keep their vows purely, and now you've made it so hard!"

Dechen looked up again and heard Tashi sobbing.

Jetsunma turned to face the little nun. Dechen stared up at her. "And *you!*" she yelled. She struck Dechen across the side of her head with the heel of her hand, not far from a few stitches. "I've taken you into my heart! *I've done everything I could for you!*" She slapped her again on the forehead. "There are words for women like you, but I won't use them!" she yelled. "It disgusts me to see you in those robes. It disgusts me to see your face!"

Dechen looked up into Jetsunma's face and never broke her gaze. Jetsunma had a look that Dechen never remembered seeing before. She was almost . . . smiling. But it wasn't a smirk as much as a leer. "What you said happened to you in India before, what you told me," Jetsunma shouted, "that isn't what *really* happened, is it? *You lied to me.*" She backhanded Dechen again.

Jetsunma began listing instructions for Dechen to follow. The young nun felt herself focusing on all of Jetsunma's words, all her advice and instructions, hoping to remember every moment. Dechen was never to look at or speak to the Monk again. She was to put her yellow robes on her altar and prostrate to them every day. She needed to get a job and pay off all of her debts. She had to stop "leaning on" the other ordained. She needed to do one hundred thousand Vajrasattva practices, but Jetsunma wasn't sure that was enough. As a punishment, she and the Monk were going to clean the temple every day—the bathrooms, the floors, the kitchen. And every moment that Dechen wasn't either cleaning or working to pay off her debts, she was to be practicing. As for reading or TV or any other "enjoyments," there were to be no more than four hours per week. She talked about how little remorse Dechen had. "You have never done a single thing that I have ever told you to do," Jetsunma yelled angrily, "so I have no confidence that you'll do it now."

Dechen followed her lama's eyes. She soaked up her lama's words. These were blessings, she told herself. Each word was a great blessing. Each slap and slug, a great, great blessing. Dechen tried to be as submissive as she could be and tried to find a posture of accepting all the blessings as they came her way. This wrathful display—as it was called—would only help to purify any negative karma that had been created by her contact with the Monk.

The Monk had been very still, but he turned slightly to see if Dechen was okay. She was cowering. She was humiliating herself. He wanted to yell at her, "Get up! Get up!"

Jetsunma turned to him again. "You may keep your robes but not wear them," she said, "and if you were in better health, I'd make you clean every toilet at the temple eighteen times a day with a *toothbrush.*" She pointed to the crowd in the chairs. "Their toilets!"

Dechen was to clean toilets, too, she said. "I can't tell you *not* to come to teachings, but if you do, sit behind an umbrella or something. I don't want to see your face. . . . And I've talked to Khenpo Tsewang Gyatso about this—*you may not keep your robes!*"

At this Jetsunma walked out. The room remained perfectly still. Alana returned to center stage. She announced that Jetsunma wanted the ordained to tell Dechen and the Monk how this evening had made them feel—sharing their anger and outrage would help Dechen and the Monk "with their remorse."

Ani Rene spoke first and addressed her comments to the Monk, with whom she had studied. "Driving in the car with you one time," she said, "you criticized some lamas and poisoned my mind with gossip!" she said, shaking with rage. "I felt sick for an hour, and I could have just ripped you apart." Tashi was so overcome with emotion that he could barely get the words out. He was horrified by what had happened, particularly by the fact that Jetsunma's life would now be shortened. Then came Konchog, the young monk who did press relations for the temple and who was a scholar. He also addressed his remarks to his friend, his housemate, his fellow monk. "I had so much faith in you," he said, fighting back tears. "You kept your vows for so long. And you talked about how the Dharma texts were more important than Jetsunma, and you almost turned my mind away from my teacher."

The nuns of Ani Farms each spoke to Dechen. Palchen said that Dechen needed to face her total irresponsibility and lack of thought for anyone but herself. Alexandra mentioned Dechen's thoughtlessness. She had never contemplated how her breakages would affect anybody but herself. Sherab was the angriest. "You're always rebellious, and everything has to be *Dechen's way!*" she yelled. Another nun talked about how she'd helped Dechen out when she broke her vows last time, how supportive she'd felt. This was different. "Countless sentient beings," she said, "will be hurt because of this."

But most of the comments were directed at the Monk, and they continued for forty-five minutes after Jetsunma's departure. In the following ten days there were two more meetings—where Dechen and the Monk were required to confess the details of their affair to the entire ordained sangha. At one point, as Dechen tried to give an account of exactly what had transpired between them sexually, the Monk began shouting, "Shut up! Shut up! It's none of their fucking business!" And it was this attitude, his indignation and pride, which seemed to fuel the anger of his peers. One by one in all three meetings, the ordained told the Monk how they really felt about him, how egotistical he was, how deluded, how he lorded his knowledge of Tibetan and all his studies and retreats and expertise in Tibetan Buddhism over everybody and made them feel bad. How he'd tried, with all his talk of tradition and other teachers and other Dharma centers, to turn them against their lama. He had taken many empowerments, but he'd somehow missed the boat.

The Monk didn't know these people well—he had been in Poolesville only eight months—and it shocked him that they would have such intense hatred for him. It also surprised him that Jetsunma should feel so strongly—to scream at him, and slug him, to threaten to throw him through the sliding glass door. He had refused to give her instruction in some high teachings, and he'd ignored what he felt had been her romantic advances; was that the explanation for her rage? But what had he done to the rest of these people to make them so angry? The attacks on his character were personal, and brutal. This is like something out of the Spanish Inquisition, he was thinking. He knew what Jetsunma would say, of course, that to strike a student was to give him a great blessing. There was a long tradition of teachers hitting students in Tibetan Buddhism. He had heard that in Tibet students were sometimes beaten unconscious with logs and clubs. Penor Rinpoche himself, the legend went, had cured one of his students of cancer by beating him to a bloody pulp—then collapsed outside on the grass and sobbed. But hitting a student in this country, wasn't that a great risk? Was this monastery life in Tibetan Buddhist America?

In the following weeks Dechen went overboard to live by Jetsunma's edicts and purify herself. She spent two or three hours a day cleaning the bathrooms or floors or whatever Rinchen told her to do. She did her Vajrasattva. She went to the bank, consolidated her debt. With credit cards, back-tithing, and what she owed Palchen in rent, the total came to four thousand dollars. She found a job right away, as a secretary in a publishing house. And since Jetsunma didn't want to see Dechen's face, she listened to her lama's teachings on Wednesday nights while scrubbing the solarium floor. She was largely shunned by the sangha but felt soothed by her mother.

They stayed up late at night, talking about how Dechen had come to veer off her intended path, how she felt dried up spiritually—and did not trust the words of her lama. Ayla Meurer spent hours with her daughter after the night at Ani Estates, going over every detail of the evening, and every word Jetsunma had spoken. Ayla admitted that she'd had difficult times at KPC over the years, too. Michael Burroughs had said and done many things to hurt her. She'd sometimes felt rejected and ignored by the inner circle. But to her Jetsunma was like Jesus Christ, a miraculous savior of the entire planet. And over the years she had felt great blessings flow from Jetsunma and she'd been able to find her own path, her own way of studying Tibetan Buddhism. She encouraged Dechen to find her way, too.

Dechen spoke a great deal with Ani Catharine Anastasia, her assigned mentor in the ordained community. Catharine Anastasia helped her see that the Monk was not her friend and had never truly cared about her; he'd only planted poison in her mind. He'd come into her life and turned her against the guru, turned her against Poolesville. In a moment of guilt and renunciate fervor, Dechen threw out all the robes that she wore while she had been with him, and she returned all the Tibetan texts and manuscripts he had given her.

The loss of her robes was too much even to consider. If Dechen wasn't an ani anymore, *who was she?* As Jetsunma instructed, she put the folded robes on her altar and prostrated to them not just three times a day, as Jetsunma had instructed, but nine. She continued to keep her vows assiduously, even after Alana made a point of reminding her several times that she was no longer a nun, and Sherab left an angry voice mail for her when she wore burgundy jeans and a burgundy T-shirt to clean the temple. "How dare you wear burgundy!" Sherab said. *"You aren't a nun anymore."* But Dechen was determined to earn her robes back, and Ayla encouraged her. She told her daughter that anything was possible, if she paid back her debts, lived responsibly, practiced Vajrasattva, and kept practicing and practicing. In every spare moment of the day, Dechen did. "I was very remorseful and sad," she said later, "but I was trying to get myself together."

When Chris Finney called her one day in late February, Dechen was surprised to hear her cheerful voice. It seemed like a long time since anybody from the temple had called her—and sounded friendly. Chris had a small business making prayer beads that were sold in the temple gift shop, and she was calling to offer Dechen her supplies. She could make some decent money string-ing the malas, and Chris said she knew that Dechen probably needed it.

"You're not making malas anymore?" Dechen asked.

"I'm not coming to Poolesville anymore," said Chris.

"You aren't?" Dechen asked. This seemed unimaginable. Chris was one of the founding members—one of the First Wavers.

"No," Chris said, and then she mentioned something about seeing a lama in Frederick, Maryland, now. "We're just going on with our life in another direction."

Dechen didn't inquire further and, frankly, didn't want to know any more. The repercussions of Chris's departure were too horrible to think about. Dechen would rather break her vows a hundred more times than *break* samaya.

Chris didn't offer any explanations, either. She just made plans to give Dechen all her beads and wire and wire cutters. The truth was, through the Dharma grapevine she had heard about the night at Ani Estates and was wondering how Dechen was holding up. News can travel fast in a temple when something un-usual happens. But when Chris asked Dechen how she was doing, she said, "Great! I'm doing great."

And that was truly how Dechen felt. Her mother was being kind and helpful. Dechen was paying off her debts. She liked her new job at the publishing house. Her boss, a woman, was sup-portive. "You don't know what you're worth, do you?" she said. And Dechen was already looking at the classified ads—to see if she could afford a studio apartment in Gaithersburg.

A few nights later Dechen was dusting the Guru Rinpoche altar in the prayer room when the sangha gathered in the Dharma room for a teaching from Jetsunma. Dechen had moved into the solarium to begin cleaning tables when she heard Jetsunma's voice. "If you could sample your teacher's mindstream," she said, "if you could sample the nectar of what your teacher actually has to give you . . . it is contained within this teaching."

Dechen could hear Jetsunma's voice almost too clearly, coming from a loudspeaker in the kitchen. "I hope that all my students who intend to remain my students are here tonight," she said, "and those who are not here, I'm afraid I'm sorry to say that it may be due to causes having been created that make it not possible or not easy for you to receive what comes directly from the mind and the intention of your teacher."

She began to read a poem she'd written to the sangha, which she explained had been inspired by the activities of two of her students. It was called "War Cry."

Bitch,
I have seen you.
I have heard your voice.
I have smelt your smell.
I have lived
    And died with you.
I know your name . . .
    Samsara.

Bitch, whore,
Whatever garment you wear
    I will know you.
Your smile is no seduction
    To me.
I know you.

You will appear
    In lovely forms,
Seductive, caressing, singing songs
    Filled with promises.
It is then I will appear
    Far more beautiful than you
Adorned with garments
    Of pure aspiration

Resplendent with gold and gems
  Of pure bliss.
From my mouth will come
  The ambrosia of Dharma
And from your
  Grasping arms
I will steal my children away,
Like a thief
  In the night . . .
And lead them to
Paradise.

Dechen felt herself sinking to the floor. She put her hands over her face. She felt her breath stop. More than the night at Ani Estates, more than anything, this poem hurt her, like a knife in her stomach.

Be warned,
  Whore-mother of suffering,
I am coming.
I am relentless!
Not one of my children
  Will I abandon to you.
I will meet you on
  Every hill and mountain.
In every ocean, in every country.
In the sky, in the six realms,
In form and formless lands,
No hell or heaven will
  Hide you from me.
I will never stop.
Like a tigress
  I will come,
Mouth dripping with blood,
Claws extended.

I will come and slay you,
I alone will defeat you.

I will rip you apart
Cut up, shredded,
*   Sliced and diced,*
No one will know
*   Which part to call Samsara.*
I will finish you.
*   You will not enslave my children.*

Then I will shed tears
*   To heal you.*
I will scoop you up
*   In my arms,*
Tenderly I will hold
*   Your head.*
My eyes will shine
*   Wisdom and compassion upon you.*
My body will be your home.
My speech will sing lullabies
*   Of pure virtue.*
Then you will remember
*   You are my child too.*
Samsara.
*   Yes, you too.*
Then, beloved child
*   Who is never separate from me,*
We will depart together.
We will be in Paradise.

Jetsunma began explaining the poem, line by line. Of course, it wasn't literally about two students, it was about the entire sangha, and it was about samsara. "*Whore* indicates an awareness that samsara is completely unwholesome," she said. "Samsara is just simply filled with degradation and unwholesomeness, with shit and garbage. There is nothing here but garbage, and so *whore* is a word that indicates the complete unwholesomeness of it."

She kept reading.

From my mouth will come
    The ambrosia of Dharma
And from your
    Grasping arms
I will steal my children away,
Like a thief
    In the night

"Skillful means are indicated here," Jetsunma said. "The bodhisattva will come like a thief in the night. And I'll tell you that there have been many times that I have stretched the truth, quite a bit, in order to hook sentient beings, that I have elaborated in order to hook sentient beings, that I have put on my chicken suit and danced in order to hook sentient beings, and I know that if *I* have done that, my humble self, then I know that the great bodhisattvas have done it much more. Whatever means are necessary! . . . When bodhisattvas meet with their students, whatever skillful means are necessary are legal!"

Dechen stayed on the floor, unable to get up. She felt a bit light-headed and confused. How long would this punishment go on? "There are many, many stories of great bodhisattvas who did not even follow the norms and traditions of the society in which they were born," Jetsunma said, "or the society in which they practiced. They threw all that out the window. And they did so because skillful means were necessary to overcome such a terrible demoness as this whore samsara."

Dechen slipped into a back room of the temple until the teaching was over and then found a ride home with Bob Colacurcio. She mentioned nothing to him about the poem. A few days later she got up the courage to talk to Catharine Anastasia about "War Cry."

"That poem—was it about me?" she asked over the phone.

"I was sure you were going to think that—you're so self-centered," Catharine Anastasia said. "It's not about you. *It's about Wib and Jane.*"

20

Come into the Fire

IN GANDHI'S CASE THE QUESTIONS ONE FEELS IN-
CLINED TO ASK ARE: TO WHAT EXTENT WAS GANDHI
MOVED BY VANITY . . . AND TO WHAT EXTENT DID HE
COMPROMISE HIS OWN PRINCIPLES BY ENTERING POLI-
TICS, WHICH OF THEIR NATURE ARE INSEPARABLE FROM
COERCION AND FRAUD?

—GEORGE ORWELL, "Reflections on Gandhi"

That winter, while continuing my reporting in Poolesville, I prepared for the trip to India. Wib phoned my house almost daily
with updates and news bulletins about Jetsunma's Pilgrimage, as
the trip was now being called. An itinerary was faxed to me, along
with helpful hints for travelers. The average temperature in India
during our stay was expected to hover around one hundred de-
grees. Shorts and short skirts were not appropriate attire at Penor
Rinpoche's monastery, in keeping with traditions of modesty, although sleeveless shirts were okay. For a small fee the monks
would wash my clothes in a nearby river, although it wasn't polite
to ask them to wash undergarments. When I told Wib that I had
gotten the first round of recommended immunizations for the
trip—diphtheria, tetanus, meningitis, typhoid—and pills to prevent malaria, I was stunned to learn that none of the Poolesville
Buddhists were getting them. "We have a homeopath who is an
herbalist," he said, "and we've been told the hepatitis shot doesn't
work anyway." Really? I said.

"And Jetsunma's acupuncturist is coming on the trip, and she
takes great care of us and protects us. She's a brilliant healer."

Wib's updates made it clear that Jetsunma had moved into another expansive phase. She was looking for a documentary filmmaker to record her pilgrimage, and Wib asked if I knew any. He was still trying to hire a helicopter to take Jetsunma to Maratika Cave so she wouldn't have to hike. He had written to the Dalai Lama's private office in Dharamsala, too, hoping that Jetsunma and His Holiness could finally meet. And, expecting throngs of Indian worshipers to follow the emanation of Mandarava wherever she went, Alana and Aileen were producing thousands of postcard-sized photos of Jetsunma—prayer cards—to hand out. "It's finally starting to feel like a reality," Wib said. The entourage had grown to thirty, including the lama, her three children, two attendants, an acupuncturist and massage therapist, as well as Wib and myself.

Over the months I'd become familiar with the manic pace of life at KPC. Expansive dreams were always followed by enthusiastic planning, followed by round-the-clock building projects and praying. The six-month stupa project was immediately followed by a pilgrimage to India, and searches for documentary filmmakers and Nepalese helicopters and hopes for meetings with the Fourteenth Dalai Lama. Jetsunma also appeared to be entering an important new phase of her life—the Princess Mandarava Phase. "The recognition is really starting to manifest," Wib said.

"Things are in transition," Alana had warned me. "Jetsunma's display is changing—the way she presents herself to the world . . . well, *you'll see.*"

In the middle of the India planning, Ladyworks had reached another crisis point. Wib called to ask if I thought the temple needed to hire a $4,500-a-month public relations person in New York City to handle the Ladyworks account, which now included a line of shampoos and conditioners that Jetsunma had created. He also wanted his memory refreshed: Why did I feel Jetsunma should not appear in the infomercial herself? Ladyworks posed all the problems that a modern-day lama has in life now, Wib said. If people had trouble with Jetsunma and the infomercial, it was probably because Jetsunma didn't fit the idea they had of a spiritual leader. She was a pioneer, he explained, she broke the stereotype and "challenged" everybody to see a Tibetan Buddhist lama in a new way. "She's a woman, for one thing," Wib said, "and she's got this long hair, and she's an American. And she's started a business. It's hard for people to grasp all that."

He was being indirect, but when he talked about "people" having trouble with Jetsunma and the infomercial, I knew he meant me.

Did Jetsunma really want to become famous as the lama who hawks shampoo? I felt frustrated by her apparent lack of wisdom. Why was she so impatient to make money? And if she was perfect, how come she had such lousy taste? In a conversation with Ani Aileen—who I thought of as a sensible person and a fellow member of the media—I found myself venting a bit and was relieved to hear her response. "Don't get me started on that infomercial," she said. "I'm not stepping into that karmic morass again. . . . I've stopped trying to train them about the real world. They'll have to make mistakes and bump up against it and learn on their own."

It wasn't long after these conversations that Wib called to say Jetsunma wanted to arrange a dinner so that "everybody could talk." Wib, Alana, and Jetsunma were gathering at the Normandy Farm Inn. I was told to bring my "questions about India," but Wib also made it clear that we would be discussing Jetsunma's "PR options" and what I expected would come her way as a result of my book. "You can talk about what you see happening," Wib said vaguely, "and Jetsunma can talk about what she sees happening." I needed to discuss "my goals," and she would discuss hers. This seemed a bit weird to me, since I thought it had all been covered months ago—and the book's release was at least two years off. Wib also suggested that I should share my ideas and thoughts about Ladyworks.

"What do you mean?"

"We're still making some decisions. . . . Ladyworks might come up."

"My thoughts about the infomercial?"

"If it comes up."

I met Wib first in the bar, where we waited for Alana and Jetsunma and had a drink. He talked about his life—his childhood in Rochester, his WASP upbringing, the country clubs and boarding schools and summers on Nantucket. He said nothing disparaging about his parents, or the way he was raised—"we're very close"—suggesting only that he and Jane were doing things differently. He had worked at the temple for eight years without a salary, and Jane supported the family with a successful graphic arts business. Their daughters were attending the Buddhist school at KPC and being taught about not killing bugs, not lying, cyclical life in samsara, bodhicitta. "In Poolesville, I'm sure they think we worship worms at the temple." He laughed. "Because every spring we take the schoolkids to the bait shop. We buy all the worms and then liberate them in the woods."

Jetsunma and Alana arrived—looking as odd a pair as ever, the lama in her designer pantsuit and nails, the nun in her shaved head and robes to the floor. In the first few minutes we discussed everything from the weather and India to Jetsunma's marriage to Michael Burroughs. "He's such a smart guy, really, and has so much going for him," Jetsunma said. "But he's got nothing to show for it, really. He always has just enough money to eke it out every month." Before I could question why Michael Burroughs's financial status should be a marker of his success in life, the conversation moved on, with tremendous swiftness, to Jetsunma's more promising future.

A documentary filmmaker had been found to join Jetsunma in India, Alana was thrilled to report. His name was Byron Pickett. He lived in Santa Fe and was the friend of a sangha member who had moved out West. He seemed to have big aspirations, too—the kind everybody in Poolesville liked. His documentary about Jetsunma's pilgrimage was going to be very high quality, shot on film, not video, and Byron was already talking about showing it at the Sundance Film Festival one day. The fact that he had no funding, or money of his own, didn't seem to bother Wib or Alana. In fact, they seemed to believe that it was their responsibility to pay for Jetsunma's documentary, and they were starting to wonder how.

Alana began asking me questions about my book—when

might it come out? How many copies might it sell? And would Jetsunma be asked to make TV appearances to help sell it? A book tour together?

"You may not be happy with the book," I said, a bit uncomfortably. "And Jetsunma may not want to go on TV to talk about it. You know, as much as I like you all, I can't be writing it to please you."

"For some reason, I'm not worried," Jetsunma said. "I'm sure I'm going to like it, and I have a feeling it's going to do really well."

I thought of all the other predictions she'd made—the surefire successes. None of them ever seemed to pan out.

"I'm glad you have such confidence," I said, "but I'm not expecting much success."

"You aren't?" Alana asked, and her mouth dropped open. She looked at Wib with a concerned expression, as if my negativity revealed a questioning of Jetsunma's wisdom.

"I'm going to try to enjoy writing it," I continued, "and not worry about the outcome."

Wib and Alana smiled and seemed relieved. Then Jetsunma chuckled.

"You're sounding like a Buddhist," said Wib.

"You're figuring out *attachment.*" Alana laughed.

"I can see," said Jetsunma, "we're starting to rub off on you."

Maybe it was true. Maybe I had started thinking more like them. Lately I had found myself paying great attention to the weather, as though it bore some message from the mystical world. I'd started shepherding bugs from my house rather than killing them. I had marked in my Filofax calendar when the planet Mercury would be "retrograde"—it was considered a bad time, astrologically, to write or travel or sign contracts. I had grown so fond of the Migyur Dorje stupa that I had taken friends out to see it, left little offerings of necklaces and rocks on the ledge of its base, and prayed many times there for my father, whose health was worsening. I had prayed for the world on occasion, then dedicated the merit of my prayers to benefit all beings. At one point I'd even called a real estate agent in Poolesville about farmhouses to buy there or rent. It was a whimsical notion, I suppose, but I had looked at a few.

I'd had a few weird dreams, too. In one Jetsunma transformed into a huge tiger—beautifully golden with thick, black stripes. She was hunched over a huge, bloody chunk of flesh. Over and over again I saw her ripping at the flesh, tearing off bits of meat, her mouth dripping with blood. And in another dream, soon after my first dinner alone with her, I dreamt that I was sitting at a table with her and her face kept changing, swelling, then growing thin, as if my vision were twisting and twisting, becoming distorted. I heard her say, "Wib and Alana are like my right and left eyes." The room began to breathe, in and out, the walls were breathing, exhaling and inhaling. I grew panicky, and a voice inside my head began to yell: "Run for your life! Run!"

Maybe I had started to enter their magical, spooky world and was enjoying some success with the concept of attachment, but what disturbed me was how much the Buddhists suddenly seemed to be living in mine. They were working out their public relations quandaries and getting deeper into debt. Money was constantly on their minds. Jetsunma didn't seem spiritual as much as driven. When I was asked what my "goal" was for the book, I said that I wanted to "tell a good story." Jetsunma's goal was somewhat grander. "I want to see Buddhism belong in America, as any religion belongs in America. I want to see it become another option, something that fits, suits us—not some exotic foreign practice, some cult that belongs only in the East."

It was probably the modesty of my goal and my lack of aspirational energy that led Wib to place the next phone call to me, a few days later, asking who owned the movie rights to my book. Had I sold them?

"That seems a bit premature," I said.

"Well, who owns them, anyway?"

I thought that I owned the rights to the book and Jetsunma owned the rights to her story. "But I'm not sure," I said.

Wib invited me to Jetsunma's house on the coming weekend. The documentary filmmaker was in town, and Jetsunma thought I should meet him. "He has some interesting ideas," Wib said. "And it would be great if the two of you could work together on some things." I could hear a hesitation in Wib's voice. As blue-blooded as he might be, he wasn't someone who could hide his anxiety.

"Has he found the money for his documentary?" I asked.

"We're still trying to help him with that," said Wib. "He seems like a nice enough guy—and Jetsunma has a strong past-life connection to him."

"Wib," I said, "can I just say something that's on my mind?"

"What?"

"You realize that if you guys pay for this documentary, it won't really be a documentary, don't you?"

"You mean if . . ."

"It's going to be considered another infomercial."

Wib called again the morning of my meeting with Byron and Jetsunma—wanting to bring me up to date on the latest developments. Byron was now actively trying to sell the feature film rights to Jetsunma's life in Hollywood, and a screenwriter named Andrea King had become very interested. She'd written a Rob Reiner movie, I was told, and something for Steven Spielberg—and her concept for the Jetsunma movie was "fictionalized" and a "romantic comedy with serious parts."

I wasn't sure what to say, but I think I managed a sound of acknowledgment that wasn't quite a groan.

"Byron came up with the idea," Wib said, "and Jetsunma got—we all got—very excited. And if he can sell the movie idea quickly, the money would help him make the documentary. And then the center wouldn't be involved."

The logic of this was somewhat skewed, I pointed out. If Byron was selling a feature film about Jetsunma to Hollywood, why would he bother with a documentary? Furthermore, did he really know what he was getting into? The story of Jetsunma didn't need fictionalizing—the truth was weird enough. And was America really ready for a romantic comedy about Tibetan Buddhism? More to the point, was America ready for Tibetan Buddhism at all? Suddenly things that had troubled me all along had become too glaring to ignore: Surely Jetsunma could have built a monastery with all the money that had gone into her houses or her wardrobe or simply the cash offerings she received for teachings. I couldn't help but think about the way her old lovers became monks and nuns to "keep the blessing intact." Would all that be in the romantic comedy, too?

Wib met me at the door to Jetsunma's house wearing his usual uniform of perfectly fitting blue jeans and a starched striped shirt. His friendly face was edged in stress. His brow was knitted, and there was a perceptible jumpiness to him.

Jetsunma was sitting on a sofa against a wall in the living room. She was wearing a black fuzzy sweater and dark pants, and, as I walked closer to greet her, I was stricken by the sight of her face. She had applied a startling amount of makeup, the amount an actress would wear for a theater performance. Rising above the dark red lips and colored cheeks, her eyes were raccooned by bright blue eye shadow. I'm not entirely sure why, but I felt afraid.

I joined Wib and Alana on the floor near Jetsunma's feet and was introduced to Byron Pickett, a young guy with a mop of brown hair and big, earnest, dark eyes. He looked amazingly like the actor Robert Downey, Jr. He wore jeans and a work shirt with the sleeves rolled up, and he had made himself so at home—stretched out on the floor like one of Jetsunma's sons—that he seemed to have been living in her house his entire life. He also appeared to be very comfortable at her feet. The entire first hour was spent helping him solve his immediate money problems and containing his excitement over the giant movie deal before him.

"I feel like I've just won the lottery," he said, smiling up at Jetsunma.

"Andrea King can't wait to start," Alana told me.

"She's really hot," Byron said to Jetsunma, and his eyes grew wider. Jetsunma nodded and smiled excitedly. "And she's ready to just drop everything and do this."

"I can't believe this is happening," said Wib.

"I know," said Alana. "I'm pinching myself."

"Gosh," I said, pathetically trying to join in and seem enthused. "It's really something else."

Byron estimated that he needed $80,000 in order to go to India with a proper film crew; he'd use that footage to raise another $250,000 to finish the documentary. The first lump of cash was something he was hoping the Buddhists could give him—and he kept directing his pleas to Wib. "I only have one month to make all these arrangements," Byron said, "and I'll need to spend five days in meetings trying to sell the feature film, and another week to finish some editing I'm doing." I got the impression that Byron was one of those people who tended to make his problems everybody else's. When the conversation would veer away from his needs, he would return to them again and again. Finally, as he was pressing Wib for money for the third time, I asked if he'd considered the ramifications of having KPC pay for his documentary.

Byron looked at me blankly. "What ramifications?"

"Well, it's not journalism if the center pays you to make the documentary."

Byron just looked at me, like I wasn't speaking English. "Really?"

"Do you understand that if these people pay for their own documentary, it won't air on PBS or wherever you had in mind?"

"Really?" he asked again, then looked down at the carpet. He pulled out two photographs that he wanted Jetsunma to see. They were pictures of the stupa, apparently taken on the day the lama and the documentary filmmaker met. "This was the day we talked and walked around the stupa," he said to Jetsunma. "And look there . . . in the sky. *Doesn't that look like a rainbow?*"

A hush fell over the room. Alana's and Wib's heads swerved to see Jetsunma's reaction. *Ahhhh . . . a rainbow.* It was Byron's final trump.

Jetsunma squinted at the picture. "It sure does. Yep," she said, nodding with great approval.

"Well, that's a good sign," said Alana.

"Very auspicious," said Wib.

"I was lying on the beach once," Jetsunma said, "and looked up, and there was a Dharma wheel made of clouds over my head—and another time, a lion-headed dakini."

The picture was passed around. I had a hard time seeing the rainbow—which perhaps said more about my state of mind than about the rainbow's actual existence. Byron didn't have a dime to invest in this project, and he had little experience, but he had a rainbow.

"Gosh, I just can't believe this is happening," Jetsunma said.

I looked up again at Jetsunma. Her blue eye shadow was glowing at me like a giant neon sign that I had refused to see all along. They called it aspiration, but it looked like desperation. They called it desire to help sentient beings, but it was just desire—in all its human glory. They talked endlessly about the danger of grasping and ego clinging, but how was this different? There was no patience, no calm or peace, no sense of a long view in that living room. *There was no emptiness.* There was only frenzy, rushing, reacting. They'd convinced themselves that they were saving the world, putting an end to suffering—and a plan as grand as that dwarfed all the obstacles and information and good sense that stood in their way.

She'd been a regular woman once—modest and kind, openhearted and well meaning, by all accounts. But now, since Penor Rinpoche had come along, she wasn't just a gifted teacher, she was an infallible saint. Every thought she had was pure, every desire sprang from a divine place. The "recognition" had brought Jetsunma many things—but it had also brought her here: She was enthroned on a sofa wearing a mask of makeup while her dearest friends had to sit on the floor at her feet. She was removed from life and kept from intimacy, from equality, from the delicious ordinariness of daily existence. Even her children had to prostrate to her in the morning. She was kept from having a real relationship or a real marriage to an equal. Suddenly, I felt an aching compassion for her, a kind of empathy—and a great sadness. Had she been ruined by all the bowing, the prostrating, the worshiping?

Pretending you are special is the most human thing of all, I thought. And it is that very urge that keeps people separate and unhappy. Being ordinary and accepting it is a great accomplishment. Doesn't Buddhism teach that?

Byron broke his lingering eye contact with Jetsunma and turned to me. "They love your title," he said. "Everybody loves it. 'The Buddha from Brooklyn.' It was the first thing that Andrea asked—if we can use it for the movie."

"Use the title to *my* book?" I asked, incredulously. "No, you can't."

"Maybe once you read the screenplay, you'll relent," said Alana.

"I can't imagine that," I said.

After Alana left to make coffee and tea, I looked up at Jetsunma again. Now that my own property—my book, my title—was threatened, I was experiencing a surge of territorial boldness, or something close to it. "Don't you want to be a little more patient about this?" I asked.

She looked back at me with a mysterious smile.

"Are you sure you want a documentary and a book and a movie all coming out at once about you?" I continued. "Aren't you concerned that this is too much?" I was thinking about the Ladyworks infomercial, too, but I didn't mention it. And I was thinking about all the things that I had learned about her—how the money for the Amitabha statue was raised in Taiwan, then used to pay for her new house. How her salary was half the operating budget. I thought about Michael Burroughs; he was out there somewhere, surely, with a story to tell. Hollywood pictures have a way of drawing all the darkness forward.

"It will bring a great deal of attention to you," I said, "probably not all of it positive."

"I'm a trusting person, and I'm not worried," she said, finally. "I have a connection with you, and I trust you. I have a connection with Byron, too, and I trust Byron. I think you both have tremendous potential, and I believe in you. I've always lived this way, as a trusting, positive person, and not worrying about things that aren't controllable . . . or being scared and cautious."

She mentioned her astrological chart. "This very week begins an inevitable public cycle," she said. "I apparently have the karma to become very famous—and there's really very little that I can do to stop it. This appears to be true for the next seven years. And my chart indicates that nothing I am involved with publicly during this period of time can hurt me."

"Well, then," I said. "I guess we can all breathe a sigh of relief."

Wib and Byron chuckled.

Alana was entering the room with a tray of mugs and said, "Anyway, if they *don't* make a good movie about Jetsunma, I sure wouldn't want to be them—with all those Dharma protectors around. They'll all start dropping dead of heart attacks."

I spent many hours trying to recover from the night at Jetsunma's house before I realized that I might never recover. I was angry at first, then, as a few days passed, I found that I was mostly sad and disappointed. And I felt silly. I had wanted to believe in Poolesville. There was so much that I had ignored, for many months, so many things too obvious to mention—things that a normal person, any journalist, would have been suspicious about from the beginning. For a long time I'd been intimidated by the newness, the strangeness, the exoticism of Tibetan Buddhism—by the beautiful and beckoning prayer room and by the lilting chants and by the magical stupa. I was a cynical person, but something about Poolesville had made me lose my cynicism. I was confident, but somehow I had lacked confidence. And I hadn't wanted to use my own judgment.

Four days after the meeting at Jetsunma's, I called Wib to tell him that I wouldn't be joining everybody in India. There were a number of reasons for this; one was that I didn't want to be out of the country for five weeks. My father was much worse, and I didn't want to be away from him. It was the truth, but only part of the truth. Most of the truth was still inexpressible: I couldn't go to India in good faith, and therefore I didn't want to go at all. The funny thing was, if I were worth anything as a journalist—a real member of the newsroom tribe—I would have wanted to go more than ever. But perhaps I didn't belong in the newsroom any more than I belonged in Poolesville.

Wib was stunned, of course. We talked for a brief time, then he called me back thirty minutes later. He'd just gotten off the phone with Jetsunma. "She says she is just rocking back on her heels with this news," he said. She offered to have the sangha do a *puja,* or prayer service, for my father. That was very generous, I said.

"She feels that you and she have entered into a great adventure together and now you are missing out on India," he said. "From her standpoint, it's the culmination of all kinds of personal changes. She said to tell you that her childhood is important, but what she's going through now is more important, and this trip is more important. She says that her *entire reason for being* is this trip to India."

I didn't know what to say.

"She understands the conventional wisdom standpoint of your dilemma, but she has a different take on the world."

"I realize that," I said. "But I have a take on the world that says my father is more important than whatever book I'm writing. And I don't have much longer to be with him. I need to be honest . . . you see, I'm not sure I believe I'll have another chance to be with him in some future lifetime."

Wib was quiet for a moment. "She wonders if there is something else bothering you, another reason you aren't coming."

I liked Wib. He'd been good to me, patient with me. It was hard not to be honest with him. "Well, I suppose I wasn't exactly looking forward to the entourage, the logistics . . . and now, with a documentary being shot, a film crew. It was becoming too much. I was turned off by all the new developments. Byron and the movie deal."

"I know what you mean," Wib said. "But she trusts him."

"I know."

"She's just looking for a big net—not fame or fortune," he said. "She's looking for the biggest net to scoop up human beings and liberate them from samsara."

Later that day he faxed me a copy of Jetsunma's long life prayer, written for her by Penor Rinpoche at the time of her enthronement. Jetsunma herself had asked Wib to send it to me— and suggest that I give it to my father. Sitting in my office, I watched the white pages come out of the fax machine, and I left them there.

I enjoyed my self-imposed exile from Poolesville during February and March. Aside from a lunch with Wib and Alana—during which Alana handed me a mysterious poem that Jetsunma had written, called "War Cry"—I heard nothing from the Buddhists. As soon as spring began to arrive, I threw myself into garden work and planting. And, again, I headed out into the countryside to look for a place to move.

While the group was away in India, I spent several weeks visiting my father in San Francisco. We watched movies and talked, and in the afternoon I sat alone in his quiet living room poring over a stack of books I'd bought on Tibetan Buddhism. They were written by various masters and monks—teachers of great renown, lineage holders with fabulous pedigrees and exotic names. Each book seemed more enticing than the next. They were slim, smooth, and had glistening jackets in vibrant colors—brilliant oranges and yellows and pinks. The face of the Dalai Lama looked out from several of them, with his shy and jolly smile.

Inside, the words were calming. The prose was clear and graceful. Suffering was discussed dispassionately, rather the way a doctor might discuss cancer, and the terrible troubles of samsara were tossed lightly about. There was a feeling of buoyancy in the pages, a *spaciousness*, as the Buddhists would say, and also a feeling of depth and clarity, as though the reader were swimming in the deepest ocean and seeing the bottom perfectly. I devoured the books and enjoyed this sort of armchair Buddhism. The books were like seductive postcards sent from a sunny and relaxed state of mind—a pure land you could only hope to visit one day. And by their example Buddhism seemed like something rational and reasonable, an unemotional and unmessy philosophy of kindness. There was no sense of struggle in the texts—none of the fumbling and bumbling that I'd seen out in Poolesville and none of the confusion and anguish that I had sensed around Jetsunma.

Perhaps these books were written from the mountaintop, I told myself, and what I'd witnessed at KPC was the dire climb to get there . . . the ugly battle toward selflessness, the ego's forced surrender, the unaccountable desires of the guru, *the razor's edge.* It was hard to imagine what Jetsunma's students had been through all these years, and none of it from an armchair. Their spiritual training had been brutal, almost cruel at times. They'd been lied to, manipulated. They'd been squeezed for money. Yet their devotion seemed profound. What was really going on in Poolesville, and what were they getting in return for their devotion?

Stories of the India trip came my way eventually. As with so many events in the life of Jetsunma, I put the puzzle together as best I could based on dribs and drabs, whispers, overheard remarks, and full-blown accounts over dinner and lunch. It had been a difficult pilgrimage—for some an absolute misery. Byron kept his film crew in a constant state of upheaval and confusion. Jetsunma seemed beleaguered and emotional. Alana described the five weeks as "lots of hardships . . . but the spiritual purposes were met."

The weather in Bylakuppe, where the group spent nearly two weeks at Penor Rinpoche's monastery, was so hot and dry and dusty that, as Aileen would put it, "we didn't know whether to open or close the windows, so we kept doing both all day long." Byron and his crew followed Jetsunma around with cameras and convinced her to wear her black leather jacket in the hundred-degree heat as a visual symbol of her "Westernness." During the day the group attended long empowerments in the main temple— all in Tibetan. And at night Penor Rinpoche invited his American students to join him on the patio of his cottage, to watch installments of a fifteen-hour videotape production, *The Life of Guru Rinpoche*, that his monks had put together themselves. It was shot in a warehouse using one camera and one microphone, and the monk who played Mandarava wore a pair of halved coconuts for breasts.

Gyaltrul Rinpoche—who was also visiting Bylakuppe at that time—kept elbowing Penor Rinpoche whenever Mandarava would appear on-screen. "Ugly! *She's so ugly!*" He laughed with his big, gap-toothed smile. And all Jetsunma's students tried to laugh, too.

But the visit to Penor Rinpoche's monastery was, according to Aileen, "something of a courtesy call." The true purpose of the trip was for Jetsunma's students to accompany their guru as she visited the famous Mandarava's pilgrimage sites in Nepal. The group numbered thirty-two, counting the film crew and a monk sent by Penor Rinpoche to accompany the travelers, and logistics were complicated. So that Jetsunma could meet up with Mandarava's spirit or mindstream, the entire group flew from Bangalore to Delhi, then took another flight to Kathmandu. After seeing the sights in small groups and circumambulating the great stupa of the Kathmandu Valley, they jammed themselves into two buses—Jetsunma alone had twenty-one pieces of luggage in India (her students were allowed one bag each)—and traveled to Pharping, where Guru Rinpoche had practiced in a cave.

Helicopters took them over terraced farms in the Himalayan foothills to Maratika Cave, where Mandarava had practiced with Guru Rinpoche centuries ago. The cave was enormous, with a wide mouth. Inside, it was dark and dank, and there were so many bats that the students had to cover their heads with hats and plastic to keep dry amid the showers of bat urine and guano. Byron and his crew set up a generator and cables and were able to flood the dark cave with eerie streams of white light. Jetsunma slowly walked around the edges of the cave, trying to connect with Guru Rinpoche and his consort—feeling for a sense of them, their spirits, their energy—and leaving white scarves in the spots where she did.

They flew again to Delhi, where another long bus trip took them to a lake that had been created when Guru Rinpoche and Mandarava had been set on fire. It was on a visit to a small grotto called Mandarava's Cave that Jetsunma finally felt a true merging with the young princess's mindstream. The place was well-kept and marked with a plaque; a lama was even living and praying and maintaining an altar there. A handprint of Mandarava's still existed on the cave wall, and after the lama pointed it out to Jetsunma, she reached up and put her hand inside the print. It fit exactly.

On another excursion, to Mandi, the group tracked down the

"pit of thorns" where Mandarava had been thrown by her father. But the pit didn't appear to be a highly venerated pilgrimage site. Located in a bad section of town, at the end of several crooked streets and an alleyway, it had no signpost and no indication that it had been visited by any worshipful followers for years. The pit was at the bottom of a small, dirty staircase, and inside it was tiled like a public toilet and lit with harsh fluorescent light. Jetsunma fell against Byron when she saw the state of the site and began sobbing and moaning. It seemed the Buddhists had simply forgotten this place—or, worse, had forgotten Mandarava. Taken back to her hotel, she was inconsolable. In the morning she told her students that she had cried all night. The "sacred energy" of the pit, she explained, was nearly gone because of neglect.

Of all the stories that came home with the pilgrims to India, perhaps the most puzzling was that, despite Wib's valiant efforts, the Dalai Lama was not available to "receive" the Poolesville group or able to meet with Jetsunma in Dharamsala. I had to wonder why the Dalai Lama didn't have a moment to meet with emissaries from the largest monastery of Tibetan Buddhists in America. Or why, in all his visits to Washington, D.C., he had never ventured to Poolesville or ever stood for a photo op with Jetsunma, the only woman tulku teaching in the West. What had the Dalai Lama heard about her? What was her rap in the larger world of Tibetan Buddhism? It wasn't as though Tibetans are so spiritually advanced that they never gossip among themselves about various tulkus and recognitions. In fact, the ones I'd met seemed endlessly fascinated with the subject.

Months after she'd left, the monks in Bylakuppe couldn't get over the brash American woman who had arrived at the monastery with her cadre of nuns and her black leather jackets and her film crew, all her makeup and luggage and helicopter rides. Jetsunma was strange, controversial—and a subject of unending speculation. It was said that she ran a "personality cult," that she "thought she was a movie star." She was a "laughingstock" in Bylakuppe, according to K. T. "Thubten" Shedrup Gyatso, an American monk who visited the monastery the following year. "She made an amazing impression," he said: "a bad one."

•

My own oasis of serenity did not last long. At the beginning of April, just a few days before the group was due home, my phone began ringing with news from another distant, magical land: Hollywood.

I grew up in Los Angeles and still have friends there—some of whom work in the movie business, some in journalism. They called to alert me to a movie deal that had been recently signed. Daily *Variety*, the trade paper for the entertainment industry, had run an article announcing that the screenwriter Andrea King was being paid four hundred thousand dollars for a feature film idea that she had pitched to Turner Pictures. It was a dramatic comedy "based on the true story about a Jewish-Italian woman with long fingernails and big hair who was raised in Brooklyn and was proclaimed a reincarnation of a Buddhist leader." Her movie was tentatively titled "The Buddha from Brooklyn."

At first when talking to my friends, I found myself defensive of Jetsunma and the movie deal. These were good people, I said, but misguided. It hadn't been intentional misappropriation of my title, just more bumbling. But as I struggled to be generous, a bad mood descended upon me. Hadn't I made it clear to Byron that I didn't want to "share" my title with him? I became overwhelmed by a vicious sort of territoriality, something journalists are taught if they don't have it naturally. And as I waited for the entourage to come home, my possessiveness about my title grew into an obsession. My title, *my book*. The days passed with this ugly feeling inside me growing. Having just read a pile of books on Buddhism didn't help; it only made me feel worse. I was now fully aware of my egocentrism but felt powerless over it.

Several days after Wib's return, I faxed a copy of the *Variety* story to his house along with a letter complaining that my title had been "stolen." Surprisingly, it was Alana, not Wib, who called me the next day. She was cheerful but impersonally so—as though she'd drawn a line in the sands of her mind about exactly how cheerful she could be.

"How was your trip?" I asked.

"There were a lot of hardships," she said. "We are certainly glad to be back in the U.S., where it's clean."

She'd read my letter, and discussed its substance with Jetsunma, who was a bit "taken aback" by my concerns and accusations. They'd all been traveling in India for five weeks—how could she know what title Andrea King was using? This wasn't her concern, and, furthermore, why didn't I just pick up the phone and call Andrea King myself? Looking back, I'm not sure why I didn't.

We scheduled a meeting with Jetsunma for the following week, but when the day came I received a call from Alana saying that Jetsunma was "having a hard day" and couldn't possibly get together. Unlike Wib—with whom I tended to chat for a while, Alana was abrupt. Trying to get her to chitchat about temple developments was like trying to sweet-talk a wall.

Soon afterward Alana set up another appointment for me to see Jetsunma, but this one was also canceled at the last minute. Jetsunma was feeling "lost and foggy and weird," Alana said. She was having a hard time "reintegrating" to America after being in India so long.

And rather than hanging up quickly, as she had done in the past, Alana dropped a few pieces of new information. These had the feeling of prepared remarks, not a casual conversation. Jetsunma and Byron were having "some problems," Alana told me. There were some papers to sign still regarding the movie deal, and Jetsunma was reconsidering whether to give Byron the rights to her story. He needed to "shape up," Alana said rather mysteriously. In India, Jetsunma had made several overtures to Byron, trying to get him to "come closer," but he had balked.

"Overtures?" I couldn't help but wonder if they'd been romantic.

"He said to Jetsunma that he needed to have *journalistic distance*."

"Huh."

"We've seen this many times," Alana said. "Being around Jetsunma brings out the worst in people, and sometimes the best. You never know which."

"God only knows what it's done to me," I said.

Alana laughed—something I was grateful for, to be honest—

and her voice became deeper and sort of hushed. "There's a real story to get, Jetsunma wants me to tell you. And the person who comes into the fire, who gets closer in, will get it. Jetsunma says, 'So far only Martha seems to have the balls.' "

In the following weeks Alana arranged two more dinner appointments with Jetsunma; both were canceled at the last minute. When I called Alana to set up others, I heard nothing back for a long time, then she left a voice mail one day saying Jetsunma was "unavailable until at least August."

The Buddhists were always talking about impermanence, but around Jetsunma impermanence was even more impermanent. It was a whole new era all over again. As the weeks passed I found myself missing the old stupa days. I missed Wib and how he used to call every few days with news and friendly updates.

I left a message on Wib's answering machine. He phoned me back a week later. "Why am I dealing with Alana?" I asked him right away. "Where have you been?"

His voice sounded rough and tired, as though he'd been up all night. "I've been through six weeks of utter hell and change since India," Wib said. "It was a total lesson." When I asked specifics, he said he wasn't really "able to talk about it." In any case, he was looking for a job in the real world, which he needed, he said, "for my self-esteem." He was also "getting out of the temple businesses, and out of the inner circle."

There was more. He and Jane had "separated," he said, something that Jetsunma had advised them to do. Wib was no longer living at his cozy house in Potomac with his wife and two daughters but in an apartment complex by himself. "Jetsunma thinks we need some time apart."

"Oh, I'm so sorry," I said. And I felt a sadness descend on me. Wib and Jane were separated? Jetsunma suggested it?

"You can always call me," Wib said, "about anything. But I'm so out of the loop now, I'm not sure how much help I'll be."

"It's been kind of weird, the last couple months."

"I feel sort of responsible," he said. "I got you into this deal, didn't I?"

"Sort of."

"Hey," he said, "whatever happened with your book title?"

"I'm going to Los Angeles next week to work on that," I said. "That was so gross of them to take it."

I didn't just look into the title when I was in Los Angeles that spring. I also began another mission, scrounging around for some other writing assignments about spiritual life in America. I had a feeling doing so might help answer some of my questions about Jetsunma and what I'd seen in Poolesville. What attracts certain people to certain leaders? More than anything, I wondered why spiritual leaders are always getting into so much trouble. Are they simply held to a higher standard—do we expect too much of them? Are they corrupted by power? And why is it that if people are charismatic enough, it seems easier to overlook their glaring faults—and the fact that they don't practice what they preach?

In an introduction to Tibetan Buddhism written by the Dalai Lama, I came across several pages devoted to the importance of finding a *pure teacher* when one begins to study. The tone is cautionary. "It is frequently said that the essence of the training in guru yoga is to cultivate the art of seeing everything the guru does as perfect. Personally, I myself do not like this to be taken too far," the Dalai Lama wrote.

> *The problem with the practice of seeing everything the guru does as perfect is that it very easily turns to poison for both the guru and the disciple. Therefore, whenever I teach this practice, I always advocate that the tradition of "every action seen as perfect" not be stressed. Should the guru manifest un-Dharmic qualities or give teachings contradicting Dharma, the instruction on seeing the spiritual master as perfect must give way to reason. . . .*
>
> *Make a thorough examination before accepting someone as a guru, and even then follow that teacher within the conventions of reason presented by Buddha.** *

* Dalai Lama, *The Path to Enlightenment* (Ithaca, N.Y.: Snow Lion, 1982).

There were similar references to this perspective in books by Gyaltrul Rinpoche and Patrul Rinpoche.* But I had to wonder how a new student who knows nothing about Buddhism could be expected to distinguish a pure teacher from an impure one. How was anyone, even a seasoned student, to feel sure she was in the presence of "the real thing"?

Charisma, according to the Dalai Lama, has nothing to do with it.† I wondered if it was like choosing a husband or anything else—you either fall in love at first sight or it takes years to reach a decision, and even then, it is an intuitive one.

I looked into writing profiles of other spiritual leaders and gurus as a way to explore this subject more, I explored practices and disciplines other than Buddhism. Frauds and saints seem to arise in every religion. I looked for leaders who were controversial, who'd tried to bridge religion and popular culture—and whose personalities and lifestyles were perhaps a bit too large.

In Palm Springs I had lunch with Tammy Faye Bakker. She wore a big, floppy straw hat; a long, white dress; and six-inch heels. Her hair had been shaved down to an inch—the length of Sherab Khandro's—and her eyelashes were so long and so fake and so coated in black mascara that each lash stuck straight out like a little black hand-dipped candle. I couldn't help but like Tammy Faye. She was fun and openhearted. And, despite the fact that she'd been recently diagnosed with colon cancer, she seemed to have only four modes of being: upbeat, bubbly, superbubbly, and sobbing bubbly. In their heyday she and her ex-husband, Jim Bakker, raised one million dollars every other day. They reached thirteen million viewers a week via satellite. She had a new book out, a memoir, so to speak, and I was struck by her accounts of the pace of her life building a ministry. She'd been driven, worked seven days a week, and focused entirely on acquiring new members, fund-raising, and building a large, impressive compound in North Carolina called Heritage USA. There was a certain need for

---

* Gyaltrul Rinpoche, *Generating the Deity* (Ithaca, N.Y.: Snow Lion, 1992); Patrul Rinpoche, *The Words of My Perfect Teacher* (Boston: Shambhala, 1998).
† Dalai Lama interview about ethics violations in America at the Conference of Western Buddhist Teachers, Dharamsala, March 1993.

an extensive wardrobe, and increasing amounts of makeup. Deep down, she said, she felt lonely and unloved. The environment at Heritage USA was full of judgment, and the larger world of fundamentalist Christian ministers was a snake pit. I read with disgust her accounts of being blackmailed by other preachers, of the politics and posturing.

These spiritual people weren't like everybody else, I said to Tammy Faye. They seemed worse.

"I know," she said. "Very terrible."

Why did spiritual leaders run into such problems? I asked. She batted her heavy lashes at me. "Let me tell you something," she said. "I think the devil can use a Christian more than he can use somebody who isn't. He's always working them."

"Why?"

"He doesn't have to spend his time on people he already has."

When I proposed that spiritual leaders tend to set themselves apart, think of themselves as good, as devoting their lives to important work—and therefore don't question their personal ethics enough, she started looking off into the next room, where lunch was being served.

"That could be true," she said. "But I don't know. Let's just turn off this tape recorder and eat!"

In Los Angeles I interviewed Dr. Laura Schlessinger, the radio talk-show shrink. Dr. Laura had brought a strict moral code and Orthodox Jewish teachings to the airwaves and was known for verbally abusing her callers. Her harsh edicts didn't seem to deter many people—in fact, they seemed to attract them. The small blonde was a black belt in karate and poised to become the most popular radio host in America. After sitting in the studio with her for a couple of hours, I started to notice that, in person and up close, she had an intensity that reminded me of Jetsunma's. Her overwhelming confidence in her message gave her a tremendous air of authority, which I had a hard time questioning. It was as though a bubble surrounded her that was impossible to pierce. She was tough and tightly wrapped, and I found myself trying to please her and compliment her in order to get her to settle down.

Far more relaxed and gentle was Renée Taylor, a legendary yoga teacher in Southern California. She was in her eighties but still teaching, and still wearing colorful floor-length saris and glamorous turbans. In the 1930s she was a screenwriter who started teaching Hatha yoga from her Beverly Hills home, and in the 1940s and '50s she was a pioneering health food advocate. She made pilgrimages to the Himalayas and wrote books about the small fiefdom of the Hunza, who she felt were the true lost people of Shangri-la. In high school I had taken yoga classes from her and had never been able to forget her soft, lilting accent—she sounded a little like Bela Lugosi—and her accounts of her exotic travels. But Renée was determined. She had come to the United States from Belgium to flee the Nazis and created a life for herself—mostly alone. Her work and teaching had influenced countless people, and she had created a little yoga empire, though it was now on the wane. In her eighties she was still driving herself in a huge red Cadillac convertible, despite the fact that she was nearly blind.

Renée tried to sell herself as soft—and there was a true softness—but she was also competitive and difficult. "I am very willful," she admitted with a laugh. When I mentioned wanting to talk to another yoga teacher, she threw out a rash of criticisms against her, and finally dismissed her technique as fraudulent. It isn't the most selfless and ego-free people who seem drawn to the role of spiritual leader. In fact, as I talked with Renée and Dr. Laura and Tammy Faye, and thought of Jetsunma, I began to suspect that it might be the most willful people who turn to spiritual measures and solutions, as a means to control and channel their own strong desires. It is a way to manage their gigantic egos. And they seem to use whatever gifts they have—charm or threat or softness—to set about refiguring the world their way.

On another trip to San Francisco, I met up with Dean Ornish, the famous heart specialist who has proven in several studies that meditation and yoga, along with a strict low-fat diet, can reverse heart disease. Dean had dark curly hair and a sweetly sad expression that made him immensely likable. Rather than being larger than life and alluring, Dean's charm was his self-effacement. He seemed genuinely modest, too, aside from the fact that the trunk of his car was loaded with copies of a *People* magazine issue that carried a flattering story about him. He and I took a hike in the

Marin Headlands and later, over lunch at my father's house, we talked about his work and his story. Like Jetsunma, he had suffered a breakdown of sorts in early adulthood—at nineteen he had been depressed and suicidal before hearing Satchidananda speak. By incorporating his spiritual lessons into his medical career, Ornish came to believe that the epidemic in America wasn't physical heart disease, it was emotional and spiritual heart disease as well. He'd taken Eastern teachings and made them American.

Soon afterward I had dinner with another medical doctor who had brought Eastern philosophy to mainstream America— and made a fortune with it. Of all the gurus I had encountered, Deepak Chopra was by far the most charismatic and fun. He had a loud and generous spirit that filled a room and an amusing way of questioning his own theories and always coming up with new ones. He had begun his work as a disciple of Maharishi Mahesh Yogi, the founder of Transcendental Meditation, but eventually left the organization to write his own books and develop his own theories. Fame came to him in the early 1990s, with his book *Quantum Healing.* He has published many best-selling books since, raced around the globe several times over giving seminars and conferences and retreats, and, like Tammy Faye Bakker, he had an infectious kind of energy that I found irresistible. But, unlike her, he found any one religion too small to accommodate his own giant spirit.

"Religion strangulates, suffocates, confines, imprisons," he told me over dinner in La Jolla. "And yet, spirituality is all about liberation. It is about freedom." All religions are based on "authentic spiritual experience," he thought, but because they are about control and largely intolerant of other beliefs, they have caused enormous damage to the world. "It's just control and drama and a form of politics, you know. It's the biggest con job of civilization," he said.

"But what's really interesting to me is that it doesn't matter what your belief system is, or how outrageous you are, there are followers."

"It does seem that way," I said.

I couldn't help but think about Catharine and Michael Burroughs, and their basement in Kensington stuffed with students. In staid Washington, D.C., of all places, they had been able to attract a group of disciples—people who sat glued to every utterance of Jeremiah, who talked about negative entities living in outer space, and who believed they'd all been together many, many times before in previous lifetimes.

"Why do certain people link up with a leader?" I asked him. "What is that attraction, do you suppose?"

"Well," Chopra said, "anytime you are attracted to someone, no matter who they are, it is because you find traits in them that you want in yourself. You just don't know this on a conscious level. So you feel kind of completed by being in their presence."

What did people see in Jetsunma that they wanted for themselves—and what was being completed? And what had I seen? What had propelled me toward Poolesville?

Turning toward Buddhism again, I began a series of long conversations with Martin Wassell, the British filmmaker who had first told me about the existence of Jetsunma and her sangha in Poolesville. Martin was protective against misunderstandings of Tibetan Buddhism but also full of savvy advice—and laughter—as I complained about having to wait endlessly to see Jetsunma. He had been involved with many Tibetan Buddhist film projects, including producing a classic documentary called *Heart of Tibet*. He knew what it was like to wait weeks, months, even years. "Many Buddhist projects are like this," he said. When dealing with Tibetan lamas, he warned me, changes and broken promises are frequent but not personal. "A lama can change his or her mind about something, and that's it—no apologies or explanations are required." It was even possible, he said, that I'd never talk to Jetsunma again.

And just as I had almost given up, Alana called one day in late June. Her voice sounded cool and certain, as usual, and, as Martin had predicted, there were no apologies for the delay.

"We're in Sedona," she said. "Jetsunma needed some downtime—just to get away and relax. She says she's been thinking about you lately, and wondered how you were doing. Would you want to just talk with her on the phone?"

•

We spoke for an hour and eleven minutes. Jetsunma's voice sounded small and meek, and kind. She did that gentle thing that Renée Taylor had perfected. She asked many questions about my father and how he was doing. When I said that he seemed the same but in very good spirits, she said, "That's perfect, just perfect. Because really it matters a lot how the person feels at the time they pass. The general feeling of happiness or regret—whichever—so that helps a lot."

"How about you?" I asked.

"I'm doing pretty well," she said. "It's funny, but I think I'm having an official midlife crisis."

"Well, you're probably entitled to one."

"That's what I figured," she said. "The worst part about it is that no one expects it of me. And if you took an opinion poll"—she laughed—"which we won't be doing, most people think I shouldn't have one. But I think it's natural and it's happening."

She was taking some time off and thinking about things, she said. She was strategizing about the future, too. Looking back, she could see that she had been trying very hard for the last eight years to find her place within Tibetan Buddhism, she said, and "trying to figure out just who I was." Early on, after the recognition, she had wanted to be more of a traditional lama—and so she wore chuba skirts and burgundy. Then she "swung to the other side" and wore business suits. "I was always just trying to figure out where I was," she said.

"Lately I'm thinking things like, well, I was born a Westerner, and if I was supposed to be a Tibetan, I would have been. And if things were supposed to be exactly the same as it was with my predecessors, then time wouldn't have moved. The truth is, you are *where* you are. And you are *who* you are. And I'm trying to move forward from that point."

She wanted to incorporate the best of everything into her teaching—and her plans for KPC. "I would never go against the traditions and what my gurus or teachers have given me, or anything to defame this lineage that I helped start. It's my home and it's my heart," she said. "And at the same time, I have to find a way to start from where I am, and take a step from the place I'm actually at. And I have to take into account that I'm a Western woman and I have certain personality traits that, you know, *we just can't dismiss our personality traits.* And when we try to, we get locked into something that doesn't feel quite real or right."

I found myself almost hypnotized by how her thoughts flowed. They never seemed prepared and ordered as much as tossed together, and there was a sense of freedom to them, a spaciousness, I guess. Listening to her was like sitting in a canoe on a river and having no idea where you were going to wind up. I enjoyed the looseness, and how she didn't seem to bother guarding her very own ordinary thinking.

We talked about the Tibetan Buddhist books I'd been reading, and how they explained some things and left out others. I was asking a lot of questions. What made sense to me about Buddhism, and what didn't?

"It's interesting that you should say that," she said, "because this is how the foundational Buddhist teachings are taught. At first, you are supposed to think through it absolutely logically. Like you are never supposed to accept a teacher until you've *logically determined* whether that teacher will benefit you. The Buddha lays down these foundational teachings, and his advice is to not accept them until they are logical to you, work them out, like equations, in your mind."

I was trying out a few fundamental practices, too, I said.

"That's a good idea," she said. "And I was telling Byron Pickett this. . . . For this story, you can't stand outside and just look at it. It's like trying to report on fires and you go to a place that's been burned by a forest fire three days before and you give a report on burnt trees. It's not the same thing as putting your hand in the fire and feeling the heat. It's not the same thing."

Byron had told her he was a "documentarian," Jetsunma said, and he needed distance. He was afraid of becoming a student of hers. "And I said, 'If you don't want to make magic or touch hearts, if you don't want to tell a story inside out—the whole story, the feel of it, the taste of it—then keep going the way you're going. But if you really want to know fire, you have to feel fire.'

"I'd say the same thing to you. You're enough of a professional. If you move in and feel the fire, don't think for a minute that you won't be able to pull your finger out if you don't like it."

She was giving two retreats in the fall, she said, a Guru Yoga retreat and a compassion retreat. "And I think," she said, "you might like to come."

It wasn't until the late summer that I heard anything about Dechen and the Monk. I was having lunch with Wib, who was talking about his new job. It got me wondering if anybody else, besides Michael Burroughs, had been in the inner circle and gotten out. And I'd started wondering whether many nuns and monks had given up ordained life and left KPC altogether.

"Not many," Wib said. "We have a pretty stable ordained sangha, compared with most Dharma centers. A very low fallout rate."

When I pressed him for specifics, he said that "years ago" a couple of monks had left. "Testosterone cases," he said. "Monks with motorcycles." I knew he was referring to Richard Dykeman—and another young monk named Chris Olance.

"Nobody recently?"

He stopped for a second. Earlier in the year, he said, a nun had "given back her robes" after breaking vows with a monk.

"Broke her vows with a monk? Wow," I said. "That's pretty serious."

"Very serious," Wib said.

"What did Jetsunma do?"

"She took it very seriously."

21.

Breaking Samaya

BREAKING TANTRIC SAMAYA IS MORE HARMFUL
THAN BREAKING OTHER VOWS.
IT IS LIKE FALLING FROM AN AIRPLANE
COMPARED TO FALLING FROM A HORSE.

—TULKU THONDUP, in *Perfect Conduct*

The time passed quickly as Dechen continued the long process of earning her robes back. She did her chores, went to work. She did Vajrasattva. She moved out of her mother's house to an apartment of her own. She felt a bit cut off from Poolesville life, and out of the loop, but happily so. In the mornings the temple was quiet and peaceful, now emptied of Jetsunma and her family, her attendants, and her entourage—who had all left for India. Little news of India found its way there in the month of March and the beginning of April, except that a movie deal had been signed with Turner Pictures. A documentary of the India trip was in the works; it would be followed by a feature film of Jetsunma's life.

Dechen passed the Monk on the temple grounds every so often. She noticed that he was smiling at her—a huge, open smile—but she looked away or looked down. And then one day in early June, Dechen heard that he had left Poolesville the way Sonam had left. Three months after the night at Ani Estates, the Monk slipped away in the middle of the night without telling anyone, even leaving some of his belongings in boxes at the monks' town house in Darnestown.

A week later he called her at home. "How are you?" he wanted to know.

"I'm great," she said.

"You are?" he asked. *"Really?"*

"Really."

They talked for a long time. The next day they talked again. And the next. There was nobody like the Monk. He knew her. He loved her. He had never meant her any harm, she realized. He had always cared about her, always been her friend. He'd been devastated when she sent those Tibetan texts back, he told her. And he'd tried so many times to catch her eye, but she was always looking down. Was she really okay? The Monk told her that he was willing to do whatever he could to get her out of Poolesville. He'd give her money. He'd find her another Dharma center. Anything. But she couldn't stay in that place.

Dechen could feel the doubts rising in her mind again, almost like bubbles that had floated to the surface. But she was also afraid. She called Ani Catharine Anastasia, her mentor, to tell her that she had spoken to the Monk on the telephone, that he had gotten back in touch with her—and she wasn't sure if that was allowed or not. "Whatever," Catharine Anastasia moaned. "I'm so sick of all this. I give up."

As Dechen kept talking to the Monk, the world began to seem larger again—it seemed to stretch well beyond the small town of Poolesville and the sixty-five acres of Kunzang Palyul Choling. The horizon seemed longer and full of possibilities. Dechen found herself full of questions all over again. Who should she believe? Who was telling the truth? She began to see that in Poolesville there had always been a choice between this world, samsara, which was supposed to be a dismal place of suffering and delusion, and the path that Jetsunma offered. *Samsara or the path:* This choice had always made Dechen feel vaguely desperate. She didn't really know very much about the outside world. She had never seen the ocean. She had no friends outside the monastery. She clung to the Guru Yoga practice, and lessons in devotion, as a way to push herself beyond the choice she didn't want to make, beyond the struggle, beyond samsara, and beyond her doubts about Jetsunma.

Was there really only one path? That was what everybody in Poolesville seemed to believe. There was Jetsunma, or there was misery and rebirth in increasingly lower realms. Were the other Dharma centers really so different? Was Poolesville really such a strange place? It was all she'd ever known.

After several months of retreat and time off in Sedona, Jetsunma returned to her big red chair in the Dharma room and began a new series of lessons that she called the Quest Teachings. She told her students that she had been in a phase of questioning and renewal, of strategizing and rethinking her life. She had felt constricted by her work at the temple and by temple life. She realized that she had been trying to squeeze herself into a role that felt unnatural and too tight.

She was in transition. Her transition was toward something even less traditional than before. "Don't be shocked if I start wearing Italian-looking clothes and big hoop earrings," she said. She talked about trying to reconnect with her Italian heritage and wanting to put everything together her own way, not fit somebody else's idea of what a Tibetan Buddhist lama was supposed to be like.

Even the way she addressed the students seemed different already. The tension—a feeling of trying too hard—was gone. "There were profound changes in Jetsunma after India," said Aileen. "And the most visible was how much more relaxed she seemed in herself, much more relaxed in her role. Before, there was much more of a sense of her sussing out the group and teaching what she felt they needed to hear," said Aileen. "She used to talk about putting on the chicken suit and having to dance for the lamas. None of that anymore . . . After India, she just sat down in her chair with a purpose. There was a deep intensity to it. . . .

"She wasn't trying anymore to be the perfect Tibetan Buddhist lama. She came back knowing what she was about— bodhicitta, compassion—and the teachings that followed were all about that."

In Sedona she had a new friend—a boyfriend—and he wasn't even a Buddhist. He was a Native American shaman. It was nice not being with a student, being with someone who was more of an equal, she told the students. And while she had been a bit skeptical of some of the practices her new boyfriend wanted to show her, she had found them very effective.

The students needed to learn to look after themselves in the same way. They were all responsible for finding their own way, too—their own path within Buddhism. Each of them had missing pieces and spiritual hungers that hadn't been met. She said that Tibetan Buddhism had everything required to fulfill those yearnings, but that the texts would never be translated into English during their lifetimes. The students needed to look elsewhere for a sense of completion and for spiritual advice. Jetsunma had begun using tarot cards again, she said, and she was relying more than ever on astrology. Whatever you needed to do to integrate your spiritual life into your culture, your daily life, your habits was a good thing. As Jetsunma had done, her students needed to nurture themselves and find ways to do this that were natural for them and their own backgrounds. She encouraged them to try new things and other traditions—Native American rituals, divination cards, yoga, or runes. She announced that she was going to arrange for an astrology class to be taught at the temple. And she was looking into having a few Native American sweat lodges.

"Start asking yourself more questions," she told them. What worked in their lives, and what didn't? What seemed to be missing? She told them that she had been questioning everything lately, even some of the Tibetan Buddhist teachings. The fundamental teachings of Buddhism call for a period of questioning. "We need to question everything, even the Dharma," she said.

Dechen sat in the back of the Dharma room, a small figure in the corner by a speaker and electronic equipment. She kept her head down and tried not to make eye contact with Jetsunma during the teachings. Four months had passed since the night at Ani Estates, and she was still cleaning the toilets and sweeping the floors. The other ordained still weren't speaking to her. How long was her punishment or *purification* meant to go on, and how long was everybody planning to shun her? How long was she supposed to sit in the back of the room with her head down? She had begun to lose hope she'd ever be able to earn her robes back.

Jetsunma seemed very different at the Quest Teachings. She seemed comfortable and in her element. She talked from her gut, confidently, candidly. Dechen hadn't seen her so comfortable with herself since before the summer of her enthronement. Dechen looked around the Dharma room and could tell that many people were feeling the same way Jetsunma was. There was almost an audible sigh of relief. The pressure was off, a pressure that they'd all felt for a long time now, to be perfect Tibetan Buddhists, to struggle up the mountain, to learn the practices and all the new words. This was a return, it seemed to Dechen, to the Jeremiah days. And while the other students seemed comforted by the new attitude, Dechen found it unsettling. It was what she had feared all along: We weren't really Buddhists. We were just some stupid New Age group.

This was the first time she had seen Jetsunma since her return from India. And the months had passed without seeing or hearing from Alana until just the week before. "Jetsunma is wondering how you're doing," Alana had told her. "Now, don't get scared, you're not going to die or anything, but she's a little worried about you. She wants you to see a doctor for depression."

See a doctor? Dechen explained that she was making payments to Palchen and had moved into a studio apartment of her own in Gaithersburg. She couldn't possibly afford therapy. A day or so later Alana called again, saying that she'd arranged for Ayla to pay for her daughter's sessions. Alana gave Dechen the name of the psychotherapist she was to see—a man she had seen several years before, who was now treating quite a few members of the sangha.

Dechen was a bit thrown off. Aside from being shunned by her friends and not being allowed to wear robes, she'd been feeling pretty good lately. She was making payments on her debts, had repaired her old Ford Tempo, and, for the first time in her life, she had a home of her own. She was thrilled to be away from the other nuns—and cooking for herself, leaving her clothes on the floor, reading as much as she wanted. But it wasn't right to argue about this with Alana. If Jetsunma wanted her in therapy, then Dechen was going to follow her advice.

In the therapist's office she still felt puzzled. Why was she there? What was she supposed to be talking about? She was not allowed to discuss the night at Ani Estates with *anyone.* The main issues on her mind—how she'd been reprimanded by Jetsunma, how the other ordained were still not talking to her, how her stepfather was furious at her for totaling the family car, and how the Monk had started calling again—were off limits. Dechen found herself telling the therapist the same old stories, mouthing all the things she'd always mouthed about herself in Poolesville. Jetsunma says I'm an approval seeker. Sherab says I'm willful. She started to think of these stories as something like "The Best of Carson"—reruns of the dramatic highlights of her life. They didn't seem to lead to any self-discoveries. Nor did the doctor have many insights to share. He gave her a list of questions to answer, a multiple-choice test for depression that reminded Dechen of something in *Glamour* magazine, and he told her afterward that her score suggested that she was "moderately depressed" and might have some success with medication. At first Dechen refused. She disliked the notion of taking any medication. She didn't even use aspirin or Tylenol at home. Also, it just didn't seem very, well, *Buddhist.* But eventually she agreed to see another doctor, a psychiatrist who immediately put her on Zoloft.

But she hated the Zoloft even more than therapy. "I was taking the tiniest amount," she said, "but it felt like champagne had been poured into my bloodstream. I got dizzy right away, and within a few days my hands were shaking. I couldn't sleep. I had this bubbly feeling. I couldn't concentrate. I couldn't even read a whole paragraph of text without getting distracted. And I couldn't practice."

As she sat in the back row at the first Quest Teaching, listening to Jetsunma encourage the students to find their own way—to nurture themselves, keep themselves spiritually alive, and ask questions—Dechen's mind felt like it was clicking into gear. *Questions, ask yourself questions.* What did Dechen want? Where was she really heading? More than anything she wanted to be able to do more Tibetan Buddhist practice, live a traditional renunciate life, and eventually do a three-year retreat. She had to be honest with herself. Was that ever going to happen at KPC? She wasn't sure that tarot cards or astrology would really work for her. She already knew what did work: a traditional Tibetan Buddhist practice. And the rest of the students would know this as deeply as Dechen did if they ever bothered to sit down on their butts long enough and just do it. Maybe they wouldn't need therapy either— or antidepressants. What was a nun doing on antidepressants?

Question everything, Jetsunma told the students. Even question the Dharma. A huge, spontaneous smile took over Dechen's face. Question the Dharma? In the nondual Buddhist universe, the Dharma and the lama and the sangha are one, inseparable. The same thing. And if she was allowed to question one, she could question them all. She could question the sangha. And she could question the lama. Dechen felt an immense weight lift from her shoulders, and a feeling of great spaciousness inside her, a freedom, a feeling of breath, of energy, of life. Her mind was suddenly alive with ideas and thoughts, and all kinds of questions. She couldn't wait to write some of them down.

She was still smiling as she watched Jetsunma walk out of the Dharma room at the end of the teaching. Alana noticed her smile and smiled brightly back. "We were told to go out and buy a Quest Book, like a journal to keep," Dechen said. And when she got hers, she pulled out a pen, opened to the first page, and quickly wrote her first entry: "I don't believe the Mandarava recognition."

She was on fire for the next two months and never stopped writing. Dechen's private mission, her own spiritual "quest," was finally facing her doubts about Poolesville. Was life at the KPC monastery as hopeless and worthless as the Monk suggested—or was it salvageable? She made up lists, drew from memories. There would be no karmic consequences of having doubts, no broken samaya, no rebirth in Vajra Hell, since Jetsunma herself had instructed her to question everything. And once the door was open, it was impossible to close it. The doubts hurled themselves at her and flooded out from within her. They stampeded. They exploded.

And they shouted so loudly she couldn't even think. How had she gone so long keeping them down? It had been exhausting always to be fighting something inside, always suppressing a part of herself. If anything had made her depressed before, it must have been that. Doubts were a part of her, the way blood was a part of her body and the air came and went in her lungs. And she was finally free—set free by Jetsunma herself—to let them flow out of her and to be herself: a person who was consumed by doubt.

First things first. She hadn't broken her vows—her root vows. She knew she hadn't. The Monk had called her at work and quoted to her the *Vinaya* teachings—the highest Tibetan Buddhist authority on the rules and regulations for the ordained. And the Vinaya said that if no orifice was penetrated, then no root vow had been broken.* Wasn't it wrong for Jetsunma to take her robes away from her? If no root vow had been broken, and the robes were still hers, she was still ordained.

Her years with the group came back to her with pristine clarity, as though she were revisiting every experience and looking at it closely again. She remembered the time she was called into a meeting with leaders of the ordained community—Alana and three others—and told that she was being kicked out of the retreat center for not doing her chores and being late on the rent. Dechen remembered how she tried to defend herself and offered to pay her back rent immediately. Everybody had trouble doing their chores, she said. "They all looked sickened as I said this, like it was revolting to hear a criminal defend herself," said Dechen. "I was supposed to make my mind like a bowl and hold every ounce of the blessing of being corrected. I was supposed to feel lucky: Most sentient beings wandered in samsara helplessly with no teacher at all, or with a teacher who wasn't as compassionate as Jetsunma."

Losing the path, losing the guru . . . it was like the terror of an astronaut losing the lifeline to the ship and drifting away into black space, the void, the deep, empty nothingness, with no way to be rescued.

---

* Ngari Panchen and Pema Wangyi Gyalpo, *Perfect Conduct: Ascertaining the Three Vows* (Boston: Wisdom, 1996).

Dechen suspected that she was afraid of losing the path—and her connection to Jetsunma—because she had no idea who she was without them. She thought of herself only in the words of others. *Jetsunma says that the problem with me is that I'm an approval seeker.* In Tibetan Buddhism the practices are supposed to bring you closer to your true Buddha nature. But in Poolesville the only true Buddha nature anybody talked about was Jetsunma's.

Dechen had spent years trying to adjust her thinking to be in alignment with something Jetsunma had said, or something Jetsunma had taught. Or something Alana had said that Jetsunma had said. After the sangha meeting about Karl, when Alana said he needed to be "broken like a wild mustang," Dechen had begun to feel differently about him. In the past she had always liked Karl and defended him. But after the meeting she drove him to the doctor's office one afternoon and found herself exasperated that he was taking so long. "Those meetings really worked," she said. And she realized that the group's opinion had always mattered more than her own.

And from above "there was a constant implication—sometimes subtle and sometimes obvious—that we were inept, helpless, shallow, and stupid," Dechen would later say. The teachings Jetsunma gave were often entertaining, but they were a rambling miasma of unrelated topics, a mishmash of Tibetan Buddhism and New Age theories, which Jetsunma called "climbing over the mountain from ten different directions." Dechen finally admitted to herself that she didn't really understand Jetsunma's teachings and didn't believe anybody else did, either. She had noticed that if students raised a logical inconsistency in a teaching, they were called "superficial" or considered "Dharma dumb-dumbs." If they insisted on thinking for themselves, they were "self-centered" and "arrogant." The will and the ego were poisonous things in Poolesville. Dechen felt they'd all been ground down—defeated by Jetsunma and her brand of Buddhism.

It reminded her of the game Wack-a-Mole at the carnivals and amusement parks on the Eastern Shore. People stood with big rubber mallets and waited for plastic moles to show the tops of their heads; the game was to clobber the moles as soon as they showed themselves. Very few students were allowed to show themselves. "It's a very subtle place, and you don't know how strong the current is until you go against the efforts to mold you," Dechen said. "The more you resist, the stronger the reaction becomes. And if you persist in going against the approved-of method, the reactions become stronger and stronger."

She found she was angry about the night at Ani Estates. It hadn't been a blessing. And it hadn't been just about Dechen and the Monk and their merit. It was a lesson in humiliation for all the students—a reminder, a warning, a theatrical presentation. And it was the result of years of decay. Dechen now saw the signs of decay everywhere. What had led a kind and generous group of people who wanted to do nothing more than make the world a better place to become in her mind a hateful, angry mob, comfortable participating in a lurid display of aggression?

A flood of questions overtook her mind. She questioned the way the temple was run and all the power that Alana had been given. They'd started out with good intentions. But the practices had decayed. The teachings had decayed. The finances had decayed. People didn't seem as happy. The prayer chart for the twenty-four-hour vigil was increasingly hard to fill. She sought out certain members of the sangha and asked them questions. In particular she approached Doug Sims and asked about the finances. Poor Doug. He seemed so beleaguered and down himself, so lost. He had tried his best to run Ladyworks and keep those books. He'd tried his best to find money for Jetsunma's business, but now that, too, had decayed. The Ladyworks business was seriously in debt, and Jetsunma was never going to be self-supporting. The temple would always be going broke trying to pay her salary and all her expenses. If the center was supposed to bring the Dharma to the West but the finances were untenable, then the Dharma was, too, which meant Dechen was wasting her time in Poolesville.

She sent an E-mail to Konchog, a monk she greatly respected, hoping to open up a line of communication with him so she could eventually talk about the future of KPC and ask him about the shedra, or monastic university, that Khenpo was starting. Maybe if the shedra was happening and was financially healthy, there would be a place for Dechen in Poolesville. Her first E-mail to Konchog was an icebreaker, however; she recounted a joke she'd heard earlier in the week. But Konchog wasn't amused. He lashed out at Dechen in a series of angry replies. She was a flirt, he told her. And she had already brought one fully ordained monk to shame. He told her to stop trying to contact him. "I'm not going to walk around in guilt and shame forever," Dechen wrote to him. "My punishment is over." But Konchog wasn't sure of that. "We hadn't gotten a sign yet from Alana or Jetsunma," he explained later, "and I guess I thought I was still supposed to shun her."

So by mid-August, after two months of investigation, Dechen felt more alone than ever—her "quest" had led only to more questions. At the heart of them sat the most colossal uncertainty of all: She doubted the wisdom and beneficence and compassion and goodness and divinity of Jetsunma Ahkön Lhamo.

"We all want to believe that the lamas are omniscient," she said. "But the truth is, Penor Rinpoche was duped."

She began to think of the ones who had left before her. In Poolesville they all told themselves that nobody ever left, that KPC had the lowest attrition rate of any sangha in America and was the most stable monastery. But if you started to look around for them, former members were in the back of everybody's mind. They were out there in the world—good people who had once loved Poolesville and been happy there, people who had come with smiles on their faces and felt like they'd found their home and later woke up and felt differently. Why had they gone? Had they lost their way, lost the path? Had they all died of cancer and gone to Vajra Hell together?

Dechen found an old phone list of sangha members and saw that Rick and Chris Finney's number was still on it. She had worked with Chris on many sewing projects and temple projects, and in the gift shop. She had known Rick since he first showed up in Poolesville; he had given her early Tibetan lessons.

Rick answered the phone when Dechen called but seemed hesitant to discuss Poolesville with her. "I was guarded, and very careful what I said," he said later. "People have to reach some of these conclusions on their own." He asked Dechen why she wanted to discuss the center.

"I just have some questions," she said.

"What kinds of questions?" he asked.

"Well, I have a feeling," Dechen said, "that KPC functions like a cult."

Rick thought for a moment. "I think you better talk to Chris."

But Chris was also hesitant to discuss details and reach controversial conclusions—she had gotten calls from other members with doubts, and they tended to pour their hearts out, only to return to Poolesville. Even as Dechen mentioned the size of Jetsunma's salary, Chris found herself explaining, "Well, Jetsunma has a lot of expenses—her wardrobe and everything."

"Ten thousand dollars a month in clothes?"

Eventually, the Finneys invited Dechen to their house, where they could discuss things more freely. Sitting in their living room, Rick and Chris asked her how things were going for her in Poolesville. She was leaving, she told them. And she wanted to find another Dharma center where she could practice and still be a nun. But what about her robes? Rick reassured Dechen that she had not broken a root vow, and therefore she was still a nun. Then he told her something that she had long suspected from her own reading of the Tibetan texts: Technically, Jetsunma had no authority to take her robes from her. He brought out a manuscript copy of *Perfect Conduct*—which he had just finished copyediting—and opened it to page 55. There were five instances that called for losing one's robes: if they were given back voluntarily to the lama who ordained you (in Dechen's case, Penor Rinpoche), if you broke a root vow, if you developed "two sex organs spontaneously overnight," if you stopped believing in cause and effect (karma and reincarnation), or if you died.

Next, Dechen talked to Richard Dykeman on the phone. He had left Poolesville in 1989 and had eventually become fully ordained in India and spent years studying with Tibetan lamas in the United States. Richard was full of passion, reassuring Dechen that things were different at the other American centers. It was more Buddhism and less guru. He told her that he'd accomplished lots of things—many practices—at the other centers, and felt good about his time in them. She shouldn't worry about life after Poolesville, he said. After a while a day would pass and she would not think of Poolesville, and then she'd go a week without thinking of Poolesville, and then it would be a month or two. She would never be sorry she left, he promised her.

While talking, Richard never once used the title Jetsunma. He called her Alyce.

After their conversation Dechen found her orange plastic bottle of Zoloft and threw it in the trash. She walked into her bedroom, slapped Jetsunma's picture off her altar, and stared at it on the floor. Rick Finney was right. Jetsunma had no authority to take Dechen's robes away. Richard was right about Jetsunma . . . *Alyce.* She didn't care about Dechen. She had never cared about Dechen. She had cared only about feeling powerful and about influencing people's lives, about making money and buying clothes and being attractive. She didn't care about the students and their spiritual lives, or even love them on a simple emotional level. She wasn't a compassionate mother to them, or even a nurturing soul. It had been an act to get everybody's devotion and win hearts. She collected them like shrunken heads. . . . All the time Dechen had wasted, all those years. Jetsunma had told them all they were only years away from enlightenment—or at least one lifetime. Now Dechen saw how far away they really were.

"It was like a dream dissipated," she said. "I was always so proud that I had managed to do something with my life, that I had started so young. . . . All those years that I worried I didn't have enough Guru Devotion, all those times we were told if we didn't practice enough that the world would deteriorate into suffering, and that the Dharma wouldn't make it in the West."

She called Sonam in Oregon and told her that she was leaving Poolesville. She tried to track down several others—Chris Olance and Don Allen, Sangye's father, who had slipped away quietly a couple of years before.

Her very last call was to Michael Burroughs. She had hesitated about calling him because deep down she still didn't trust him. For years she had blamed him for all the problems at KPC. But maybe she needed to rethink that, too. Through the grapevine

of former KPC students, Dechen discovered that Michael was living in Colorado and still a Tibetan Buddhist. For years he had remained bitter about his time in Poolesville and felt his life had
been largely wasted. He had done public relations for the Naropa
Institute in Boulder for a couple of years, then drifted back into
professional organ playing and choir directing. Dechen wanted to
ask him about a Tibetan program at the Naropa Institute—maybe
Michael could help her get in.

When Michael came on the line, she heard his familiar Tennessee drawl and realized, suddenly, how much she'd missed him.
"They all call me," he said. "Everybody calls. And I help everybody
get out."

"I'm already out," Dechen said.

They spoke briefly about the Naropa Institute, and about
KPC. He didn't seem to have much to say, and spoke mostly in
sound bites. "You know, her channeling was faked," he claimed.
"She wasn't happy with the recognition as Ahkön Lhamo. It
wasn't flashy enough."

Michael urged Dechen to write to Penor Rinpoche and detail
some of the things she had seen over the years—particularly the
night at Ani Estates. There were abuses in Tibetan Buddhism, but
Michael reassured her that there were also some very good lamas
around in the world that she could study with. "You can drag
fame and girls and money in front of them and they won't even
bite," he told her.

"I've wasted so much time," she said.

"What about me?" he said. "I was married to her. I find it all
really embarrassing."

Then, he asked for a favor. Michael had a letter he'd written to
Atira that he wanted Dechen to deliver. He hadn't seen or spoken
to the girl for six years, but he wanted Atira to know he still loved
her. Dechen said she wouldn't be able to do this herself, but she
had some ideas.

At the end of the brief exchange, he said, "You know, you are
still a nun."

"I know," she said.

That night she went home and saw the photograph of Jetsunma's smiling face on the floor of her bedroom, where it had

landed two days before. She pulled the picture out of its frame and ripped it into tiny pieces. She flushed them down the toilet. She took her gau off her neck and pulled out the relics—little tufts of Jetsunma's hair. At first she planned to burn them, but she decided that was "too respectful." She flushed them down the toilet instead.

Then she shaved her head. She put her robes back on. And she bought a bus ticket to New York City.

She believed what Michael and Rick and Richard and the Monk and *Perfect Conduct* had told her—she was still a nun—and now she wanted to hear it from a higher authority, Khenpo Tsewang Gyatso.

Khenpo was giving a series of teachings from an apartment in the Bowery that had been converted into a small Dharma center. It was the last day of teachings, and at first he seemed very happy to see Dechen—dressed in her dark burgundy robes. When she offered him a white scarf, she said quietly, "I'd like to meet with you, if I could."

Khenpo nodded. "After the teachings."

She waited for hours to see Khenpo alone. There were many students milling around the apartment and much conversation about a new Dharma center that Khenpo was helping to organize in New York. Eventually he caught Dechen's eye and led her to a small bedroom in the apartment, which he was using.

She came right to the point. "Jetsunma took the vows away from me, and I don't believe that she can do that, but I don't know," Dechen said. "I cannot read the Dharma texts, and this is a very dangerous situation for me. If I believed her that I was no longer an ani, then I could be breaking vows and not even know or have a chance to purify."

Khenpo had a strained and sad look on his face. The creases between his brows were wider than his thin black mustache. "Even the Buddha, even Guru Rinpoche," he said, "cannot take your robes away."

Dechen nodded and tried not to show any feeling. She was relieved, though—not just for her sake, but because, in spite of her fears about how political the world of Tibetan Buddhism could be, Khenpo had told her the truth. "But perhaps," he said, "you should not wear the robes at the temple. People might be upset."

"I don't think I'm going back to KPC," she said.

"Okay. Study and practice on your own," he said.

He invited her to join a group of students who were going out to dinner that night. A few of them—members of a rich Taiwanese family—were sponsors of Penor Rinpoche's monastery in India, and others were sponsors of the center in New York Khenpo was helping to start. They would be holding a committee meeting later to discuss their plans. Over dinner Dechen was asked about KPC. She was a nun there, right? Yes, she said. The committee members seemed curious about Poolesville. It was known to be such a beautiful temple, and very successful. They hoped to use it as a model.

After dinner Dechen returned to the Bowery apartment with the other students, and, since it was too late to take a bus home, she was invited to remain there overnight. As she listened to Khenpo's students discuss how to start a new Dharma center, Dechen found herself wanting to contribute some ideas. Rather than speak at the meeting, she curled up in a corner and wrote out a list of recommendations that ran for six pages. Her advice had not been directly solicited, but she felt it was important that this new center not run into some of the problems she'd seen in Poolesville. She was careful not to mention anything about KPC, but it would have been possible, based on her suggestions, to guess that her experience in Poolesville had not been entirely positive. And quietly, when the committee meeting was over, Dechen handed the notes to one of the members, an American woman.

From across the room Khenpo watched Dechen hand the notes to his student. He looked alarmed. He asked to see her alone again, but the meeting kept being delayed.

She stayed another day in the apartment, waiting to see Khenpo again. There were many people around to talk to while she waited, including a few Tibetans she'd met in Bylakuppe. Finally, Khenpo gave Dechen an opportunity to speak with him, but not alone. He sat in the teaching room along with other Tibetans and asked about her decision to leave KPC. After she reassured him that she had great devotion for Penor Rinpoche, she made open complaints about Poolesville. Knowing how family-oriented Tibetans are, she made sure to mention how she'd been discouraged from being in contact with her father. She described how, when she was only eighteen, she had been removed from her mother's care and told to live with another sangha member. She was also concerned about her brother and wondered whether his involvement with KPC had been healthy for him. She felt Jetsunma had directly harmed her family, she said bluntly. The other Tibetans in the room, who couldn't help overhearing the story, nodded their heads in sympathy and looked horrified. Khenpo looked horrified, too—but mostly that Dechen would speak this way, so boldly and so negatively about a Palyul teacher in a public setting.

She continued. She told Khenpo about the KPC finances—the amount that Jetsunma was paid, and how money was raised for temple projects but spent on her instead. Khenpo shook his head and seemed speechless. She was planning to launch into her theories about how KPC wasn't a Tibetan Buddhist center as much as a personality cult, but she could tell from his face that she'd already said enough. "He didn't have much to say after that," she said, "and I got the impression that he didn't want me around anymore, either."

The next morning, as she prepared to leave New York, Dechen was told that Khenpo wanted to meet with her *again*—but this time he spoke angrily to her in front of many people, including several of the sponsors of the new Dharma center. "You need to purify!" he yelled. "You need to do lots of Vajrasattva, and learn more about your vows, and study the Vinaya!" To Dechen, the conversation didn't make sense—it was advice that Khenpo had given her days before but now in a different tone. She could only surmise that this was a political move to discredit her. Dechen had become too negative, too threatening. And it was possible that Khenpo believed she'd written damning things about KPC in her six-page memo. Soon afterward he arranged for her to be taken to the bus station by three of the Taiwanese sponsors, and he joined them in their Mercedes. As she got out of the car at the bus station, and was standing in the street, Khenpo got out, too. "I have more to say to you!" he yelled in a voice so loud that all the Taiwanese could hear. "You have broken your vows, and you need to study the Vinaya, and then *maybe*, in the future, you can retake vows."

It was during the five-hour bus ride back to Maryland that Dechen's rage and confusion multiplied. She had hoped that Khenpo would be supportive of her—and, at first, he had. But now she could see he would always protect the Palyul tradition and Penor Rinpoche and Poolesville. Somewhere along the way the truth had become irrelevant. There was nowhere to go to make complaints about Jetsunma. Nobody wanted to hear them.

She imagined what Khenpo would say about her in the future—how she'd be discredited. She imagined that before long nobody would believe there'd ever been a night at Ani Estates. It would be dismissed as gossip, as the wild delusion of an irresponsible girl. Dechen decided to do three things upon returning to her apartment in Gaithersburg: She would call Alana's voice mail to say she was leaving KPC for good, she would call her mother to say she was leaving of her own accord—and wasn't being kicked out. And then she would call the police.

That way Khenpo wouldn't be able to lie about what had happened to protect Penor Rinpoche. There was another reason, too. "I just wanted to make sure," Dechen said, "that Jetsunma never hit anybody again."

It is hard to know exactly how Jetsunma reacted when she was arrested by the Maryland State Police on charges of battery. Later on she would say, "Oh, I wasn't too frightened. The police have far worse people than me to worry about. I was more afraid for the Dharma."

Dechen only learned that Jetsunma had been arrested a day later, when her family was sent to her apartment. Alana had called Ayla Meurer and suggested that Ayla attempt some kind of "family" intervention with her daughter. Dechen needed to see the lack of wisdom behind leaving Poolesville and filing criminal charges against her root guru.

Ayla and Dechen had never really fought much—or ever struck each other—but the day Ayla came to the studio apartment, things became overheated quickly. Dechen pushed her mother, and then Ayla pinned Dechen against the wall. Scared by the intensity of their emotions, the two women soon sat down at the kitchen table and began to talk calmly. Ayla told her daughter that Jetsunma loved her, that Jetsunma was divine, and that the negativity Dechen was seeing was only a reflection of her own mind. Jetsunma was incapable of harming anyone, and her every action brought benefit to countless beings.

"If she was a guru *at all*, that would be true. But she's not."

"Of course she is! Don't say things like that."

"I've thought this over carefully," Dechen said, "and I consider KPC a *cult*. And Jetsunma is out of control."

Ayla seemed ruffled and embarrassed. "There are good cults and bad cults. Like anything in life. You're making a terrible mistake."

"Stay out of this, Mother. This doesn't concern you."

"Of course this concerns me," Ayla said. "This is my teacher you are talking about."

Hoping to ward off similar "interventions"—and to make sure her fellow ordained learned of the police charges she'd filed—Dechen began leaving messages for sangha members on the temple voice mail system. She used the word *cult*, well aware of the impact it would have. She called Sangye Dorje and left a long message describing her strange encounter with Khenpo—in particular his early assurance that "nobody" could take her robes away. Her messages to Alana were hateful and angry, deliberately intended to rile her. The idea was to light so many fires that there'd have to be a major sangha meeting where the police charges would be discussed.

Within a few days Karl Jones showed up at the apartment to try to reason with Dechen, but her landlords turned him away. Then the letters started coming. Some were hand-delivered outside her apartment door. Others were sent by certified mail. They were from sangha members who had received voice mails from Dechen. Each letter contained one particular sentence—"Stop leaving these slanderous voice mails or I will consider this harassment and file charges"—but the rest was often very personal. Sangye Dorje wrote her, telling Dechen that she suffered from "paranoia" and was "certainly a borderline schizophrenic." He recommended that she find a good psychiatrist. Bob Colacurcio urged Dechen to study Guru Devotion more. Alana's letter was beautifully written—and designed to nail Dechen deftly in a vulnerable place. "You have succeeded in your quest to take revenge against your mother. Your childhood rage now controls you, and you have now, indeed, broken her heart. Not just your birth mother, but your spiritual mother as well."

Alana offered to meet with Dechen privately, saying she was opening her hand and reaching out to Dechen because she had bitten the hand of all her teachers and, "having been there myself in the past, I know that sometimes you need someone to just say, it's okay, we can stop this now." At the bottom she said, "I don't think you want to end up institutionalized or on medications. Help yourself or ask for help."

Dechen moved into the Finneys' place for a few nights to escape what she feared might be a deluge. Ayla began calling the Finneys, asking to speak to her daughter, and, when they wouldn't hand over the phone, Alana called for Chris.

"I have a message from Jetsunma for you," Alana told Chris. "She wants you to know that she's thinking about you, and she's really worried because she sees that your karma is running out and great obstacles are headed your way."

Chris felt she understood what Alana was saying: You are going to die.

"I'm not sure what you need to do," she told Chris. "Maybe you can have some tsogs [purification prayers] done for you at Frederick. We could do some for you. You could pay some money to the ordained and they could do some."

"Okay," Chris said quietly. Then she suddenly felt something very unexpected. She felt bad for Alana.

"You take care of yourself, too, Alana," Chris told her. "And thank Jetsunma for thinking of me, but I'm doing really well."

Michael Burroughs called Dechen at work to talk about the charges she'd filed. He had heard about them from Rick Finney.

His voice was full of mischief and amusement. It was "hilarious" and "wonderful," he said, but he wasn't going to get involved—he didn't want to get on Khenpo Tsewang Gyatso's "bad side." Michael told her that he had seen Khenpo recently in Colorado, in fact, and when the subject of Dechen's charges came up, Khenpo said he needed to get in touch with her. Could she take a call from him at work?

Khenpo had a deal to offer Dechen. He was worried about potential embarrassment to Penor Rinpoche if word of the police charges or some of the other activities he'd heard about in Poolesville became public. If Dechen agreed to drop the charges, Khenpo was willing to arrange a formal censure of Jetsunma, and she would be sent into retreat immediately. To discuss the details, both Michael and Khenpo called Dechen one afternoon from a speakerphone. The censure, according to Michael and Dechen, included a demand that Jetsunma no longer call herself a Tibetan Buddhist teacher or a Palyul lama, and she would be asked to stop using the title Jetsunma.

"Michael did most of the talking," said Dechen, "and then Khenpo confirmed it."

But Dechen had stopped trusting Khenpo at this point, and she agreed to drop the charges only if the letter of censure came from Penor Rinpoche, was signed by Jetsunma, and then a copy of it was delivered to Dechen. None of them seemed to realize that, because the charges were criminal and brought by the state of Maryland, it wasn't up to Dechen to drop them.

Soon after, a letter censuring Jetsunma was drafted in Bylakuppe and approved by Penor Rinpoche. Two American monks who were visiting Penor Rinpoche's monastery during the fall of 1996, K. T. "Thubten" Shedrup Gyatso and Tenzin Chophak, were asked to assist in the wording of the letter and to help clean up Khenpo's English. They also had long talks with Khenpo about Poolesville, since Thubten had spent three months living in one of the monks' houses there.

"He's a very reserved guy," said Thubten of Khenpo. "But we had very relaxed conversations, and he spoke to me as openly as possible. He already knew exactly what was going on in Poolesville. Her salary was unheard of. Her monks were living in crummy conditions, and some were giving fifty percent of their salaries to her. Jon Randolph couldn't even afford a pair of new shoes."

The tone of the final one-page letter was "really harsh" and "scolding," according to Thubten, "the way a father would reprimand a naughty daughter." There was no mention that Jetsunma should drop her title or stop calling herself a Buddhist teacher. Instead, the letter admonished her for neglecting her ordained sangha. Penor Rinpoche wrote that his first priority was always taking care of his monks and nuns—making sure they were fed and housed and receiving teachings. Jetsunma, the letter scolded, was clearly not doing that. There was another complaint: She wore too much makeup and needed to "tone down her appearance."

But in the end it appears the letter was never mailed. It didn't have to be. The state of Maryland officially dropped its charges against Alyce Zeoli on November 8, 1996, and Penor Rinpoche no longer had a public scandal to worry about. The prosecutor called Dechen to tell her that the case was weak. The witnesses—the members of the ordained community in Poolesville—were considered "hostile." The Monk was uninterested in testifying because he felt that Dechen's case might turn people away from Tibetan Buddhism. Dechen had even suspected that her mother would have testified against her.

In many ways Dechen was relieved. "I was just tired," she said. "And I had taken on a lot. I had very little support, with the sole exception of Rick and Chris Finney—neither of whom thought I should have filed the charges originally."

Two days later, on November 10—a crisp, clear day—Dechen packed up her Ford Tempo with all the belongings she could fit in it, within inches of the ceiling. She drove to her mother's and left a basket of flowers on the sundial in her garden. She put the basket on the point of north, as a way to tell Ayla that she was heading north, to her dad's house in Toronto.

Ayla saw Dechen out front and stepped out to approach her. "It's a terrible thing to lose a daughter," she would say later.

Dechen waved good-bye from the car and drove off. She told nobody where she was heading. She left no forwarding address, no phone numbers. She drove through Pennsylvania and New York. She stayed in motels and at old friends' houses. She ate in coffee shops and at McDonald's. Every night she called the Monk and told him where she was and described the day.

When she got to her father's place, she told him that KPC was a cult. "I know," he said. Together they drove to Detroit and spent Thanksgiving with his mother. Dechen hadn't seen her grandmother for nine years. She saw her cousins, her aunts and uncles. Her father got out his guitar and sang folk songs. Dechen sat on the floor and played with little cousins she had only just met. Her grandmother pulled her aside and asked about her brother. Was there any way of getting him out, too?

Dechen headed off again, alone. In early December she found herself driving through the Badlands, the black hills of South Dakota. Late in the afternoon, as the sun began to set, she got out of her car and stood in the vast expanse of space in the center of the United States. She felt good and free and sure of one thing— what she was doing. She thought back on all her years with Jetsunma, all the teachings, the hard work, the practice, the stupas, the beautiful prayer room . . . The time hadn't been wasted, not entirely. Dechen could see that she'd made progress. And she'd done some remarkable things. Everybody there had. Perhaps that was the invisible reward of devotion. But in the end Poolesville wasn't what it appeared to be, or thought it was, and that was the saddest fact of all. It wasn't the Fully Awakened Dharma Continent of Absolute Clear Light any more than Disneyland was. It was a fantasy place as powerful and seductive and delusional as samsara, and just as corrupt. "It was like the end of *The Truman Show*," Dechen said. "Me alone in the sailboat, breaking through that illusion."

22.

Approaching the Nondual

ANYONE UNABLE TO UNDERSTAND
HOW A USEFUL RELIGION CAN
BE FOUNDED ON LIES WILL NOT
UNDERSTAND THIS BOOK EITHER.

—Kurt Vonnegut, *Cat's Cradle*

I had moved out to the country by the time of the compassion retreat in late September 1996. My boyfriend and I had gotten engaged and found a house in a quaint and well cared for little
village in Virginia called Waterford. For years I had been telling
myself it was time to move on, to withdraw from city life, from the
crowds and noise, the smell of money and politics, and the sight of
lobbyists sitting around big dinner tables at expensive restau-
rants. I wasn't sure that I believed that my life on earth was samsara—a place of delusion and suffering—but existence in
Washington, D.C., came pretty close.

The funny thing was, as much as I had moved farther away
from D.C.—and in what seemed to be the opposite direction from
the state of Maryland—I was now closer to Kunzang Palyul Choling. Alana had called to ask if I needed a place to stay in
Poolesville over the four-day retreat and made arrangements for
me to use a spare room at a sangha member's house. But after the
first commute I realized that this wasn't necessary. About eight
miles from my house was a small ferry that crossed the Potomac.
It left from a little wharf tucked into the side of the river—and was

marked by a hand-painted sign that said, WHITE'S FERRY, with an arrow; it shuttled three cars at a time. Once on the Maryland side of the river, I found myself in the farthest reaches of Poolesville, at the end of River Road. The rest of the drive was poetic. Traveling along a narrow country lane, passing woods and fallow fields and open farmland, in just ten minutes or so I found myself at the driveway to the temple. I had returned again to the land of the Tibetan Buddhists, to the big white plantation facade, to the wind chimes, the flapping prayer flags, and all the friendly faces I had come to know. I hadn't moved far away, it seemed, but come full circle.

It had been nearly three months since I'd talked to Jetsunma or visited much with her students, except by phone. My summer had been spent settling into a new house and hand-wringing about my book. I had talked to theologians and religion professors and other Tibetan Buddhists. I had read up on everything from crystals and cults to the Church of Jesus Christ of Latter-day Saints. I had been trying to figure out the difference between a cult and a religion—and had decided it was only two things: a matter of time and conformity.

The prophet who began the Mormon Church, Joseph Smith, received revelations from a white salamander on a rock. In these visions he claimed he was told how the universe worked, how heaven was arranged—the ideas and stories that became the foundation of a new religion. Smith and his followers seemed like strange people when *The Book of Mormon* was first published in 1830 in Palmyra, New York, and Smith himself was later sent to jail and then lynched. The Mormons were driven west to Salt Lake City to escape persecution and prospered there. Of course they were seen as a cult, and a group of fanatics who didn't smoke or drink coffee or liquor, hoarded food in their basements, and believed they would become gods of their own kingdoms someday. Smith's successor, Brigham Young, had twenty-seven wives. But over the last hundred years their church had matured and become an elegant cruise ship of a religion. It is the richest and most successful church in America. It owns the most land, has the most stable membership; it had built the most temples and attracted the most new followers. And it had joined the mainstream by carefully abandoning certain practices not in sync with society's norms. Polygamy, for instance, was dropped overboard along the way.

If KPC was a cult, maybe it would mature beyond that. It sure looked like a cult and smelled like a cult—and was often managed the way cults are. But the tulku system was long established in Tibet, where the divine lamas seemed to be a law unto themselves. In the East there are ways of dealing with abuses—gossip and quiet ostracizing, and other correctives that are too subtle and imprecise for Americans. We expect accountability, open books, and fewer secrets from our religious leaders. As the Monk had told Dechen, and would ultimately tell me, democracy is a very good thing, and Americans expect it, deserve it. Wasn't there a way for Tibetan Buddhism to comply with these ideals?

There would always be determined people like Dechen who would tell their stories. Others—people like Kathy Coon, Bonnie Taylor, and Bob Denmark—would be quieter victims of a bad system, would leave peacefully and try to figure out for themselves why they were ever in Poolesville. Bonnie Taylor left in 1996. She had given nearly two hundred thousand dollars to KPC in five years and found herself pressured to donate another one hundred thousand to Ladyworks.

Kathy Coon and Bob Denmark would leave in 1997, after serving on a financial committee and seeing the budget for the first time. When the committee sent a letter to Jetsunma asking her to take a reduced salary from her sangha, she refused. She claimed that great negative karma would be caused by rescinding an offering to a lama, and the temple would fall to ruin.

In 1996, Kathy transferred a hundred thousand dollars in stocks and bonds to the temple, with a specific written request that the money be restricted to helping build a monastic university in Poolesville. But it never went to the shedra. According to Konchog Norbu, the shedra administrator, it went into the giant pot that paid for everything. And Kathy received a thank-you card from Ladyworks. "From the point of view of intention, I got what I wanted, I guess," Kathy said. "I gave money and wanted power—wanted to buy power—and I did." Ultimately, Kathy came to believe that Jetsunma was corrupt and that the monks and nuns involved with KPC's board and finances were breaking their vows by misleading people.

If KPC was a cult and not Tibetan Buddhism at all—as some of its detractors suggest—it would surely die with Jetsunma. But I had hope that wasn't going to happen. I had hope that eventually the books would be opened, amends would be made, a new board of directors would be elected and not appointed. Monks and nuns would stop fund-raising—and strong-arming potential donors. The children of members would receive immunization shots, not be discouraged from attending college—or ordained before they were mature enough to handle the vows. There wouldn't be secret sangha meetings. The manipulation tactics, and the desperation, would end. Jetsunma would support her monks and nuns in the traditional way and not the other way around.

Somebody would step in, I had to think, and save these decent people from themselves, from Jetsunma, or from an imported medieval system that surely could work better. Maybe Khenpo Tsewang Gyatso would step in—although he would tell me eventually that he had no interest in doing that. Running a Dharma center was a headache and too political. As for the problems in Poolesville, "What problems?" he said. I liked Khenpo and enjoyed talking to him. He was a traditional Tibetan monk and saw things from a traditional point of view. I could see his hands were tied. And while Buddhists are not supposed to lie, he explained to me that it was okay to lie if you were protecting your teacher. "If this comes from devotion," he said, "and pure motive, then it is okay."

Maybe Penor Rinpoche himself—the man Khenpo protected so purely—would step in. Maybe Penor Rinpoche would publicly apologize for the ethical violations that had occurred at a Palyul center under his guidance—something many former students at KPC would appreciate. But in the three interviews I conducted with him, he revealed no such plans. He was an optimist. All new Dharma centers have difficulties, he explained. And this was America, where the Dharma is in its infancy and "pride is a big problem." But he spent a great deal of time with me and was en-

couraging about my book, which was perhaps his way of dealing
with these things. Besides, he was a very busy man. Penor Rinpoche had monasteries to run, and eighteen hundred monks to
feed. And, like all good Buddhists, he had a long view of begin-
ningless time—a few squabbles and problems didn't add up to
much. He also had his hands full talking to reporters after 1997—
kindly and delicately trying to explain his recognition of the Hollywood action-picture star Steven Seagal as the reincarnation of a
Tibetan terton.

The moon was rising when I arrived at the temple the night before the retreat. I parked my car on River Road, took the shortcut
into the woods, and found the narrow dirt road that led to the Migyur Dorje stupa. Over the years, I could see now, I had become the
sort of person who needed to know the worst about a place—or an
individual—before I could balance it with the best. Maybe that is
what journalists do for a living. We live in the mess and ugliness,
look for problems and weakness, for things that need to be improved. An experienced Tibetan Buddhist would strive to have a
nonjudgmental perspective. Penor Rinpoche and Khenpo, they
lived in the sunshine. *What problems?* When they looked at something, it was neither good nor bad. They saw goodness and perfection, the Buddha nature.

As I began to walk around the stupa, I thought about Jetsunma. "The lotus has its roots in the mud," one of the lamas had
once said to me, when we were talking about KPC. You could add
up all the negatives, all the worst things that could be said about
Jetsunma, and, still, that wasn't the whole story either.

"I see this as a pattern of mine," she had said to me on the
phone, earlier in the summer. "I am a religion builder and I tend to
build structures that others can use. It's like an archetypal response I have. It's like being a natural-born teacher or a maternal
type, personality-wise. And what happens to me is that a lot of
times I will build a structure that really works and it's useful and
people seem to move into that structure. But at some point I find
that I'm carrying it on my shoulders and I'm kind of weighed
down by it. . . . So I'm feeling . . . a little buried under it. You
know?"

She presented her central dilemma quite lightly but made no attempt to hide it: She had started a religion and now had to run it.

Each morning of the retreat began with an hour of traditional prayers. Otherwise, I had been told that the four days would be an assortment of assignments and workshops created by Jetsunma in her "nontraditional" mode. As usual when Jetsunma was teaching, there was a line of cars parked along River Road the next morning. I caught sight of Wib's mane of white hair across the temple foyer, and when he saw me he smiled and made his way through the crowd. "I hoped you'd come," he said. He was tan and rested, looked handsome in a dark denim shirt. We hugged and laughed and shared news. He asked about my new house—and carefully inquired about the title of my book. "Oh, don't worry," I said with an embarrassed chuckle. "I took care of that.

"What's going on with you?" I asked. Wib closed his mouth and winced slightly. He and Jane were thinking of writing a letter to Jetsunma, asking her blessing to start repairing their marriage. Wib wanted to move back home. Not only had he grown tired of living by himself, away from his family, but he was already disenchanted with a corporate marketing job in Northern Virginia. "I miss being at the temple all day," he said.

"Really?" I asked. "You'd come back and fund-raise and all that?"

"The real world is overrated," he said with a shrug. "At least here I'm doing something meaningful with my time."

I took my seat inside the Dharma room. It was filled to capacity—maybe eighty or one hundred people—and there was a buzz of anticipation. Jetsunma had been even more than usually elusive of late. Wib confirmed my suspicion that she was beginning to pull away from Poolesville—talking of going into a permanent "semiretreat" and spending a large part of the year at her house in Arizona. Her public teachings had become very rare.

She entered wearing a head-to-toe burgundy outfit, but not official robes. The room of students all rose and began finding places on the floor to prostrate to her, three times. I stayed in my chair.

She looked different—altered in some way. She was thinner than ever before and seemed very toned. Since India, according to Wib, she had started working out ninety minutes a day. There were signs of muscles under her tight velvet knit top, and her burgundy wraparound skirt was fitted against a flat stomach. The rigorous exercising had even changed the planes of her face. She had visible cheekbones and a slightly sunken look underneath them. Her eyes looked different, too—very different. But from the back of the room it was hard to say why. For one thing she appeared to be wearing hardly any makeup.

The weekend was about bodhicitta, she said, after the Seven Line Prayer was finished. It was about compassion. And this meant that mostly the weekend was about suffering and the exploration of suffering and our reactions to suffering. She didn't want people to sit passively for four days. "You aren't here to just watch movies and listen to teachings and be entertained." This was a weekend for work, for digging and questing and brutal self-honesty, she said. She also wanted students to "resist the temptation to think of this as some kind of quick fix, a patch-up job on your spiritual life. And resist thinking you are going to come away from this weekend feeling good, on some kind of high.

"The way to understand other people's suffering," she said, "is to first recognize your own." We tend not to want to think about these things. We make an enemy of suffering. But the point of Tibetan Buddhism is to learn how to take the negatives of samsara and the failings inside us and transform them. You can use your suffering as a way to ascend—to build character and depth, so that the suffering becomes your mentor and your blessing. Or you can see it "as a way to become angry and bitter and jealous and a victim—as though suffering was uniquely yours alone—and no one else experiences it.

"People say that Buddhism is a downer religion," she said, "but I just think it's realistic. It teaches the full equation. It teaches that cause and effect are interdependent, one giving rise to the other. We have funny superstitious notions that if we do something nonvirtuous that we'll be punished immediately . . . this lifetime. And in fact, there is no delay. The cause and the effect arise together, interdependently, but because of the way we see time, we think there's a delay."

She drew a diagram on the board, a "time and space grid," she called it—and explained how karma ripens. "If you are handicapped in this life, you had a nonvirtue of the body in the past. Mental illness and mental trouble, or neurosis and instability and depression, is from nonvirtuous mental activity of the past," she said. "There's no magic about this."

I thought about how unfashionable all this was, this talk of suffering and punishment, the tough explanation for the handicapped: They deserve it. And the psychotic: They deserve it. And the poor: They deserve it, too. I had grown used to it after a year of coming to Poolesville, but it had nothing to do with the notion most Americans had of Tibetan Buddhism. We only knew what we knew by looking at the cheerful face of the Fourteenth Dalai Lama. And when he said, "My religion is kindness," we had gotten it into our heads that Tibetan Buddhism was just niceness. If we did a little meditation and held some brown beads like Richard Gere wore on the cover of *Esquire*, maybe we could smile like the Dalai Lama, too. But the truth is, the Vajrayana path is brutal and the struggle to surrender one's ego can seem endless. If the Tibetan lamas seemed cheerful and giggly all the time, it wasn't because they held a view that life is fun. They laughed because there was almost no choice.

"Christopher Reeve, it turns out, really is Superman," Jetsunma was saying. "He has turned this experience of suffering into a way to help others and a vehicle for his life to become truly meaningful. How meaningful is being a movie star and an equestrian? Suffering alone is not important. How you react to suffering is. Making the choice is the important thing—whether you suffer from a big splashy accident or tragedy or just from moment-by-moment sorrows—you must realize you have a choice. And the choice begins by experiencing suffering and allowing yourself to feel it."

Afterward I dropped in on a lesson that Ani Rene was giving in the prayer room—a sort of introduction to Tibetan Buddhism for newcomers, about Ngöndro and the Four Thoughts that Turn the Mind. I wanted to listen to Rene describe these concepts, and, frankly, I just liked hearing the sound of her voice and being in the same room with her. She was an accomplished practitioner—revered by all in Poolesville and by those who weren't anymore. She exuded intelligence and precision. She had a wonderful air of warmth mixed with detachment. If anyone had achieved a feeling of egolessness—without losing a sense of self, strength, and inner direction—it was Rene.

She stood in her dark burgundy robes with her back to the altar and, in a soft and gentle voice, described the purpose of prostrations and led the small group in a test run. Rene was in her midforties, I guessed, and her face was round and had very wide cheekbones. Her eyes were green and gray and brilliantly clear. As I watched her demonstrate a prostration—lifting her strong, bare arms to the crown of her head, to her throat, to her heart, then down to the ground—I realized that I had never once tried to do a prostration. What a funny oversight on my part, I thought. How unprofessional and weird, after one year of coming to the temple. *These people have done hundreds of thousands of them, and I couldn't be troubled to do only one.* And I found, as I wobbled through a few, that they are physically hard to do—something like a multi-stepped yoga pose called the Sun Salutation. You were up, and you were down, you were stretching, and you were bending. And after just a few, it was odd, but I felt loosened up, kind of flowing.

Jetsunma talked about her childhood in the evening teaching, and she pondered the question I had been asking myself for a year now. What had a greater impact on her life and behavior now: her lousy, abusive childhood—the cigarette burns on her body, being beaten with a radiator brush—or all the past lives she had spent praying in a cave?

"My pedigree is long and impressive—but that's not what gave me my strength," she said. "My empowerment came from seeing the suffering of others . . . and when people say that tulkus know how to choose their next reincarnation, I think, *What fresh hell I picked.* But I wouldn't trade it. It was empowering, a training . . . and I know suffering so well now that I can see your own suffering even when you can't see it. And I can see you try to rise above it. I can see you go into the zone, hanging on to some idea of happiness that you think you could have.

"I can walk into a situation, a room, and get it just like that," she said, snapping her fingers. "My teachers tell me that's because of my lifetimes of practice, but I don't know that's true. My days as a child were unbelievably long, maybe never-ending."

The effects were still with her, the results of years of being hungry and being beaten, of being told she was ugly and worthless. And, apparently, even the lama hadn't found a way to heal herself. Nor had the big white house in the woods that she'd dreamed about as a child—the house that was perfect and beautiful and safe, where she promised to take her little brothers someday—been an answer to her problems. "I'm still scared," she said. "I'm afraid all the time."

And she often felt fragile and worthless. "It wasn't until the last few months that I decided that I wasn't half bad looking," she said. "Before, I thought I was a troll or a dwarf or something. . . . It's taken me this long to feel I'm worthy, that I'm okay-looking, that I can be confident in rooms full of people and feel capable."

She didn't like her job as lama, she admitted. "I don't like being the authority, being in front of you, being in charge. I don't like this chair and the clothes that go with it. . . . But I have a need to be of benefit to sentient beings. And if you'd been empowered as I have, there's nothing you would rather do at any moment of the day than care for the suffering of sentient beings . . . and every night and every day you have to remember that there are people who have hopes of you, who are waiting for you."

The next morning there was a sign taped to the glass window in the temple door. It was a warning of obstacles arising, a lesson in nonattachment and impermanence, and a reminder that at KPC the unexpected regularly happens:

Jetsunma is experiencing muscle spasms in her back and is receiving treatment . . . sked has been changed.

While I tried to decide how to spend the next couple of hours—either watching *Dead Man Walking* in the Dharma room or "self-questing," I browsed in the temple gift shop and loitered in the foyer. I noticed for the first time that there were baskets everywhere I looked, with little signs asking for money for one worthy cause or another. One basket said, BROWNIES FOR THE TEENS. Another said, ALYCE'S RESTAURANT. Another sign said, HELP BUILD A STUPA, another basket was for "KPC," and, finally, there was a basket on a pedestal by the door to the Dharma room with an index card that read: WE SENT JETSUNMA TO THE BEACH THIS SUMMER. NOW HELP US PAY FOR IT.

It was a sad assortment of pleas. And it made me feel sort of sorry that Alana had arranged for me to attend the retreat on an "editorial waiver" and skip paying the $140. As I hovered around the baskets, I realized that I had always felt vaguely bad about not giving the Tibetan Buddhists much of anything for their time and generosity and kindness to me—the hours of interviews they'd endured, the transcriptions of teachings they'd E-mailed me, the books and ideas they'd shared. They'd been generous with me— and answered all my questions with unfailing honesty. I'd bought them dinner and lunch when I could. I had shown up at their houses with flowers and cookies—and at Christmastime sent Jetsunma a few novels, which I was never sure she'd actually gotten. (One monk confessed to me that he found his ordination day offering to Jetsunma—one year after he'd given it—still wrapped and stuck in an upstairs temple closet.) Looking around at the baskets, I pulled out my wallet, wrote a check for two hundred dollars, and dropped it in the beach-fund basket.

As I watched *Dead Man Walking*, it was touching to hear the nuns giggling and laughing at all the nun jokes—and even more so to hear them sobbing at the end. Afterward I ran into Alana on the front porch.

She didn't seem to be at the workshops or movies that weekend—or doing much self-questing at the stupa. She was busy attending to Jetsunma, who, I would discover later on, had been arrested only days before on battery charges for hitting a nun who had broken her vows. When I caught Alana she was wearing a pair of burgundy jeans and a burgundy T-shirt and clearly between errands of some kind. She had just returned from taking Jetsunma to the acupuncturist and now carried a few envelopes and papers in her freckled hands. Realizing that we might not find a chance to visit again over the weekend, we decided to sit for a few minutes inside, where it was warmer.

The solarium was a large, glassy room that led to the kitchen and community room. Bulletin boards were covered with announcements and pictures of new ordained. Four round tables were set up with chairs, for lounging and eating meals—for people who'd been crowded out of the dining room. A few cardboard boxes filled with old newspapers and magazines had been dropped on the tables. The boxes contained library books, too—mostly oversized coffee table books, travel books, picture books.

"What's all this?" I asked Alana.

"An idea of Jetsunma's," she said, "part of tonight's teaching."

Alana looked tired but relaxed. Her blue eyes still twinkled with some kind of energy and readiness. I realized that she always had this look—vaguely tired, vaguely pleased, like the way the mother of the bride looks the day after the wedding. I wondered how much work the retreat had been for her.

"You have a hard job," I said.

"I guess I do," she replied.

We caught up on some things, and then I asked her a few questions about Michael Burroughs. I was going to be calling him, I said. There were things that needed to be cleared up, accounts to confirm—his side of the story needed to be heard. She sipped on a Diet Pepsi and took a deep breath. "I suppose you have to," she said. "Just be careful about what you're hearing."

I said I would.

"I think about Michael a lot," she said, then sighed. "And he's a good teaching for me. I used to be more like him. I know for sure that five years ago I was more like Michael."

"Hard on students?"

She nodded. "Gyaltrul Rinpoche said to me recently, 'Take care of yourself. You're the pricker point.' 'What's that?' I asked. 'People don't get mad at her,' he said. 'They get mad at you. And you have to be careful not to get angry in return—because the negativity will shorten your life.' "

There were things that Jetsunma's students weren't supposed to resent Jetsunma for—the mothering vibe, the control they'd granted her over their lives, the money they'd given over the years, the failure of Ladyworks and the other temple businesses. Deep down, people must have been ambivalent about her. Many times I had heard students suggest that the inner circle was responsible for the problems at the temple. Sometimes it was Wib and Jane who were blamed, or Tashi. But most often it was Alana.

"When Michael left," she said, "nobody was sorry. Not one person. That's sad. I can't imagine leaving here and having nobody miss me."

She had thought about leaving. This seemed inconceivable to me. "We joke about my being a Virgo with Scorpio rising," Alana said, "a perfectionist with a sting. But, actually, I've had people say how much I've improved these days. They used to refer to me as Ice Maiden. But Jetsunma has softened me, really has softened me. I am a little bit more compassionate than I used to be." She laughed. "But mostly, you know, I just can't stand people. But I'll do anything for them. It's a strange kind of personality that I have."

Her personality didn't seem as strange as her relationship with Jetsunma. She seemed capable of unfathomable devotion. She had once been Jetsunma's closest friend and lover and was now her servant. She wasn't just the go-between and gatekeeper, she was Jetsunma's private secretary, housekeeper, and cook. Along with Atara and Ariana, she made all the appointments that Jetsunma would eventually cancel, made airplane reservations that Jetsunma would cancel, and then, when she rescheduled the appointments and airplane tickets, Jetsunma would cancel again. "On all levels everything is stirred up when you're around her," Alana said. She did Jetsunma's laundry, her Christmas shopping, her mail-ordering, her grocery shopping, and she sent out all the flower arrangements to students on their birthdays or when their parents died or their children were born, with a card that said, "Love from Jetsunma."

"Being a nun wasn't a natural fit for me," she said. "Not like it's been with some of the others. . . . I look at my daughters' lives, their little town houses and their husbands, and sometimes I still long for that. . . . I have days, lots of days, when I just want to get a town house and play with my grandkids and *forget all this.* . . .

"And it's hard sometimes . . . well, you know it'd be nice to just *have someone to hold.* I have that want, that skin hunger, or even the intimacy of being really good friends with somebody. I've been instructed not to weigh Jetsunma down with emotional problems. That's not what the guru is there for—mundane living. She is supposed to lead us on a spiritual path. . . . But as a sentient being, I have ups and downs. But I don't want to burden her, or distract her. So I'm not as open."

When I asked Alana how she thought she'd spend the rest of her life, she smiled sort of wistfully.

"Think you'll stay with Jetsunma?" I asked.

"Forever, I hope," she said.

In the evening Jetsunma's face looked swollen and waxy—like a flesh-colored mask she'd put on. She began talking about how people lose compassion, how they stop having an open heart. The teacher's role in Tibetan Buddhism is "to help the student understand the enlightened mind," she said. Her way of helping her students was sometimes to share her experiences.

When she was younger and living in North Carolina, she said, she began praying for the continent of Africa. She became obsessed with Africa for a year or so, and started buying African clothes and African music and put pictures of sad-faced African kids on her refrigerator to remind her about the suffering there. Eventually her life changed because of this practice. She realized that if you pray for something that intensely, with your whole heart, you can begin to feel different inside. It was as though you were becoming the thing you were praying for. You could feel it in your bones. And it stayed with you, with every breath, every thought, everything in your day became that thing you were praying for. And it took you beyond ego and self to a place where you became unseparated from the rest of the world. It was a way to approach experiencing things as nondual.

"Emotion is just ego and conceptualization," Jetsunma said. "Compassion is way more fundamental, and unconnected to ego and negativity."

Each of us had to find a place to pray for, she said. This was our assignment. The boxes in the solarium were there to help us with ideas. We were to pick a subject that was dear to us—not necessarily something big or important or really current like Bosnia. It didn't have to be a place, either. It could be an issue or a cause, like rain forests or toxic waste or abortion. "Find something that moves you deeply," she said. "Something that will motivate you—because you will need that kind of emotion and energy to keep focused."

Afterward Ani Rene described a meditation and visualization—a "practice"—that was meant to accompany our praying. We began by doing three prostrations, and by reading the Bodhisattva and Refuge vows three times. Then we closed our eyes and imagined ourselves with the subject of our prayers. We visualized a lotus blossom in the middle of a lake before us, and a bodhisattva on the blossom, and then a sky of buddhas and bodhisattvas with their dakini consorts before us. We imagined that we were gathering all the earth's treasures, and all the treasures of all the universes, piles of jewels and riches, and, along with our subject, we made an offering of all this wealth to the bodhisattvas and dakinis.

"Stay deeply focused," Rene said, "and feel utterly and completely responsible for this place you are praying about—as though you would exchange your life for theirs, gladly."

We were to say *om* while we visualized inhaling all the suffering and misery and discontent of our subject and *ah* while we meditated on the absolute Buddha nature, pure wisdom and emptiness, then *hum* as we made an exhalation of bliss. We had inhaled the suffering of our subject and purified it. "Your exhalation should pour out like nectar," Rene said softly. "Bliss going out into the world."

We took our new practice out to the stupa the next morning after an hour of prayer in the prayer room. Jetsunma arrived in casual clothes—black jeans, cropped beige sweater, and boots—and led the group across River Road to the woods. We each brought pieces of fruit to make offerings at the stupa, and I fumbled with an apple and orange and tried to be solemn, beginning to realize how uncomfortable I felt with the enormity of Jetsunma's ambitions for saving the world. Others in the group approached the stupa with great confidence and intimacy, reverently bumping the tops of their heads up against the concrete and clutching their prayer beads. I bent over to begin a prostration in front of the stupa but found, in the open air and in the company of Jetsunma, I was unable to. I was worried about falling over, or doing it awkwardly. And I was too proud.

Afterward we watched a documentary of animals being tested in labs, kittens being injected with flea spray, monkeys struggling against restraints while medical researchers smashed their skulls with a giant cow puncher as a way to study head trauma. After that there was a movie about lambs being slaughtered.

At the night's teaching Jetsunma arrived and quickly began, as though she had so much to discuss she might run out of time — or lose track of all the things she was keeping in her head. The teaching was long and meandering. When she was done, going way over the scheduled amount of time, she got up from her throne, and I saw that she had a stripe of dark sweat bleeding through the back of her burgundy dress.

She spoke of the "practice of bodhicitta" as it is viewed in traditional Tibetan Buddhism. There are several levels to the practices, each one bringing a deeper and subtler understanding of the Buddha nature. It is a recurring theme in Tibetan Buddhism—this need to separate students on the path by their ability with the material, by the level of their understanding. There is a hierarchy in place at all times, which says that some are better, more evolved, more enlightened, and presumably closer to realization and Buddhahood. But, essentially, everybody is a zero on the rungs of this well-defined ladder compared with a fully realized master.

"When I went to India this last time, Penor Rinpoche said to me that he normally doesn't establish and enthrone tulkus who have not been trained," she said, "but he said in my case he was willing to do that because, from the first moment that he met me, he knew that in the past I had been a *very great bodhisattva* and that I have *truly mastered bodhicitta* so that I had truly expressed bodhicitta in every way. He said that . . . it would be an impossibility that I would appear in the world unarmed and unable to be of benefit to sentient beings, that I would *always* be able to teach sentient beings and lead them on the path of the bodhisattva into enlightenment. He said that he's always had that confidence in me, and so even though I was not trained, he did the unheard of. He enthroned me and recognized me and made me, in fact, not only enthroned but very public because he had full confidence in the bodhicitta that I would express."

She talked about Mandarava's Cave near the lake at Tso Pema, and how she had encountered a lama there who was "greatly moved" by a meeting with her. He had "tears in his eyes and could hardly speak," she said. "He couldn't believe that the day had come when he had met Mandarava's reincarnation."

Once she was alone in the cave, Jetsunma's mindstream and the mindstream of Mandarava met and "became like one river," she said. "I felt her, her mindstream, what she was. I felt that everything that was said about her was true. . . . *She really was like a living Buddha.* She had all the major and minor marks. She really was like that. And I felt her relationship to me. I understood it very well, in a way that I never understood my relationship with any of the other predecessors that I have been recognized as . . ."

She came to understand that "Mandarava's blessing was everywhere"—"every time a child was nurtured, every time someone who was sick was healed, every time some mental disturbance had been pacified."

Finally she brought the lesson around to its point. The story of Mandarava was the story of just one great bodhisattva with great compassion, she said. There were many others.

"What will your story be?" she asked the students. "How will your compassion express itself? . . . In some future life, I hope and pray that I will have the opportunity to read stories of the modern Ahkön Lhamo and her disciples. And to hear these great stories about the enormous deeds of her disciples and even further down in the future to realize that her disciples have been reborn great bodhisattvas that single-handedly, armed with courage and love, brought about the end of suffering. . . .

"I think it's time to start writing your story, and it's time to stop being little children who are looking to me to supply your happiness and to supply your motivation and to supply some way of making your path easy. Now it's time for you to look within your heart and fan the fire of love until it is greater than anything you have ever known, even greater than your own self-absorption."

I closed my eyes. I couldn't look at her anymore—or listen anymore. And I found myself instead drifting off into the meditation that Ani Rene had taught the night before. I thought about my subject—the place dear to my heart, the place I would be praying for night and day.

I began to imagine myself at the entrance of a long driveway. It led to a large plantation house with white columns. I walked through the doors at Kunzang Palyul Choling and sat down in the Dharma room. I was surrounded by monks and nuns, by the First Wavers and the new faces. I was with the ones who'd been brave enough to stay and with the ones who'd been brave enough to leave. Jetsunma was standing with us, too. And in my meditation we made our offering of great riches to the buddhas and bodhisattvas and dakinis. . . . *Om.* I inhaled the suffering and misunderstanding and sadness of Poolesville. *Ah.* I meditated on the feeling of emptiness and wisdom and open space. *Hum.* I made an exhalation of pure bliss. As Rene had instructed, I imagined myself responsible for the plight of my subject. And I felt as though I would gladly exchange my life for theirs. Somebody had to be looking after these people who spent so much time worrying about everybody else.

On the last day of the retreat, coming over on White's Ferry, I put the windows down in my car and stared at the river water rushing on either side of me. The water was dark and gray and muddy, and I realized that I would never know the truth about Jetsunma, whether she was a good leader or a very bad one. And I realized I was sad. Someday, maybe not tomorrow or next month, or even next year, but someday, I would have to stop going out to Poolesville. Someday it would be over, and that already made me sad. And as the water swirled and the shore of Maryland grew closer, I thought about devotion and what it means. There is nobility in sacrifice—any sacrifice. And as much as I didn't want to admit this, there is in fact a sort of ladder that people seem to ascend in order to be liberated from self-concern and experience themselves as part of something larger. And sometimes people do ridiculous things to get there.

Inside the warm temple foyer I ran into Sherab, and we visited a bit. It was funny how the retreat was nearly over and we'd not seen much of each other. "I haven't been out and about, exactly," she said, and laughed. I noticed that her eyes looked swollen and red. She admitted that she had been crying all weekend. "This has been a rough one," she said. "I'm kind of a wreck. Call me Ani Basketcase." Later, after a showing of *Leaving Las Vegas*, I saw her sobbing in the hallway.

On my way into lunch I saw Doug Sims and stopped to say hello. His strawberry blond hair was cut short, he was thinner, and his freckled face looked drawn. When I asked him what he was up to, he said, "I got a job in the real world. I needed it for my self-esteem." I remembered how he'd looked just a year before, a giant sunbeam of a man who was painting the tree of relics behind the prayer room during the golden days of the stupa. "Why hasn't the stupa been painted yet?" I asked. "Don't ask me," the accountant said a bit sourly. "They ran out of money."

I stood in the lunch line with Bob Colacurcio, and he asked how things were going. He was a big friendly bear, a former Jesuit who had moved his family from Michigan to be closer to Jetsunma. Anytime I wanted to call him or come see him, he said, he'd be happy to help explain things. Help me see how it was. "You know, the mind wants to understand things simply. And the conventional mind wants to understand things even more simply," he said. "And it's not easy to get out of a comfort zone. But on the Vajrayana path, it is my understanding that the teacher is supposed to do whatever he or she can to get the student from the comfort zone. And the teacher would use any means to get this to happen—for the student's own benefit."

At the end of the lunch line, I found Eleanor Rowe collecting money for lunch. And I found Kamil, the monk from the Virgin Islands, serving. I looked around the room and saw Sangye eating with Jon Randolph and David and Sylvia Somerville. I saw a cluster of nuns, and the great yardage of burgundy fabric hanging on them. I overheard Rene saying, "It's funny, but I didn't identify with her as much as the Sean Penn character. Watching the movie, I really felt the angry little man inside me."

I found a table and sat next to Wib's wife, Jane Perini. We talked about "flow"—how sometimes things just seem meant to be and go smoothly, almost as though you've tapped into some current you were meant to ride. I told Jane I was sorry about her and Wib, and her eyes filled with tears. When we said good-bye she gave me a hug. Afterward Jon Randolph and I bumped into each other on the front porch. The tall thin monk had always seemed puzzled by my job of writing about KPC. "You could make Jetsunma look pretty bad, if you wanted," he said.

"I know."

"Because people don't understand."

"I know."

We agreed to talk later on, and have lunch. And then he said, "You're a part of this, Martha. *Can't you feel that?*"

It seemed an unimaginable crime, if Jetsunma wasn't going to lead these people to liberation—if she wasn't able to meet up with her students in the bardo like she promised. Jon Randolph looked into my eyes, and I looked into his. It was the kind of prolonged soul-searching exchange that I usually avoided, and was embarrassed by. But something inside me felt different, sort of open and unscared, and as though the monk were taking me somewhere I was suddenly ready to go.

Jetsunma took the throne for her last teaching of the retreat. I stood up and found a free spot on the floor where I could try out a few prostrations in public. It wasn't that hard or embarrassing, really. In fact, it was kind of a thrill.

The weekend was shaping up to be important, Jetsunma said after we were all done. She had seen some very auspicious signs in the sky. "Did you see that little rainbow around the moon last night?" she asked. There are *nagas* or nature spirits who exist on earth and communicate with us through rainbows, through certain-shaped clouds and lightning. "Virtue does manifest itself in the world," she said. "And our compassion and caring has been noticed by these natural spirits."

As she was talking I remembered an old Tibetan Buddhist story called "Miraculous Tooth."* There was an old woman whose son was a trader. He often joined caravans and traveled on business to far spots in India. When his mother learned that her son was going to be near Bodh Gaya, where the Buddha became enlightened, she asked him to bring her a relic from there—something she could use as a focus for her devotion. Her son went to the holy place, and when he returned to his mother, he realized that he had forgotten her request. Seeing a dead dog on the street, he tore a tooth from its mouth and wrapped it in silk.

When he presented the tooth to his mother, he told her it was one of Buddha's canine teeth. It was a true holy relic. The old woman put the tooth on her altar and began praying and prostrating before it. Soon the tooth began to emanate countless tiny pearls, and rainbows bounced about the room. The old woman, for the first time in her life, found the unshakable peace of mind that she had always sought. And when she died soon after, an aura of rainbow light surrounded her, a sign that she'd attained enlightenment.

Jetsunma was making an announcement. Something about the people in the audience who were going to be taking Refuge and Bodhisattva vows—the initial pledge to become a Tibetan Buddhist. They needed white scarves, she said. I walked out of the Dharma room and pulled Rene aside. What did the Refuge and Bodhisattva vows really entail? What was one committing to?

"Have you read the vows?"

I nodded. "But is this a promise to start practicing?"

"I hate to tell you," she whispered, "*but you already are.*"

---

* Surya Das, *The Snow Lion's Turquoise Mane: Wisdom Tales from Tibet* (San Francisco: Harper San Francisco, 1992).

I returned to my seat at the back of the room and felt a rush of heat into my face. I had a feeling that was on top of another feeling that felt more important than a feeling. It was an urge or drive—something like an instinct. It wasn't rational—it didn't have anything to do with actual thinking. It wasn't a choice as much as something that simply *happened.* And it didn't come from a place where doubt exists or where one spends an enormous amount of time wondering what the lama is being paid or whether she buys too many clothes. It is a generous place. An unselfish and forgiving and unconditional place. It is not the place where I am a journalist. And, I hate to admit it, but it's a nicer place to be.

The vows are simple. Anybody could have said them, and we did, in fact, all say them together. A commitment to living things and life, to kindness and selfless efforts to end suffering. These are things that all people would hope for themselves in their better moments. We walked in a line toward Jetsunma's throne. And we filed past a large clear bowl of water with a flower floating in it.

I handed Jetsunma the white scarf that Wib had lent me. She took it in her hands and held it up to her forehead. And then returned it to me. Up close she looked really pale, sort of nude, without all her makeup. And something else was different about her—something about her eyes. They weren't brown anymore. They were bright blue. *She was wearing colored contact lenses.*

She handed me a folded white piece of paper. I smiled and turned toward Rene, who was standing next to me. Rene reached up and began tying a blessing cord around my neck. It was a string of red thread, tied with a blessed knot in the middle.

Rene's head bent close to mine, and I looked down on her hair, cut short but thick and clean and rich, speckled with gray. She finished tying the cord and looked at me.

"So you did it," Rene said.

"I did."

Her eyes were so green, so naturally green and so gray. Her face was so open and gentle and kind, so beautifully plain. It would break your heart, the kindness in that face. And it was everything to me in that moment, and made me feel the way I always felt about the stupa, kind of humbled and encouraged and uplifted at the same time. Rene's face gave me hope. And many times since I have thought, maybe Jetsunma isn't the real Buddha. Maybe it's Wib or Jane. Maybe it's Sherab or Sangye or Alana. But more often than not, I think, *Maybe the Buddha is Rene.* Jetsunma is the dog's tooth, the decoy. The one who draws the fire. The one who throws her weight around. The one who can be loud and demanding and get attention. The one who has the nerve to ask for money.

I opened the piece of paper that Jetsunma had given me. It was my new name, Karma Drolkar. For a long time I kept it in my desk, half forgotten, and then late one night when I was on the phone with Dechen—we were sort of laughing and talking together about Poolesville—I asked her what the name meant.

"Literally, it means, 'action of White Tara,' " she said. "But that's not a very poetic translation. Really, it's something like 'the wisdom of the emptiness of all phenomena.' "

The wisdom of emptiness. Despite all I knew, I liked that.

Epilogue

In the winter of 1996, Dechen moved to the West Coast, where she still lives, in a city that she does not wish to disclose. She calls her mother once a year, around Christmas, and works as a secretary.

The Monk continues to teach and travel, and study with Khenpo Tsewang Gyatso.

In the spring of 1997, Jetsunma announced to her students that she was moving permanently to Sedona, Arizona. Certain students—including Rene Larrabee, Sangye Dorje, Sherab Khandro, Alana Elgin, Atara Heiss, Alexandra Johnson, Ariana Kreitsmeyer, Sophia Windolph, David Somerville and his family—were asked to move there, too. They found houses and work in Sedona. The ordained among them were told by Jetsunma that they no longer needed to wear their robes except during Buddhist prayers and ceremonies. I visited them there in 1998.

In October 1998, Jetsunma came to believe that certain Hopi prophesies, which predict that floods and famine and great earthquakes would nearly destroy the United States in April 1999 and again in November 1999, were true. She told her students that Washington, D.C., would likely be underwater at that time. After much preparation for self-sufficiency and survival, many of Jetsunma's remaining students in Poolesville joined her in Sedona—where they would be on high ground and survive catastrophes. A 150-acre farm was purchased outside Payson, Arizona, where her followers could live together, self-sufficiently if need be. She also announced plans to build a stupa and a new temple in West Sedona. In October 1999, Jetsunma turned fifty. In the year 2000 she plans to make a world tour and give a series of teachings.

The temple in Poolesville still has an active and growing sangha. In 1998 the Jetsunma-appointed board of directors resigned following the publication of a critical article about KPC in *Mirabella* magazine by Will Blythe, and a new board of elected members replaced them. It was announced that the temple had been paid off.

Karl Jones moved to Ireland after his separation from Jetsunma in 1996. He was reunited with her in the fall of 1997, then separated again from her in spring 1998, and reunited with her again later that year, only to be again separated in 1999.

Sangye Dorje gave back his monk's robes in the summer of 1997, during a visit to Poolesville by Penor Rinpoche. He had never been a good monk, he told me, even though everybody thought he was. "You become ordained and hope to become a perfect monk someday, to grow into the robes. I could tell that wasn't happening to me." He wanted to get married someday, he told me, and have a family.

Wib Middleton and Jane Perini were reunited in December 1996 with Jetsunma's blessing. They moved to Sedona, Arizona, in March 1999.

Khenpo Tsewang Gyatso continues to travel, teach, and open new Palyul centers. Twice a year he comes to Poolesville and gives instruction to shedra students there.

His Holiness Penor Rinpoche remains the throneholder of the Nyingma School and oversees and supports a monastery of eighteen hundred monks in southern India. He recognized the actor Steven Seagal as the reincarnation of a terton or treasure revealer named Chungdrag Dorje in 1997 and was met with a storm of complaints by Tibetan Buddhists around the world. In an interview with me in the summer of 1997, Rinpoche said that he would not be recognizing any more Americans as tulkus because of their "problem with pride." He also made a point of telling me that, in India, the Tibetan teachers feed and clothe and house their monks, not the other way around. He has established his own Palyul Retreat Center in the Catskills. He has hopes that this book will help Dharma in the West and be of benefit to all sentient beings.

Gyaltrul Rinpoche remains in retreat in Half Moon Bay and was not available to verify the accounts of his conversations with Alana Elgin, Jetsunma Ahkön Lhamo, Michael Burroughs, Richard Dykeman, or Aileen Williams.

Andrea King's comedic screenplay based on the life of Jetsunma was written but never made into a film.

Ladyworks Inc. stopped all operations and was $650,000 in debt by the summer of 1997, according to Alana Elgin. The second infomercial was never aired.

At the time of this writing, Byron Pickett was still at work on his documentary about Jetsunma's India pilgrimage.

Kathy Coon continues to be a practicing Buddhist. Bonnie Taylor and Bob Denmark do not.

Rick and Chris Finney became the proud parents of a third daughter in 1998 and named her themselves. Only Rick remains a practicing Tibetan Buddhist.

•

Richard Dykeman, after ten years as a monk living in India, Oregon, and Northern California, gave back his robes in 1998 and is doing construction work in the Baltimore area.

Sonam, the nun who left Ani Farms in the middle of the night, died of cancer in 1998. She was thirty-six.

Catharine Anastasia moved to Sedona in October 1999.

Rinchen remained in Poolesville and is making plans to do a three-year retreat at Penor Rinpoche's center in New York.

Aileen remains in Poolesville and works at NBC.

Michael Burroughs moved to Nepal in 1998 to be tutored privately by several tulkus. He has been identified as a lama in the lineage of Northern Treasures and a branch terton in several lifetimes. He agreed to be interviewed for this book in the hope of getting back in contact with Atira.

The Migyur Dorje stupa was painted gold in February 1998 by Sherab Khandro, who is otherwise living in Sedona, Arizona, and supports herself as a painter. She remains a nun.

Acknowledgments

It is a courageous thing to sit down with a writer and allow her to tell your story for you. It becomes more courageous when you realize, midway, that your story is not going to be all that flattering in places. For their stoutheartedness and lack of vanity I would like to thank Jetsunma Ahkön Lhamo and the monks and nuns and lay practitioners of Kunzang Palyul Choling—both past and present. They were never anything but kind and generous to me, despite all my arrogance and egotism and fear. I hope they will understand why this book became what it did.

I would also like to thank His Holiness Penor Rinpoche for spending time with me and for giving me advice and guidance when I asked for it. And for finally saying, "You need to stop talking to people and just write."

Who should I thank next—the people who loved me, the ones who inspired me, those who fed me, or the people who actually paid me money to write this book? In the order of hours spent resuscitating my tired spirit, I would like to thank my indulgent and understanding husband, Bill Powers; my irrepressible cousin, Leslee Peyton Sherrill; my wonderful literary agent, Flip Brophy; and my most enthusiastic fan and father, Peter Sherrill, who clapped so hard and so often for me while he was alive that I can still hear him. I would also like to express unending thanks to Joel Achenbach, Bob Barkin, Tess Batac, Ron Bernstein, Geraldine Brooks, Richard Ben Cramer, Susan Davis, Marydale DeBor, David Del Tredici, Amy Dickinson, J. D. Dolan, Barbara Feinman, Marc Feldman, Rose Jean Goddard, Larry Hass, Tony Horwitz, Tammy Jones, Laura Marmor, Billy McClain, Jeanne McManus, Danielle Mirabella, Lou-Ann Nixon, Mary Powers, Bob Rosenblatt, Sally

Quinn, Jack Shafer, Anina Sherrill, Marilyn Sherrill, Nathaniel Sherrill, Steve Sherrill, Sally Bedell Smith, Lyn Sommer, Mit Spears, Lincoln Spoor, David Stang, Mary Stapp, Lauve Steenhuisen, Elsa Walsh, Mark Warren, and Carolyn White. They gave me good ideas and encouragement—and sometimes a glass of wine—when I most needed it.

Writing this book would not have been possible without the magnanimous support of *The Washington Post.* I have been influenced and inspired by its publishers, Katharine Graham and Don Graham, and encouraged and rescued by its many talented editors, especially Ben Bradlee, Steve Coll, David De Nicolo, Len Downie, Janet Duckworth, Ellen Edwards, Mary Hadar, Brian Kelly, David Von Drehle, Gene Weingarten, and Bob Woodward. In this book, my descriptions of life in the newsroom should not be read as criticism of the *Post* in particular. The truth is, a newsroom is a newsroom and people are people, wherever you go.

The Virginia Center for the Creative Arts is a magical place where I was able to work on this book—during stays in 1997 and 1999—and also find great camaraderie. I would like to thank the board of directors and benefactors of VCCA for making that possible. Also, I would like to thank John Gregory Brown for bringing me to Sweet Briar College to teach and the winter term class of 1997 for their energy and honesty; I will never forget their stories.

I owe a special debt to Martin Wassell, who first told me about Jetsunma and KPC and stuck with me, inspiring me to be fair. It would be hard to find a nobler or more loyal guide into the heart of Tibetan Buddhism in the West.

And then there's David Rosenthal, who originally saw a book in my stories about KPC and then promptly, thanks to his good fortune, vanished from sight. Ann Godoff bravely stepped in and gently shepherded me and my enormous herd of characters to the finish. She made this book as fine as it could be, and for this I am forever grateful.

—*Martha Sherrill,*
October 1999

Index

About the Author

MARTHA SHERRILL has been a staff writer at *The Washington Post* since 1989. She has also written for *Esquire, Vanity Fair,* and other magazines. She lives with her husband and son in the Washington, D.C., area.

About the Type

This text was set in Photina, a typeface designed by José Mendoza in 1971. It is a very elegant design with high legibility, and its close character fit has made it a popular choice for use in quality magazines and art gallery publications.